Economic Reconstruction

This book is produced in full compliance with the government's regulations for conserving paper and other essential materials.

This volume is based largely on a series of lectures delivered at the Graduate School of Public Administration of Harvard University in 1944.

ECONOMIC RECONSTRUCTION

EDITED BY
SEYMOUR E. HARRIS
Associate Professor of Economics, Harvard University; formerly Director, Office of Export-Import Price Control

CONTRIBUTORS

EDWARD M. BERNSTEIN
JOHN D. BLACK
ROY BLOUGH
EVELINE M. BURNS
JOHN M. CLARK
GERHARD COLM
HOWARD S. ELLIS
MORDECAI EZEKIEL
WILLIAM HABER
GOTTFRIED HABERLER
ALVIN H. HANSEN

SEYMOUR E. HARRIS
CHARLES D. HYSON
A. D. H. KAPLAN
S. MORRIS LIVINGSTON
EDWARD S. MASON
GLENN McLAUGHLIN
JACOB L. MOSAK
CHARLES D. STEWART
ALAN SWEEZY
ARTHUR R. UPGREN
DONALD H. WALLACE

HENRY C. WALLICH

First Edition
SECOND IMPRESSION

McGRAW-HILL BOOK COMPANY, INC.
New York　　　　　　　　　　　　　　　　London
1946

ECONOMIC RECONSTRUCTION

COPYRIGHT, 1945, BY THE

MCGRAW-HILL BOOK COMPANY, INC.

All rights reserved. This book, or parts thereof, may not be reproduced in any form without permission of the publishers.

PRINTED IN THE UNITED STATES OF AMERICA

Prefatory Note

Early in 1944 I suggested to Dean Williams of the Graduate School of Public Administration at Harvard that a series of lectures on economic reconstruction might make a valuable contribution to the solution of one of the most difficult economic problems ever to confront this country. With his enthusiastic approval I arranged a series which was given at the school over several months in 1944. The contributors, including the five members of the faculty of the Graduate School of Public Administration and one member of the Faculty of Columbia University, are or have been until recently government servants holding key positions.

This book is based on these lectures. To present a well-balanced discussion of the important economic problems of the transition and later postwar periods, several economists who had not participated in the lecture series were invited to contribute to this volume.

The Graduate School of Public Administration paid the expenses connected with the lectures and with the preparation of this volume for publication. I am indebted to Miss Penelope Hartland, and especially to Miss Lillian Buller and Mrs. Rita Wilfort for their assistance.

SEYMOUR E. HARRIS, EDITOR.

CAMBRIDGE, MASS.,
    June, 1945.

Contents

	PAGE
INTRODUCTION	1
Seymour E. Harris	

Part I

GENERAL ASPECTS

CHAPTER
- I. POSTWAR EMPLOYMENT OUTLOOK 15
  Alvin H. Hansen
- II. AGRICULTURAL AND INDUSTRIAL PROBLEMS IN CONVERSION FROM WAR TO PEACE 21
  Mordecai Ezekiel
- III. POSTWAR AGRICULTURE IN THE UNITED STATES: PROBLEMS AND POLICIES 36
  J. D. Black and C. D. Hyson
- IV. WAGES AND EMPLOYMENT IN WAR AND POSTWAR 59
  Seymour E. Harris
- V. FORECASTING POSTWAR DEMAND 78
  Jacob L. Mosak

Part II

SPECIAL PROBLEMS OF RECONVERSION

- VI. MAN POWER AND RECONVERSION 95
  William Haber
- VII. LIQUIDATING WAR PRODUCTION 124
  A. D. H. Kaplan

CHAPTER	PAGE
VIII. THE REDISTRIBUTION OF THE LABOR FORCE . . . . *Charles D. Stewart*	146
IX. REGIONAL PROBLEMS OF INDUSTRIALIZATION . . . . *Glenn McLaughlin*	163

Part III

CONTROLS

X. ECONOMIC CONTROLS IN POSTWAR TRANSITION . . . . . . *John M. Clark*	181
XI. DEVELOPMENT OF PRICE CONTROL AND TRANSITION PRICE PROBLEMS . . . . *Donald H. Wallace*	196
XII. INTERNATIONAL COMMODITY CONTROLS; CARTELS AND COMMODITY AGREEMENTS. . . . . *Edward S. Mason*	217

Part IV

MONETARY AND FISCAL PROBLEMS

XIII. CENTRAL AND COMMERCIAL BANKING IN POSTWAR FINANCE . *Howard S. Ellis*	237
XIV. FISCAL POLICY IN ECONOMIC RECONSTRUCTION . . . . . . *Gerhard Colm*	253
XV. POSTWAR TAX STRUCTURE . . . . *Roy Blough*	275
XVI. A POSTWAR TAX PROGRAM . . . . *Alvin H. Hansen*	292
XVII. POSTWAR FINANCING OF BUSINESS ENTERPRISE . . . . *S. Morris Livingston*	301

Part V

INTERNATIONAL ECONOMIC RELATIONS

XVIII. SOME FACTORS AFFECTING THE FUTURE OF INTERNATIONAL TRADE AND INTERNATIONAL ECONOMIC POLICY . . . . . . *Gottfried Haberler*	319

CONTENTS

CHAPTER	PAGE
XIX. MONETARY STABILIZATION: THE UNITED NATIONS PROGRAM. *E. M. Bernstein*	336
XX. INTERNATIONAL CAPITAL FINANCING . . . . *Arthur R. Upgren*	353
XXI. THE PATH FROM BRETTON WOODS . . . . *Henry C. Wallich*	366

Part VI

SOCIAL SECURITY AND THE CONTRIBUTIONS BY THE GOVERNMENT

XXII. SOCIAL SECURITY . . . . *Eveline M. Burns*	381
XXIII. GOVERNMENT CONTRIBUTION . . . . *Alan Sweezy*	397
INDEX	413

Contributors

(Arranged in the order of their chapters in this book)

I. **Alvin H. Hansen.** Littauer Professor of Political Economy, Harvard University; former President of the American Economic Association; author of *Full Recovery or Stagnation?*; *Fiscal Policy and Business Cycles*; *State and Local Finance in the National Economy*; *America's Role in the World Economy*, etc.

II. **Mordecai Ezekiel.** Adviser to the Secretary of the Department of Agriculture; author of *$2,500 a Year*; *Jobs for All*, etc.

III. **John D. Black.** Professor of Economics, Harvard University, and **Charles D. Hyson,** Harvard University. Professor Black has contributed to the formulation of agricultural policy in the thirties and is the author of *Production Economics*; *Parity, Parity, Parity*; *Food Enough*, etc. Dr. Hyson is Resident Consultant at the Graduate School of Public Administration.

IV. **Seymour E. Harris.** Associate Professor of Economics, Harvard University; formerly Director of the Office of Export-Import Control, Office of Price Administration; editor of the present volume and of *Postwar Economic Problems*; author of numerous volumes on economics.

V. **Jacob L. Mosak.** Chief, Economic Analysis and Forecasting Branch, Office of Price Administration; author of *General-equilibrium Theory in International Trade*.

VI. **William Haber.** Professor of Economics, on leave from the University of Michigan; formerly in charge of Planning and Program Development of the War Manpower Commission; now Adviser on Manpower in the Office of War Mobilization and Reconversion; author of *Industrial Relations in the Building Industry*; *Unemployment, a Problem of Insecurity*, etc.

VII. **A. D. H. Kaplan.** Professor of Economics, on leave from the University of Denver; Adviser to a Congressional Committee dealing with postwar economic problems; author of the C.E.D. study on *The Liquidation of War Production*.

VIII. **Charles D. Stewart.** Chief of the Occupational Outlook Division, Bureau of Labor Statistics, Department of Labor.

IX. **Glenn McLaughlin.** War Production Board; formerly Expert on Regional Problems with the National Resources Planning Board; author of *Growth of American Manufacturing Areas*.

X. **John M. Clark.** Professor of Economics, Columbia University; former President of the American Economic Association; formerly economic adviser to the Price Administrator; author of the C.E.D. study *Demobilization of Wartime Economic Controls*; *Studies in the Economics of Overhead Costs*; *Social Control of Business*; *The Costs of the World War to the American People*, etc.

CONTRIBUTORS

XI. **Donald H. Wallace.** Associate Professor of Economics, on leave from Williams College; Special Economic Adviser to the Deputy Price Administrator; formerly Acting Deputy Administrator in charge of Price; author of *Market Control in the Aluminum Industry* and of numerous studies in the area of pricing.

XII. **Edward S. Mason.** Professor of Economics, on leave from Harvard University; Special Assistant to Assistant Secretary Clayton of the State Department and is making a study of Business Arrangements in Foreign Trade for the C.E.D.; author of *Steel Railway in Massachusetts* and *The Paris Commune*.

XIII. **Howard S. Ellis.** Professor of Economics, on leave from the University of California and visiting Professor at Columbia University; Assistant Director, Division of Research and Statistics of the Federal Reserve Board; author of *German Monetary Theory, 1905–33; Exchange Control in Central Europe*, etc.

XIV. **Gerhard Colm.** Bureau of the Budget; author of *Economic Consequences of Recent American Tax Policy*, etc.

XV. **Roy Blough.** Director of Tax Research of the Treasury Department; has made many contributions to the theory and practice of taxation.

XVI. **Alvin H. Hansen.**

XVII. **S. Morris Livingston.** Chief, National Economics Unit, Bureau of Foreign and Domestic Commerce, Department of Commerce; author of *Markets after the War* and numerous other studies on our current economic situation.

XVIII. **Gottfried Haberler.** Professor of Economics, Harvard University; has served on the staff of the League of Nations and the Federal Reserve Board; author of *The Theory of International Trade; Prosperity and Depression; Quantitative Trade Controls*, etc.

XIX. **Edward M. Bernstein.** Professor of Economics, on leave from the University of North Carolina; Assistant Director of Monetary Research, Treasury Department; has played an important part in the formulation of the plans at Bretton Woods; author of *Money and the Economic System; Public Utility Rate Making and the Price Level*.

XX. **Arthur R. Upgren.** Associate Editor, *Minneapolis Star Journal*, and Professor of Economics, University of Minnesota; formerly Vice President and Economist, Federal Reserve Bank of Minneapolis; author of *Reciprocal Trade Agreements, Raw Materials and Latin American Solidarity*.

XXI. **Henry C. Wallich.** Economist in the Research Division of the Federal Reserve Bank of New York; has written numerous articles on current economic problems.

XXII. **Eveline M. Burns.** Visiting Professor of Economics at Bryn Mawr College; on the staff of the National Planning Association; is largely responsible for the American Beveridge Plan published under the auspices of the National Resources Planning Board; author of *Social Security in Our Postwar Economy; Toward Social Security; British Unemployment Programs, 1920–1938*.

XXIII. **Alan Sweezy.** Associate Professor of Economics, Williams College; is the author of numerous articles on the relation of government and the economy.

Introduction

The Issues

by SEYMOUR E. HARRIS

I

MORE than two years ago the writer edited a volume on postwar economic problems.[1] At that time it seemed necessary to apologize for the diversion of any energies from the immediate job of waging war to a consideration of postwar problems. That the postwar economic problems were going to be of unprecedented difficulty and require the energies and time of our best economists was nevertheless apparent even then.

Some may ask: Why should the writer edit a book on reconstruction when postwar economic problems have been explored? To borrow a military analogy: Whereas the earlier volume was perhaps 75 per cent strategy and 25 per cent tactics, this volume is at least 50 per cent tactics. We have had more than an additional two years in which further to appraise our war efforts and the better to understand the readjustments which will be required. Whereas the wartime rise in our national income had been but $50 billion by 1942, by 1944 it had increased by about $90 billion above prewar levels. Whereas the Treasury had spent $32 billion in the fiscal year 1942, it spent $95 billion in 1944, and expenditures are estimated at $100 billion in the fiscal year 1945. To carry comparisons further: Federal taxes had yielded $14 billion in the fiscal year 1942, and their estimated yield in the fiscal year 1945 is $44 billion; total deposits adjusted and currency outside banks were up $18 billion by June, 1942, or almost 30 per cent over 1939, and were up $87 billion, or 135 per cent, by Dec., 1944. Whereas by the summer of 1942 the labor force

[1] *Postwar Economic Problems*, now in its fifth printing.

had risen by only 3.2 million over the total for July, 1940—and total civilians employed, plus the armed forces, had risen by 9.7 million—the respective estimates for the summer of 1944 were increases of 8.9 and 17.2 million, respectively.

We have watched our war program go into high gear and reach dimensions predicted in 1942 but not generally accepted as likely to be realized. Impressed by the significant gains, we are also now in a better position to envisage the magnitude of the problems of readjustment and of maintenance of a healthy economy than were the writers of the earlier volume. Now we can study with some precision—as those writing in 1942 were unable to do—concrete proposals for liquidation of government property, for the postwar tax structure, definite programs for international reconstruction, patterns and magnitude of spending on consumption and investment, the speed of demobilization of workers, of the military, and of controls, the manner of dealing with the plethora of cash and liquid resources, the possible contribution of the government. In 1942 we were able to consider many of these problems but, not knowing how far we would go, we were not in a position to know how far we might descend or how high the plateau we might cling to, given appropriate policies by government, business, labor, and agriculture.

II

The next decade may well decide a vital issue: Can this country afford the luxury of a free-economy society? Of course our free economic system has been administered many drugs and has even had some surgery. Yet there are still large elements of freedom in it. That it has survived for 10 generations in this country does not prove, as many optimists seem to hold, that it will outlive them. Whether an economy, half free and half regulated, can survive is another issue.

What is needed is not exhortation or intuition or expressions of faith in our economic institutions. It is now necessary to study facts and to draw conclusions from them. This is essentially what the 22 economists who have contributed to this volume do. They are all hopeful that the system of private enterprise will survive; but they are also aware that the system faces a period which will test its strength and resiliency as never before.

Our 22 collaborators are not members of any one school. They are stagnationists and anti-stagnationists; New Dealers and critics of at least a substantial part of New Dealism; supporters of deficit financing and adherents of a balanced budget.

The editor has the temerity to suggest that most economists would agree on the following propositions:

1. Our system of free economic enterprise will not survive unless we can find employment for at least 90 per cent of those genuinely seeking work. We may tolerate unemployment of 5 to 10 million for brief periods; but it is unlikely that the country will stand by again while 10 million or more are unemployed for a decade. There are not a few who contend that we must have full employment; but all will agree with the position that we must have a high level of employment.

2. Any failure to spend a significant part of our income in a given year on consumption and investment goods will start a downward movement which, unless it is stopped, will be cumulative in its effects.

3. Our most perplexing problem of the reconversion and postwar period is, therefore, to prevent the reduction of Federal expenditures by around $75 billion from producing a downward spiral from which the system will never recover. More than one-quarter of this contraction of Federal expenditures, according to current estimates, will take place after victory in Europe, now popularly referred to as VE-day; and the remainder after victory over Japan, now popularly referred to as VJ-day. It is indeed fortunate that the large readjustments required will not be forced upon us all at once by a simultaneous ending of the warfare on both fronts.

III

We are not suggesting, because a national income of $160 billion or a gross national product of $200 billion has now been attained, that a full-employment economy will require an equal income or gross national product. Much will depend on the numbers on the labor market, changes in productivity, hours of work, the wage and price level, and the like. The reader will find in this volume some estimates of income for a postwar year (Chapters V and XIV by Drs. Mosak and Colm) that equal approximately the amounts attained at the peak of the war effort. Assuming relatively little unemployment, a large labor force, and continued gains of productivity, they arrive at these highly satisfactory results. The Brookings Institution, on the other hand, emphasizing the effects of national downgrading, substantial departures from the labor market, loss of overtime, and, disregarding the historical trends in productivity, arrives at a much lower estimate of national income—$123 billion.

Recent estimates by Dr. Kuznets, the country's leading expert on income, are also not cheering. He obtains his results by projecting incomes of the past into the future. Whereas most economists estimate national income on the basis of what might be achieved—under a full-employment or high-employment income—Dr. Kuznets assumes that we shall continue to manage as badly as we have in the past. Most of the other estimates offer us something to shoot at or, according to many, what we must attain; Dr. Kuznets draws inferences from history.[1]

All these estimates are for an early postwar year. Our attainable income continues to gain as we probe into the future. If we continue to raise man-hour output at the same rate as in the past fifty years, the net national income will soon be $200 billion. On the assumption that productivity and production rise every twenty years from 1940 on at the rate they did from 1920 to 1940, the results would be as follows: (This is not a prediction.)

	1940	1960	1980	2000
Productivity	100	200	400	800
Industrial production	100	166	276	458

IV

If there is a leading theme in this volume, it is this: a substantial decline of spending cannot be tolerated and, when it has occurred, corrective measures must quickly be taken. There are few, if any, chapters in this volume that do not deal with this problem directly or indirectly. The general problem of the maintenance of a high level of spending is dealt with by Profs. Hansen and Sweezy and Drs. Ezekiel, Colm, and Mosak. According to these writers, an adequate level of spending is not likely to be attained without substantial contributions by the government. Essays dealing with special aspects of the economy also treat, directly or indirectly, of the support of demand. In the chapters on agriculture, labor, social security, taxation, and international economic

[1] Dr. Kuznets' estimates of 1942 discussed here are more gloomy than those in a study by him to be published (1945) by the National Bureau of Economic Research.

relations, the reader will find discussions which are related to demand.

Those responsible for these chapters would agree on the significance of the magnitude of spending. There is no general agreement among economists, however, as to the government's contributions. Economists today are divided into two camps: (1) those who maintain that, given a healthy milieu—a tax system that does not weigh too heavily on business enterprise, a flexible price and wage policy, healthy relations among government, business, and labor, relaxation of trade barriers—given these, this country will support its population at a high standard of living and at high-employment levels; (2) those who contend that irrespective of the improvements along the lines adumbrated above, the government will have to make a significant, if varying, contribution to total spending and employment.

The editor would not claim that this issue has been resolved. Our experience in the thirties seems to him to count in favor of the stagnationists. It is hoped that the experience of the fifties will help clarify the issues. If in the next decade free enterprise is given the support of a strong and able government, if a much needed change in the tax structure on lines suggested here is effected, if a flexible price and wage policy and the improvements in international economic relations proposed here are accomplished—then if large amounts of unemployment still prevail, the position of the stagnationists will attract increased support. They will, however, naturally lose support if, in the absence of a large measure of government intervention, the fifties prove to be a period of sustained prosperity.

Of this much one can be certain: Against the $75 billion of government spending to be replaced annually, current estimates of deferred demand, unfilled orders, and new markets for durables seem to be a pittance. Even the optimistic estimates of the Chamber of Commerce put deferred demand at but $20 billion; and clearly a large part of this is in fact current demand.

V

From all of this the reader should not infer that large amounts of unemployment will prevail unless, in the early postwar years, we attain a gross national product of $200 billion or a net national income of $150 to 160 billion (1943–1944 prices). The required income which will yield full employment will depend upon the productivity changes from

1940 to 194x. Here we assume a net change for the forties at the rate given by the previous fifty years. This is not, however, the only relevant factor. Among other factors which will determine the amount of unemployment will be the numbers on the labor market and the number of hours in the working week. Most estimates are based on a 40-hour working week. Since, however, the working week was 37 to 38 hours in manufacturing before the war and since over the last few generations there has been a reduction of the working week of around 20 hours, there is much reason for setting the working week at 35 hours. A reduction of hours of work by 5 hours from the 40 hours generally assumed *may* account for 7 to 8 million additional jobs.

Another relevant consideration is the numbers on the labor market. Enrollment in high schools might rise by 1 million (around 15 per cent of the total now in these schools), in schools of higher education by 1½ million (a rise of about 100 per cent, or from 15 to 30 per cent of the total number of those aged nineteen to twenty-two and from more than 1 to more than 2 per cent of total population). An additional 1 million or more might be added in the elementary and other schools.

It is easy to see that potential unemployment might be cut by 10 million or more through a reduction of hours to 35 and increased schooling. If the public prefers work to schooling and leisure, this is obviously not an ideal solution. But since in the past the public has taken its gains partly in leisure, there is no reason why they should not continue to do so. If they could make a conscious choice, would they not continue as in the past? At any rate, if private demand does not provide 55 to 60 million jobs at 40 hours per week and if, fearing governmental participation and public deficits, we do not supplement private and public demand sufficiently to yield a high level of employment, then here is a way out of widespread unemployment. It is clearly to be preferred to the unemployment, breakdown of morale, maldistribution, and low-income levels of the thirties. We may then well have full employment at an income of around $125 billion instead of $150 billion, if we assume the withdrawal of several million additional from the labor market and a 35-hour week in manufacturing and corresponding reductions elsewhere.

VI

In this volume we are concerned with two groups of problems: the transitional and the long-run. They are not, however, independent.

A failure to solve our transitional problems will aggravate the long-run situation. Many of the problems are, moreover, both short- and long-run.

First, there are the monetary, financial, and savings problems. They will plague us in the immediate future and, if unsolved, will still be with us in the fifties. We were confronted by the end of 1944 with a wartime rise of liquid assets (deposits, cash, and government securities) of about $106 billion, or 130 per cent; of deposits and currency of more than 85 per cent; of United States securities held by individuals of 360 per cent.[1] These raise baffling questions which Drs. Ellis and Livingston discuss. What can the banks do to control the flow of money when corporations and individuals hold unprecedented amounts of cash and securities? What can the reserve banks do to control the banks when the latter can allow billions of dollars of securities to run off as a means of adding to their reserves? Can industry finance the transition without further recourse to banks and the capital market? These and similar problems are under consideration in this volume.

Related to these problems are the tax issues. Drs. Hansen, Blough, and Colm consider taxes not merely from a purely fiscal viewpoint; they are interested in the effects of a given tax system on enterprise, consumption, investment, employment, income, and total spending. What kind of tax system will meet minimum tests of adequacy of revenue and justice and yet strain our system the least?

VII

In general, a wide extension beyond the controls extant in 1930–1940 is not compatible with a system of private enterprise. This means that most wartime controls must go, once the maladjustments brought by war have disappeared. (Too rapid termination of wartime controls, however, may account for distortions which will aggravate the difficulties of attaining postreconversion stability and high levels of employment.)

Our war experience attests that controls spread: from one segment of the economy to another; from one type to another, and complementary type. There is no halting this process. Price control of selected commodities releases surplus purchasing power which endangers stability in

---

[1] Figures are estimated for the 3 years ending Dec. 31, 1944, and relate to individual holdings. *Federal Reserve Bulletin*, October, 1944, p. 953.

uncontrolled areas. Effective price control requires control of demand through rationing, allocations, and limitations on consumer credit and control of supply conditions through export control, conservation measures, limitation orders, standardization, simplification, and the like. Price control alone, of course, does not account for all these controls; but the pressure of the price administrator frequently is felt. This is not all, however. Price control requires control of wages and farm prices. Once wage control is achieved, it is necessary to rely upon compulsory transfers of man power to achieve the optimum distribution; or be satisfied with a far less than optimum distribution (for wage control removes an important stimulus to movement).

In this volume Profs. Clark, Mason, and Wallace discuss the problem of controls. They are interested primarily in the reconversion and demobilization period. A premature removal of controls will, in the opinion of Profs. Clark and Wallace, bring about serious distortions. Our government is already beginning to feel the pressure of businessmen for hasty removal of controls and, fearful of their retention, they are disposed to argue that, with the removal of controls, economic factors will once more begin to move where they are most needed and output will expand. Perhaps if these businessmen read this volume, they will not then be so certain that premature removal will be to their interest. They will learn that controls are interrelated; that an early removal may bring inflation, use of scarce factors for nonessential purposes, excessive inventory accumulation and exports, unfair distribution as between big and small business, etc. Would they, for example, favor a free market for automobiles before supplies are reasonably in relation to demand, or construction on the basis of price bids irrespective of scarcities, say, summer resorts as against the need of housing for medical purposes?

Professor Mason treats a problem which is of both immediate and long-run interest. Cartels and international commodity agreements are planned by governments abroad. Business and governments fearing excessive supplies and falling prices, loss of markets, and scarcity of exchange are inclined to resort to programs for protecting their markets, raising their prices, and, therefore, improving their terms of trade. This country is faced with the difficult question as to whether it should join in this division of markets, restrictionism, and the like—a program incompatible with our liberal trade program—or stay out and thus perhaps frustrate those who plan a division of markets at the expense of consumers.

VIII

As a result of the war, there have been significant changes in the structure and ownership of industry and in the composition and size of the labor-supply market. One should not expect that, with peace, these must necessarily revert to prewar conditions. Our regional pattern of industry is significantly different from that of the prewar: the Far West, the Tennessee Valley, and some regions of the Southwest have tended to increase their relative command of manufacturing facilities. Our labor force has grown greatly. It remains to be seen whether the composition, size, and regional distribution will once more return to normal. Our government owns perhaps $75 billion of property and exercises a great threat over our system of private enterprise through its control of this property as well as through its policy in the field of termination of contracts. We await with interest its policy toward manufacturing facilities that can survive in the postwar only if Treasury help is forthcoming. Are we to move workers out of war areas as war business gradually disappears and the slack is not taken up by private enterprise, or is the government, as the British government has announced it intends to do, to move facilities into depressed areas or subsidize industry in the depressed regions? Furthermore, while these large deficiencies of demand and substantial amounts of unemployment may develop in special industries and localities, the *aggregate* demand of the country may be adequate relative to supply. Thus it is not enough to discuss the problems of the postwar in terms of over-all supply and demand conditions. In the war period, pressures on particular markets have increased more than those on others. This is reflected in the varying rate of increase in population, employment, income payments, bank deposits, and the cost of living.

In connection with this the following is of interest. From December, 1939, to December, 1944, the percentage increase of deposits was a minimum in the New York Reserve District (71 per cent) and a maximum in the San Francisco District (248); in the spring and summer of 1943, wage rates in selected manufacturing industries in Detroit were as much as 31 per cent above the average in all urban areas; from 1941 to 1943, incomes in Oregon and Florida were up 97 and 95 per cent;

in New Hampshire and New York, only 23 and 30 per cent. According to a study of the Bureau of Labor Statistics, the required demobilization as a percentage of April 1940 employment was 40 per cent or more in the states of Washington, Connecticut, Michigan, California, Indiana, Nevada, Oregon, and Ohio and but 17.2 per cent for South Dakota and 28.4 per cent for New York.[1]

If total demand should be deficient in the postwar period, the net effect of maldistribution and immobility will be that the incidence of unemployment will be unevenly distributed—it will be concentrated disproportionately in certain areas and on a limited number of individuals; and the distribution of the working population according to the maximum productivity will to this extent be impaired. If, on the other hand, total demand should be more than high enough to assure full employment, the effect of maldistribution will be unfilled vacancies in some areas and unemployment in others.

The troublesome problems mentioned here will give the reader an indication of the range of subjects discussed by Drs. Haber, Stewart, McLaughlin, and Kaplan. Upon the manner in which these problems are solved will depend in no small part the success of the reconversion and also, to some extent, the long-run economic conditions.

IX

Let us assume that the reconversion policies will be wise—even as judicious as those proposed in this volume! Let us also assume that the proposals for price policies, controls, wages, labor, disposal of property as recommended by our collaborators will be accepted. In a world of group pressures, less than perfect government, widespread ignorance of economics and, even worse, the acceptance of economic fallacies—in this kind of world we are expecting too much if we anticipate that the final decisions will not, at least in part, be based on economic nonsense. Again let us also assume that the governments of the world will follow the advice of Prof. Haberler and Drs. Bernstein, Upgren, and Wallich and will encourage exchange stability, relaxation of trade restrictions, and renewal of foreign lending. Even under these very favorable circumstances, the government may have to do more.

This is the theme of Profs. Hansen and Sweezy and it is supported

---

[1] For assumptions, etc., see *Bureau of Labor Statistics Serial No. R 1691*, "State Variations and Post-war Demobilization," September, 1944, especially pp. 4–13.

INTRODUCTION

by several others: Drs. Ezekiel, Colm, and Mosak.[1] Professor Hansen, for example, estimating postwar savings at 10 per cent of disposable national income, concludes that the required volume of investment is much larger than the country will probably be able to absorb. (Professor Hansen's estimate of individual savings is modest. He apparently is anxious to understate his case.) Many would put savings at substantially more than 10 per cent of disposable income at an income of $140 billion —the percentage in 1944, under unusual wartime conditions to be sure, was around 27 per cent. It will also be necessary to increase consumption by at least one-half above the 1940 amount. Insofar as consumption or investment fails to reach its goal, it will be necessary to accept declining demand and unemployment or encourage further investment. Professor Sweezy discusses the form which these investments might take. An adequate social-security program, as envisaged by Dr. Burns, may also contribute to a higher volume of spending and to that extent reduce the need for public investment.

Public investment at the rate of $10 billion annually may be required if a downward spiral is to be averted. Growth of the public debt at this rate will be unfortunate only if national income does not rise correspondingly to support it. An annual rise of national income of 2 per cent, or $3 billion—a rate less than that of the past fifty years—would yield additional income of fifteen times the debt charge on new debt accumulating at the rate of $10 billion per year; and the $3 billion of new income each year should yield Federal revenue equal to three times the cost of financing the new debt. This growth of debt and public investment may be the price that will have to be paid if a cumulative decline is to be prevented. It is surely to be preferred to a reduction of national income by 20 to 40 per cent. And perhaps we shall be able to get on without much additional public investment. So much the better. It need hardly be added that there should be periods of debt repayment, as well as of debt expansion.

This volume then is an attempt on the part of 22 economists (gov-

---

[1] The reader will find an appraisal of postwar demand by Dr. Bissell in the aforementioned *Postwar Economic Problems*. He largely dismisses additional public investment as a necessary condition of full employment. The reader should also consult Dr. Livingston's *Markets after the War*. Here, by a projection of the relation of gross national product and consumption in numerous markets over the years 1929–1940, Dr. Livingston envisages an adequate level of consumption and private investment to support a full employment income. More has, however, been claimed for these results by many (who found support in them for optimistic estimates of postwar demand) than the author had intended. See the fuller discussion of these issues in the editor's *Inflation and the War and Postwar Economy* (1945).

ernment servants past or present) to study the major economic issues confronting this country in the immediate future and in the longer run. We have assembled here the analyses of experts in the fields of income, agriculture, social security, fiscal policy, controls, money, business finance, etc. And from it all we draw this conclusion: The problems are difficult and will be soluble only if the country gets better leadership than it had in the interwar period. Our number one problem is not the nineteenth-century one of production, but the twentieth-century problem of demand. Somehow we must learn to take the goods which are produced off the market. There is scarcely a chapter in this volume which does not make some suggestion along these lines. This problem of adequacy and maintenance of demand falls to the lot of the economist. Let it not be said of him, if the problem fails of solution, that he has not given the best advice he had to offer and that he has not with energy and courage urged his views upon those who determine policy.

Part I

GENERAL ASPECTS

Chapter I

Postwar Employment Outlook

by ALVIN H. HANSEN

SO MUCH has been written recently on postwar employment in the United States that the subject is perhaps becoming somewhat threadbare. Foreign economists, I find, are particularly inclined to be somewhat wearied of American speculation on the subject, while at the same time a little disturbed that we do so little about it. By and large my own contacts with foreign colleagues leave me with the impression that they are distinctly pessimistic about our outlook. The article by Gunnar Myrdal in the November, 1944, issue of *The Atlantic Monthly*, although not necessarily representing an analysis to which most foreign economists would subscribe, does represent the general pessimistic attitude.

I myself am inclined to think that my foreign colleagues exaggerate the problem. At the same time I am disposed to think that many American economists are altogether too complacent about it.

The war experience has, I think, left all of us more or less stunned with the magnitude of the employment problem. We have actually witnessed a volume of civilian production higher than that of any peacetime year, despite the drastic decline in consumers' durables. On top of that we are producing almost $90 billion of war matériel, while at the same time there are 11 million of our best working force in the military forces. Although the Army and Navy pay roll is indeed considered as part of the national income, it is nevertheless true that their per capita receipts are relatively low compared with those of the civilian population. Their employment in civilian pursuits would yield a higher national product. On the other side, there is a net addition of 6 to 7 million to the labor force of women, young people, and older people not normally in the labor force. There is also the overtime. Full employment—which means in a dynamic society as large as ours perhaps 3 million unemployed—would, however (after deducting the overtime and the excess labor force) mean a very substantial increase in civilian employment beyond present levels. Civilian employment should rise in the postwar by 4 or 5 million above the current 51.5 million.

The mere enumeration of these data shows what it means to have full employment in the United States. Even during the prodigious war effort no serious labor scarcity developed, and foreigners, coming from tighter labor markets, are continually amazed at the "unessential jobs" that they find being performed all around in our vast country—the cleaning of dust and smoke from the outside walls of stone buildings and the like.

To maintain the national product at a level commensurate with our capacity to produce, the American people will have to advance their standard of living as a whole by somewhere around 50 per cent. So large an advance in the standard of living has never before been made in a short interval of time. If we could achieve a full-employment income, are we prepared to spend enough to maintain that income for long?

A substantial and sudden rise in the standard of living of a people requires not merely the power to produce; it also involves an educational process. There is considerable danger, it seems to me, that we shall experience a distinct lag in our standard of consumption behind our extraordinary capacity to produce, of which we have only recently become fully aware.

In order to achieve a high consumption standard we cannot neglect the fact that a large proportion of the population receive extraordinarily low incomes. Minimum wage rates must be raised and everywhere wages must be increased to the highest possible level consistent with the cost-price situation. If we are going to solve reasonably well our employment problem, we must become high-wage conscious. I hasten to add that it makes no sense to raise wages if this involves price increases. While we need to be high-wage conscious, we must guard against becoming wage inflationists. Inadequate purchasing power leads to deflation; but we must also guard against inflation. Always in economic matters we are compelled to steer a difficult course.

Before the war, many industries had learned to make fairly satisfactory profits while operating at low capacity levels. Full employment requires a pricing policy that permits expansion. At full capacity utilization, unit costs are low. Accordingly, either prices can be lowered or wages increased. Price policy and wage policy must be adapted to the requirements of high production levels.

Much can be done to raise our standard of living and to reach a higher consumption economy through expansion of certain public services. Foremost among these are educational facilities, where these are seriously deficient, and also public-health facilities and services.

With respect to education, it is not generally recognized how large a percentage of American children is growing up in states with intolerably low educational standards. In 1939–1940, in eight of the most advanced Northern states, the average educational expenditure per pupil was $140 per annum. In contrast, 22 states fell below an expenditure of $84, while 11 states spent less than $60 per pupil, and 8 averaged less than $40. At least 40 per cent of our children are growing up in areas that do not meet modern accepted standards of a minimum public-school education, and 25 per cent are growing up in areas under intolerable conditions which result in widespread illiteracy. Illiteracy in the United States is gravely underestimated in the census. The Army authorities tell us that, typically, persons with less than 4 years' education are "functional" illiterates. A high standard of living commensurate with our modern productive power cannot be achieved if such conditions are perpetuated.

The military records show how far we fall short of the minimum health standards which modern science makes possible. About 40 per cent of the selected-service registrants were not able to qualify for full military service. Here, again, the divergencies in different parts of our country proved to be very great.

With respect to housing, nearly a third of our urban community lives in slum or seriously blighted areas. Juvenile delinquency, crime, tuberculosis, and the general death rate are typically from four to six times higher than in the rest of the community. We cannot achieve a standard of living commensurate with our productive capacity until we have removed low-standard slums and provided decent housing standards for the entire population.

There appears to be no difference of opinion regarding the need of our social-security system for overhauling and substantial expansion. The Wagner-Dingell bill should be adopted, but the financing features of the bill require drastic change. We should not permit receipts from pay-roll taxes to exceed current benefit payments. We should not continue to permit the social-security program to draw from the mass of the people a vast amount of compulsory savings. We should not permit social security to act in a deflationary manner upon the economy. Beginning with an even balance between receipts from pay-roll taxes and benefit payments, as costs increase they should be carried by the Treasury. Eventually, we should thus approach a reasonable sharing of social security by the government, the employer, and the employee.

Something substantial can be done to achieve a high-consumption society by means of the tax structure. Sales taxes should be completely eliminated, while excises should be reduced, and, as Messrs. Ruml and Sonne have pointed out, the course of events may eventually justify their complete elimination. I discuss a postwar tax program in a later chapter of this book.

Finally, we cannot escape a consideration of the over-all savings-investment problem. The standard of consumption and the distribution of income, already referred to, will indeed affect this problem. I am doubtful, however, that the savings pattern in this country in the next decade with all these reforms is likely to show any very substantial change. Any fundamental change is likely to take time.

It is perfectly true that war has brought new impacts which cannot be overlooked. The masses of the population have accumulated a nest egg in government bonds and cash. These holdings, however, are frequently enormously exaggerated. Close to two-thirds of the total Federal debt outstanding is held by financial institutions, inclusive of government agencies and corporations, while nearly two-thirds of the rest is held by nonfinancial business concerns and by well-to-do individuals. Probably not more than 15 per cent of government bonds is held by the mass of the population. Nonentrepreneurial individuals held about 20 per cent of the amount outstanding on June 30, 1944.[1]

Nevertheless, in terms of former standards the amounts are large. How will this affect the propensity to spend out of current income? About this there is difference of opinion. My own view is that, while millions will dispose of some of their holdings to buy durable consumers' goods, others will be making new purchases of bonds and that on balance the nest egg of savings will largely be maintained.

[1] *Cf.* H. S. Ellis in Ch. XIII and Mordecai Ezekiel in Ch. II. It should be observed that savings of individuals are close to $100 billion. These figures, however, include bonds, net additions to cash and deposits, reduction of debt, and investments in real property. Moreover, these figures apply to individual entrepreneurs and farms and include the savings of the rich and the considerably well to do.

Postwar taxes on individuals will be higher than in prewar. This must affect the percentage saved from the income receipts of individuals, but it will not necessarily affect the percentage of disposable income (income after taxes) saved. It will be very interesting to see how it works out, but I think it is a reasonable assumption that at high-income levels individuals will continue, as in the twenties and in the prewar, to save around 10 per cent of their disposable income.

Depreciation and other reserves for capital replacement will amount to about $10 billion or more. Add to this $3 or $4 billion of net corporate savings and $2 or $3 billion of unincorporated business net savings. Gross business savings are thus likely to run around $15 to $17 billion. Individual savings, after deducting the net savings of individual entrepreneurs, are likely, I think, to run around $11 billion. Thus, total gross savings on these assumptions would amount to from $26 to $28 billion at high employment levels.

What are the prospects that gross private-capital formation can be maintained year in and year out at a level adequate to provide outlets for $26 or $28 billion a year of savings? Whereas this is certainly possible for a year or two, I think no one will deny that there is no comfortable prospect that investment outlets of such magnitude can for long be maintained.

Twelve billion dollars per annum invested in business plant and equipment, with $1 billion for net addition to inventories and $2 billion net foreign investment (after deducting for foreign funds invested in this country) represent very large magnitudes. But these figures would scarcely permit sufficient outlets for the savings of business alone. There remain the $11 billion or so of individual savings, entrepreneurs excluded. The only significant remaining outlets are residential housing and new government issues.[1]

These figures, rough though they be, do, I think, in a broad way present the dimensions of the problem. Myrdal, in the article referred to above, dared to predict that we would not witness in the United States a balanced budget in this decade.

There is every evidence that we shall in fact have a large Federal budget in the postwar years and that neither business nor the public generally will be eager to pay high taxes. It is probable that the public debt may, except for periods of very high private investment, continue to rise. *I believe, however, that the debt will not rise in relation to the national*

---

[1] *Cf.* Messrs. Colm and Mosak in Chs. XIV and V.

income. It is not mere wishful thinking to look forward to a secular rise in the national income of 2 or 2½ per cent per annum. But this requires not only efficient use of productive resources, but also generous outlays, both public and private, on research relating to new products, new resources, and new methods of production.

We shall, I think, experience a wholesome public pressure in favor of development and expansion. We shall not achieve perfection, and at times the volume of unemployment may be considerable, but the nation will not tolerate stagnation. The resolution presented to the President and the Congress by the eight Missouri Valley governors for a Missouri Valley Authority is indicative of the new trend of thinking. Urban redevelopment, public housing, and transportation, together with river-valley development, are the great areas for development and expansion. A program along these lines, combined with the measures indicated above to raise the consumption function, will, I think, profoundly change the character of industrial fluctuations. Under a program of development and expansion, the business cycle will prove to be something far different from what it has been in the past. Nevertheless, we should strive to combine with a developmental program a compensatory program designed to minimize cyclical fluctuations. The British White Paper on Employment Policy represents a major landmark in cycle policy and it cannot, I think, fail to have an important effect upon our own country.

Chapter II

Agricultural and Industrial Problems in Conversion from War to Peace

by MORDECAI EZEKIEL

ECONOMIC progress after this war depends much more on what happens in industry than on what happens in agriculture. The impact of the war has been enormously greater in industry than in agriculture, owing to the highly mechanized character of modern warfare. Unless ways are found to solve the industrial postwar problems, what we do on the agricultural side will make little difference.

Changes during the War

AGRICULTURAL

What happened during the war includes both the impact of the war and the adjustment to it. The dominant element in adjustment to the war, both in agriculture and in industry, has been the enormous expansion in production of which our economy has shown it is capable. The expansion in agriculture alone is phenomenal enough. The physical volume of agricultural output increased steadily in this war by about three times as much as during the corresponding period of World War I. A part of the increase was due to favorable weather, but the large and continued increase year after year shows that better production methods and better varieties, such as hybrid corn, deserve a large share of the credit. The average yield per acre, by 5-year periods, has been going up steadily. If we take all the recent yield increases and say that all the increase is due to favorable weather, increased productivity will be underestimated.

The production of agricultural products is now approximately 28 per cent above the 5-year average before the war. With that increase in output has gone a shift in its composition. The biggest increase has been in the products most needed during the war. A great deal of effort has been made to speed the production of peanuts and soybeans, and their production has been multiplied several fold. Meat is up 51 per cent, dairy products 13 per cent, and poultry 52 per cent. How much agricultural labor it has taken to produce this output is difficult to say. The total number of people working on farms is no larger now and possibly is smaller than it was before the war. They are working harder now; the figures on average hours worked per week have increased about twice as much on farms as in factories, according to the census surveys. Great emphasis has been placed on expanding the protective foods: meat, livestock products, and the things especially needed for the war. Some things have been expanded to meet the special overseas demands such as cheese, dry beans, and dehydrated products in general.

Despite the enormous increase in output, consumer rationing has been needed for many food products. Most of the increased production has gone overseas. The increased consumer buying power has greatly expanded the ability of civilians to buy food. If it were not for price ceilings, ration coupons, and war-savings drives, the great excess of food demand over food supplies would have driven their prices far higher than they now are. Despite the war shortages, civilian per capita consumption of most foods—including such essentials as eggs, meats, fresh and canned vegetables, and fluid milk—is now well above prewar averages. Only in butter, cheese, and canned fruits have war needs cut average civilian consumption materially below previous averages.

INDUSTRIAL

On the industrial side, the expansion has been enormous. Our factories are producing today at least twice as much in physical volume as they produced before the war. To make a comparison of that volume, we must add together food and clothing and airplanes and tanks and guns. Yet that does not tell us what we shall be able to make when we get back to peacetime production, in plows, automobiles, and other things that we were already making on a peacetime basis. Taking the date of 1940 as a basis for comparison—it was a record year in peace-

AGRICULTURAL AND INDUSTRIAL PROBLEMS

time output—we have expanded 90 per cent in industrial production since 1940. There has been a great difference in the composition of what we are producing. Nondurable-goods output has expanded 53 per cent, but production of durable goods is up 159 per cent. In transportation equipment, which, prewar, included automobiles and locomotives and during the war includes ships, aircraft, and other mobile military goods, we are producing more than seven times the volume produced before the war. In these lines the postwar problems of readjustment will be very great.

In the movements of goods, the figures are startling. The total volume of goods moved has been just about doubled. Increase in the transportation of individuals is even more startling. It is now 275 per cent of prewar levels. Transportation facilities like trucks and streetcars, which constitute internal transportation, were heavily influenced by war shortages, of course. Rail transport of individuals alone is now 426 per cent of prewar. Part of that is replacing the automobile. In addition to that, there is a lot of moving around on the part of the civilians. These figures indicate how much more transportation we can use when we have the means to buy it.

Shifting from War to Peace

Looking into the future, into the period of postwar adjustment, the fundamental question, of course, is whether our economy can maintain a production for peace equal to this enormous production for war. Adjusted for price level, we have today at least 50 per cent more production of goods and services than we had in our best prewar year. Here is the fundamental problem to be faced for a prosperous period after the war: How can we shift over from a war to a peace economy and still maintain that level of activity?

INTERNATIONAL PROBLEMS INVOLVED

This chapter does not consider the international aspects in any detail. Obviously, any attainment of prosperity here and in the other countries must be part of a process of postwar adjustment in which political adjustment and economic adjustment are of equal weight. We cannot have a prosperous world, an upsurge of production, and maintained employment here and in other countries, unless the businessmen or the other economic units operating in the countries feel safe in continuing the arrangements they set up. This means that international arrangements for security, international arrangements for resolving political disputes, international collaboration, must be taken as a hypothesis if we are going to talk about effective domestic economic activity. There are great problems of political structure involved, of plans and groups for world-wide security organization, world-wide trade arrangement, world-wide collaboration in a number of different fields. We have some sorts of that already, *e.g.*, in the International Labor Office, now definitely in existence. Other organizations are needed. An international bank would speed industrialization and industrial development. Something in the way of an international transportation organization is needed, international health service, international welfare, etc. As far as the political declarations of the leaders go, the four major United Nations are all committed to a postwar world that does emphasize expansion and cooperation. The international conferences at Hot Springs, Bretton Woods, and Dumbarton Oaks have moved on toward reaching these goals. I am hopeful that we have learned from the last war that there is no use in fighting one war, writing a bad peace, then fighting another one. There are many women who want to establish a world where their sons will not have to fight another war.

If we move in this international field, to real collaboration, I think there is a possibility that the period for the generation after this war may be of quite a different quality from the two decades that most of us have grown up in. Before World War I there was considerable freedom of international trade. There was a good deal of interdependence among the nations for a time even after that war. After 1920, especially from 1925 on until 1940, there was a period of increasing isolationism. Trade barriers and other restrictions on trade were raised and intensified. Many people think that there might be a continuance of that autarchic situation after the present war period. Yet if the forward-looking international plans work, the coming time will be more like that before the first war. It does not necessarily mean we are going to become completely free of trade restrictions or that there will be a disappearance of governmental institutions to control and direct international trade that developed during recent decades. But it may be a period where government controls of foreign trade will continue but will be used for the continuous expansion of international cooperation rather than for restriction. It is only on the assumption that something like that can

AGRICULTURAL AND INDUSTRIAL PROBLEMS

happen in the international sphere that we can talk about maintaining full production and full employment here at home. Making that assumption, what do we have to do here at home in the postwar period to maintain levels of income and employment, to use the capacity we are using during the war?

PEACETIME DEMANDS FOR PRODUCTS

Guesses have been made as to how much people could use of various products. Perhaps the best over-all study yet available is the one made by Livingston, which is based on what happened during the prewar period as national income increased. He assumes that we would have about as much annual increase in output per hour as before the war, that workers will be working about the same hours as before the war. His study probably understates the necessary expansion of consumers' perishable goods and overstates the production of durables. In other words, he projected what happened between 1929 and 1940, inclusive of the low period of 1933 and the high boom period in 1929, and carried it up to a super boom. As his estimates stand, they show the need in peace for 43 per cent more food, 47 per cent more textiles, around 69 per cent more consumers' durables, about 66 per cent more producers' durables, and 144 per cent more in housing projects, than in 1940. The bill of goods our people would like to buy in peace, according to these estimates, differs greatly in make-up from what we are producing for war. In some lines, ships and aircraft notably, production would have to be much smaller. In metal fabricating as a whole, we would need only about one-third as much as we were producing in the middle of 1944. For basic steel and iron, however, we might need almost as much as the war output, but it would not be so highly fabricated into such close precision products. In consumer goods like clothing, textiles, lumber, paper, printing, and miscellaneous small industries, expansions in output of one-fourth or one-third over peak war production might be needed. In construction, trade, and service industries, the expansion above wartime levels would be still larger.

STRUCTURAL CHANGES MUST BE MADE IN OUR ECONOMY

That brings us to the question as to what kind of shift we must make after the war. Strangely enough, there has been very little talk on that problem. The war has greatly expanded our capacity to produce certain products. Twenty billion dollars has been spent in building new plants to make the things we need in the war: aircraft, ships, chemicals, armament, and the other things that are of special use. The net result has been to increase enormously durable goods capacity. We have many more metal workers, probably twice as many welders, and many more workers in most of the other metal-products trades than we will ever be able to find employment for in time of peace. Little expansion has been made in our capacity to produce the soft things people need in peace: clothes, processed foods, textiles, printing, and paper products. So that means that the major change to be made at the end of the war is to cut down the volume of production and the number of people who are working on metal products. Hard goods, durable goods, must be reduced. The number of people who are producing soft or nondurable goods must be expanded. That involves something more than a process of factory conversion. We hear a lot as to how long it will take to convert tank arsenals to automobile production. There is no possible type of conversion that can enable you to produce clothing in a shipyard. Some of the plants can produce the sort of things we need in peace. They are perfectly good to produce automobiles and pleasure boats, but the truth is they are good to produce twice as much metal products as we can possibly use. We are going to have to build new plants to produce other peacetime products, and pretty fast, so that people can be employed in them. That is part of the postwar problem. These are physical aspects of remaking our economy, while trying to maintain the same level of output.

The normal total factory production in peacetime is about 45 per cent durable goods and 55 per cent nondurable goods. In a condition like the peak of a boom in 1923 or 1929 the rate was 50–50. Today, at the wartime peak, the production oi durable goods is 63 per cent of the total. In order to maintain the same output but get the proper peacetime proportion, we need to cut down at least one-third in output of durable goods and add at least 50 per cent to our present production of nondurables. That is the over-all physical problem.

FINANCIAL ASPECTS

The financial problem is equally difficult although, of course, very different. In the postwar period we shall have a great many new factors whose effects no one can forecast. The biggest one is the accumulation of wartime savings, already running into about $100 billion, in the hands of

AGRICULTURAL AND INDUSTRIAL PROBLEMS

individuals, two-thirds of that in the hands of lower income individuals. About $50 billion of war-accumulated funds are in the hands of business. These figures will be larger when the war ends. No one knows what people will do with that eventually. No economist can say positively whether the greater probability after the war is an extreme inflation or an extreme deflation. There are possibilities that we might have either. This enormous fund of savings, spent rapidly, could create a heavy inflation. On the other hand, when the government stops buying the products now being produced by business, if that war demand is cut off suddenly and if unemployment rises to 8 or 10 or 15 million, people might hesitate to spend their income or their savings. So we could have a very sharp deflation and depression after the war. There are many things which might influence this—tax policy and government expenditure policy, etc., but those are the underlying factors with which the national policy will have to deal. In trying to talk about this problem and in trying to think constructively about the postwar period, we need to break it into two parts: the period of readjustment and the longer time period.

Steps in Reconversion in Industry

The war will not end quite so suddenly as last time. We have two enemies this time, and their collapse is not simultaneous. Germany has surrendered already, and the question left is, How much longer will Japan hold out? We have an interim period in which we can start some of the readjustment. Some 2 million men or more may be demobilized in the year ending May, 1946. War contracts have begun to be cut. Quite a considerable range of civilian production is being started. Perhaps even the building of some of the newly expanded peacetime plants can be begun. Possibly we may be able to maintain fairly full employment through the period from the defeat of Germany to the defeat of Japan.

RATE OF RECOVERY

Then the reduction of armed forces will begin. There will be a very rapid cutting down of military production. Possibly we shall still be producing one-third of the total national production for war. In the first half of 1944, war was taking 40 per cent of the nondurable output, 76 per cent of the durable goods. When we get the final cut after the defeat of Japan, when we lose most of the last quarter of our current war production, how long will it take to come back? How long a low period shall we have? Here are some rough calculations on that. Industry expanded production during the war period at a rate of about 20 per cent a year. It takes time for industry to recruit personnel, train management, build the plants. It may be from 2 to 3 years after the low before industry can get into full production again, even with the best sustained demand. In the intervening period, with unemployment running as high as 6 to 10 million, there is the danger that, if we are not careful, business might go into a tailspin. All this is assuming that industry will expand for the future unknown and uncertain demands of peace just as rapidly as industry has expanded in the last few years for the positive orders of the government.

Steps to Speed Conversion

What are the things we can do to render the demands less uncertain so that businessmen will feel more confident, so that industry will retool and expand capacity, reemploy people as far as is technically possible? It will be necessary to retool and build new factories to produce soft goods. Enormous amounts of material are ready to produce machines, and these will be greatly needed to industrialize China, South America, and India. If we can export, say, $5 billion a year of industrial equipment, even if for only a couple of years, that would help greatly to ease the shock; so we could taper off present production of metal products instead of stopping almost overnight. If our businessmen were ready to go into action, to build more clothing factories, more shoe factories, more building-material plants, that also would help to provide continued utilization right after the end of the war. So we can put down as two items:

1. A very large volume of industrial-equipment exports,
2. A very large volume of industrial-equipment production for internal use for things we ought to have ready.

We should be encouraging businessmen to start now. We should start building new plants as promptly as engineers can be spared from the war effort. We ought to put them to work, planning the details, specifications, and blueprints, so that they can take over the work and build our new buildings, as promptly as declining war needs permit.

A third field is public works. This period of slack employment right after the guns stop will be a time when public works can be put through, especially public works of a rather light character: work on streets, roads, and forests. They should be works of types that can be started promptly and stopped promptly. Public works also require long advanced planning. Not merely the national government but the state governments and municipalities should set up public works, making the arrangements ahead of time. All this can help make jobs, can prevent postarmistice unemployment.

A fourth step is assurance of income. There should be a program of separation payments. We ought to have compensation not only for people in the military service but also for people in war work so that both will be assured of income during the transition period until they can get jobs again. The present social-security unemployment payments average only $60 a month. A war worker who has his income reduced from $200 to $70 a month is certainly going to cut down sharply on what his family spends and will hesitate to spend his savings. Assured income until a new job is ready will make him a better spender and help prevent a contraction in the markets for goods.

Finally, there is need for a series of measures to assure businessmen as to the conditions under which they will have to operate in the postwar years. This would involve prompt decision and action by legislative and administrative bodies on tax, wage, and price policies and clear decisions as to the sequence and order of steps in modifying or removing wartime controls such as those on materials, prices, exports and imports, and transport. The desire of the businessman and investor for certainty as to the future conditions under which he will operate cuts across the administrative and economic need for flexibility in adjusting fiscal and financial policy to current economic conditions. Some compromise will have to be found between these conflicting interests.

DANGER OF INFLATION

It is very important, once postwar production is reestablished, that we prepare for the possible longer time period of subsequent boom. Once we get over the transition and get something like full employment again, people may start spending their war savings too rapidly and produce an acute price inflation. That brings up a political problem. Have we enough courage in this country to go through a period of rather slack business, when there is no problem of increasing prices, and still keep the price control, rent control, and credit controls on the books?

Or shall we end the controls as soon as the upward price pressure ends and then face a possible later inflation without the measures to check it? When we get to the subsequent period of inflation, shall we have controls ready or shall we move fast enough to create new ones? We could have other different controls, such as taxes, but the speed of Congress in imposing new taxes during the war was not very impressive. The real issue is this: The savings we have in our system are enough to maintain full employment for perhaps 7 or 10 years if spent bit by bit over a long period. There are not only savings to provide the buying power but also wartime shortages of goods, housing, industrial equipment, to stimulate demand. All that backlog of postwar demands plus the money to spend can last for a substantial period. But we can get that only if the inflation danger is avoided. If the money is thrown in too rapidly, we may dissipate the savings in rapidly soaring prices and then, of course, there will be an enormous smash after the bubble bursts.

Problem of Full Employment

The preceding paragraph relates to the period of the possible postwar boom, perhaps running for several years. After that period we may again come face to face with the chronic problem of unemployment we had during the thirties. Then we may once more have to face a tendency toward a chronic underemployment equilibrium. There is, however, a possibility that the large volume of war savings may leave us with a permanent willingness to consume more and save less, and less danger of unemployment. Of course, if the present income-tax structure is maintained, the situation may be different. The high progressive tax structure has a tendency to reduce savings more than consumption and to reduce somewhat the tendency for savings to exceed investment outlets. Still other measures may be needed to maintain markets equal to full production. Unless these measures are taken, after the boom we may have another period of chronic underemployment like that of the thirties.

No one can be sure that the sequence of conversion slump, postwar boom, and possible subsequent great depression will work out just as suggested above. Just how consumers will use their great accumulations of wartime savings is one of the unknown questions of the future. If the problems of conversion are not met swiftly and effectively and if unemployment rises to great heights shortly after the fighting stops, people may hesitate to spend their savings and may hoard them to cover their expenses over a feared long period of unemployment. Such a reaction could cause a deflation rather than an inflation, with a contracting cycle of activity rather than the hoped-for expansion. Even if the reconversion goes well, many people may decide to hang on to their wartime savings as a permanent investment and continue to save large portions of any new income. In this event investment outlets may soon fail to keep up with funds available for investment, and business activity may start to collapse in consequence. The nation would then face the problem whether to permit national income and employment to fall because of the inadequate markets for the products or whether to take publc action to provide supplementary markets, such as in social services of education or medical care, in public works, in urban reconstruction, or in regional developmental programs—to absorb the production which private purchasers were not prepared to buy.

The magnitude of the wartime savings is so much greater than ever before and our industries are in war production so much deeper than in any previous war, that past experience gives only a limited guide to probable future developments. Despite the possibilities of immediate catastrophe, however, the facts as to war depletions of goods and inventories, and the reports to date as to postwar uses that individuals intend to make of their savings, support the view that if the reconversion period is handled well, a boom period of fairly high employment of several years' duration is at least a reasonable probability.

Reconversion in Agriculture

DOMESTIC

The reconversion of agriculture from war to peace will involve less drastic structural changes than have been shown to be necessary in industry. Although our agricultural production has been greatly expanded during the war, most of that increase has been in products that would also be needed in time of peace, such as meats, dairy and poultry products, and vegetables. If reasonably full employment and high national incomes can be maintained in time of peace, most of this increased output can be used by our own consumers, though possibly at moderate reductions below wartime peaks in the real prices of food. Sharp reductions may be needed in output of certain war-specialty products, however, such as navy beans, soybeans, peanuts, and hemp. As a whole, farmers increased output of these products only under strong urging from the government and can reduce production readily by shifting the land to other uses.

The initial readjustments to peace may be easier in agriculture than in industry. Wartime purchases of food will not drop quite so suddenly as will those of munitions. The armed services can be demobilized only slowly; meantime they must be fed. Relief requirements will take large volumes of some foods, though not so large as was expected at one time. Food production in the warring countries has been maintained during World War II better than it was in World War I. The reduction in war demands will thus be slower in food than in industry. If the process of industrial reconversion and the reestablishment of peacetime industrial activity on a high level make good progress, domestic consumers may be ready to buy increased quantities of food almost as fast as they are released from export needs. If industrial activity is not kept operating at high levels of production and income, however, farm prices will soon fall to or below the support levels and it will be difficult to move all the increased food into consumption.

The levels of industrial activity, here and abroad, are even more important for wool and cotton than they are for foodstuffs. Stocks of these products are heavy; in wool, phenomenally heavy. Competition from synthetic products and from foreign production has been increasing. The increase in the demand for clothing as family incomes rise is relatively larger than is the increase in the demand for food; its "income elasticity" is higher. High and expanding levels of industrial activity here and abroad could step up all textile consumption to the point where both the stocks and the current production of natural and synthetic textiles would move into consumption readily and at good prices. If this optimistic result is not secured, however, cotton producers in the United States face serious postwar problems, involving a decision either to continue to reduce output while maintained prices continue to encourage the substitution of other products, or else to reduce prices to competitive levels. In the latter case, arrangements to shift production to low-cost areas and to encourage shifts of resources to other products in high-cost areas might ease the readjustment.[1] A positive conversion program, to carry through such shifts in Southern agriculture, was suggested by Secretary Wickard to the Pace Committee in December, 1944, and has been developed further by the Bureau of Agricultural Economics.[2]

[1] Messrs. Black and Hyson discuss the agricultural problems more fully in Ch. III.
[2] Mordecai Ezekiel, "Agricultural and Industrial Opportunities for the South," Bureau of Agricultural Economics, mimeographed, speech before Southern Regional Council, Inc., Atlanta, Ga., Apr. 11, 1945.

FOREIGN

The postwar readjustments in foreign agriculture will vary in different countries, depending on the impact of the war on them and their farm adjustments to war needs. As a whole, the food-importing countries, especially those directly affected by military operations or shipping shortages, made themselves more self-sufficient by cutting down on their production of feedstuffs and meat animals and by increasing their acreage and output of crops for direct human consumption, notably grains, potatoes, and vegetables. Given prosperous industrial conditions after the war, these wartime shifts would be reversed. In addition, forward-looking plans are being made to raise levels and efficiency of food production and consumption throughout the world, through the operations of the proposed Food and Agriculture Organization (FAO) of the United Nations. One glimpse of some of the agricultural reorientation it may be supporting can be given by some quotations from the writings of two English economists on the subject of what is needed to make European agriculture prosperous: [1]

> Accordingly, it would seem essential to set up some regional authority to establish a power supply for the entire Danube area. The slogan "A Tennessee Valley Authority for the Danube Basin" has been coined, and, indeed, the analogy of the T.V.A. is peculiarly apposite. What is needed is a regional commission with powers to replan not only the power supply, but also the industries and the layout of agriculture in cooperation with the local governments of the area. We shall see in Chapter V the importance that this might have in the diversification of farming and the overcoming of climatic disadvantages, but its most immediate importance would be in facilitating the establishment of new industries. . . .
> Put briefly, the plan for Eastern Europe is in two parts. One involves raising the productivity of industrial workers and providing a steadily increasing supply of consumption goods which the peasants want. The other involves a reorganization of farming, also greatly raising productivity and providing a bigger surplus of food than hitherto for consumption in the towns (and incidentally by the peasants themselves, too). That is the plan. The problem is to create a hinge which shall link the two halves of the plan together. Contact being once assured, there is no reason why mutual exchanges should not continue in an upward spiral of prosperity.

This conception of an expanding economy, agricultural and industrial, after the war is squarely contrary to the kind of thing we had in the interwar period. The characteristics of that period were expressed in trade restrictions, commodity agreements, and internal agricultural

[1] P. L. Yates and D. Warriner, *Food and Farming*, Oxford University Press, London and New York, 1943.

controls like the British agricultural schemes and our AAA. One of the real problems after the war is the inertia of such institutions. The fact of having established one type of institution has the result that people get used to its carrying on one particular function. They cannot visualize its doing something quite different. Yates has a very interesting point of view on this also. He is talking about production controls.

By asking for security and stable prices, the peasants have brought upon themselves a great deal more: a vast number of forms to be filled up, inspectors to placate, and fines to pay for infringements of regulations of which they often have not known the existence. Hence, it seems reasonable to expect that by the end of the war the cultivators of Europe will have an intense dislike of governments and all their works—even before the war the relationship was hardly cordial—and they will be firmly opposed to all schemes of planned production in so far as these involve individual quotas assigned to each farm. They quite naturally expect the community to guarantee them their fixed profits; they are unwilling to guarantee the community a fixed quantity of output in return. . . .

One of the biggest problems in psychology after the war is whether we can reorganize our institutions to expand the economy on the agricultural as well as on the industrial side.

Conclusion

There is much hope in that there has been a lot of talk about, and recognition of, these problems of postwar adjustment. The publication by the Department of Commerce of *Markets after the War*,[1] and the work of the Committee for Economic Development have served to dramatize the possibility of a much larger market in terms of specific things: electric fans, washing machines, and other things manufacturers could make and think of. They have done a great deal already to make businessmen aware of the fact that there can be much larger markets than before, to have them think about setting their sights for a much higher level than before, and to prepare to build factories for production that will meet that higher market in the agricultural and industrial field. They are attempting to take as many measures as possible on the industrial side to encourage private planning for postwar industrial development. Some legislative steps have been taken ahead of the need, *e.g.*, on contract cancellation, surplus property disposal, and veterans' rights.

[1] S. M. Livingston, *Markets after the War*, 78th Congress, 1st Session, *Senate Doc. 40*, Washington, 1943.

AGRICULTURAL AND INDUSTRIAL PROBLEMS

Beyond what private industry can do, there is also need for a definite public policy of assuring sufficient outlay, private and public combined, to maintain markets for high activity and full employment. The Murray Bill (Senate 380, Seventy-ninth Congress) is one proposed measure which would definitely establish such a policy.

In the Atlantic Charter and in various other governmental discussions, much of what has been done to ensure industrial expansion after the war will stop a lot of bad things we did before—stop having too many trade restrictions, stop interfering with foreign trade. Whether that will be enough remains to be seen. Many would like a great many positive actions added—actions to speed the industrialization of underdeveloped nations, to encourage the growth of production and trade, to assure higher levels of activity. Some of the more recent international conferences have begun to develop positive institutions to this end—the Fund, the Bank, the FAO.

Whether all necessary steps are taken or not, the idea of a much higher level of production is actively abroad in the world. Every country has seen how under the stress of war it can produce much more than it was able to before. After the war any government that folds its hands and says, "There is nothing we can do to maintain prosperity," will find it very difficult to stay in power. Our task is to help agriculture, industry, and government find ways to use for the constructive ends of peace the great productive powers developed for the destructive uses of war.

Chapter III

Postwar Agriculture in the United States: Problems and Policies[1]

by J. D. BLACK
and C. D. HYSON

THE INTENT of this chapter is to study a few of the major problems that will confront American agriculture after the war and briefly to indicate possible lines which any attempts to deal with them may follow. The one overmastering problem of American agriculture in this period will be that of an outlet for its production. All the others are more or less ancillary to it. The magnitude of this problem depends in a large measure on the level of business activity and urban employment that is maintained. In the discussion following, two assumptions are made with respect to this, which will be referred to as high-level employment and low-level employment. Probably the most reasonable expectation is a level somewhere between these extremes. The reader can adopt the analytical results here presented to fit his own particular set of expectations somewhere between these extremes.

The period to which these results apply is after the relief and reconstruction of European agriculture are virtually completed. This will be the third crop after the war in Europe is ended. Reconstruction will be completed in the second crop, except that herds of all types of livestock will not be restored.[2] They will not be fully restored in the third year but

---

[1] The Committee on Research in the Social Sciences of Harvard University assisted in the financing of the research upon which this analysis is based. This is *Publication 10* in the publication series of the Seminar in Agriculture, Forestry, and Land Use Policy.

[2] More time will be needed on the flooded lands of Holland and in a few other areas. The first crop after the war in Europe is here considered to be that of 1946.

will be enough so that the lack will not be significant. The best judgment of those who have been following closely the war developments in agriculture is that numbers of cattle are now only 25 per cent reduced, of sheep scarcely at all, and of hogs not more than 40 per cent.

High-level Employment

Under assumed conditions of postwar high-level employment, what will the demand for food be like in the United States? Unfortunately, the available data do not furnish any sound basis for preestimates. Table 1 presents two series of data on the physical volume of food consumed in this country by years from 1922 to 1943. The first is that compiled by the Bureau of Agricultural Economics (BAE) from its data on tonnages of food apparently moving into consumption, with some adjustment by weighting for the fact that when consumer incomes are higher, more expensive types of foods are consumed. The adjustment for this is very small—not more than two points in any year. The second series was obtained, for the period 1929–1943, by dividing the Department of Commerce series on per capita retail food expenditures by the Bureau of Labor Statistics (BLS) index of retail prices of food for the same years.[1] This resulting series, therefore, has all the errors and omissions in it that are in both of these series, some differences in items included, and, most important of all, some significant differences in conception.[2] The Department of Commerce has tied its series to the census data of 1929 and 1939. They include sales of food in retail stores and restaurants and values of foods produced and consumed at home. No comparable series has been prepared for 1922–1928.[3] The figures since 1939 are for civilians only.

[1] The series for deflated per capita civilian consumption of food is a simple expenditure and price relationship. Expressed mathematically, it is $q/p = v$, where q = total expenditure for food, p = price, and v = physical volume consumed in terms of purchasing power in 1935–1939 dollars.

[2] The limitations of a series derived in this way are discussed in detail in the reply of the BLS to the Meany-Thomas report on the cost of living, released on Feb. 25, 1944, under the title, *The Cost of Living Index of the Bureau of Labor Statistics*. There is also some discussion of the subject in Milton Gilbert, Simon Kuznets, and others, "National Product, War and Prewar," *Review of Economic Statistics*, August, 1944.

[3] In Table 1 the derived series has been extended back through 1922–1928 by using, as a basis, the farmers' cash income from farm marketings, plus agricultural imports, less agricultural exports. The series thus derived corresponds roughly with the Department of Commerce series in the period 1929–1943. It does not include certain margins of middlemen, and certain other errors are introduced by carry-overs. It is believed, however, that the percentage change reflected by the series computed on this basis shows the trend in domestic consumption of food through the period 1922–1928.

A sizable difference appears in the amplitude of the fluctuations in the two series: even in the prewar years 1929–1939 when Commerce figures are available, the BAE series swings only from $113 to $123,

TABLE 1.—FOOD CONSUMPTION PER CAPITA, AND GROSS NATIONAL PRODUCT PER CAPITA, 1922–1943 *

(In 1935–1939 dollars)

	BAE series	Derived series	Gross national product
1922	$117	$103	$ 513
1923	119	112	584
1924	120	115	575
1925	119	120	581
1926	120	107	611
1927	119	115	602
1928	120	119	613
1929	120	118	667
1930	118	113	617
1931	118	115	559
1932	116	109	487
1933	114	108	495
1934	117	106	526
1935	113	109	566
1936	117	117	648
1937	118	120	659
1938	118	120	616
1939	123	124	684
1940	124	128	733
1941	127	136	864
1942	126	161	1,000
1943	125	159	1,175

* Gross national product (GNP) figures for 1929–1943 are Department of Commerce estimates. Department of Commerce estimates of GNP prior to 1929 have not been published. For the years 1922–1928, GNP estimates are those of S. Kuznets which, although different in concept from Department of Commerce figures, are designed to represent the gross value of goods and services in terms of current factor earnings. The GNP for 1941–1943 are Department of Commerce estimates, deflated by the BLS Index of Cost of Living. The GNP for the years 1922–1928 were also deflated by the BLS Index of Cost of Living. The Department of Commerce series of GNP for 1929–1940 were deflated by special Department of Commerce price deflators for consumer commodities and capital equipment. Refer to Henry Shavell, "Price Deflators for Consumer Commodities and Capital Equipment, 1929–1942," *Survey of Current Business*, May, 1943, pp. 13–21.

whereas the derived series swings from $106 to $124—$10 as compared with $18. Since 1939, the BAE series has risen only from $123 to $125, whereas the derived one has risen from $124 to $159. This wide difference in the recent years could of course be explained if the Commerce retail expenditures series reflects much of the purchases of food in black or irregular markets and much upgrading of foods and the like, and the BLS series does not. Another factor of importance could be the increased consumption of foods in public eating places. But these explanations do not cover 1929–1939 and seem inadequate to cover the wide differences since. The judgment of the writers is that the BAE series does not sufficiently reflect shifts between cheap and expensive foods with changing

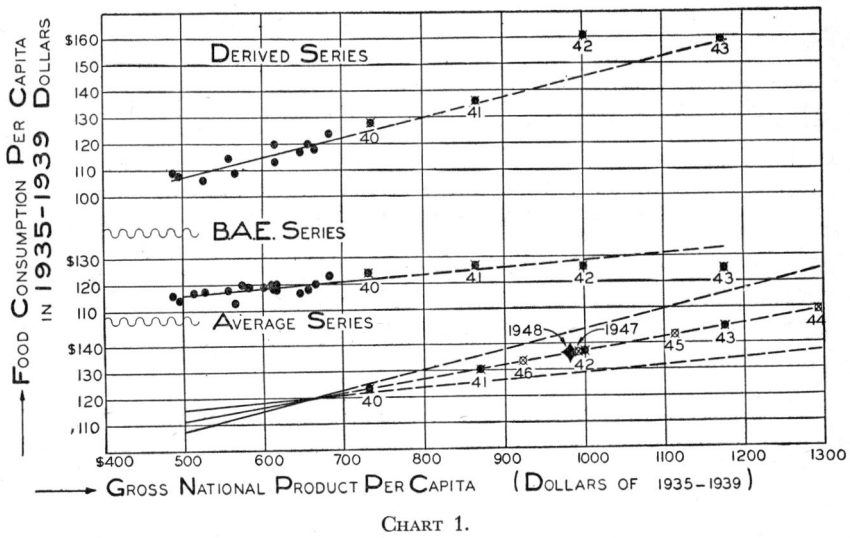

CHART 1.

employment—between cereals, potatoes, and cheap vegetables on the one hand, and meats, dairy products, and fruits on the other—and that the derived series contains some large errors that exaggerate the fluctuations.

In Chart 1, these two series are shown in their relation to changes in national income, expressed in terms of gross national product (GNP), reduced to a per capita basis (civilian population) in the third column of Table 1. The line of average relationship (regression line) for the BAE series is fitted to the years 1922–1939 in the middle section of the chart; that for the derived series, to the years 1929–1939 only, in the upper section. Then the two regression lines are extended as broken lines far enough to include the high GNP of $1,175 in 1943.

To preestimate the food consumption for 1944 to 1948 required making certain assumptions about the GNP for these years.[1] The usual preestimates of GNP in these years, assuming a high level of employment, range around a figure of $140 billion in 1935–1939 dollars, or $170 billion in 1942 dollars. The writers are undertaking no estimation of their own but merely take a sort of modal figure out of the various preestimates, excluding some of the recent ones that range around $200 billion in 1942 dollars.[2] It happens to agree closely with that of Prof. Alvin Hansen. Following a similar procedure as to the course of the war, probable employment, and incomes in the intervening years, a series as follows is obtained, all in 1935–1939 dollars: 1944, $165 billion; 1945, $146 billion; 1946, $124 billion; 1947, $139 billion; and 1948, $140 billion. Should the European war not end so promptly as now expected, or the Japanese war fold up in less than a year afterward, or last more than a year afterward, these preestimates would need to be modified somewhat. The reason that these figures are made in 1935–1939 dollars in this case is that the writers wish to make their comparisons of food consumption and food production with the period 1935–1939 as a base. In 1942–1943 dollars, the series would run $200, $180, $140, $165, and $170 billion, respectively.[3]

[1] Questions may be raised about GNP as a measure of national income for the purpose in hand. Alternative series, such as income available for consumption, affect somewhat the location of the points for individual years but do not change the slope of the regression line significantly. Present predictions of income and GNP are largely based on historical experience, postwar man power, its capacity to produce, and unemployment estimates. Because of the inclusion of certain taxes paid by business enterprise, particular reserves set up for depreciation and depletion, GNP forecasts are higher than comparable estimates of national income.

[2] Those used were by S. M. Livingston, S. Kuznets, Sumner Slichter, R. M. Bissell, A. H. Hansen, and the National Resources Planning Board. S. Kuznets, "National Income and Taxable Capacity," *Proceedings, American Economic Association*, March, 1942, pp. 37–53. S. M. Livingston, "Postwar Manpower and Its Capacity to Produce," *Survey of Current Business*, April, 1943. A. H. Hansen, *After the War—Full Employment*, National Resources Planning Board, February, 1943. A. H. Hansen and H. S. Perloff, *State and Local Finance in the National Economy*. S. M. Livingston, *Markets after the War*, p. 3, Department of Commerce, Washington, March, 1943. R. M. Bissell, "Postwar Private Investing and Public Spending," in *Postwar Economic Problems* (edited by Seymour E. Harris), pp. 92–97. Dr. Bissell does not specify whether his forecast is in 1942 dollars or in those of the current year. S. H. Slichter, "Present Savings and Postwar Markets," *Harvard Business Review*, Autumn, 1943. Higher recent estimates of around $200 billion in 1943 dollars have been made by E. E. Hagen and N. B. Kirkpatrick in the *American Economic Review*, September, 1944, and by Jacob Mosak and Gerhard Colm in Chs. V and XIV in this volume.

[3] The civilian population preestimates for 1944–1948 used to reduce the GNP series to a per capita basis were as follows: 127.5, 131.0, 134.5, 140.0, and 142.5, respectively. Making these of course requires certain assumptions as to the number of persons maintained in the armed services in each of these years.

Projecting per capita civilian food consumption on the basis of the BAE and the derived series, and the foregoing GNP preestimates, would give the results in the second and third columns of Table 2; on the basis of halfway between these two series, the results in the fourth column. These results are presented in the middle line in the bottom series in Chart 1. The authors offer no defense for splitting the difference between these two series. The true series surely lies somewhere between the BAE and the derived series. The series halfway between is presented merely as an example of what the true series might be like. One of the writers thinks it is nearer the BAE series; the other, nearer to the derived series. The consumption forecast for 1940–1943 by the average regression line is intermediate between that shown in the BAE and the derived series.

TABLE 2.—FOOD CONSUMPTION PER CAPITA IN THE UNITED STATES, 1944–1948, BASED ON PREESTIMATES OF GNP, THE BAE SERIES, THE DERIVED SERIES, AND A SIMPLE AVERAGE OF THE TWO

(In 1935–1939 dollars)

	GNP, billions	Food consumption per capita		
		BAE series	Derived series	Average of these two
1944	$165	$137	$167	$153
1945	146	132	154	143
1946	124	127	139	133
1947	139	129	145	137
1948	140	128	144	136

It may be helpful to see what these three series mean in terms of percentage of GNP that is spent for food according to these three series. Table 3 makes such a determination for selected years. Further calculations yield the following: According to the BAE series, out of each $100 additional GNP, only $2.50 is spent for food; according to the derived series, $6.30; and according to the third series, $4.40.

It is apparent also that a straight-line relationship is here assumed and that the percentage of income spent for food does not fall off at a higher rate at high incomes than at low incomes. There is no basis in the experience from 1922 to 1941 for any assumption to the contrary. But it may be that at the high GNP's of 1942 and 1943, such a decline has appeared in the BAE series in the middle section of the chart and that the regression line flattens out above $900 GNP per capita. But food shortages and rationing could account for much or all of this. Who knows how much meat, butter, fruits, and other relatively expensive foods our people would have bought in these years if they could have obtained them? The derived series shows none of this flattening, except possibly in 1943, but a large part of the increasing expenditures

TABLE 3.—PERCENTAGE OF GNP SPENT FOR FOOD IN SELECTED YEARS, ACCORDING TO THE THREE REGRESSION LINES, AND GNP PER CAPITA

	GNP per capita	BAE series, per cent	Derived series, per cent	Average of these two, per cent
1922	$ 515	22.0	20.0	21.2
1929	670	17.5	17.7	17.6
1935	570	19.4	18.6	19.0
1939	685	17.4	17.5	17.5
1942	1,000	12.2	14.2	13.2
1944	1,300	10.2	11.3	10.8
1946	905	14.0	14.1	14.1
1948	1,000	12.5	13.2	12.9

for food at the higher levels in this series may be due to services added—*e.g.*, more eating out—and may not mean more actual food consumption.

According to the BAE series in Table 3, more than twice as large a percentage of the low GNP of $515 per capita of 1922 was spent for food, as of the high GNP of $1,300 per capita in 1944. The derived series shows 11.3 per cent of the 1944 GNP spent for food, and the BAE series 10.2 per cent. Even if all the high expenditures on food in 1948—$136 per capita according to the average series—would be for actual food, the consumption in that year would be only 26 per cent above the 1935–1939 level, allowing for an increase of the population to 143 million. Agricultural production in 1944 is 33 per cent above that level. Production of food in 1944 (excluding fibers, etc.) is 36 per cent above that of the 1935–1939 level. If the BAE series were taken as a guide, the food consumption in 1948 would be still lower, and the surplus larger.

LOW-LEVEL EMPLOYMENT

All that remains to be said on the subject of food consumption under the assumption of low-level employment is that, given a GNP of, say,

$100 billion in 1935–1939 dollars in 1948, the total food consumption would be 16 per cent above that of 1935–1939 on the basis of the average series; with a GNP of $120 billion, it would be 20 per cent above that of 1935–1939. It would be still lower if the BAE series were taken as a guide. The kind of recession that set in in 1920–1921 could reduce employment enough to cut the GNP to the $120 billion level and, unless there were forces in the total situation sufficient to bring about a business revival like that of 1923–1925, such reduced income and food consumption could persist as it did from 1931 to 1939.

Agricultural Output

Now let us consider what agricultural output is likely to be in postconversion years, and between now and then. Nothing much more than conjecture is possible on this subject. The major factor in it is the government support which farm prices receive. The government is committed to full "parity" prices for cotton and wheat and most other products for another year, and if the Congress of 1944 could put this over, why not the Congress of 1945? The Price Stabilization Act passed in the fall of 1942 contains a guarantee of 90 per cent of parity for two years after the end of the war, and if disorder still persisted in Europe or Asia, making it necessary to continue military occupation there, the President could under the law extend the period still further. Moreover, considering the strategic political position which the corn-belt and cotton-belt congressmen and senators now hold and will continue to hold so long as the party balance is about even in Congress, what reason have we for thinking that the 90 per cent guarantee will not be extended? Indeed, it may very well be raised to a 100 per cent guarantee, its present level, when the time comes to apply it.[1] The recent surplus-property legislation authorizes the sale of farm products abroad at the world price and the making up of the deficiency below parity out of the public treasury, and this may very well be the pattern for future price control for farm products in this country.

If prices of farm products are sustained at such levels and the farmers have confidence that such prices will be provided and really made to stick and if no restraints on production are applied, the authors' judgment is that the agricultural production index by 1948–1950 will rise from the 133 level of 1944 to 140 or 145, on the 1935–1939 base. They

[1] The same result may be attained by raising the parity base.

make this prediction, after allowing adequately for the part played by the unusual weather of 1942–1944 and for the accumulated stocks of feed for livestock that were drawn upon in those years. Farm labor, farm power and machinery, commercial fertilizer, and other farm supplies will be much more available in 1946 and afterward than in the past three years.

Such an increase in production, however, is not likely to occur. There is much talk of food surpluses already developing. This is mostly without foundation. Europe and Asia will need all the food that this country can spare in 1945 and surely also in 1946. The city populations of Europe have suffered much more from underfeeding than early press reports have indicated, and if order is to be established in the various European countries, food must be provided more liberally than thus far in Italy and France. But cotton is already in surplus. A few other small items will become surplus in 1946, and some important ones in 1947. By 1948, this country will be definitely on a food-surplus basis, even with high-level employment, unless measures have been invoked that are potent enough to prevent it. What the writers expect is that two things will happen that will serve to check the expansion of agricultural production. The first is that production-restriction devices will be reinstituted by 1948, if not sooner, and that they will be temporarily effective in holding down total production. Although they will reduce the acreages of major crops, as did the controls of the 1933–1940 years, increases in yields and/or expansions of outputs of other farm products will within a few years make the specific restrictions largely impotent so far as the effect on total agricultural output is concerned.

More important will be the circumstance that the government will not be able to impose a rigorous price-support policy, and farmers in consequence will not have enough confidence in the future to go ahead and make commitments like buying machinery and livestock and erecting buildings to house additional livestock. First of all, it is difficult to support prices of any product well above the equilibrium price with the accumulation of stocks that surely ensues. This proved to be true with eggs in 1943–1944, even in wartime. Second, the efforts to hold prices at such levels will come under vigorous attack in the urban press and in Congress, and the political support will be so weakened that farmers will become dubious about the outlook. The difficulties of raising enough money by taxes to meet the current expenses of government will be an important contributing factor.

The reasonable prospect is therefore that agricultural output will not rise to the extent first suggested and that perhaps an index of 135 to 140 per cent for 1948–1950 is a better conjecture than one of 140 to 145.

The Probable Surplus [1]

Whether a surplus will actually develop of course depends upon two other factors: (1) the net balance of food export-imports and (2) the extent of use of supplementary food-distribution measures, like school lunches and the stamp program. Let us, at this stage, assume that these will be maintained at the level of the peak year 1940–1941. The aggregate expenditure in that year for the stamp program, school lunches, and all the others was $162 million, which is less than 2 per cent of our total food production. The expenditures for the two preceding years were at only half this rate. Value of exports in 1937–1939 averaged 3.3 per cent of the total value of food production; imports of competing products, 4.7 per cent; and of all products, 6.8 per cent. The imports, it is apparent, are mostly of types that will not contract but rather will expand with the growing population and increased income. If nothing else develops in the world to expand our exports of food, they will do well to maintain their prewar relation to our imports.

Given domestic food-distribution measures such as those maintained in 1937–1939 and the same foreign-trade balance, we can then look forward to production at least 35 to 40 per cent greater than that of 1935–1939 and consumption not more than 26 per cent greater with high-level employment, and 16 per cent greater with low-level employment. Our agriculture was already on a surplus basis in 1935–1939, with large stocks of cotton, wheat, and some other products in the "ever-normal granary."

Price Measures

Even though the general economy solves its problem of maintaining a high level of employment and national income and of financing the war debt, there will be again, as in 1921–1929 and in 1931–1939, an agricultural problem left to be solved. Let us briefly review the different possible approaches to its solution.

The one that the political leaders of the farmers keep to the front is

[1] The reader will note that the term surplus is not enclosed in quotes. This is a true market surplus—a quantity of goods that does not pass through the channels of trade into consumption.

always a price solution. They stand ready to approve prices that will give the farmers a reasonable level of income, even without supporting measures in many instances. The facts of the situation are that the agricultural statesmen have discovered that price-pegging loans will hold the price of a farm product at a level set not too far above the equilibrium price and that many of them are prepared to vote such loans and let the rest of the country worry about preventing excess stock-piling. They will accept production control as a supporting device, if forced to, and with still less enthusiasm a program of domestic distribution of the surpluses among needy groups in the population. They are more inclined to dispose of the excess stocks in other countries than at home, and in this they have the support generally of those who trade in foods and fibers.

The general acceptance among these leaders of "parity prices" as a yardstick is more or less incidental. It happens to be a device that serves their general purpose of securing price-supporting loans, and in terms of which they can negotiate among themselves—corn vs. cotton vs. wheat, etc. By 1937–1940, the process by which parity payments were distributed among the commodity groups had taken on the form that the distribution of tariff benefits takes in Congress when a new tariff law is being enacted.

Proposals to abolish the parity yardstick are therefore more or less beside the mark. It would help to abolish it, especially to abolish it as a yardstick for the relative levels for the different products, if some worse yardstick would not be substituted for it. The most likely substitute would still be "cost of production" or a near relative of it, and then surely the price program would be in a mess.

The rational price level for any product is of course the equilibrium price. The writers believe that if a competent quasi-judiciary agency, like the Interstate Commerce Commission, were created and given authority to establish a set of loan guarantee prices for farm products at 10 per cent below the price that would call forth the supply consumed and exported in normal years, it would come near enough to the level defined to make the procedure workable. They would vote for the creation of such a board without a qualm if they were congressmen. The difficulty is that their fellow congressmen would not—not if they really understood what they were voting for, not 20 cents a pound for cotton but 12 cents (at 1942–1943 prices), not $14 a hundredweight for hogs but $9.

Proposals to use parity as a yardstick to determine the average level of farm prices, and something like equilibrium prices to distribute it among the different products, would stand a better chance of being accepted by Congress, but not much of a chance at that. In that case, the base period had better be shifted to 1925–1929, because it can be demonstrated that returns to agriculture, labor, and capital were more nearly in balance then than in any recent period before or since.[1]

Expanding the Foreign Market

It thus appears that any farm-price measure that will receive enough support to be enacted into legislation will set prices so high that surpluses are bound to accumulate. The problem then becomes one of disposing of these surpluses. The outlet most likely to be favored is export. As already stated, the new surplus-property-disposal legislation authorizes such a procedure. Exports have been of great importance to our agriculture in the past and could well be in the future. There can be no doubt that we needed a foreign market for farm products before the war. Chart 2, Small Crops vs. Large Crops, makes that conclusion very clear. It throws into contrast two periods: a recent one, 1934 to 1940, when the nation almost lived unto itself agriculturally, and then 1910 to 1919, when it had large exports. In the recent period, agricultural exports were only 6 per cent of our production; in the earlier period, 13 per cent of it. Going up on this chart means more farm income; going to the right, more farm output. There is no escaping the fact that the farmers were much worse off in the thirties when they did not have much of a foreign market. Their incomes were much less than in all the years from 1910 to 1919 except 1916 and 1917.

By this time the reader may be worrying about the fact that price levels were much higher in some of these years than in others and that the country was bigger and had more production in the 1930's than in the 1910's. Both of these have been allowed for in the chart. The dollars have all been reduced to a common level, and the production has been reduced to a per capita basis. There was also a good deal of unemployment at home in 1934–1940 and consequent reduced buying power. But this also has been allowed for in making the chart. The farm incomes

[1] J. D. Black, *Parity, Parity, Parity*, Harvard Committee on Research in the Social Sciences, 1942. J. D. Black and C. A. Gibbons, "The War and American Agriculture," *Review of Economic Statistics*, February, 1944.

in the chart are what they would have been if nonfarm income per capita had been the same in all years.

The second thing to notice in the chart is that in 1910–1919 the larger the output generally, the more real income it brought. The peak-year output of 1912 sold for a fifth more than the small output of 1916. In those years, it was more than safe to expand our agriculture. It

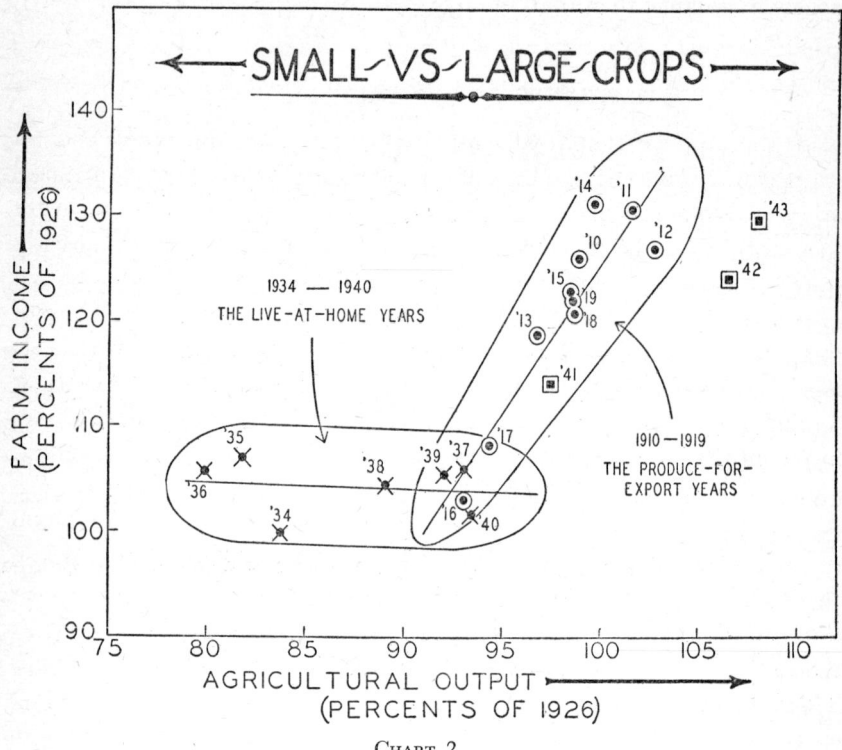

CHART 2.

yielded big dividends to do so. But after 1934 this was not true any more. The year 1940 had the largest crop in this period. But it did not sell for so much money as the short crop of 1936. One could not honestly say to the farmers of the country in 1934–1940: Go ahead and produce all you can; the more you produce next year the more money you will get for it. What actually seems to have happened is that the large outputs sold for about the same as the smaller ones. But since the costs of the larger crops were more, the net returns to the farmers were less.

If the years 1920 to 1933 had been put in the chart, they would have appeared in a halfway position between those of the periods before and after, with incomes ranging mostly 115 per cent of those of 1926 and with their general direction sloping upward gently. We were still in the foreign market in these years, with farm exports equaling 11 per cent of agricultural output.

Now let us see how the new war years fit into this scheme. The last two appear to the right in the chart with the largest outputs in our history and also with near-the-top incomes. In other words, we are pretty well back in the pattern that prevailed in 1910–1919. The year 1941 is halfway back into this pattern. Everything is just as one would expect. Our lend-lease shipments and greatly increased military demand are taking the place of our former export outlets.

The remaining war years should stay within this pattern. But what then? The first year after the last war, 1919, saw very large food exports at good prices even after adjusting for the high price level. But 1920 was a bad year, with exports and prices both low. And 1921 was only slightly better. Exports and domestic demand picked up gradually after that, 1928 being the best year in this period. This war has destroyed more agriculture than the last one. But given 2 or 3 years for rehabilitation and we can surely expect as much of a shrinkage of export demand for food as in 1920–1921—if this postwar history follows the same course as the last one. It is also important to remember that Europe was more nearly self-supporting in foods in 1939 than it was in 1914.

Nevertheless, this country is going to need foreign markets for its farm products. How can we obtain them?

The first answer is in terms of what not to do. We can refrain from measures that will take us out of foreign markets increasingly. It is now apparent in retrospect that, most of the time since the Federal Farm Board was set up in 1929, we have been engaged in measures which have had that unfortunate result. In 1929–1931 we were holding back our exports of cotton for European mills until our cotton was selling at a premium of 40 per cent over Indian cotton as compared with the normal ratio of 23 per cent. The British mills met this challenge in three ways: (1) by using up accumulated stocks, (2) by making over their equipment to use more short-staple Indian cotton, following the lead of the Japanese in this matter, and (3) by encouraging more cotton production within their own empire.

Other countries have met it in still other ways, including substitution of artificial fibers for cotton. The effect of all these developments has been that the cotton crop of 1935–1939 sold on the average for

$640 million compared with $1,043 million for that of 1925–1929. To be sure, in single years taken one after the other in immediate succession, the short cotton crops sold for more than the large ones; but this was not true after time enough had elapsed for our foreign customers to work out ways of beating our monopoly.

Our policies with wheat and corn since 1929 have been of the same general order and less disastrous in degree only. Before 1929 it had paid us to raise and sell all the farm products that we could in the foreign markets. The more we sold, the more money we received for our farm output. But some short-sighted persons began pointing out that when we sold in the foreign market we had to sell at world prices and that this set the level for domestic prices. So we decided to use methods that would set our domestic prices above the world prices. Tariffs would not do it for any products that were exported. The McNary-Haugen program that held the stage in the 1920's would have raised domestic prices above the world level and would still have permitted exports at world prices. But, no doubt, competing countries would have called this export dumping, or paying export duties, and would have retaliated.

So what finally came out of these demands was straight restriction of output. This in itself would not have been very serious because there would still have been plenty of cotton, wheat, corn, and hogs to export. There was a threat in it for the future, but that was all. The device which finally did the job of killing off our foreign customers effectively was the "ever-normal granary" as it worked out in practice. At the start, the loan values were down around 52 per cent of parity, and these still left prices on an export basis most of the time. But when the loan values got up to 72 and finally 85 to 90 per cent of parity, no nation would buy from us except under dire need from war or prospect of war, as happened in some volume from 1937 on. We also resorted to export subsidies and some dumping, it will be remembered.

There is only one thing to say about the measures followed from 1929 on: if we want to soak our own consumers by raising domestic prices and think we can get away with it over a period of years, well and good; but we must figure out some way in which we can still produce for and sell in the foreign market at world prices. There are measures that will do this. The task is to find the one with the least bad and the most good in it. In effect, all that is needed is that we stop shutting ourselves out of the foreign market by insisting on selling in it only at the monopoly prices which we set.

The positive measures that may be adopted are more important than the negative ones. They include, first of all, the reducing of costs of production to a point where our products can compete with those of other exporting countries. There is every reason for believing that our corn and hog production can stand up against that of almost any part of the world which can be named. This was not true before the war, but power and machinery have been making great strides on corn-belt farms in the last few years. We shall not export so much wheat as we once did, but that is because we have found a better use for some of our former wheatland and not because of labor and machine costs. As for cotton, there are large acreages in the South that lend themselves to low-cost production through the use of more machinery and power. Developments in these directions are certain as soon as machinery is freely available after the war; and they can bring costs down to a level where the bulk of our production can hold its own with anybody's.

Nor are these the only ways of reducing costs. There are recent developments in new varieties of crops and in the use of fertilizers and methods of cultivation that may save as much expense per bale or bushel as do power and machinery.

Someone may say that we cannot afford to make these changes, that they will throw millions of farm workers out of jobs and spell the doom of the family farm. They need not do either of these things. As for the family farms, they surely are doomed unless they become large enough to use the new family-size tractor outfits which farm machinery companies are getting ready to make by the hundreds of thousands. The way to kill off the family farm is to keep it poor. As for laborers on farms, it is high time that they shared in the general shortening of hours that came to factory workers in the 1930's. The machines will make this possible.

Finally, the world is getting ready for some positive measures, both international and national, to prevent the recurrence of hunger in the midst of plenty. The United Nations Conference on Food and Agriculture at Hot Springs laid this down as its cardinal principle and said many important things relating to it. But it did not work out any definite procedures for accomplishing this end. The Interim Commission no doubt will be equally cautious. However, the permanent food organization will have to meet this problem the moment that the United Nations Relief and Rehabilitation Administration lays down its burdens. The Hot Springs group was surely right in saying that each nation must assume the major responsibility for seeing that its low-income and other vulnerable groups have enough food to keep them reasonably healthy and able to work. But the central body will need to help in developing the international movement of food that will be needed.

One of the immediate obstacles to larger exports of food to many of these countries is that, in the short run, they are more desirous of industrializing than of feeding their people better. They are setting more income in the long run above better nutrition in the immediate future. They wish to use their purchasing power in foreign markets to buy manufacturing equipment and, in some cases, are hoping to export food in order to obtain more foreign exchange. Of course, in the longer run, these countries will be better markets for food after they industrialize than now.

It is to be doubted if the kind of two-price system authorized by present legislation will prove to be acceptable. The deficits made up out of the public treasury—arising from selling products at foreign prices that are bought from farmers at parity prices—are essentially export subsidies. Other exporting nations will pay similar subsidies, and our exports will be very little larger after all. International agreements already drawn contain commitments not to pay such subsidies. The most feasible type of two-price proposal is still that suggested by Dr. Beardsley Ruml in 1928 and presented to Congress and the public by the senior author (J. D. Black) as the Domestic Allotment Plan in Chapter 10 of his *Agricultural Reform in the United States*.[1] Under this plan the grower would have received the export price for the part of his product that was exported, and a higher government-supported price for the part of it which was used at home. He would have received a quota covering only his share of the domestic market. He would have been free to produce as much or as little as he wished at whatever price the export market would bring. Thus no direct subsidy would have been paid on exports. The government would need to make no subsidy payments out of the public treasury. If such a plan were to be applied, the prices of the different products could be held at parity or some other desired level in the domestic market and the country would still be in a position to export freely and to take part in international efforts to make staple foods more available to the underfed millions of Europe, Asia, and South and Central America.

[1] McGraw-Hill, 1929.

Expanding the Home Market

Desirable as may be measures for helping the underfed of other countries to obtain more nearly adequate diets, surely it is more important to use our resources to provide good diets for our own underfed millions. The 1936 consumer purchase survey showed that three families in every four were consuming less than recommended amounts of one or more of the following: protein, calcium, iron, vitamin A, thiamine, riboflavin, and ascorbic acid; that half the families consumed less than enough calcium (milk the most important source); 30 per cent of the families less than enough of vitamin A (especially from oranges, tomatoes, and green and leafy vegetables); 60 per cent, less than enough of thiamine (from meat, eggs, milk, and the whole kernels of cereals, beans, and peas); and 65 per cent, less than enough of ascorbic acid (from fruits and vegetables, including potatoes).

The reason for these deficiencies was about half lack of income and half unwise use of their incomes. Only a sixth of the families in the lowest income groups had *good* diets, and two-fifths had only *fair* diets. Thus nearly a half of them had *poor* diets. On the other hand, a sizable fraction of those with high incomes had *fair* or even *poor* diets. Supplementary food-distribution measures correct these conditions in two ways: by helping out those who do not have the means to buy the needed foods and by helping people to form habits of eating the foods needed. The latter is the more important of the two.

If food is to be made available to foreign consumers at less than the prices prevailing in the regular channels of trade, why not to needy families in our own country? The argument against it has been that such distribution unavoidably cuts into the regular consumption of food and reduces the demand. Dr. F. V. Waugh and others in his original article on "The Controlled Distribution of a Crop among Independent Markets," in the *Quarterly Journal of Economics*[1] pointed out the need for keeping the two markets separate. This was done under the stamp program by making only families definitely on relief eligible for the stamps and applying them only to additional purchases of foods. Under the school lunch program, the children who can afford to pay for their lunches are required to do so. No devices of this sort for keeping the two markets separate will work perfectly, but something can be devised which will work well enough for the temporary loss in demand in the

[1] November, 1936.

regular market to be more than offset by the gains from forming habits of eating the foods provided.

The following is offered as a general outline for a program of supplementary food-distribution measures:

1. School lunches. They should be more general, and improved in quality.

2. Penny milk and other milk-distribution schemes. Improved and expanded.

3. Special distribution of milk, orange juice, and the like among preschool children of families unable to buy them. Distribution should be upon recommendation of medical or public-health authorities and home demonstration agents.

4. Food stamps for families unable to buy needed foods, upon recommendation of relief agencies, public-health authorities, and home demonstration agents. The foods covered by stamps should be prescribed for each family on the basis of needs, and the free distribution should apply only to purchases in addition to those already being made.

5. Distribution of unpreventable emergency surpluses through these channels by adapting the foods furnished to the supply situation. But such adaptation should be kept within bounds—particular foods should not ordinarily be made into school lunches or distributed through stamps merely because they are in surplus.

6. As a last resort, direct distribution of unpreventable emergency surpluses through depots.

Four major principles should guide all forms of supplementary food distribution:

1. It should be handled as a matter of public health and nutrition and not of relief. It should be presented to the public in terms of the importance of having its people able-bodied and efficient and of giving the new generation coming on a chance to be healthy.

2. It should supply the foods which will make up the specific deficiencies of the families receiving them and which at the same time are most readily available in the area or community and will make up the deficiencies at the least cost. This means that these families will form habits of eating which are fitted to their incomes and which they will be able to finance themselves when their earning power improves somewhat.

3. Supplementary food distribution should make education, in the form of *learning by doing*, its controlling technique.

4. Responsibility for such distribution should be decentralized in very large measure so as to ensure proper adaptation to local conditions.

The more of the surplus food of the country that can be distributed through such channels as the foregoing, the less will be the need for distribution abroad. If the country persists in paying the producers the same price for food that is distributed abroad as for that which is sold at home through the regular channels of trade, then the government and the taxpayers should make up the difference in price on that distributed as surplus domestically the same as on that exported. If it accepts the more reasonable proposal, two prices for producers—one for the part consumed at home and another for that exported—it should follow the same practice for the two parts consumed at home.

Shifting Production to Other Foods

The most efficient of all methods of reducing surpluses of food products is to shift the use of the land into the production of those foods which have low yields of calories and proteins per acre and per man-day

Table 4.—Calories and Proteins from an Average Acre of Land and Day of Man Labor in the United States Used in the Production of Different Foods *

	Per acre		Per man-day	
	Calories	Proteins †	Calories	Proteins †
Wheat, used as white flour......	835	56	740	50
Corn, used as meal.............	1,880	96	550	28
Soybeans, used as human food..	1,545	340	1,030	226
Dry field beans................	1,250	150	335	46
Potatoes......................	2,285	118	270	14
Sugar beets...................	6,250	0	545	0
Dairy products ‡..............	235	22	50	48
Beef.........................	45	7	25	3.6
Pork.........................	500	18	30	4.6
Eggs.........................	145	26	25	4.5

* From J. D. Black, *Food Enough*, pp. 133, 139, Jacques Cattell Press, October, 1943.
† Grams.
‡ The dairy enterprise as a whole.

of labor. Table 4 makes clear the type of shifts called for. Thus shifting 1,000 acres of wheatland in central Kansas into dairy production will have the same effect on surpluses of calories as taking 700 acres out of production; shifting it to beef will have the effect of taking 950 acres out of production.[1] The effect on labor would be mixed—more labor is used when grain is fed to livestock instead of sold for cash; less when the livestock is kept on pasture. The net effect is a releasing of labor.

Diets with more dairy products, meats, and eggs in them are of course more costly, and families with low incomes cannot buy them freely. They are, however, exactly the foods needed to improve the diets of our needy families. Supplementary food-distribution plans need to be built around introducing these into school lunches, the stamp program, etc. Surplus-food distribution becomes much more effective from the standpoint of both the consuming and the producing groups when it is geared in thus with production adjustment.

Proposals to deal with surpluses by shifting to livestock production were made in this country as early as 1934.[2] They were blocked by opposition of the livestock producers; but at that time no supplementary food-distribution measures had been introduced.[3] Coupled with such provisions at this time, they ought to be much more acceptable.

Subsidies

The AAA program, from 1933 on, was a heavily subsidized program. In the later years before the war, direct subsidies were made per pound and bushel to make up for deficiencies in prices below parity. This may seem strange in view of all the opposition to subsidies that has come from some of the agricultural statesmen since 1941. The price-pegging loan is of course only a concealed subsidy. The concealment is now rather thin with the Commodity Credit Corporation funds being used to make up "losses" on surpluses sold at export prices.

More important than the fact that these subsidies have been paid, and are continuing to be paid, is the manner in which they have been paid. When paid by the AAA, they were "conditioned," *i.e.*, the farmer had to adjust his acres toward "soil-conserving" and away from "soil-depleting" crops. This was highly desirable, and no doubt has been a factor in the high production of the war years. The recent trend is

---

[1] The figures in Table 4 are average acres in the United States; for the central Kansas land, the effect would be somewhat more or less, but not enough to invalidate the comparison in any way.

[2] W. C. Waite and J. D. Black, "Nutrition and Agricultural Policy," *The Annals of the American Academy of Political and Social Science*, November, 1936.

[3] The Boileau Amendment passed in 1940 prohibited AAA conversion of any land to forage and grass and feeding it to dairy cows if this increased the number of dairy cows.

away from this conditioning. The trend should be strongly reversed. Moreover, the conditions set should take into account more than soil conservation. They should contribute to shifts in production that will reduce surpluses and provide foods needed for improved diets. Most important of all, they should not have the effect of causing farmers to continue growing certain basic crops for fear of losing their historical bases or quotas.

Adjustment Credit

Coupled with such subsidies will be needed a type of credit that will enable farmers to make the desired shifts in their production. Shifting to livestock requires initial investments that many farmers cannot make unaided. Likewise does establishing pastures in many parts of the South and West.

Surplus Farm Population

A high level of urban activity may be important for agriculture because of its effect on demand for food; it is much more important as creating a demand for the excess population of our farms. Around 5 million (gross) very able-bodied workers have left our farms since 1939, and still we have turned out 33 per cent more farm products than in 1935–1939.[1] Some of these workers are needed back on the farms. In 1940, only 12 per cent of the farm working force of this country was female; in 1944, over a fifth of it was female. Also many old men are now at work who want to retire, and boys who should go back to school. But the cities will need to keep or absorb three-fourths of these 5 million workers.

Moreover, power and machinery are going to replace labor on farms at an unusual rate in the next decade. Also certain farming areas in this country are still overcrowded and have too many small or poor farms that will not provide a real living for a family.

Ten years of thriving industry and trade that would provide jobs at present wage levels or near them, for all the farm people who would leave the farm for such jobs, would do more for the agriculture of this country than all the measures described above put together. Such a migration would leave some major adjustment problems in its wake, but they could all be handled with relative ease. At the end of these 10 years, prices of farm products would

---

[1] *Cf.* the figures by Dr. Haber in Ch. VI. The net reduction is much less, for many young and old male workers and many female workers have been substituted—Editor.

not need to be so high relatively as now; the product per worker would have doubled in many sections as the result of the economies associated with a larger scale of output and increased equipment.

Many groups in this country are fearful of the effects of such a migration. Some of them have a set of ideas about the need for keeping a considerable fraction of our people on the land, perhaps as a seedbed for population, perhaps to conserve the virtues of rural life, or what not. Others expect depressions like that of 1930–1933 to recur at intervals with 20 million workers out of jobs, and it is better to have them living in a shack on a patch of land than standing in the bread lines. Others say that urban industry and trade can never really provide work for more than three-fourths of our population; or, if they do, it will be a useless kind of activity of which the cities already have too much. What these groups say makes some sense. But still, the way to recognize its validity is not to keep a large stand-by population living in squalor or else on subsidy. The family farms of a good agriculture will be large enough to provide a living for the farm family equal to that of the union-labor families in cities. They will provide income enough for the boys and girls to go to high school. There will always be some families preferring to work a small patch of land and live simple straitened lives, with no ambition for their children for anything more. Let them have what they want, but do not condemn to this sort of a life the millions of farm families capable of much more. There will also, let us hope, be a million or more of little part-time or residential farms for those who have another major source of income and like to do a little farming on the side. But the main pattern of American farm life should be something very different from this.

Chapter IV

Wages and Employment in War and Postwar

by SEYMOUR E. HARRIS

THE ISSUES [1]

IN THIS war, labor has improved its position substantially. Average hourly earnings are up much more than the cost of living; and pay rolls a fortiori. With the support of the government, trade-unionism has made notable advances. Employers have learned how to make the most effective use of skills, and the government and business have done an effective job in moving industrial workers from job to job, region to region, and industry to industry. In the postwar, labor is likely to be confronted with serious problems of downgrading, loss of overtime, substantial reduction in pay rolls, and pressure to migrate.

In the writer's opinion, there will be little justification for a general reduction of basic wage rates. In particular instances, the case for a reduction of wage rates may be strong; in others, rises may well be in order. As the country once more climbs to higher levels of productivity, the upward movement of basic wage rates should be resumed.

Under the pressure of unemployment, entrepreneurs will undoubtedly press for lower wages. Reductions not justified by changes in productivity will be fatal to the economic system. With the loss of overtime, general downgrading, movement into lower paying industries,

---

[1] The reader should consult S. H. Slichter, "Labor after the War," in *Postwar Economic Problems* (edited by Seymour E. Harris), pp. 241–262. Professor Slichter discusses there many of the changes in the labor situation resulting from the war.

and withdrawals from the labor market, wage payments will be reduced substantially. The net reduction, after allowance for social-security payments, demobilization pay, and reduction of tax payments, will be of the order $10 billion after VE-day and $15 billion additional after VJ-day.[1] These are significant declines, which may have serious effects upon total spending. It is easy to jump in our analysis from a full-employment economy that provides $160 billion of national income to a full-employment income of $125 billion, the latter reflecting the losses enumerated above and others to be mentioned. We should, however, take into account the transitory effects of the decline in wage and salary payments and accompanying decline in other forms of income. Total spending may be affected by a larger amount than the actual reduction in these incomes; and the pressure may be felt especially in consumption-goods industries (inclusive of construction), which many of us hope will take up a large part of the slack associated with the decline of war expenditures. For this reason, among others, vigilance should be exercised lest incomes are deflated even more than the amount corresponding to the reduction in man-hours and downgrading. Any excessive reduction in wage rates, moreover, insofar as it contributes toward reduced demand and output, will lead to further cuts: at reduced levels of output, productivity will indeed suffer.

In that period, price policy will be a relevant factor. The Office of Price Administration (OPA), for the immediate post VE-day period, has already gone on record as opposing significant rises in prices and yet supporting prices high enough to pay current wage rates.[2] Profits at present are clearly high enough to support present wage levels. They will not be if the decline, which is feared or which may be brought on by wage cutting, materializes. Labor, on the other hand, will also contribute to falling employment if it insists upon rises in basic wage rates corresponding to the reduction of total pay rolls.

Our long-run price policy should be toward stability. Our gains from continued improvements should be taken in stable prices and rising wage rates, not in falling prices and stable wage rates. Aside from the increased burden of fixed charges associated with falling prices, rising wage rates are to be preferred to falling prices because labor prefers to take its gains in that manner.

[1] *Cf.* S. M. Livingston, "Magnitude of Transition from War Production," *Survey of Current Business*, August, 1944, pp. 6–11; and J. Mayer, *Postwar National Income*, p. 11, Brookings, 1944.

[2] *Cf.* Dr. Wallace, Ch. XI.

Our War Experience [1]

The rise of wages and salaries in 1939–1943, 1944, is given in Table 1.

TABLE 1.—PERCENTAGE RISE OF PAY ROLLS, 1939–1943, 1944

	1939–1943	1943–1944
1. Total compensation of employees.........	131	9
2. Salaries and wages.....................	119	9
3. Salaries and wages, exclusive of government	109	..
4. Pay rolls covered by old-age and survivors' insurance and railroad retirement.......	126	..

SOURCE: *Survey of Current Business* and Social Security Board.

Series (2) in the table excludes supplementary payments (relief, social security, etc.); the rise is less than under (1). These payments have become of declining significance. Since the rise of government pay rolls has been particularly sharp, their exclusion in (3) accounts for the smaller rise in (3) than in (1) or (2). Finally, the marked rise in (4) may be associated with the relatively large increases for those receiving less than $3,000 and with the marked gains made by the aristocracy of labor, who are disproportionately covered under social security.

In the 5 years from January, 1939, to January, 1944, wage payments in manufacturing industries rose by 250 per cent. Average weekly earnings were up 95 per cent, and the number of employees by 78 per cent. The most important factors accounting for the rise in manufacturing pay rolls are revealed in Table 2.

TABLE 2.—FACTORS ACCOUNTING FOR CHANGES IN MANUFACTURING PAY ROLLS, JANUARY, 1939, TO JANUARY, 1944

	Per Cent
1. Increased employment................	31.3
2. Increased hours......................	16.3
3. Increased overtime premiums..........	9.5
4. Redistribution among industries........	11.3
5. Other, chiefly increased rates...........	31.6

SOURCE: E. C. Bratt and C. H. Danhof, "Components of Wartime Wage Changes," *Survey of Current Business*, September, 1944, p. 18.

[1] This analysis of wartime changes is based largely on Chs. XIX–XXII, XXVII of my forthcoming *Inflation and the Postwar Economy*. (See this book for a much fuller discussion.) See especially E. C. Bratt and C. H. Danhof, "Components of Wartime Wage Changes," *Survey of Current Business*, September, 1944, pp. 17–18, and H. M. Douty, R. J. Myers, and H. D. Block, "Wages in Manufacturing Industries in Wartime," *Bureau of Labor Statistics, Bulletin 756*, November, 1943, and WLB, *Report to the President on the Relationship of Wages to the Cost of Living*, etc., mimeographed Feb. 12, 1945.

Table 2 suggests that the most important factors were a rise in manhours of employment [(1) and (2) above] and a rise in average rates [(3), (4), (5)]. The latter is, however, made up of many components. In particular, the rise of overtime premiums and the redistribution of workers in favor of higher paying industries account for about two-fifths of the increase in the average hourly wage. Item (5) is an omnibus one which includes a rise in basic wage rates. It is related also to changes in the proportion of workers on late shifts with wage differentials; those resulting from the shifts of workers from low-wage to high-wage occupations (and the reverse); upgrading and promotions; rises in incentive pay. It is difficult to appraise the importance of these last items as against the change in the basic wage rate.

The results of another official study check pretty well with the results in Table 2.

TABLE 3.—AVERAGE MONEY EARNINGS OF WORKERS IN MANUFACTURING
(January, 1939 = 100)

	July, 1941	July, 1942	July, 1943
1. Average weekly earnings....................	127.7	157.1	184.4
2. Average hourly earnings....................	116.3	135.4	152.4
3. Estimated straight-time average hourly earnings	113.6	129.9	145.1
4. (3) adjusted for interindustry shifts...........	110.6	121.8	132.1

SOURCE: H. M. Douty, et al. "Wages in Manufacturing Industries in Wartime," *Bureau of Labor Statistics, Bulletin 756*, November, 1943.

Table 3 suggests that

1. From January, 1939, to July, 1943, increased overtime and adjustments for interindustry shifts account for two-fifths of the rise in hourly earnings.

2. The year of largest wage increases was July, 1941, to July, 1942 (approximately 25 per cent for the average weekly wage).

3. The annual *rate* of increase for *weekly earnings* was less in the following year and less still in the 6 months ending January, 1944.[1]

4. Estimated straight-time hourly earnings *adjusted* continued to rise almost as rapidly in the year ending July, 1943, as in the preceding year. This should not be taken as a reflection on the War Labor Board (WLB) which had some control over wages in the latter year; in fact,

[1] Based on a comparison of figures in Table 3 and those in the *Survey of Current Business* studies.

the explanation is undoubtedly largely upgrading, rise of incentive pay, movement to higher paying plants, and the like. At least for the 6 months ending January, 1944, there may even have been a decline in straight-time hourly earnings adjusted. Now let us consider the rise of pay rolls according to types of industry.

Pay rolls in war industries accounted for about 80 per cent of the total rise of pay rolls from January, 1939, to January, 1944; nonwar industries accounted for about 20 per cent. Whereas in war industries, the rise in straight-time hourly earnings accounted for less than one-third of the total increase in pay rolls, this factor accounted for more than one-half in nonwar industries.

An increase of employees is responsible for more than two-fifths of the rise of pay rolls in war industries, and less than one-fifth for nonwar.

It is interesting also that these components account for relatively the same part of the rise in pay rolls in war and durable goods industries, on the one hand, and nonwar and nondurable goods, on the other.

In nonmanufacturing industries, the rise of wages has not been nearly so large as in manufacturing industries. This is evident from the fact that total wages rose little more than 100 per cent, whereas in manufacturing they rose by 250 per cent. *Rise of employment, redistribution among industries, and premium overtime pay weighed more heavily in the total gains for manufacturing; the rise of rates and hours was relatively more important for nonmanufacturing industries.*[1] This does not, of course, mean that wage rates rose more in nonmanufacturing than in manufacturing. Rather the reverse occurred. The figures account for relatively large gains for manufacturing and small ones for nonmanufacturing.

Steady Rise of Pay Rolls

1. Salaries and wages have continued to rise in increasing absolute amounts since 1939 and until 1943, and in increasing relative amounts until 1942. Even in 1943, despite the stabilization of the total amount of employment since the middle of 1942 and despite heroic wage-stabilization policies introduced in 1942, the percentage rise was no less than 28

[1] *Survey of Current Business*, September, 1944, p. 19. *Cf.* Senate Hearings to *Continue the C. C. C.* (1943), pp. 189–190. It is estimated that from August, 1939, to September, 1943, the hours of employment rose by 11.3 per cent for all nonagricultural employment and 18.6 per cent for manufacturing; and average hourly wage rates rose 20.3 per cent in nonmanufacturing and 59.1 per cent in manufacturing.

per cent and the absolute rise, $22.6 billion. [From July, 1940, to July, 1942, nonagricultural employment had risen by 5.5 million; from July, 1942, to July, 1944 (estimated) there was a decline of 300,000.] Approxi-

TABLE 4.—PAY ROLLS, 1939–1944

	Total, billions	Rise, billions	Rise, per cent	Rise, manufacturing pay rolls, per cent	Rise, average annual wage, manufacturing, per cent
1939	$ 44.2				
1940	48.6	$ 4.4	10	17	6
1941	60.8	12.2	25	40	15
1942	80.5	19.7	32	32	22
1943	103.1	22.6	28	33	17
1944 *	112.8	9.7	9		

SOURCE: Calculated from materials in *Survey of Current Business*.
* Estimated.

mately $8 billion of the $23 billion rise, however, is associated with the expansion of the government pay roll, and that largely for the armed services.

2. A measure of stabilization was obtained by 1944. Nevertheless, even in that year, with total employment downward, the redistribution of workers affected, and the hours largely stabilized, the rise in the wage bill was estimated at $9.7 billion. Here, again, the growth of military forces was relevant.

3. As might be expected, the relative gains in manufacturing are not quite twice as great as for all pay rolls in 1940 and 1941, and substantially larger in 1942–1943. This is explained by factors already enumerated. In the years July, 1942, to July, 1944, employment in munitions industries (a large part of manufacturing) rose by almost 3 million. This gain was made possible by reductions in construction and nonindustrial employment. Employment elsewhere (with the exception of Federal war agencies) was relatively stable.

4. A rise in the average annual wage in manufacturing of 17 per cent in 1943 clearly reflects strong inflationary pressures. In that year the rise of hours was about 5 per cent or, if overtime additions are included, a rise of about 7 per cent in the pay roll is explained. The remainder must be accounted for by continued movement into high-paying occupations and industries and further rises in basic wage rates (to

be commented on later). In that year, we should note, the cost of living rose by 6 per cent.[1]

We have thus far commented on the causes of the increase in pay rolls. In the spring of 1942, the government began to try to control wages. How successful were they?

Responsibility of the WLB

First, it is clear that the authority of the WLB is circumscribed. On the basis of estimates of the WLB for the first year of stabilization, rises in basic wage rates ordered or approved by it accounted for but 20 per cent of the increase in *straight-time average hourly earnings* in factories and but 7 per cent of the *total* rise of factory pay rolls (see Table 5).[2] For a somewhat shorter period, increases in basic wage rates accounted for but 6 per cent of the increase in *gross average* hourly earnings, and all other adjustments affecting hourly earnings authorized or directed by the WLB accounted for an additional 6 per cent.

Second, the upward movement of wage pay rolls continued at a rapid rate, though somewhat diminished in the first year of the WLB's stabilization program. We have commented on the figures above.

TABLE 5.—Percentage Rise in Various Economic Variables during First Year of Wage Stabilization, Year ending September, 1943

	Per Cent
All income payments	17.9
Wages and salaries	19.6
Factory:	
a. Wage-earner pay rolls	21.2
b. Factory man-hours	8.7
c. Weekly wages	15.4
d. Hourly earnings	10.8
e. Straight-time average hourly earnings	7.3*
f. Adjustments in basic wage rates ordered or approved by the WLB	1.5

* The rise for hourly earnings is reduced by about 18 per cent to allow for increases resulting from additional overtime and about 16 per cent for the shift of workers to more productive industries. In this manner 10.8 in (d) is reduced to 7.3.

At least some part of the rise other than that associated with decisions of the WLB must be associated with increases in basic wage rates.

[1] For hours, see "Hours of Work in Manufacturing, 1914-43," *Bureau of Labor Statistics,* Serial No. R 1635, p. 7; for man power, see *ibid.,* "Manpower Requirements in 1944," Serial No. R 1598, p. 5.

[2] Figures in this section are from monthly reports of the WLB. The history of the WLB is given in my *Inflation and the Postwar Economy.*

From October, 1942, to May, 1943, "all other factors" accounted for 40 per cent of the rise in gross average hourly earnings. There can be little doubt but that a significant amount of spurious upgrading and promotions not justified by changes in the tasks assigned are included here. When employees are denied increases in basic wage rates, they, in collusion with employers, find ways of evading WLB regulations.

Third, the largest part of wage inflation is associated with factors over which a government, not prepared for total war, has no control. Inclusive of the premiums for overtime, the rise in man-hours accounts for almost 60 per cent of the increase; and movements into higher paying industries, an additional 10 per cent. The remainder—30 per cent—includes rises in basic wage rates (in part as an offset to the increase in the cost of living) and any rise of productivity not reflected in shifts to war industries, other forms of upgrading, higher pay for late shift differentials, promotions, merit increases, etc.

Wages and the Cost of Living

Fourth, a word should be said concerning the rise of wages in relation to the cost of living.[1]

From 1939 to 1944, total compensation of employees rose 140 per cent. This compares with an increase in the cost of living of 25 per cent. Clearly there is no justification for raising further the total wage bill, which has gone up five to six times as much as the cost of living, on the grounds that wages must keep pace with the rising cost of living.

Many will point out, however, that the appropriate relation is between the pay envelope of *each* worker and the cost of living. We therefore present in Table 6 figures for *real* (money corrected by the rise in the cost of living) weekly earnings. There has been a substantial rise.

TABLE 6.—REAL EARNINGS, WEEKLY, 1942–1944
(January, 1939 = 100)

	All manufacturing	Nondurable goods
July, 1942	133.8	114.3
July, 1943	148.5	127.0
June, 1944	159.0	

SOURCE: Bureau of Labor Statistics.

[1] Based on Douty, *et al.*, *op. cit.*, p. 16, and *Survey of Current Business*.

WAGES AND EMPLOYMENT

Weekly earnings are larger in part because of the increased number of hours, the relative growth of overtime premiums, and the shift to higher paying industries. Defenders of the thesis that wage rates should move with the cost of living will, therefore, contend that the straight-time average hourly wage adjusted for interindustry movements should rise as rapidly as the cost of living. The fact is that it has risen more rapidly. Real hourly wages so adjusted (1939 = 100) were as follows (and they have gone up since):

	All manufacturing	Nondurable goods
July, 1943	106.4	105.3

Even basic wage rates may well have gone up as much as the cost of living. No one really knows how much basic wage rates have increased. A guess based on the WLB estimate would be that factory workers in the first year of stabilization had a rise in their basic wage equal to 7 per cent of the total increase in pay rolls. To this we might add an additional 7 per cent for the concealed rise included in "all other factors." This increase of 14 per cent would offset a rise of about 35 per cent in the cost of living in the case of manufacturing labor and substantially less for nonmanufacturing labor.[1] In 1945 the WLB estimated the rise in basic wage rates for 1941–1944 at 20 per cent.

Labor's case for a parallel movement in basic wage rates and the cost of living is not strong. Under the Little Steel formula, rises up to 15 per cent are generally allowed; and the increase in the cost of living by summer, 1945, may well be 30 per cent. (This allows for some understatement in official index numbers.) Should the Little Steel formula be abandoned, a further rise in basic wage rates of 15 per cent might be involved. In view of the large rise in weekly earnings and in the total wage bill, labor's command over goods has substantially increased in the course of the costliest war of all times. Labor has been able not only to maintain its position but also to increase its purchasing power in terms of both present and future goods. Labor has done at least as well as all other groups with the exception of farmers; and the latter's position in 1939 was rela-

[1] The total rise in pay rolls of manufacturing is 250 per cent. Fourteen per cent of 250 comes to 35 per cent. If basic wage rates account for the same relative rise in nonmanufacturing as in manufacturing, the increase in basic wage rates would be less than 14 per cent in the former. We have here applied a percentage (14) for a period of several years, which quite properly is related to a briefer period.

tively unsatisfactory. Any further rises in basic wage rates justified by an increase in the cost of living beyond 15 per cent will further raise the cost of living, contribute toward the breakdown of price control, stimulate the farm bloc to increase its demands, and further accentuate the problems of postwar readjustment.

Any rises granted in the future should be on a selective basis. Above all, the increases should be granted, in substandard cases, to groups whose total income has not gone up so much as the cost of living and not to factory labor in general which has gained disproportionately from war demands.

This raises a very important problem. Since we have discussed manufacturing wages, the case against further wage increases has been clearly overstated. Hourly earnings in various industries are shown in Table 7.

TABLE 7.—HOURLY EARNINGS INDEXES, 1943
(1939 = 100)

Manufacturing	152
Anthracite coal	116
Bituminous coal	129
Building construction	134
Railroads	116
Composite index, New York FRB	137

SOURCE: S. Kuznets, *National Product in Wartime* (preliminary ed.).

WAGES AND PRODUCTIVITY

Fifth, there is the relation of wage payments and productivity. Most will agree that if the productivity of the worker rises, he should obtain compensation in higher wage rates. Man-hour output in civilian goods industries had risen but 7 to 8 per cent by 1942 and since has been reduced a few per cent. Hourly wages have gone up more than the 4 per cent rise in these industries plus an allowance for the rise of unit prices. That is, wages seem to have kept up with productivity in nonwar industries. *One must not assume, furthermore, that a parallel movement of wage rates and productivity would exclude inflation. The important fact still is relevant that the workers produce almost as much of war as of nonwar goods. The former are not available for purchase.* In short, even if wages rise with (and only with) increased productivity, inflation would still be a threat.

Much can be treated under productivity. There is, for example, the 11 per cent of the total rise in pay rolls in 5 years, which is accounted for by the shift of workers to high-paying industries. High-paying industries, let us observe, do not here mean correspondingly high physical productivity. These gains in productivity reflect in no small part the willingness of the government to pay adequately high prices to attract the necessary factors. A rather large rise in productivity of war industries is associated with important economies of expanding output as well as with the higher rewards offered on war contracts.

Upgrading, increases of incentive pay, shifts to higher paying occupations and factories within an industry, and the like may all be included under payments for higher productivity. We do not include upgrading and promotions which are in fact disguised increases in basic wage rates. Total rises in payments under the general head of productivity may total 20 per cent of the rise in wage payments. This is a figure which seems much larger than any rise in physical productivity; but it is not larger when corrected for the increase in unit prices.

Let us summarize the discussion of the last few pages: (1) The largest rises in pay rolls are explained by factors over which the WLB has no control. (2) The rises in basic wage rates have been substantial. They may correspond roughly to the increase in prices corrected for changes in productivity. (3) Aside from postwar considerations, little is to be said for a parallel movement in wage rates and the cost of living. (4) The case for further wage increases in wartime is strongest in nonmanufacturing and low-paid occupations. (5) A parallel rise of wages and productivity would not preclude inflation during wartime.

We turn now to a few additional statistical aspects.

The Case for and Against Higher Wage Payments

We have already noted many of the arguments advanced in support of higher wage payments. Some contend that the worker is entitled to a stabilization of his wage rates in terms of the products he buys. In other words, as the cost of living rises he should obtain a corresponding compensation in the wage rates per hour or per week if the number of hours does not change. Others comment on the increased productivity of labor—in part, associated with improved efficiency of labor—and hold that labor should get its fair share of this increase of productivity. Then, if productivity rises, they contend that wage rates per hour should rise. Upgrading, too, has been given as a reason for the payment of higher wages. If the average worker is doing a higher class job where more skill, more training, and more ability are required, he should have a higher rate of pay. (This factor is related to productivity.) In this manner, the increase in the average rate of pay per hour of work is explained away by the higher general average of skills used today than in the prewar period. Labor interests have also pointed to the fact that workers are entitled to time and a half for overtime because the entrepreneur gains in a reduction of overhead costs per unit of output as a result of overtime work. Since the entrepreneur gains in this sense and since overtime subjects the worker to inconvenience and additional fatigue, the worker claims that he is entitled to a higher wage rate when he works longer hours. Undoubtedly, as has been noted by the WLB, overtime accounts in part for the increase in the average hourly wage rate.

Many who support high-wage policy use other arguments. They emphasize the fact that in our war economy mobilization of economic resources has not been carried to an extreme. *Since government will not move labor from one industry to another or from one job to another, the only possible method of obtaining the maximum mobility of labor resources in accordance with war needs is to allow the incentive of higher wage rates to operate fully.* Once wage rates are stabilized, the aircraft factories that need more workers will find it increasingly difficult to spirit them away from other and less essential enterprises.

There is also the interrelationship between wage rates and other costs. Unless the cost of living can be stabilized, the pressure for increased wages becomes overwhelming and, with inadequate control of farm prices and hence rising prices, stabilization of wages becomes most difficult. It is, therefore, imperative to control not only wages but also farm costs and any other costs that tend to raise prices.

Finally, there are the incentives required not only to move labor but also to increase the total supply. Our main objective, after all, is to increase output; and in a period in which output has risen by three-quarters it is not easy to refuse requests for higher wage rates. The worker needs some inducement to increase output: the patriotic urge, the various banners bestowed by the government, and the competitive urge to outdo other plants in achieving war objectives will also help. Many workers, however, need the additional incentive of an increase in the wage rate or hourly earnings in order to produce more goods and work longer hours. Much of the absenteeism is associated in no small part with the lack of interest of the worker in producing more goods. At the present high-wage rates and with the scarcity of consumer goods, he is frequently satisfied to work 5 days instead of 6, or 40 hours instead of 48. In order to induce him to work longer hours or produce more goods, it may be necessary either to give him a bonus in the form of war bonds or a higher wage rate (part of which will be used to buy war bonds), or to make available to him a larger supply of consumption goods. Many will not work harder merely to obtain a stake in future goods which is their reward insofar as they receive war bonds in payment for longer hours or more intensive production. In many cases it may be helpful to make more civilian goods available to workers. If, by releasing $5 billion worth of additional civilian goods, workers may be encouraged to produce $10 billion more of war goods, the net effect would be salutary.[1] In summary, incentives are a *sine qua non* for full participation by workers in the war effort.

What, then, can be said against the high-wage policy of the war period? First, the larger these income payments are, the greater the pressure on consumption markets. This is evident in the statistical analysis of an earlier part of this chapter. Second, the larger this excess of income over supplies of goods available at current prices, the stronger the case for taxation of the low-income groups. However, such taxation brings great difficulties and, even if the tax program is imposed, it is not likely to be imposed in an equitable way and will cause considerably more grumbling on the part of those who are subject to the heavy taxation than if the income had not been earned.

Third, it is patently clear that the net effect of these large payments to all groups of income recipients has been that the government has not had so much available for the war economy as it otherwise would have had. For example, in 1943 consumption was $20 billion in excess of consumption for 1943 as anticipated in 1942 and of what was clearly desirable from the viewpoint of the war economy. In other words, priorities, allocations, and conservation and limitation orders had only a limited success, and entrepreneurs under the pressure of large supplies of purchasing power on the market have done everything possible to divert resources into consumption-goods industries. High-wage payments have contributed toward that pressure.

Fourth, an excessive rise of wages and prices aggravates postwar problems of readjustment; particularly if productivity should decline or prices should decline.

Finally, the payment of high wages, even though consumption goods are not available, results in strong pressure on commodity markets,

---

[1] *Cf.* House Hearings on *Price Control Bill* (1941), pp. 1554, 1629, 1846*ff.*; Senate Hearings on *Emergency Price Control Act* (1944), pp. 301*ff.*

making enforcement of price control and rationing more difficult and, therefore, the equitable distribution of goods more difficult to achieve.

In summary, arguments for higher wage rates are the increase of productivity, the contribution of pecuniary rewards to an optimum allocation of labor as between essential and nonessential industries, the need of maximum incentives, and the urge to improve labor's postwar position. Against the high-wage policy are to be listed especially the increase of inflationary pressure and the excessive output of consumption goods.

Productivity in the Postwar

Our postwar national income will depend on productivity, and the basic wage rate will be determined largely by changes in productivity. There has been a steady increase in productivity, both before and during the war, and the extent of the rise has exceeded expectations. In the years 1899 to 1937, for example, physical output of manufacturing rose by four times, employment by two times, and the number of hours was reduced from 60 to 40 per week. The net effect of these changes was that the man-hour cost of a unit of output had been reduced by two-thirds.[1] For the period 1919–1940, output per man-hour rose from 58 to 139 (1929 = 100). This is an average rise per year of almost 4 per cent. In the same period, unit labor cost, despite a rise in wage rates, fell from 145.4 to 81.2.[2] The rise of output per man-hour for 1929–1941 equals 34 per cent, or a rise of 2½ per cent, annually compounded.[3] Finally, the Department of Commerce, basing itself on a new revised index of the Federal Reserve Board (FRB) and using for its series of hours of employment the same weights as are used in the FRB index, finds an implied increase in man-hour output of 3.1 per cent from 1939 to 1943.[4]

Recently the Bureau of Labor Statistics commented on the probable trend of productivity. Its conclusions, based on past experience, differ radically from the pessimistic view taken by Dr. Mayer of the Brookings Institution.[5] The following is quoted from a statement of the BLS:

During the entire period 1909–1941 productivity in all manufacturing industries increased at the rate of about 3½ per cent per year. With regard

---

[1] S. Fabricant, *Employment in Manufacturing, 1899–1939*, pp. 153–154.
[2] *Productivity and Unit Labor Costs in Selected Manufacturing Industries, 1919–1940*, U. S. Department of Labor, February, 1942, p. 1.
[3] *Markets after the War*, p. 3.
[4] *Survey of Current Business*, October, 1943, p. 8.
[5] Cf. pp. 3–4.

to the first World War period, no measures were available between 1914 and 1919. However, since our economy was not initially substantially affected by the war, we have no reason to suppose that the increase between 1909 and 1914 stopped at the later date. However, since the figures for 1914 and 1919 were identical, it appears that there was probably first some increase and then a decline. This is indicated by the dotted line between 1914 and 1919 on the chart. Beginning in 1919 productivity measures became available on an annual basis, and the increase for three years was at the rate of 10 per cent per year. After 1922, the general trend was resumed. [Chart omitted here.]

Approximately the same behavior is expected during and after World War II. In the manufacture of civilian type goods, productivity generally has declined during the present war period. The productivity index for 23 civilian type industries combined increases from 100 in 1939 to 107.6 in 1941 and then declined to 104.6 in 1943. Some further decline during the war period is expected.

The reasons for the decline in productivity in the civilian industries during the war include the following: Perhaps most important, new equipment and machinery have not been available and to a certain extent the capital structure of these industries is declining, using the word "capital" here in the physical rather than the financial sense. In addition, the civilian industries have received less protection from Selective Service than the war industries. Because of their generally lower wage structure they have found it more difficult to attract or retain competent workers. Where materials were limited, the civilian industries have had to use inferior grades or substitutes. They have been most affected by transportation difficulties. Looking at the whole picture, the maintenance of productivity at even the present levels must be considered a creditable job.

After the war most of the factors which tended to hold back productivity in the civilian industries will disappear. Replacement of old equipment at greater than the usual rate and installation of many new processes and methods is expected. It does not seem unreasonable to suppose that productivity will increase at a rate approximating 10 per cent per year as it did after the last war. The two dotted lines on the chart after 1941 indicate the area within which productivity is expected to fall, depending on different assumptions regarding the extent of the decline during the war and the length of the war.

In a discussion of productivity, we should distinguish the period after Germany's defeat and that following Japan's defeat from the later periods. In the former, productivity in civilian-goods industries might well decline. Output may be at a subnormal level; many of the industries will receive less favored treatment by government agencies in control of supplies, capital, and man power; labor turnover will continue to be high; and the inflow of inexperienced help will continue. For these and other reasons, productivity may decline in 1945 and 1946.

Over all these periods, the volume of output will be decisive. At a high employment level, productivity will almost certainly continue to be high and to improve. At a level that yields only 35 to 40 million jobs, man-hour output will be low. In this discussion, since we assume a high level of employment, we also assume that output per man-hour is likely to be high. There is, of course, a point beyond which any expansion of employment yields declining output per man-hour.

In later periods, industry will be supported by renovation of plant, the availability of new plant and new processes, the return of skilled workers, a reduction of labor turnover, and the weeding out of the most inefficient workers who will either desert the labor market or, in a relatively small number of cases, become unemployed. There will also be much downgrading.

These are the factors that will account for a continued rise of man-hour output. [The rise in gross national product (GNP) will correspond on the assumption that basic wage rates and prices remain unchanged.]

Two factors should, however, be considered offsets. The first is the improvement in the quality of the product at a given price once conditions are normal again. A given supply of factors will then yield a smaller GNP. Dr. Mosak estimates the resulting loss of product at $7.5 billion. This is, however, not a loss in any real sense. A given number of dollars of GNP corresponds to a substantially larger real product when the quality of the product rises.

A more important problem is the changing composition of the employed. In wartime, workers gravitate toward high-paying industries. In manufacturing industries, for example, annual wages in war industries as of 1943 were 50 per cent higher than in nonwar industries. These higher rates of pay reflect higher physical productivity; but they also largely reflect the government's willingness to pay sufficiently high prices to attract workers to war industries. The redistribution of workers as between occupations and industries will undoubtedly result in a reduction of the average pay roll. A cut in pay rolls associated with the redistribution of workers, though it is reflected in a reduction in the money GNP, does not account for a corresponding fall in the *real* GNP. This follows because in part the rise in wartime is not associated with an increase in physical product but rather with inflated rates of pay offered by the Treasury. The rise in real product does not correspond to the increase in pay; correspondingly, the fall will not be so large as the decline in the average pay roll.[1]

---

[1] Dr. Mosak, however, concludes that the GNP per man-hour of work in the postwar will not be reduced as a result of the changing composition of the labor forces. *Cf.* Ch. V.

When we add it all up, the conclusion seems to be that after a temporary pause, man-hour output should continue its rise of the last few generations. The rise in money GNP may not be quite so large as in the prewar; but the rise in real GNP should continue unabated. The larger numbers of new workers, the new skills, the improvements in plants and techniques, the maintenance of a high level of output—all these will be decisive. There is then every reason for continued increases in basic wage rates.

Other Problems of the Future

In the opening paragraphs, we briefly discussed several issues of the future. Here we shall develop points raised there and consider a few additional issues.

In general, wage rates should conform to productivity. If rates are too low, the individual entrepreneur may be tempted to expand too far, but he will soon be deterred by the general contraction of demand. Each employer and industry will be affected in varying degrees by the profit inflation associated with reduced costs and the deflation associated with declining demand.

We enter the early stages of demobilization and reconversion with a price-wage relationship that is not far from the appropriate one. To those who have followed the wage and profit history of the war, it will be apparent that basic wage rates are not too high. Pay rolls will fall substantially, and even hourly earnings will suffer. But if productivity continues to climb as we predict, there will be every reason for a continued rise in the basic wage rate. Whether productivity continues to rise, however, will depend in no small part on the success of the reconversion program. If, for example, the total wage bill is cut drastically, the resulting effect on demand and employment may be a further reduction in average productivity. Wage rates that are not too high at a $140-billion income become excessive at a $100-billion income.

As the total of wage payments and the "take-home" pay envelope is reduced in response to downgrading, loss of overtime, and movements into nonwar industries, labor may be a little overzealous in its attempts to offset declines by corresponding rises in the basic wage rates. This temptation may be strengthened if (as we hope) the government introduces a comprehensive and adequate social-security program.[1] Excessive rises in wage rates—especially if prices are not allowed to respond—

---

[1] See Ch. XXII. There Dr. Burns discusses the appropriate relation of wage rates and payment rates under social security.

may also contribute to declining employment and output. If, on the other hand, prices are allowed to respond, maldistribution of income may result and large accumulated savings may not be spent or will be absorbed in rising prices rather than give rise to expanding output.

Our policy should be one of high wage rates and low prices. Only in that manner shall we be able to obtain and maintain a high level of output. Monopolistic and restrictive policies on the part of business can have only one result: high prices and reduced output. American industry has advanced on a policy of high productivity, high wages, and low prices.

In its report to the President on the Little Steel formula, the WLB made some concrete suggestions concerning future wage policy. Although the labor members of the WLB argued that since the cost of living had risen by 45 per cent and basic wage rates by only 20 per cent, a substantial rise in the latter should be granted, nevertheless, the WLB refused to break the Little Steel formula. The labor members had also pointed out that once *hourly earnings* were reduced to a point where their percentage rise above prewar was no greater than the percentage rise of *basic wage rates*, labor's position would deteriorate—this on the ground that basic wage rates had risen less than the cost of living. Apparently impressed by this argument, the public members of the WLB proposed that Congress set minimum wages in numerous key occupations and that labor and capital agree on wage principles that would assure the retention of some of the wartime gains obtained by labor.[1]

Employment levels will be determined by the flexibility of our wage and price system and (related to them) the magnitude of demand. The amount of employment and unemployment will also be determined by the numbers on the labor market, length of the working week, and similar considerations. We should not leave out of account the mobility of workers and their willingness to move into areas or occupations of high demand. On this score, the expansion and vitalization of our employment service are important. In view of the changed geographical distribution of manufacturing facilities and employment, geographical mobility is especially important.[2] Unless workers show a willingness to move in response to demand and unless the government shows a greater

---

[1] See especially WLB, *Report to the President on the Relationship of Wages, etc.*, mimeographed, Feb. 12, 1945; and C.I.O. members of WLB, *Report to the President on the Relationship of Wages to Consumers' Prices and the Cost of Living*, mimeographed, Mar. 7, 1945.

[2] For further discussion of these issues, see Chs. VI, VIII, and IX.

interest in mobility than it has so far displayed (*e.g.*, Congressional opposition to payment of travel expenses of stranded workers), we may well experience at one and the same time areas of unemployment and of unfilled vacancies. Total employment depends not only on total demand and wage rates, but also on the distribution of workers. If they do not move, then we may be confronted with distressed areas or with the need of subsidizing industries there.

Chapter V

Forecasting Postwar Demand

by JACOB L. MOSAK[1]

Introduction

THE PURPOSE of this chapter is twofold: (1) to estimate the level of the gross national product which the nation will be able to produce in the postwar period and (2) to estimate the combined amount of government expenditure and private capital formation that will be necessary to maintain full employment. The analysis employed permits us to determine (1) the amount of government expenditure and private capital formation that is required to yield any given gross national product under specified conditions, and inversely (2) the amount of the gross national product that will be produced with given amounts of government expenditures and private capital formation.

The analysis is confined to the year 1950 so as to eliminate the special reconversion problems which must be treated separately. It is based on certain income and expenditure relationships which prevailed in the period 1929–1940. The projection of these relationships implies that the war and the reconversion period to follow will have no significant long-run effect on the producer and consumer habits with which we are concerned. This is, of course, a questionable assumption, but there seems to be little reason to believe that the distortions which may occur during this period will significantly reduce the magnitude of the problem of maintaining full employment.

[1] The author is indebted to Messrs. Michael Sapir and Neal Potter for their assistance in the development of the estimates. This chapter is republished by permission of editors of *Econometrica*.

I. Labor Force and Capacity of Output in the Postwar Period

In 1950 the nation will be able to produce a gross national product of about $200 billion in 1944 prices under "full" employment conditions and 1939 average hours worked per week.[1]

This estimate is based on the following projections of labor force, employment, and productivity:

a. LABOR FORCE AND EMPLOYMENT

The civilian labor force in 1950 will probably exceed the 1944 total of 52.5 million persons by 7.8 million persons, even if we maintain 2.5 million men in our postwar armed forces and even if over 4 million of the abnormal entrants withdraw from the labor force.[2]

If we allow for 1.5 million unemployed under full employment conditions, we shall have an increase in employment of 7.2 million, or more than 14 per cent above 1944 levels of 51.6 million. Even under full employment there will be no need to increase agricultural employment above the present level of 8 million. The entire 7.2 million will, therefore, serve to increase civilian nonagricultural employment by 16.5 per cent from 1944 levels of 43.6 million. Civilian government employment —Federal, state, and local—will decline by 1.5 million men after the war even if the government establishments are maintained at the levels attained during the height of the defense program in 1941. We shall, therefore, have an increase of 8.7 million, or 23 per cent, in employment in private nonagricultural industries under full-employment conditions.

Average hours worked per week in all private nonagricultural establishments in 1944 are approximately 10 per cent above 1939 levels. A return to prewar hours would, therefore, leave us with approximately 11 per cent more civilian man-hours to be worked in 1950 than in 1944.[3]

---

[1] The Department of Commerce concept of the gross national product is generally accepted as the best available over-all measure of the total product or income of the economy.

[2] This estimate is about 1 million higher than that made by the National Planning Association. The latter estimate, however, was made at an earlier date when the number of "war extras" was lower than it is today, and apparently it did not assume compulsory military training. If we were to reduce our estimate of the labor force by 1 million, we should reduce our estimate of the gross national product by about $4 billion.

[3] This estimate is not precisely correct because the percentage increase in total man-hours obviously depends upon the percentage distribution of employment by industry. See, however, the discussion in part c.

b. GROSS NATIONAL PRODUCT ON ASSUMPTION OF 1944 PRODUCTIVITY

In 1944 the gross product of all private nonagricultural industries will be about $150 billion. If average output per man-hour in 1950 remained only as high as in 1944, the gross product of all private nonagricultural industries under full employment would be about $166 billion in 1944 prices.

Assuming present average rates of pay to prevail in civilian government employment, compensation to civilian employees in government will amount to $8.5 billion if employment is reduced to 4.5 million persons. Interest payments for Federal, state, and local governments will probably be $5.5 billion and pay to the armed forces about $3 billion. The gross product in government will, therefore, amount to about $17 billion.

We assume that under present farm prices and present agricultural employment the gross product in agriculture will be at least as high as in 1944, or about $17 billion.

Adding all of these components together, we obtain an estimate of $200 billion in 1944 prices for the gross national product in 1950 on the assumption of 1944 productivity per man-hour in private industry.[1]

c. CONSIDERATIONS ON POSTWAR PRODUCTIVITY

Is it reasonable to assume that under full-employment conditions the average output per civilian man-hour worked in 1950 will be at least as high as in 1944? What are the factors that may be expected to change productivity from current levels?

1. FACTORS WHICH MAY REDUCE PRODUCTIVITY. On the side of lowered productivity, four major factors may be considered:

a. First, there is the possibility of diminishing marginal returns as employment increases.

I think that this factor is of little significance. If the economy is given adequate time to adjust plant and equipment to the larger numbers of workers, any tendency to diminishing marginal returns can readily be overcome. I believe no one can doubt that, if we are fortunate enough to have full employment in 1950, we shall have more than sufficient plant and equipment to overcome this tendency. Clearly the average volume of plant and equipment per employee will be larger in 1950 than it is today.

---

[1] The fact that the estimate of the gross national product is measured in 1944 prices does not imply, of course, that the 1944 price level will in fact prevail in the postwar period.

b. Second, productivity in the metal and metal-products industries may decline when production is shifted from war goods to civilian goods.

Although there is little evidence on this point, I am inclined to the belief that this factor is also not of much significance. The great strides in munitions production appear to have been made primarily through the application of techniques long familiar in the production of machinery and equipment and of consumers durable goods. Furthermore, many of the new techniques developed for munitions production should be equally applicable to peacetime production of civilian goods.

c. Third, there will be a shift from munitions industries where physical output per man-hour has increased at a remarkably rapid rate to nonmunitions industries where the growth has been moderate.

The importance of this factor has, I believe, been generally overrated. Despite the much greater growth in physical output per man-hour in the munitions industries, the dollar contribution per man-hour to the gross national product in the metal and metal-products industries in 1943 appears to have been about equal to the average for all private nonagricultural industries. Apparently other industries made up through war-induced economies, through quality deterioration, and through greater price increases what they failed to accomplish through comparable increases in productivity. If this is also approximately true of 1944, then clearly a shift in man-hours worked from the metal-products industries to other industries will not in itself reduce the total gross private product if the men are absorbed in the other industries in proportion to present man-hours worked.

Although we cannot predict in what proportions the men will actually be absorbed in the various industries, it does not appear that the shift out of the metal-products industries will have a depressing effect upon the gross private product. Only in the textiles, lumber, paper and printing, rubber, and miscellaneous manufacturing industries and in trade was the gross national product per man-hour in 1943 lower than for the metal-products industries. In the food and tobacco and chemicals manufacturing industries, in mining, construction, transportation, and public utilities, and in the finance, services, and miscellaneous industries the gross national product per man-hour in 1943 was greater than in the metal-products industries. It appears probable that the gain in employment for this second group will be more than in proportion to the total.

As a test of the possible effect of a shift in employment we have calculated the effects on the gross national product of a restoration of the 1939 percentage composition of employment both under present hours and under 1939 hours.[1] In both cases the effects of this change are negligible.

d. The fourth factor which might lower productivity per man-hour is the most significant one. Many industries, particularly the transportation, trade, and service industries, have experienced a partly fictitious increase in productivity through deterioration in the quality of their goods and services. If, after the war, competition compels them to restore the peacetime quality of their goods and services without any change in prices, this fictitious portion of the increase in their productivity will be eliminated.

It is practically impossible to evaluate the quantitative effects of this factor, both because there are no adequate data on the extent of quality deterioration during the war and because it is impossible to determine how much of this quality deterioration will be eliminated after the war without an offsetting increase in price. All the industries which might be affected in this manner, however, probably will not account for more than $75 billion of the gross national product, even after the shift to a peacetime composition of employment and production. It is probably not too bad a guess to assume that these industries will not in any event reduce their gross national product by more than 10 per cent through the elimination of quality deterioration without increases in their prices. On this basis we would get a maximum effect of $7.5 billion for this factor.

2. FACTORS WHICH MAY INCREASE PRODUCTIVITY. Offsetting these factors are a number of others which will tend to raise productivity above current levels. To some extent the current levels are depressed by overtime work, by the replacement of the youth with marginal labor, by the exceptionally rapid rate of labor turnover, and, in some industries, by the necessity to use old machinery and equipment which would otherwise have been discarded. The elimination of all of these factors should have a significant effect on productivity in the postwar period.

In addition, we must take into account the probable effects of the normal growth in productivity. Mr. Livingston has estimated that in the

---

[1] In these calculations the gross national product per man-hour within each industry was assumed to be unaffected by the shift in employment.

period 1929–1941 the physical gross national product per man-hour increased at an average rate of 2½ per cent per annum. For 1929–1940 he estimates the rate of increase to be just under 2 per cent per annum.[1] If it were assumed that all the productivity factors discussed in the preceding paragraphs canceled themselves out, then output per man-hour in 1950 would be approximately 12 per cent higher than in 1944 on the basis of normal growth alone. This would add about $20 billion to our estimate of the gross national product.

Taking all of these factors into account, we obtain an estimated range for the gross national product in 1950 of from more than $190 billion to about $220 billion in 1944 prices. To be conservative we may assume that the productivity will remain unchanged from current levels and adopt an estimate of $200 billion.

II. The Demand for the Gross National Product

Unfortunately the mere existence of the capacity does not provide an assurance that we shall have the production. We shall not have a $200 billion gross national product unless the economy will spend $200 billion per annum on finished goods and services. Can we count on this amount of expenditures? What, in other words, is the nature of the demand for the gross national product?

The economy may be divided into three main groups of buyers: (1) individual consumers, (2) business concerns, and (3) government.

The demand analysis adopted in this paper with respect to these three groups is based on the following assumptions:

1. That the volume of consumer expenditure is a function of the disposable income in the hands of individuals, which in turn may be determined from the gross national product when the tax structure, dividend policy, etc., are known.

2. That government expenditures for goods and services are determined autonomously by social-political considerations and except for the very long run are, practically speaking, independent of the gross national product.

3. That business demand for private gross capital formation, although partly dependent upon the gross national product, is significantly affected by too many other factors to permit any reliable forecast

[1] S. M. Livingston, "Post War Manpower and its Capacity to Produce," *Survey of Current Business*, April, 1943.

of the amount demanded at any given level of the gross national product. We are, therefore, compelled to treat private gross capital formation in our analysis as a residual.

Given these assumptions, we can determine the amount of government expenditures and private capital formation combined that is required to yield any given gross national product, under specified conditions or, inversely, the amount of the gross national product that will be produced with given amounts of government expenditures and private capital formation.

a. CONSUMER EXPENDITURES

The projection of consumer expenditures at each given level of the gross national product is derived in three major steps: First, the level and composition of the national income before taxes is projected corresponding to each volume of gross national product. Next, we estimate the level of disposable income in the hands of individuals corresponding to each level of the national income, under specified assumptions as to corporate and personal taxes. Finally, we project the aggregate volume of consumer expenditure corresponding to each level of disposable income.

1. NATIONAL INCOME BEFORE TAXES AND THE GROSS NATIONAL PRODUCT. The national income projections in this report are based on the following assumptions:

a. That the gross national product originating in Federal, state, and local government in the postwar period will amount to no more than $17 billion. This consists of $8.5 billion in compensation to employees, $5.5 billion in interest payments, and $3 billion in pay to the armed forces. The gross private product is, therefore, equal to the gross national product minus $17 billion.

b. That for every $10 billion increase in the gross private product the volume of business taxes other than Federal corporate profits taxes will increase by something over $0.5 billion. Beginning with a level of $11.2 billion at a gross private product of $83 billion (corresponding to a gross national product of $100 billion), it rises to $16.4 billion at a gross private product of $183 billion or a gross national product of $200 billion. This is a crude estimate based essentially on the current levels of Federal, state, and local tax rates. For want of a better term we shall refer to these taxes as "indirect" business taxes.

c. That the distribution of the gross private product less "indirect" taxes into its component income shares will bear a stable relationship to the aggregate level, and that this relationship can be adequately approximated on the basis of simple gross correlations between each of the components and the aggregate level in the period 1929–1940.

This assumption is an extreme oversimplification for many reasons, amongst which the following ones may be mentioned:

First, it implies that the gross national product will be distributed by industry in accordance with the prewar pattern. This assumption appears to be reasonable as there is little reason at present to expect any significant postwar change from the prewar pattern of the composition of the gross national product by industry.

Second, it implies that the price-wage structure within each industry will not be seriously distorted from its prewar relationship to the gross product of the industry. In this connection, it should be emphasized that the price-wage structure in most major industry groups has remained rather stable even during the war, despite the enormous increase in the level of income and despite the existence of wartime controls. The indications are, in fact, that if it were not for overtime premium pay, labor upgrading, and the wartime shift of employment to the higher paid industries, salaries and wages would be somewhat below the levels derived from the prewar relationships. Our use of the prewar relationships as a basis for postwar projection may, therefore, result in some overstatement of salaries and wages unless basic wage rates in the postwar period are raised sufficiently to offset the effects of the elimination of these wartime factors.

Finally, it implies that the relationships which prevailed when the gross national product was under $100 billion and was subject to serious fluctuations may be used as a basis for postwar projections with respect to fairly stable values of the gross national product up to $200 billion.

With respect to the validity of the relationships for the higher levels of the gross national product, we have already pointed out that they appear to have held even during the war when the gross national product stood at comparable levels. To test the effect of *changes* in it on the distribution of income by type of share, we experimented with multiple regressions, using as independent variables the gross private product less "indirect" taxes of both the current and the preceding years. The estimates of salaries and wages and of profits before taxes [1] obtained from these regressions on the assumption that the product remained the

---

[1] Inventory profits were excluded from the total throughout the analysis, thus eliminating one element that is greatly affected by *changes* in prices and production.

same in both years did not differ materially from those obtained by the use of the simple regression.

Taking all these factors into consideration, it appears that the simple regressions for the period 1929–1940 do yield very useful first approximations, particularly for aggregate private salaries and wages, aggregate corporate profits before taxes, and aggregate entrepreneurial income.

2. DISPOSABLE INCOME AND THE GROSS NATIONAL PRODUCT. With appropriate assumptions concerning the tax structure, we may pass from national income to estimates of disposable income in the hands of individuals. This involves estimating, first, income payments to individuals and, second, personal income taxes. We have made three assumptions concerning the corporate tax structure: (*a*) that present taxes prevail in the postwar period, (*b*) that the excess-profits tax only is repealed but that income tax rates remain at present levels, and (*c*) that income taxes are reduced to 1940 levels. We have likewise made three assumptions with respect to the personal tax structure: namely, 1944, 1941, and 1940 Federal rates, giving us in all nine sets of disposable income corresponding to each level of the national income before taxes.

It should be noted that the projections for corporate savings out of profits after taxes, though estimated conservatively in the light of past data, are necessarily arbitrary since there is no really adequate basis for projecting them. The estimates of government transfer payments and of contributions to social security are based on the assumption that there will be no change in the present structure of social security. This assumption is, of course, extremely unrealistic for low levels of output and high levels of unemployment. It is used only to indicate the magnitude of the problems that would face us in the event of our failure to maintain a high level of income in the postwar period.

3. CONSUMER EXPENDITURES AND DISPOSABLE INCOME. It is assumed that the volume of consumer expenditures in the postwar period will bear a stable relationship to the aggregate volume of disposable income. This assumption also represents an extreme oversimplification, since clearly many other factors, particularly prices and the size distribution of disposable income, are important factors in determining consumer expenditures. Within the range of variation to which these two factors were subject in the past, however, their effects on aggregate consumer expenditures do not appear to have been very important. Their primary role in the past seems to have been to determine not what the

total volume of expenditures will be but how a given total volume of expenditures will be distributed among individual commodities.[1] In the absence of any drastic change in prices or in the distribution of income in the postwar period, the simple linear relationship of consumer expenditures to disposable income for the period 1929–1940 may be used as a first approximation for our postwar projections. There is reason to believe that this equation may yield values of consumer expenditures that are too high at high levels of disposable income.[2]

b. PRIVATE GROSS CAPITAL FORMATION AND GOVERNMENT EXPENDITURE

The difference between the gross national product and the corresponding volume of consumer expenditure represents the amount of private gross capital formation and government expenditure necessary to maintain the given gross national product.

The amounts necessary to maintain a full-employment gross national product of $200 billion are staggering. Under 1944 Federal personal income-tax rates, $85 to $87 billion of private gross capital formation and government expenditure are required, according as corporate tax rates are maintained at present levels or are reduced toward 1940 levels. Under 1941 personal rates $75 to $78 billion are necessary, and under 1940 rates $71 to $75 billion are required.

Can such expenditures reasonably be expected in the postwar period? If not, what range of expenditure appears to be more reasonable and what gross national product range would it yield? Under what circumstances could such a range correspond to "full employment"? Let us consider each question in turn.

1. PROBABLE LEVELS OF GOVERNMENT EXPENDITURE. *a. Assuming no positive government expenditure or investment program.* In the absence of any positive government expenditure or investment program, there is no

---

[1] This is suggested by the following two facts:

a. A regression of per capita "real" consumption on per capita "real" disposable income yields results that are very similar to those obtained from the regression of aggregate money consumption on aggregate money disposable income.

b. Multiple regressions, using the ratio of salaries and wages to total income payments as a rough index of income size distribution, were examined for the three major classes of consumer expenditure: durable goods, nondurable goods, and services. Although the separate effect for each class of expenditure appeared important, the combined effects on aggregate consumer expenditure substantially canceled out.

Both of these questions, however, need to be explored more fully.

[2] Consumer expenditures for 1941 fell considerably below the value calculated from the equation, despite the absence of any important shortages and the absence of price control.

reason to believe that the Federal government will spend more than $15 billion on goods and services. It is generally estimated that state and local government expenditure will not exceed $10 billion, making a total of $25 billion for all government expenditure on goods and services. In that event private gross capital formation will have to be $60 to $62 billion under 1944 Federal personal income-tax rates, $50 to $53 billion under 1941 personal tax rates, and $46 to $50 billion under 1940 personal tax rates, if we are to maintain a gross national product of $200 billion. These figures may be compared with the peak level of private gross capital formation of $19.6 billion reached in the year 1941, when the nation was equipping itself for war production.

b. Assuming balanced Federal budget. At a gross national product of $200 billion, Federal government taxes other than social-security receipts are estimated at approximately $45 billion under 1944 tax rates, and at $22.5 billion under 1940 tax rates. If the government adopted a policy of spending on goods and services as much as it received in such taxes, private gross capital formation would have to be $32 billion under 1944 tax rates and $38.5 billion under 1940 tax rates at a gross national product of $200 billion.

2. PROBABLE LEVELS OF PRIVATE GROSS CAPITAL FORMATION. Unfortunately, there appears to be no adequate basis for estimating the demand for private gross capital formation at varying levels of the gross national product. Any attempt to estimate it on the basis of the correlations existing in the past between these two variables, with or without the use of a time trend, almost inevitably ends in failure. The demand for private gross capital formation, as has already been indicated above, is too unstable a function to permit of such an approach. The regression equations obtained in this manner closely approximate the supply function for saving (*i.e.*, they represent the demand function for consumer expenditure in a disguised form) rather than the demand function for private capital formation.[1] If the equations are treated as demand functions for private gross capital formation, *i.e.*, if they are used as the basis for estimating the demand for capital formation at varying levels of the gross national product, then they raise the estimated combined marginal propensity to consume and invest out of a given gross

[1] This is another example of the problem treated repeatedly in the literature on statistical demand and supply functions, namely, the problem of determining both the demand and supply functions from a given set of observed data on actual purchases. See the article by J. Marschak in *Studies in Mathematical Economics and Econometrics*.

national product to such high levels as to yield fantastic multipliers.[1]

We seem compelled, therefore, to resort to more or less arbitrary guesses of private capital formation based on considerations of the orders of magnitude that prevailed in the past, and on the quantity and quality of our present plant and equipment. Such considerations lead to rather pessimistic conclusions. In the absence of any revolutionary inventions which might render our present plant and equipment obsolete, and in the absence of a large export program, it is difficult to see how capital formation can average in excess of $20 billion per annum.

With a $20 billion annual average level of private capital formation and $10 billion of state and local expenditures, Federal government expenditure will have to be $55 to $57 billion under 1944 personal tax rates, $44 to $48 billion under 1941 personal tax rates, and $41 to $44 billion under 1940 personal tax rates, if we are to maintain a gross national product of $200 billion. Federal expenditure on goods and services in excess of its taxes would then amount to $12 billion under 1944 corporate and personal tax rates and $19 billion under 1940 corporate and personal tax rates.

The more optimistic reader may substitute his own higher estimates for private capital formation and reduce correspondingly the estimate of required government expenditures.

3. PROBABLE GROSS NATIONAL PRODUCT IN ABSENCE OF POSITIVE PROGRAM. With total government expenditures of $25 billion and with private capital formation of $20 billion, we would obtain a gross national product in the neighborhood of $120 billion under 1944 personal tax rates, $130 billion under 1941 personal tax rates, and $140 billion under 1940 personal tax rates.[2] Under 1944 corporate and personal tax rates, Federal receipts would exceed expenditures by approximately $6 billion at the $120-billion gross national product level. Under 1940 corporate and personal tax rates, however, receipts would fall short of expenditure by approximately $2 billion.

---

[1] A notable example of this type is the Department of Commerce and Committee for Economic Development study of *Markets after the War*, which has become the bible of the optimistic postwar planners. If the regressions in that study are interpreted as demand propensities to consume and invest out of a given gross national product, then they yield a Keynesian multiplier of about 21.6. A $1 billion increase in autonomous expenditures would then increase the gross national product by $21.6 billion. If the regressions are not interpreted as demand functions, then they provide no basis for projecting the demand for consumer goods and for private capital formation and no basis for the optimisim which the study has generated amongst postwar planners.

[2] These figures are rounded to the nearest $10 billion.

If prices remained at current levels, a gross national product of $140 billion would reduce employment by about one-third below full employment levels. Not all these people would show up in the unemployment figures, since many would withdraw from the labor force and many others would be partly employed. One way of maintaining full employment with a gross national product of $140 billion at current prices would, of course, be to reduce average hours worked per week rather than to reduce employment. Such a solution can hardly be considered adequate, however, unless average weekly earnings are sufficient to maintain a decent standard of living.

It is quite unrealistic, of course, to assume that prices would remain at current levels if the gross national product fell to $140 billion. The lower the level of prices associated with the $140 billion gross national-product level, the smaller will be the reduction in employment. It should be noted, however, that the lower the level of prices, the more difficult will it be to achieve a gross national product of $140 billion. But since money expenditures would not fall in proportion to the decline in prices, it is probably true that we could have a higher level of employment and real income at lower prices than at higher prices.[1] This is a strong argument for reductions in excise taxes and for gradual reduction in prices without offsetting wage reductions. It is not an argument, however, for promiscuous price and wage cutting on a large scale which would reduce rather than increase employment by creating an atmosphere of highly unfavorable business anticipations.

III. Summary and Conclusion

The nation will need to produce a gross national product of about $200 billion in 1944 prices—approximately the same level as prevails today—in order to maintain "full" employment in the postwar period. If certain past relationships prevail, consumer expenditures at this level of the gross national product will amount to about $113 billion under

---

[1] The money volume of national income originating in government would probably be only slightly reduced as a result of price declines in the private economy. The demand for private capital formation, though probably inelastic with respect to price, is not completely so; consequently real capital formation would probably be higher at low prices than at high prices. Likewise, if our relationships are correct, money disposable income would fall less than in proportion to money gross national product and money consumption would fall less than in proportion to money disposable income. Consequently, real consumption too would be higher at low prices than at high prices. Thus real expenditures of government, business, and consumers would all be higher at low prices than at high prices.

1944 Federal, corporate, and personal tax rates and to $129 billion under 1940 rates. (These are about $18 and $34 billion higher than current levels.) Private capital formation plus government expenditures on goods and services will, therefore, need to be between $71 and $87 billion in order to maintain full employment.

If the Federal government confines itself to "normal" expenditures only, it will need to spend approximately $15 billion. State and local

TABLE 1.—INCOME PAYMENTS, DISPOSABLE INCOME, AND CONSUMER EXPENDITURES, UNDER 1940 CORPORATE INCOME TAX RATE
(In billions of dollars)

Gross national product	100	110	120	130	140	150	160	170	180	190	200
Income payments.....	82.8	90.1	97.6	105.1	112.6	120.6	128.4	136.3	144.4	152.3	160.5
Personal taxes:											
Federal income:											
Under 1944 rates..	7.8	9.2	10.6	12.0	13.5	15.1	16.9	18.7	20.7	22.8	25.1
Under 1941 rates..	2.7	3.4	4.1	4.9	5.7	6.6	7.6	8.6	9.7	10.9	12.2
Under 1940 rates..	1.3	1.7	2.2	2.7	3.2	3.8	4.5	5.2	6.0	6.9	7.9
State and local and Federal estate, gift, and automobile.........	2.4	2.4	2.5	2.6	2.6	2.7	2.8	2.9	3.0	3.1	3.2
Disposable income:											
Under 1944 rates....	72.6	78.5	84.5	90.5	96.5	102.8	108.7	114.7	120.7	126.4	132.2
Under 1941 rates....	77.7	84.3	91.0	97.6	104.3	111.3	118.0	124.8	131.7	138.3	145.1
Under 1940 rates....	79.1	86.0	92.9	99.8	106.8	114.1	121.1	128.2	135.4	142.3	149.4
Consumer expenditures:											
Under 1944 rates....	66.9	71.7	76.5	81.3	86.1	91.2	95.9	100.7	105.5	110.1	114.8
Under 1941 rates....	71.0	76.3	81.7	87.0	92.4	98.0	103.4	108.8	114.4	119.7	125.1
Under 1940 rates....	72.1	77.7	83.2	88.8	94.4	100.2	105.9	111.6	117.3	122.9	128.6
Government expenditures and private capital formation:											
Under 1944 rates....	33.1	38.3	43.5	48.7	53.9	58.8	64.1	69.3	74.5	79.9	85.2
Under 1941 rates....	29.0	33.7	38.3	43.0	47.6	52.0	56.6	61.2	65.6	70.3	74.9
Under 1940 rates....	27.9	32.3	36.8	41.2	45.6	49.8	54.1	58.4	62.7	67.1	71.4

government expenditure will probably not exceed $10 billion. Private capital formation will, therefore, have to average between $46 and $62 billion or between 2¼ and 3 times the 1941 peak level in order to maintain full employment. It seems evident, therefore, that private capital formation will be inadequate to assure full employment, even under low tax rates such as those which prevailed in 1940.

Only the government is in a position to provide positive assurance of full employment. To do so, it must (1) establish a price and wage policy and a broadened social-security program which will raise the postwar propensity to consume out of a given gross national product far above the levels which prevailed in the prewar period, (2) stimulate private capital formation by appropriate tax legislation, underwriting of loans to small business, support of industrial research, and related measures, and (3) increase its expenditures on social and other public services and engage in a large-scale construction and developmental program sufficiently flexible to fill any gap that may remain in private expenditure.

Part II

SPECIAL PROBLEMS OF RECONVERSION

Chapter VI

Man Power and Reconversion

by WILLIAM HABER[1]

I. Introduction

THE ACHIEVEMENT of full employment after the war is the prime objective of public policy and the goal most eagerly sought by government, business, and labor. Whether or not we shall have full employment will be determined by policies which go far beyond the problems in the field of man power. Contract-settlement policies, revision of the tax structure, disposal of surplus property, wage- and price-control policy, and international-trade policy—subjects covered elsewhere in this volume—will all directly influence the speed with which civilian production is resumed and the total level of output and employment which can be reached.[2] The wisdom with which these complex issues are handled will determine the total number of jobs available.

This does not mean, however, that man power is a "dependent variable" and that wise action in other major fields of policy will automatically and smoothly place all persons who want jobs in gainful employment. Even if the demand for goods and services is so high that the wartime labor force, including those in the armed forces, could be absorbed in gainful employment, a substantial volume of unemployment will nevertheless exist.

Unemployment in the face of a demand for goods potentially high enough to ensure full employment is paradoxical but probably inevitable. When the war-production machine is dismantled, all the workers

---

[1] The writer is indebted to Charles V. Kidd for assistance in the preparation of this chapter.
[2] See also, B. M. Baruch and J. M. Hancock, *Report on War and Post-war Adjustment Policies*, February, 1944.

released will not be immediately placed in civilian production. Many communities are going to have far fewer jobs to offer in peacetime than they had in wartime. All the returning veterans are not going to move directly from demobilization centers to gainful civilian employment. Unemployment arising from these causes, often labeled "frictional" unemployment, is one price that must be paid for a rapid transition from war to peace. There is general agreement that, on balance, there is more to be gained by a speedy transition than by gearing the transition to a pace that would superficially lessen the cost of the change-over by spreading it over a longer time. We are not going to keep intact either the armed forces or the war-production structure as an unemployment relief measure.

As soon as this premise is accepted, the obvious questions are: (1) How can the volume of frictional unemployment be minimized? (2) What degree and kind of assistance and protection should be offered to those who are released from war jobs or the armed services? (3) How can these measures be designed to promote full employment?

"Reconversion" unemployment, which is a particular variety of frictional unemployment, has received public attention since 1943. By it is meant the physical inability of plants to use a full staff on production while war plants are being ripped apart and put together again for civilian production. Although reconversion unemployment will probably be relatively light, means of minimizing loss of earnings during this period deserve serious consideration.

If the economy will run at full tilt once temporary maladjustments of one kind or another have been ironed out, we can move quite easily from war to peace. The real threat, of course, is not these temporary maladjustments but the possibility of a substantially lower level of economic activity. If jobs are not available because the demand for goods has dried up and the volume of new investment has fallen off, the problem of man-power transition will be different in both nature and size. We shall then be forced to decide such fundamental questions as the extent to which the government expenditures must supplement private investment in order to ensure full employment, and the extent of the government's obligation to provide the necessities of life to workers unemployed for long periods through no fault of their own.

A discussion of a comprehensive program for dealing with either frictional or "depression" unemployment which may develop during the transition period can be made more concrete if we have some picture of the probable volume of unemployment which we will have, and of the timing and location of this unemployment. Although such an analysis is in no sense a prediction, it can indicate in general terms the lower and upper limits, as well as the timing and location, of transition unemployment.[1]

II. Man-power Mobilization, July, 1940–July, 1944

We are engaged in total war. Our armed forces consist of over 12 million men, not 4 or 5 million as in World War I. The war consumes about 60 per cent of our national income, not 20 to 25 per cent as in 1919.[2] Our labor force has reached 65 million, the highest in our history. Including those in the armed forces, over 50 per cent of our labor force is producing for war. Millions of new workers have come into the labor market. Large-scale migration of workers and their families has been necessary in order to build and man the shipyards, aircraft plants, and other rapidly constructed war-production facilities. Production of the metal goods which make up most of our war production has required an expansion of manufacturing industry which boosted 1944 factory employment to over 16 million workers in comparison to some 11 million in the prewar period.

The heavy in-migration of war workers and the geographical concentration of war contracts expanded the population of dozens of communities and produced serious problems of congestion and community facilities. Hours of work increased sharply in many industries; a 54- or 60-hour week was not uncommon. Weekly earnings increased substantially as a result of a longer work week, some increase in hourly rates, and the penalty overtime rate. Traditional hiring practices were discarded in war establishments; Negroes, older workers, and handicapped persons were employed in unprecedented numbers. The number of women workers reached new heights; over 18 million were employed in October, 1944, compared to 13 million in October, 1940. Women workers were brought into the shipyards and into many trades heretofore barred to them. Unemployment fell to less than 700,000 in Septem-

---

[1] For a discussion of the factors affecting the volume of employment in the transition, see S. H. Slichter, "Jobs after the War," *The Atlantic Monthly*, October, 1944; see also Robert R. Nathan, *Mobilizing for Abundance*, 1944.
[2] National Resources Planning Board, *After the War, 1918–1920, Military and Economic Demobilization of the United States. Its Effect upon Employment and Income*, June, 1943; and "Demobilization of Manpower, 1918–1919," *Monthly Labor Review*, April, 1944.

ber, 1944, far below the "irreducible minimum" assumed during prewar years.

The end of the war will have an immediate and drastic effect on the employment situation and the labor force. Remarkable success in expanding the labor force, in drawing in new workers, and in inducing millions to migrate, has created the demobilization task which faces the civilian labor force. The size of the transformation which must take place when the war is over is measured by the tremendous changes which occurred during the mobilization period.

a. GROWTH OF THE LABOR FORCE

A total of 19,400,000 persons was added to war-expanded activities and the armed forces between July, 1940, and July, 1944.[1] These millions were obtained by a large increase in the national labor force, by the reemployment of those who were unemployed in June, 1940, and by the transfer of workers from other employment.[2]

The labor force, including the armed forces, reached a total of 66.6 million persons in July, 1944—a peak which 2 years earlier was generally assumed to be unattainable except through the application of rigid controls under national service legislation. About 5.5 million women and 4.2 million men entered the labor force during the 4-year period. This increase is about 7 million workers in excess of the normal increase which would have resulted from population growth and the long-range tendency for a larger proportion of women to enter the labor force. The civilian labor force declined by 1.4 million. This is another way of saying that the addition of 9.7 million persons to the total labor force

[1] The gains are as follows:

	Millions	
Armed forces........................	11.1	(from 0.5 to 11.6)
Munitions industries..................	5.5	(from 4.0 to 9.5)
Other manufacturing.................	0.5	(from 6.5 to 7.0)
Federal war agencies.................	1.5	(from 0.1 to 1.6)
Transportation and public utilities......	0.8	(from 3.0 to 3.8)
Total........................	19.4	

[2] The sources from which these 19.4 million came are

	Millions	
Additions to the labor force............	9.7	(from 56.9 to 66.6)
Reductions in unemployment..........	7.4	(from 8.4 to 1.0)
Contraction in employment:		
Agriculture.......................	0.9	(from 10.6 to 9.7)
Construction......................	1.3	(from 2.0 to 0.7)
Mining and other..................	0.1	(from 21.8 to 21.7)
Total........................	19.4	

was not sufficient to offset the 11 million increase in the armed forces.

Many millions of workers have shifted from less essential activities to the munitions industries and the armed forces. Nevertheless, the net loss in the declining segments of nonagricultural employment was only 1.7 million, and all but 400,000 of this net decline is accounted for by a shrinkage in new construction. Employers in less essential activities were, therefore, generally successful in obtaining replacements, in spite of varied efforts and "controls" designed to induce workers to desert these activities for essential jobs. Most of these employees in less essential activities were new entrants into the labor market, chiefly women, who replaced the persons transferred to war activities or the armed forces.

In no other nation at war have employment levels in trade and service activities been maintained at nearly prewar levels. We have been able to build an armed force of nearly 12 million fighters, to develop a munitions industry employing at its peak 10.4 million workers, and at the same time to maintain at nearly normal levels the civilian economy of the United States.

To the amazing record of military production and the maintenance of the civilian economy must be added the record of agriculture. Despite the decrease of 900,000 in agricultural employment between July, 1940, and July, 1944, farm output rose substantially. Many workers have left low-productivity farms to go to higher output farms, as well as to enter industry and the armed forces. Seasonal agricultural needs, particularly at the peak of harvesting activities, have at times been difficult to meet. However, fuller utilization of available farm residents, together with the seasonal services of school-age youths, townspeople in rural areas, vacationists, and others, have contributed to the attainment of food-production record.

These changes in the distribution of man power between 1940 and 1944 are summarized in Chart 1 on page 101.

b. SOURCES OF ADDITIONAL WORKERS

At the beginning of the defense program in July, 1940, there were 56.9 million persons in the labor force, including armed forces. Normal labor-force growth would have increased this figure to about 59.7 million persons 4 years later, but the actual level was 66.6 million. At the time of the attack on Pearl Harbor, $1\frac{1}{2}$ years after the beginning of the defense program, the actual labor force exceeded the normal labor force by only 1 million persons. Thereafter, however, the total labor force has exceeded the normal force by a rapidly increasing margin. By the middle of 1942, this excess over normal had jumped to 2.4 million, and by July, 1944, induced to a large extent by a very rapid induction of persons into the armed forces, the excess in the actual labor force reached 6.9 million.[1] Since July, 1944, the labor force has continued to increase faster than normal but at a much slower rate.

Contrary to popular impression, the wartime increase in the labor force has not consisted primarily of women. Of the total 6.7 million excess over normal in April, 1944, 3.7 million were men and 3 million were women.[2] Over 2 million boys and young men who would normally be in school or college were serving with the armed forces or were in the civilian labor force. The remaining excess over normal among males consisted about equally of older men who normally would be retired and of handicapped and other marginal persons who normally would not be a part of the labor force.

Among the 3 million women workers who would not normally be in the labor force, about one-half were young women under twenty-five, about 1 million of whom would normally be in school. About 0.5 million of these younger women were estimated to be servicemen's wives who normally would not be working or seeking work. The remaining 1.5 million "excess over normal" among women were housewives over thirty-five who normally would not be in the labor force.

c. EXTENT OF INTERSTATE MIGRATION

Production of war goods is concentrated in a relatively small number of areas. Shipbuilding contracts were necessarily placed in coastal cities, especially on the Pacific Coast; aircraft assembly was concentrated in the established centers of the West, as well as in large plants in a few

[1] Increase in the labor force, July, 1940–July, 1944 (in millions of persons).

Period	Actual increase		Excess over normal increase	
	For year	Cumulative	For year	Cumulative
July, 1940–July, 1941	1.5	1.5	0.8	0.8
July, 1941–July, 1942	2.3	3.8	1.6	2.4
July, 1942–July, 1943	4.6	8.4	3.9	6.3
July, 1943–July, 1944	1.3	9.7	0.6	6.9

[2] "Sources of Wartime Labor Supply," *Monthly Labor Review*, August, 1944.

additional areas; the highly centralized auto industry and other producers of metal products were quickly converted to war production. Large-scale migration was necessary to man these expanding establishments. Economic and patriotic incentives to induce migration appeared

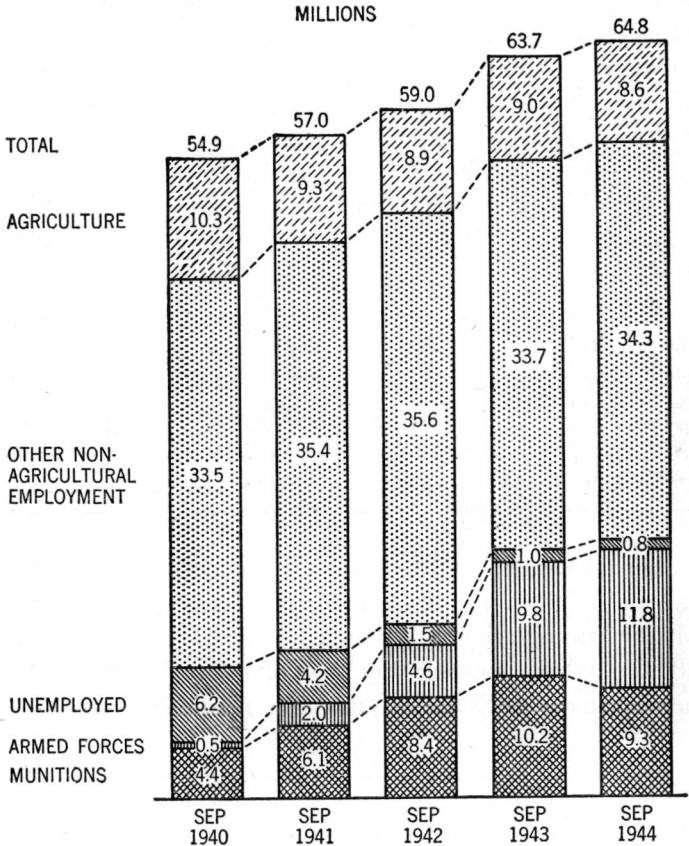

CHART 1.—Distribution of man power, September, 1940–September, 1944. (*Source: War Manpower Commission, Bureau of the Census, and Bureau of Labor Statistics.*)

adequate, and several million workers moved hundreds of miles to provide the expanding war-production man power.

The Bureau of the Census estimates that *net* migration of civilians from one state to another amounted to about 3.5 million from April, 1940, to November, 1943.[1] This net population migration of 3.5 million probably includes some 2 to 2.5 million workers. The total number who

[1] Bureau of the Census, Department of Commerce, *Interstate Migration and Other Population Changes: 1940 to 1943*. Special Population Report, Series P-44, No. 17.

migrated from one state to another exceeds the net figure by an unknown amount. It is probable that the gross migration of workers, including an intrastate movement that probably exceeds interstate migration, has amounted to as much as 6 or 7 million.

In-migration has been highly concentrated geographically. Thus, of the net migration of 3.5 million for the country as a whole, nearly 1.5 million was into California alone. No other state shows net in-migration of as much as 300,000.

TABLE 1.—NET IN-MIGRATION, SELECTED STATES, APRIL, 1940–NOVEMBER, 1943.

State *	Net in-migration April, 1940– November, 1943, thousands	State	Net in-migration April, 1940– November, 1943, thousands
California	1,369	Florida	187
Michigan	281	New Jersey	185
Washington	245	Virginia	155
Maryland	235	Oregon	138
Ohio	231	Connecticut	127
District of Columbia	205		

* Indicates states in which net in-migration of 100,000 or more has occurred.

Net out-migration has been much less concentrated. Thirty states show net out-migration as against 19 (including the District of Columbia) with net in-migration. Oklahoma had the largest net out-migration, over 300,000, while four states lost a net of 200,000 to 300,000 each and 11 others lost over 100,000. Wartime patterns of migration were thus in

TABLE 2.—NET OUT-MIGRATION, SELECTED STATES, APRIL, 1940–NOVEMBER, 1943.

State *	Net out-migration April, 1940– November, 1943, thousands	State	Net out-migration April, 1940– November, 1943, thousands
Oklahoma	304	West Virginia	140
North Carolina	263	South Carolina	138
Kentucky	263	Georgia	131
Arkansas	225	Missouri	117
New York	223	Alabama	116
Mississippi	194	Pennsylvania	112
Iowa	193	Wisconsin	103
Minnesota	192	North Dakota	100

* Indicates all states having net out-migration in excess of 100,000.

general toward the East and West Coasts. This centrifugal movement was an acceleration of peacetime trends.[1]

d. HOW MAN POWER HAS BEEN MOBILIZED

The demobilization process will be affected not only by the extent but also by the means of man-power mobilization.

By and large, the transformation and expansion of the labor force were brought about by means other than control or direction of workers or employers.[2] Migration and shifts to munitions work within the same community were primarily in response to job opportunities at relatively high wages. Delay in establishing effective wage control may have increased the cost of the war and may render peacetime wage adjustments more difficult, but the delay also permitted the growth of a wage and earnings differential that enormously facilitated man-power mobilization.

Job opportunities and wage differentials would not, however, have done the job unaided. Guidance to jobs through the information provided by the United States Employment Service, through recruitment activities of private employers and governmental agencies, and through advertising, has been indispensable. The duty of all persons to serve where they can best help the war effort has been drummed into the public by posters, movies, and community drives. Control over hiring has been necessary to prevent pirating of workers and to ensure that the short supply of workers is directed to most urgent employers. Employment ceilings have been imposed on less essential employers at a level requiring release of workers for more essential work; ceilings have been set on the employment of essential employers at a level requiring the full use of the existing work force. The net effect of these measures has been to supplement the forces that assisted man-power mobilization, to direct these forces into the most useful channels, and to provide a degree of precision in man-power allocation that could not be expected if wage differentials and job opportunities alone had been relied upon.

III. MAN-POWER DEMOBILIZATION

As we enter the first stages of demobilization, we have munitions employment of about 9 million workers, armed forces totaling over 12

[1] W. S. Woytinsky, *Internal Migration during the War*, Social Security Board, November, 1944, p. 3.
[2] John M. Clark, *Demobilization of Wartime Economic Controls*, p. 65.

million, a total labor force expanded beyond normal by about 7 million, an occupational pattern distorted by concentration in munitions work, and at least 3 million workers who moved to a new state during the war. Each of these facts high-lights a set of man-power demobilization problems. Before these problems are indicated and a program for coping with them is outlined, it would be well to suggest the size and nature of the labor-market changes that will come during the successive stages of demobilization.

Some phases of demobilization begin while the mobilization process continues. It is already clear that the demobilization of our resources—man power and facilities—will not be a sudden catastrophic event. It is more likely to be a process extended over a period of time. By the end of 1944, for example, while the two-front war was being fought at a furious pace, munitions employment had already declined by about 1.3 million from the peak of 10.4 million in November, 1943; by the end of 1944, about 1.5 million members of the armed forces had been released to civilian life.

The rate at which further demobilization proceeds will be jerky and unpredictable but, to give some form to speculation, three phases of the transition can be identified. These are from peak munitions production to VE-day, from VE-day to VJ-day, and after VJ-day.

a. PEAK MUNITIONS PRODUCTION TO VE-DAY

We are now in the first phase of reconversion and demobilization. Since the peak of 10.4 million in munitions employment was reached in November, 1943, employment in the munitions industries declined at an average rate of over 100,000 workers per month to a level of 9.1 million in November, 1944. This decline was due, in part, to the increasing productivity of the industries producing war goods—to the decline in man-hours per unit of product. It was due also to the induction of men into the armed forces. The primary reason, however, is found in the decline of the industries' total man-power requirements as a result of production cutbacks, and completion of contracts.

Two significant policy problems became important during this period. The first was concerned with the location of production cutbacks and the second with the volume and location of civilian production. With regard to the location of cutbacks, the Office of War Mobilization and Reconversion has determined that, barring other considerations, cutbacks should be placed in a manner designed to relieve the existing labor shortage.[1] With regard to the resumption of civilian production, it was decided after a premature beginning in the summer of 1944, that large-scale reconversion would have to await the end of the European war. The war requirements were too high and the economy too taut to permit any actual diversion of man power and facilities for reconversion. Planning had to be in the paper stage.[2]

b. VE- TO VJ-DAY

The first significant impact of demobilization will come within 2 or 3 months after the defeat of Germany. Reductions and shifts in war activities as well as an increased rate of release from the armed forces, following the defeat of Germany, are posing the first test of our ability to minimize the shocks of transition from total war to peace.

1. LABOR REQUIREMENTS, LABOR FORCE, AND UNEMPLOYMENT. The key to the volume of man-power requirements during the year following the defeat of Germany, assuming that Japan is not defeated during that period, is the decline in the munitions production for the Army. In all likelihood, the production of goods for the Navy will continue at about the same rate as before the defeat of Germany. As a working assumption, we can count on a decline of 35 to 40 per cent in the total munitions program by the end of this period.[3] A precise estimate of this crucial figure is impossible because many decisions cannot be made until well after the defeat of Germany.

For example, the volume of supplies and equipment which can be shipped from the European area for the Pacific war cannot now be determined. If a large volume of the supplies is transferable, a lower level of munitions production will be called for and the rate of home-front demobilization will be correspondingly increased.

On the assumption that the estimated rate of decline in munitions production is accurate and that releases from munitions production proceed at an even rate throughout the year following the defeat of Germany, roughly 1.5 million workers would be released from munitions employment during each half of the year after VE-day.

In addition, as a working hypothesis, it can be assumed that the armed forces will discharge a total of about 2.4 million—900,000 in the first half and 1,500,000 in the second half of the year.

[1] Office of War Mobilization and Reconversion, "War Contracts, Policies of Contract Curtailment, Non-renewal and Termination," Jan. 20, 1945.
[2] See *First Report*, by the Director of War Mobilization and Reconversion, Jan. 1, 1945, p. 12.
[3] See *Second Report*, by the Director of War Mobilization and Reconversion, April, 1945.

The supply of man power which must be absorbed in civilian production may, therefore, approximate 5.4 million.

Although the reabsorption of 5.4 million persons in one year may appear to be a difficult task, there is every likelihood that the volume of unemployment will remain quite low in the year following the defeat of Germany. First, about 800,000 persons will be inducted to provide replacements for the armed forces. Second, the release and reabsorption of many munitions workers will entail no change of jobs. As the steel and textile industries, for example, begin to deliver for civilian uses the same products now delivered to the armed forces, the workers released from munitions production will be reabsorbed in civilian production. This process may well account for 1.5 million of the 5.4 million available workers.

Finally, more people are going to leave the labor force than will enter the labor market in the year following the defeat of Germany. As indicated below, the net withdrawal can easily reach 700,000.

The sum of these three offsetting factors is 3 million workers. Thus, 2.4 million workers must be absorbed in civilian production or be out of a job. This figure, added to the one million workers who will probably be unemployed at the beginning of the period, represents the probable maximum amount of unemployment in the year following the end of the war in Europe.

Actual unemployment will, of course, be considerably below that amount. The reconversion of civilian production will get under way. Its volume and speed will be limited by the availability of materials and facilities, by the supply of tools, and by the success in overcoming inevitable bottlenecks. Many workers to be released in war-expanded areas cannot be reemployed except by migration to expanding communities. As a result of these and similar situations, unemployment, local in character and of varying duration, may exist in many communities. There is no basis for estimating the numbers who will be reemployed in civilian production during the year. It can be assumed, however, that the actual volume of unemployment will be considerably below the maximum indicated above—perhaps between 1.5 and 2.5 million workers.

2. SHRINKAGE OF THE LABOR FORCE.[1] The proportion of the 7 mil-

---

[1] The time of the year when the war in Europe ends will have a considerable effect on the levels of employment in agriculture and other highly seasonal activities. The time of the year will also affect the size of the labor force since, for example, the labor force expands with the close of schools in June. Seasonal factors are omitted from this analysis since comparisons are made on a 12-month basis.

lion persons not normally in the labor force who will leave the labor market after VE-day is a most important factor in evaluating the size of the transition problem. The assumption that most of these persons who normally would not be in the labor force will immediately withdraw after VE-day is probably not true.

First, it cannot be assumed that the young men who may be separated from the armed forces and the younger men released from war jobs will immediately return to school to complete their education. Experience indicates that a relatively small proportion of persons who withdraw from school to accept employment with the intention of returning later ever do so. The provisions of the G.I. Bill of Rights, providing subsistence pay simultaneously with free education, will induce a considerable number of armed-force dischargees, whose education had been interrupted, to return to school. However, the announced policy of discharging first those who had been in the armed forces longest, and those who are married and have dependents, will greatly reduce the number likely to return to school during the period of partial demobilization. Only after the defeat of Japan can large numbers of discharged veterans be expected to return to school.

Nor can it be assumed that a large proportion of the older workers employed in the munitions and other industries will voluntarily withdraw from the labor market. Workers will be laid off from munitions plants, but only a small proportion of the older workers are presently employed in munitions plants. Moreover, it is unlikely that many of the older workers now employed in nonmunitions industries will voluntarily leave the labor force until they become unemployed.

The assumption of rapid and extensive withdrawal from the labor market cannot even be made generally for female workers. A large proportion of those laid off by munitions plants may return to their domestic and other duties but, as is true of older workers, the majority of working women normally not in the labor force are employed in nonmunitions plants. Employment of women in trade, service, and nonmunitions manufacturing establishments has increased very substantially. Although a large proportion of the women released from employment will probably not seek new jobs, those who are not released will tend to hold on to their jobs. Most of the women added to the wartime labor force are working because their income replaces the earnings of husbands, brothers, and sons who are in the armed services. Other women in households with relatively fixed incomes found it necessary to seek employment as an aid in meeting the rising cost of living. The economic status of many of these households will not suddenly change so that the women will wish to stop working. In addition, a large number of women who have tried paid employment prefer it to keeping house. During the year following the defeat of Germany, therefore, no extensive voluntary withdrawal of women from the labor force should be expected.

The wartime labor force includes a good many handicapped and marginal workers who would not have been employed or seeking employment under peacetime conditions. Most of these workers will keep their jobs until they are laid off and will seek new work after they are laid off. Public opinion and the necessity for the rehabilitation and employment of large numbers of returning disabled veterans will tend to keep handicapped workers in the labor market as employees or job seekers.

In summary, only about 1.3 million of the abnormally expanded wartime labor force will probably withdraw during the year following the defeat of Germany. Offsetting these prospective withdrawals from the labor force will be the normal growth of 600,000 per year in the labor force. On the basis of these assumptions, the net withdrawal from the labor force during the year following VE-day will probably not exceed 700,000 workers.

3. THE UNEVENNESS OF DEMOBILIZATION. As was true during the period of man-power mobilization, over-all figures on production requirements and man-power demands are deceptive. These totals are the net result of a multitude of factors, and the net figures provide no measure of the impact of demobilization on specific industries and geographical areas.

Moreover, the estimate that not more than 2.5 million workers will be unemployed *at any one time* during the year following the defeat of Germany does not mean that only 2.5 million workers will experience any unemployment during this period. There will be rapid turnover in the composition of the unemployed group.

Finally, the impact of unemployment will vary. In response to new technological developments, some industries will expand; new boom towns with all the gold-rush atmosphere of crowded war-production centers may be created; as certain munitions programs decline, some one-industry munitions towns will become ghost cities. It is these specific, acute, localized situations that constitute the primary man-power demobilization problem during the first reconversion period. Until Japan is defeated, we shall be faced with the difficult task of maintaining certain types of munitions production at constant levels, or even expanding the production of some, while civilian production is being slowly resumed.

The unevenness of the demobilization can be suggested by indicating how various war-production centers will be affected.

a. One-industry Communities. Relatively hardest hit will be the towns and labor-market areas which have boomed because of a single war industry. Among these are Milan, Tenn., and other towns supported almost solely by shell-loading or explosive plants; Orange, Tex., and other communities working almost exclusively on merchant vessels; Wichita, Kan., with aircraft; and a number of other one-industry towns with greatly expanded populations. Some of these one-industry communities, however, will be able to reconvert, probably at a level of employment lower than wartime peaks.

b. Areas with Favorable Reconversion Possibilities. The important prewar industrial areas of the Great Lakes, Middle Atlantic, and New England regions will face serious readjustment problems even though the eventual prospect of a high level of employment is favorable. Detroit is the outstanding example of this type of area. A wide variety of war products—10 per cent of the nation's combat material—is made in Detroit. Aircraft tanks and parts for these weapons constitute more than half the output of the area. VE-day will hit Detroit hard, but the duration of unemployment will depend entirely on how soon automobile plants can be released from war production and converted to the manufacture of automobiles. This in turn will depend on how fast other industrial areas manufacturing components such as tires, axles, bearings, fractional horsepower motors, and machine tools can reconvert.

Delays in reconversion resulting from technical and engineering problems may cause large-scale unemployment of several months' duration in areas like Detroit. At the same time, man-power shortages will continue in other areas producing goods needed for the Japanese war. West Coast cities, for example, may be loaded with vital war work for the Pacific campaign. The inevitable exodus of war workers out of the West Coast communities or their transfer to civilian production may in fact lead to a tight man-power situation in spite of some cutbacks. Critical shortages may also develop in key skills, with surpluses in other skills. It is possible that the pirating of key workers needed for reconversion may recur. Needless large-scale cross migration of the displaced workers during the interim period—for example, from Detroit to the West Coast—may also be a problem.

c. Areas with Moderate or Limited Reconversion Possibilities. Different problems will arise in areas such as those in the South and on the Pacific Coast which had diversified prewar industries but which were not among the key industrial centers of the nation before the war. Employment in these areas is concentrated in new government-owned war plants (as contrasted with the reconverted, privately owned plants of the key industrial cities) engaged largely on products for which the postwar demand may be insignificant. Some of the facilities, however, will have post VE-day conversion possibilities. Employers in these areas, in many instances relative newcomers in the field of industrial civilian production, will be anxious not to be left behind in the rush to conversion. The problem is complicated by the fact that many of the facilities, such as shipyards on the West Coast, produce goods vitally needed for the war against Japan.

d. Communities Not Drastically Affected on VE-Day. Finally, there will be a number of labor-market areas that may not be directly or drastically affected by cutbacks on VE-day—areas such as Washington, D. C., with government employment and service and trade; New York City, with a large total but a small relative volume of war work. Some of these areas have industries of a character that are important to civilian as well as war work (St. Louis and Chicago). They may be expected to experience a short period of moderate labor surplus, after which reemployment of continuing war and expanding civilian work may absorb most of the unemployment. Others (such as Pittsburgh, Pa., Gary, Ind.) will have relatively little difficulty in reconverting, because their major industries are vital for peacetime as well as for war production. In some areas, existing labor shortages may become more acute because of outmigration to areas with better postwar prospects.

c. AFTER VJ-DAY

The impact of demobilization will become most acute with final victory in the Pacific. At that time there will probably still be 6 million persons engaged in munitions production, most of whom will be released from munitions work within a few months after the defeat of Japan. Over a longer period, depending upon the availability of transportation and the size of our occupying forces, an additional 7 million persons will be released from the armed forces—assuming that the armed forces remain at 2 or 3 million for some time after the end of the war.

It would be erroneous to assume that the number of persons released from war jobs and the armed forces will remain unemployed. "Evaporation" from the labor market, which will have begun with VE-day, will continue at a more rapid rate. Older workers will retire in greater number. The wives of servicemen, who entered the labor force for economic or patriotic reasons, may also be able to assume their domestic responsibilities with the return of their breadwinners. The average hours of work per week will be much closer to 40 than to 45, thus absorbing many displaced war workers. And the limitations on the expansion of civilian production will have been removed.

These developments will at the same time reduce the number of job seekers and increase the number of jobs in a revived civilian economy.

It would be futile to attempt to estimate the volume of employment and unemployment with which we are likely to be confronted under such circumstances. We cannot avoid extensive layoffs from munitions production. We must anticipate the return of veterans at the rate of ¾ million per month for many months. Jobs will not be available immediately for these displaced war workers and released veterans. An unemployment level of 5 or 6 million workers is therefore to be anticipated.[1]

Whether this unemployment will disappear in a postwar boom and reappear later in a postwar slump, or whether we can reach stable full employment after a relatively short period of readjustment is a question that the future alone can answer.

IV. Planning for Man-power Reconversion

Policy formulation in the man-power field can proceed without precise quantitative estimates of employment and unemployment. It is clear that an expanding economy is a changing economy and that one cost of the expansion will be temporary unemployment for a very substantial group of workers. That is the lower limit of our transition problem. If we do not have an expanding economy, we face a return to the conditions of 1933. That is probably the upper limit of our problem.

Although the dimensions of the problem which we face cannot be established, we do have enough guideposts to indicate both the general

[1] R. A. Lester, *Providing for Unemployed Workers in the Transition*, 1944, p. 17.

requirements and the specific elements of a program for man-power reconversion.

The fact that the volume of unemployment may range from a low level of unavoidable "frictional" unemployment to a very high level of long-run "depression" unemployment immediately establishes *flexibility* as one prime requirement of a man-power program for the transition. Such a program must contemplate a series of measures to be applied when and if needed, and on the scale needed, in response to different levels of unemployment. As a guide to specific action, this criterion would indicate, for example, that we should have ready both a shelf of small projects and an array of big public works projects.

Since the ultimate objectives of a man-power program for the transition is full employment, the measures adopted should be designed so as to supplement rather than offset the effect of other measures designed to promote a high level of production and employment.[1] A well-designed man-power program must contemplate more than caring for workers thrown out of jobs. Proper policy related directly to man-power considerations can reduce the volume of unemployment. This objective offers a guide to the specific content of man-power transition measures. It suggests, for example, that in planning for civilian production, employers should go as far as possible in making advance offers of jobs to specific workers. It suggests that unemployment compensation payments should last long enough to supply a stream of income that will add substantially to current purchasing power. It suggests that weekly benefit payments should be set at a level which will not make idleness compete in attractiveness with suitable work.

The volume of frictional and transition unemployment will depend to a great extent on the skill with which labor-market factors are taken into account in determining when and where production is cut back and civilian expansion authorized. A good program for man-power conversion must therefore be a *coordinated* program.

More is involved in man-power reconversion than guiding workers to jobs and supplying their basic needs if jobs are not available. Training and retraining programs, carefully considered to be of practical value to those who must change their occupations, must be set in operation. Vocational guidance and counseling can both aid the individual and increase the productivity of the labor force. After all these steps have

[1] See E. E. Witte, "What to Expect of Social Security," *American Economic Review*, March, 1944.

been taken, there remains the fundamental task of providing a basic subsistence to workers out of jobs, primarily by payment of unemployment benefits. A *comprehensive* program is therefore essential.

Finally, the man-power reconversion program must be *adequate*. The elements of the program must have depth as well as breadth.

With these criteria in mind, the outlines of a specific program for man power in the transition period can be drawn up.[1]

a. MINIMIZE UNEMPLOYMENT

1. TIMING AND LOCATION OF PRODUCTION ADJUSTMENTS. Until the summer of 1944, virtually every element of the war-production program was expanding. Since that time, changes in requirements have necessitated large-scale contractions in some items of production, while the production of others was increased. As a result, production adjustments requiring the layoff of tens of thousands have been necessary in many areas. Such downward readjustments in production will increase as we approach the close of the war. By the end of the year, after VE-day, as we have seen, munitions production may have been cut by as much as 40 per cent. Whenever a choice is possible and after due consideration of such factors as strategic requirements, the reduction should be made where workers can be placed in other war production or in civilian production. Until the war is over, such a policy will ease the man-power shortage in tight labor areas. As the end of the war approaches, the proper location of cutbacks is essential if local pools of unemployment are to be kept to a minimum.

Smaller one-industry and one-plant communities, with a war-expanded population for which few jobs will remain, present the problem of production adjustments in the most acute form. A program designed to guide re-migration, especially if accompanied with the payment of transportation costs "back home" or to a community where job opportunities exist, would go far in stimulating the orderly movement of war workers. With or without such a program, however, production should be reduced as early as possible in such areas so as to induce the out-migration of workers at a time when alternative job opportunities exist elsewhere. Otherwise, the end of the war is likely to create a local stranded population, subsisting first on unemployment insurance bene-

---

[1] Even after allowing for all of the differences between this country and Great Britain, social insurance and public works policies developed for Great Britain form a stimulating point of departure for thought about our problems. See, for example, W. H. Beveridge, *Full Employment in a Free Society*.

fits and later on local public relief, while jobs are available in other localities.

The keys to successful coordination or man-power and production policies are (1) adequate administrative arrangements and (2) strong action by man-power authorities. The machinery for coordination has been established, but whether man-power factors will be given adequate consideration when the industrial war machine is dismantled remains to be seen. Since the consequences of inadequate consideration of man-power factors in the letting of contracts and construction of facilities have been evident for some time in the form of congested production areas, there is some ground for optimism that man-power factors may be given greater weight in reconversion.

2. PRERECONVERSION PLANNING. VE-day and VJ-day will be the occasion, for the largest cancellation of production contracts and mass layoff of workers in the nation's history. The speed with which civilian production can get under way will vary, depending upon the technical and engineering factors in each industry and in each plant. In some industries 6 to 12 months may be necessary before production levels requiring a full work force will be reached. Prereconversion planning and preparation can help to shorten this period. Authorization for such prereconversion planning would pay dividends in speedier reemployment after VE-day and VJ-day, but the scope of activities diverting man power and materials from urgent war work will have to be limited so long as war production remains the nation's primary business.

Authorization for such planning would permit manufacturers to prepare material specifications, dies and tools, and model types for later production. Completion of these preproduction steps will ensure the speediest possible return to full-scale civilian production once controls can be released.

3. HOURS OF WORK. Wartime requirements made it necessary to set aside the established prewar standard work week. The 40-hour week was discarded, except in some nonwar activities where a longer work week would fail to release man power for more essential activities. As a result, wartime hours of work in the manufacturing industries expanded about 14 per cent. In many establishments the 55- to 60-hour week was common, except where the three-shift system was in operation.[1]

---

[1] Max D. Kossoris, "Studies of the Effects of Long Working Hours," United States Department of Labor (*Bureau of Labor Statistics Bulletin 791*), August, 1944.

Immediate post VE-day layoffs will not be extensive enough to permit a general return to the 40-hour week. When the war is over, however, a rapid return to the 40-hour week will help to absorb displaced war workers and returned veterans.

Substantial unemployment will lead to many proposals for the 30- or 36-hour week. Such work spreading can equalize the burden of unemployment, but it does not represent a solution for the problem.

A reduction of the hours from the wartime peak will immediately introduce problems of wage adjustment.[1] The "take-home" will be drastically cut once overtime work is discontinued. The question of the extent to which this reduction can be offset by an increase in hourly rates will then become acute, particularly in certain industries where the wartime wage controls were rigidly applied. In many situations, increased production resulting from the reduction in the work week and from technological developments will permit an upward adjustment of wage rates which will not result in a rise of production costs.

4. PUBLIC WORKS PROGRAMS. During the decade of the 1930's, we developed extensive work programs for the unemployed—the Civil Works Administration, the Works Progress Administration, the National Youth Administration, the Civilian Conservation Corps, in addition to the more regular types of public works. We relied upon these measures as well as direct relief to provide cash and work opportunities for the millions of unemployed. Since 1935, social insurance methods, particularly through unemployment compensation, have been developed as the primary device to provide cash benefits for short-time unemployment. A liberalized insurance program should be sufficient to meet the problem for "normal" unemployment. However, mass unemployment, for relatively long duration, will reintroduce the question as to whether cash benefits alone are enough. On the basis of the estimates of labor displacement in the reconversion period, it appears that we should be able to avoid the establishment of a reconversion WPA, or its equivalent. Cash benefits, through social insurance, may be adequate and the work relief issue postponed for some time.

Prereconversion planning must, however, include the planning for public works. These have been deferred during the years of war. Their deferment will undoubtedly be continued while the war with Japan is being fought. Later, when postwar layoffs and rapid demobilization of the armed forces create large pools of unemployment, public works

---

[1] See, for example, S. H. Slichter, *Problems of Wage Policy after the War*, p. 79.

projects may become an indispensable method of providing useful work. The large inventory of unmet needs accumulated by local, state, and the Federal government, represents a potential demand for materials and man power. The preparation of plans, the selection of sites, the completion of engineering details represent necessary elements of preconversion planning. VE-day should see the release of small projects in areas where local pools of unemployment have been created by war-production cutbacks and where fairly rapid reabsorption of the unemployed seems probable. VJ-day should find us ready with the larger projects capable of expanding the demands for materials and construction labor.

Postwar planning, extending beyond the reconversion period, must also contemplate public works as a compensating device to help fill the gap in employment if private investment does not provide an adequate number of jobs.

b. EMPLOYMENT ASSISTANCE TO WORKERS

1. ASSIST RE-MIGRATION. Some re-migration of the 3.5 million persons who left their homes for new jobs during the war will take place before the war is over. As war contracts are cut back in certain areas, many workers will return to their home communities, to the farm, or to self-employment. The end of the war will nevertheless find hundreds of thousands of workers ready to get on the move, headed for home or for areas where they think jobs will be easy to get. The greater the volume of unemployment, the greater will be the extent of migration.

To avoid aimless wandering in search of work, this re-migration should be guided and, to some extent, assisted. The United States Employment Service should be prepared to provide accurate and current information on employment prospects in the most important labor-market areas. This information should make it possible for any worker to check on the job prospects in the community to which he intends to move.

2. JOB COUNSELING AND OCCUPATIONAL ADJUSTMENT. Not only have millions of workers changed their homes, but hundreds of thousands of them have left their usual occupations. Millions of new workers have been trained for jobs which will be nonexistent in the postwar period. Job opportunities in many occupations vital to war production, particularly those related to fabrication of metal, will decline in importance as we return to peacetime activities. On the other hand, we may

look for many new trades, particularly in the service occupations.[1] In addition, returning veterans will need some aid in translating their wartime technical experience into peacetime jobs and activities. Finally, several million veterans will return from military life to seek their first jobs in competitive employment.

Where shall they go? What is the occupational trend? How make the adjustment from war job to peace job; from military life to a competitive occupation? [2]

These questions suggest the importance of vocational counseling and adjustment. Our counseling services will need to be expanded and strengthened if veterans, war workers, physically handicapped, and others are to be guided into productive employment with the greatest possibility for occupational adjustment. These services must be based on the most accurate available employment information, must be provided on a national basis, and must grow out of the day-to-day operating experience of the public employment service.

3. TRAINING AND RETRAINING. Many of the considerations just outlined apply with equal force to the vocational training problem. The war has required us to overtrain millions of workers in metal-working occupations. Peacetime industry will need, for example, but a fraction of the welders who have been trained for war production. Useful retraining for war workers and war veterans must be based on comprehensive occupational information, must grow out of concrete demand for and supply of particular skills or types of workers, and must be geared to industrial employment trends and occupational outlook. Training programs must avoid training for the sake of training. The administration of such a training program and the selection of the courses should be local, in the plants, in the vocation and technical schools, but it can be adequately administered only if based on comprehensive information concerning the national as well as the local labor market.

A training program must also be flexible. If we face only "frictional" unemployment, training programs should be inaugurated only in the areas where there are substantial numbers unemployed. The courses should be designed, so far as possible, with specific jobs in specific plants

[1] E. F. Denison, "Service Industries—Trends and Prospects," *Survey of Current Business*, January, 1945.

[2] See War and Navy Department manuals for conversion of military occupations to civilian occupations—Special Aids for Placing Military Personnel in Civilian Jobs (Enlisted Army Personnel), February, 1944; Special Aids for Placing Navy Personnel in Civilian Jobs, May, 1943.

in mind. Since most jobs require very little training, most of the burden of training can be financed by private concerns and done on the job.

More complex policy questions will arise in the establishment of a training program if unemployment is more extensive. Only in the long run, as a result of raising the general productivity of the labor force, can training increase the number of jobs. The immediate effect of a training program during a period of extensive unemployment is, therefore, to place the trained individuals in a better position to compete with their untrained fellows for a limited number of jobs. So long as the courses are open to all comers, this is not inequitable, but neither does it increase the number of jobs.

When jobs are scarce, training for jobs which may not be available is justified. Good training courses are probably better designed to preserve unemployed workers' self-respect than leaf raking. Moreover, the existence of a large group of workers who do not have the basic knowledge of subjects such as English and mathematics required for any but the lowest paid jobs, justifies the establishment of such courses during a period of mass unemployment.

c. FINANCIAL ASSISTANCE TO UNEMPLOYED WORKERS

1. UNEMPLOYMENT COMPENSATION. The subject of jobless benefits for veterans and war workers and the role of social insurance in the reconversion and postwar period is covered elsewhere in this volume. Unemployment benefits are not a substitute for full employment. Nevertheless, we are certain to have a substantial amount of unemployment during the transition. Everyone is agreed that we cannot afford mass unemployment of long duration, but few are so bold as to claim that we know how to, or will be able to, avoid it in peacetime.

A sound social insurance program, designed to provide cash benefits for involuntary unemployment, is, therefore, an indispensable part of a reconversion program for man power.

Unemployment benefits are the best means yet devised for providing a subsistence payment to workers who are temporarily out of a job through no fault of their own. The obligation of the government to make such payments is now generally accepted. Aside from the immediate assistance which adequate unemployment benefits can provide to individuals, these payments are a means of averting a precipitous decline in consumer purchases that might touch off a descending spiral of deflation.[1]

[1] See S. H. Slichter, *Social Security after the War*, p. 29.

The present provisions for jobless benefits, contained in the 51 state unemployment compensation laws, are inadequate for either purpose.[1] About 30 of our 43 million civilian workers are not protected, including those who work in government industrial establishments. The duration of weekly payments is too low. The maximum duration of benefit payments in most states is 16 weeks or less—less than the duration of unemployment for a large proportion of the workers who will be unemployed during the reconversion period. The weekly benefit is inadequate in terms of minimum requirements, in relation to average wages and in relation to the benefits provided by the Congress for unemployed veterans. The disqualification provisions are unduly restrictive.

The $6 billion reserve accumulated in the accounts of state unemployment compensation funds is probably sufficient to meet the demands upon such funds during reconversion. But a long period of large-scale unemployment will put the funds in some states under a severe strain.[2] Such a danger is in part responsible for the failure to liberalize the duration and benefit features of the state laws. The apparent solvency of the state unemployment reserves is, in part, due to the inadequacies from the viewpoint of benefits and duration. Greater coverage, fewer disqualifications, more liberal benefits, approximating, for example, the weekly payments under the state workmen's compensation laws, and payment of benefits over a longer period would introduce serious doubts about solvency, especially if the estimates of reconversion unemployment should turn out to be too optimistic. To fail in correcting these recognized deficiencies is to fall short of the minimum requirements for providing protection during the reconversion period.

How to correct these deficiencies is a subject of heated controversy concerned less with the substantive character of the insurance laws than with the issue of state rights. The states can be relied upon to improve the existing legislation over a period of years. Federal loans to the state funds, as have been provided in the Mobilization and Reconversion Act of 1944, can avoid insolvency.

If we wish to deal directly and more rapidly with the shortcomings in the 51 state laws, we can provide for minimum Federal standards, particularly in relation to the amount and duration of benefits. A uni-

---

[1] See, for example, *Ninth Annual Report of the Social Security Board, 1944*, pp. 1–16; also, Richard A. Lester, *Providing for Unemployed Workers in the Transition*.

[2] See, for example, Economic Problem of the Reconversion Period, Fourth Report of the House Special Committee on Post-war Economic Policy and Planning, Pursuant to H. Res. 408, 78th Congress, 2d Session, pp. 15–30.

form Federal unemployment insurance law would correct the weakness most quickly, but there is little prospect of its adoption in advance of a period of severe unemployment.

2. DIRECT RELIEF. Statutory benefits dependent upon fixed conditions of eligibility, generally requiring a prior period of substantial employment and earnings, inevitably lead to the denial of such payments to many persons. This group will vary in size directly with the volume of unemployment. Some workers will exhaust their rights to unemployment benefits even if the unemployment compensation system is made adequate to carry the load which it is designed to carry. Some workers will not be qualified to work in either public works projects or in private industry. For these persons a direct relief program becomes necessary.[1]

Direct relief grants, payable upon a demonstration of need, should be available to all persons in this category as long as the need exists. The program should be financed by Federal grants matched by state funds. Minimum standards, relating to such matters as residence requirements, should be established as a condition precedent to the Federal grants.

Although there is much to be said for work relief as opposed to direct relief, experience during the great depression points fairly conclusively to the need for a supplementary direct relief program. Overhead costs of work relief are high; the utility of made-work projects is often doubtful.

In addition to advance provision for relief, the public-assistance programs provided for in the Social Security Act should be strengthened. Even in July, 1944, 2.8 million old persons, children deprived of parental support, and blind persons received aid under the special categories of public assistance; in addition, 0.5 million individuals were receiving general assistance.[2] During the transition, this load will increase. The programs are deficient in a number of respects. Maximum payments in a number of states are low; provision for medical care of recipients of public assistance is inadequate; residence requirements for the receipt of public assistance are excessive in a number of states. Correction of these deficiencies will be of material assistance in providing for need generated primarily by loss of jobs and income during the transition.

[1] See *Security, Work and Relief Policies*, National Resources Planning Board, Washington, 1942.

[2] "Public Assistance Goals: Recommendations of the Social Security Board," *Social Security Bulletin*, November, 1944.

d. ADMINISTRATIVE MACHINERY—THE UNITED STATES EMPLOYMENT SERVICE

The wartime experience has amply demonstrated the necessity for unifying the executive agencies dealing with man-power problems. The best program can be emasculated by ineffective administration. Administration by appointment of successive layers of "coordinators" is at best a makeshift, and the cost of relying upon a disjointed administrative man-power structure during the transition period will be a greater degree of unemployment than is necessary and less effective provision for those who are unemployed.

The logical place for centralizing the man-power functions is in the Department of Labor. As soon as the concurrent demands for man power by both the armed forces and for war-production activities slacken off, such a reorganization should be undertaken.

In such a reorganization the key element is the maintenance of a national employment service. Other steps, such as consolidation in the Department of Labor of functions relating to training and labor relations, are also desirable, but the Employment Service is the key to successful man-power demobilization.

Wartime mobilization of man power required a national public employment service.[1] The 1,500 local offices of the United States Employment Service have had the responsibility for administering the man-power mobilization program of the War Manpower Commission. This includes programs for recruitment, placement, and transfer of workers; for the control of labor turnover. It also includes the collection, analysis, and dissemination of more adequate local labor-market information than has ever been available. Without a national employment service these vital activities could not have been performed.

While the war continues, serious man-power problems arising from national policies and nationally determined production requirements will continue to exist. Interstate and interregional transference of workers will continue to be important even though local pools of unemployment may exist. To relinquish unified administration of the National Employment Service while a war-production program of great magnitude is still to be completed would be a blunder. During the reconversion period, man-power problems will continue to stem largely from national decisions, and the repercussions of the decisions will not be

---

[1] International Labor Office, *The Organization of Employment in the Transition from War to Peace*, Montreal, 1944, pp. 116–123.

limited by state boundaries. The end of the war, therefore, will not reduce our dependence upon an employment service organized on a nation-wide basis, covering all sections of the country, and prepared to provide those services without which the reconversion of the nation's man power from war to peace cannot be facilitated in an orderly manner.

Specifically, a United States employment service designed to deal effectively with the man-power problems of the reconversion and postwar period must:

1. Maintain a national network of local employment offices at least as extensive as the present system.

2. Collect comprehensive labor-market reports and information on labor supply and demand, by occupation, for the use of these local offices in referring displaced workers and veterans to where they are needed.

3. Administer a nation-wide system of job clearance to advise local employment offices of job openings in other parts of the country so that the offices can indicate to workers in areas of labor supply the areas of job opportunity.

4. Assist in transferring workers during the emergency transition period to new jobs in other localities or to their former places of residence.

5. Provide an occupational and job-counseling program designed to aid new workers, returning veterans, handicapped workers, and displaced war workers.

6. Establish special placement programs, particularly designed to aid in the placement of handicapped workers and other groups in the labor market who require special assistance.

7. Administer a veterans' placement program as provided for in the Veterans' Readjustment Act of 1944.

8. Register and place workers as required under the 51 state unemployment compensation laws.

9. Participate in community employment planning.

As a result of the war experience, a much broader conception of the Employment Service's place in the community and national economic life has developed. Around it should be grouped all the other agencies dealing with questions of labor supply and training. It is essential, in view of the critical problems of the reconversion period, that the Employment Service be strengthened by salaries adequate to attract a highly trained personnel, selected on the basis of competence.

At the same time, it is important that the present close contact between employers, labor organizations, and the Employment Service on a local, regional, and national basis be continued. Their advice and assistance during the period of war has been invaluable. The support given by management and labor to the Employment Service has made possible the administration of man-power controls on a voluntary basis during the wartime period. The continuing participation and consultation with advisory management-labor groups will be even more necessary in dealing with the community labor-market problems during the reconversion period.

Chapter VII

Liquidating War Production

by A. D. H. KAPLAN

IN THE liquidation of our war production we may clear or clog the way to a satisfactory postwar economy. The policies and administrative practices governing the termination of war contracts and the disposition of the government's war stocks and industrial facilities will color the outlook for enterprisers, workers, and consumers. They will to that extent determine whether we move confidently toward expansion of our peacetime economy, to realize the greater potentials in production and consumption, or whether we retrench in a defensive attitude toward an unfavorable prospect.

The settlement of claims on canceled war contracts and the transaction of surplus disposals are only the mechanics of the liquidation. The economics of liquidation is concerned with major policy questions which are political as well as economic. It involves sensitive timing of cancellations and freeing of surpluses to dovetail with the resumption of civilian production; the tapering off of priorities, consumer rationing, and controls over prices and wages, as new civilian facilities and supplies become available. It questions the infiltration of government war plants into the structure of private enterprise, the strengthening or deemphasizing of wartime monopoly, and the desire in some quarters for a geographic redistribution of industry. It is concerned with resolving the conflicts of interest among manufacturers, distributors, and consumers, with respect to the channeling and expediting of surplus disposal.

Our production for global war has been on so large a scale that it has room for a wide range in estimates of the area of claims on canceled contracts and the magnitude of the surpluses that will emerge from the war. The size of the estimates one accepts will in turn influence one's point of view on how cautiously or how freely to wind up the war con-

LIQUIDATING WAR PRODUCTION 125

tracts and dispose of the surpluses. This chapter will, therefore, attempt first to translate the volume of war production into workable concepts of the magnitude of the contracts and surpluses to be liquidated. From those estimates as a base it will proceed to questions of economic policy and administrative machinery for the liquidation program.

I. Magnitude of the Liquidation

From July, 1940, to the end of the calendar year 1944, procurement under war contracts totaled roughly $200 billion. About five-sixths went into munitions; the other sixth represented construction and equipment, almost equally divided between military installations and industrial facilities. At the peak, passed early in 1944, war production was running close to $7 billion per month.

CONTRACTS TO BE LIQUIDATED

There are no available control data giving the total number of contracts and subcontracts currently in force, or the amount of unfinished contractual business outstanding at any one time. Indeed, such data, if available, would be of limited value for our purpose, because the production program is in constant flux, because listed contracts may be within several hours or several years of completion, and because advance payments by the government may be a negligible offset to claims in some cases and almost 100 per cent in others.

The question of what is a separate contract is debatable enough to permit estimates of the total number of prime contracts—those directly with the government—to have ranged from 100,000 to 250,000 at the peak of war production. Several agencies of the government cooperated in an effort to arrive at the total number of contracts in the fall of 1943. They found that the bulk of the war procurement was represented by approximately 105,000 contracts for $50,000 or more. These contracts were held by approximately 17,000 establishments, and their aggregate face value was slightly under $150 billion. The smaller prime contracts, adding at least another 100,000, accounted for an aggregate of around $4 billion, or less than 3 per cent of the total number of contracts in the books. As to the number of establishments which held the prime contracts, no reliable figure was obtainable. It was learned, however, that three out of four of the contracts in the $10,000 to $50,000 class were held by the firms which were also engaged on the larger contracts.

Back of the prime contracts are an indeterminate number of subcontracts. Studies of samples have indicated that there are, on the average, not less than 10 subcontracts per prime contract; and that they total in value between 35 and 40 per cent of the prime contracts. The conceivable grand total of 2 million subcontracts has involved—indirectly, if not directly—some 70,000 establishments engaged in the kind of manufacture that goes into war contracts.[1]

Small contracts and subcontracts tend to clear themselves more or less currently; many of them are in effect informal purchase orders which are invoiced in the ordinary course of business, supplied from regular stocks, and hardly recognizable as war contracts rather than as civilian contracts. Yet the network as a whole is so large and complex that, even if the great majority of contracts are clear of liquidation problems, there will still be thousands of firms left whose difficulties with cancellations and claims will require first-aid treatment. This observation is particularly applicable to the subcontractors who have not had the benefit of direct contact with the government procurement agencies and are dependent on the ability of their prime contractors to make prompt settlement. Both during and after the war many of them will have to be supplied with working capital with which to carry on while the prime contractors are settling their cases with the government.

The total of the unfinished contracts is many times the total of the claims which will emerge from cutbacks and terminations. Following the Armistice of 1918, less than $0.5 billion in final settlements on claims resulted from the total of $4 billion which represented the unfinished portion of the then terminated contracts. Early in 1944, when cutbacks and terminations already totaled nearly $16 billion of unfinished contracts, the claims were only 2 per cent of the face value, although the government was allowing about three-fourths of all claims up to that time.[2]

---

[1] The Census of Manufactures (1939) gives 184,230 establishments with manufactures of $5,000 or more per annum; 95,000 of these were in food, apparel, and the printing industries, of which only a very small fraction would have war contracts; 80 per cent of the remainder is the most liberal, informed estimate of the number of war contractors and subcontractors.

[2] In the report rendered in March, 1944, by the Army to the War Contract Subcommittee of the Senate Committee on Military Affairs (Print 2 of the Subcommittee Reports) the status of Army contract termination as of Dec. 31, 1943, was summarized as follows:

1. Number of contract terminations.................... 9,509
2. Canceled portion of contracts....................... $7,915,000,000
3. Number of claims pending as of Dec. 31, 1943........ 4,215
4. Number of claims pending over 6 months............ 570

LIQUIDATING WAR PRODUCTION

The claims experience on wartime cancellations, especially the early ones, is not to be taken as indicating what will develop by the end of the war. Early cancellations were covered so largely by substitute contracts in connection with changes of specifications and military tactics that many firms did not bother to present termination claims at all. Nevertheless, the chances are good that the ratio of claims to total cancellations will be lower in this war than it was in the last. War production was in an advanced stage by the end of 1943, with payments and contracts relatively current, whereas in the last war the Armistice hit us while inventory was being accumulated and production was gathering momentum for the expected big push in the spring of 1919. Notable also is the tighter government control of inventories in this war as compared with the last; war contractors' inventories remained stable at an aggregate of less than $10 billion for raw materials, goods in process, and finished goods, while production was rising to its peak.

The most practical basis for estimating the size of contractors' claims is in the contractors' war inventories. Obviously, we do not know how far production and inventories will have tapered off by the time the war is over. A conservative official estimate, based on the assumption that war in the Pacific will continue for a year after the European armistice, has placed production at the war's end at about 60 per cent of the peak war production of $7 billion a month at the beginning of 1944. Inventories of the war manufacturing industries began to decline in the spring of 1944.[1]

Let us take, however, for the sake of argument, the maximum position that prevailed early in 1944 when monthly war production was up to $7 billion. At that time the aggregate inventory in the hands of war contractors was estimated to be about $10 billion, including $2 billion in finished goods.[2]

Under the policies set by the Joint Contract Termination Board in February, 1944, and reemphasized by the Contract Settlement Act passed in July, 1944, invoices for finished goods are to be paid promptly

5. Value of claims presented..........................	$155,000,000
6. Value of claims pending as of Dec. 31, 1943..........	$112,000,000
7. Value of claims settled, Sept. 1 to Dec. 31, 1943.......	$43,000,000
8. Amount of settlements for claim value shown in (7)...	$32,000,000
9. Percentage of settlements to claims..................	0.74

[1] *Cf. Survey of Current Business,* October, 1944.
[2] Estimates of the National Economics Unit, Department of Commerce, released in November, 1943, for the third quarter of 1943, were: raw materials and goods in process, $8,090 million; finished goods, $1,194 million.

at contract prices, without awaiting negotiation of other claims. Goods in process are likewise to be treated as invoice items at cost plus a maximum of 6 per cent, where other terms were not specifically stated in the contract. Raw materials in general are invoiced at cost plus 2 per cent. There will also be certain permitted allowances to cover design, engineering costs, and other preparation charges; costs of removal and storage of machinery; excess depreciation and related loss factors resulting from the inability to finish the contract and forward commitments with subcontractors—in general those items of additional cost not covered in the predetermined contract or invoice prices. On a few early war-contract terminations nearly 100 per cent of the claim consisted of preparation charges which had not been translated into output at the time of termination. With the standardization of contract terms and the progressive nearing to completion, the percentage of loading for special costs progressively declines. It would, therefore, probably overstate the maximum figure for these additional charges to place them at 15 per cent of 1943 contract inventories, or $1.5 billion.

As offsets to the claims of the contractors the government has two types of credits. One will be the advance payments made by the government. The other offset is in that portion of the inventory which the contractors may be able to retain for civilian production. Retention may run as low as 20 per cent of the total inventory, owing to the specialized character of the war goods, which would render them unsuitable for civilian products.

The area of settlement requiring negotiation may be expected to represent only a small fraction of the inventory held by the contractors. The area of dispute requiring formal adjudication would be correspondingly less.

If we can assume that the Contract Settlement Act, calling for immediate payment of uncontested items, will be carried out in practice, there is no reason why the area of conflicting views in negotiation should exceed $0.5 billion. Thus, the magnitude of contract claims does not, of itself, appear as an insuperable problem in the liquidation of the war production. Rapid clearance of this phase of liquidation is feasible if the staffs of both the contracting agencies and the contractors are conversant with the procedures which have been laid down and are forehanded in predetermining the values of potential claims.[1]

---

[1] Before the Military Affairs Committee in the fall of 1943, Undersecretary Patterson testified that the average length of time for settlement of claims by the War Department up

LIQUIDATING WAR PRODUCTION

Settlements between the prime contractors and the government will not, of course, take care of the loose ends in the unfinished business between primes and subcontractors. It was an eye opener to the public when, in the summer of 1943, the cancellation of a single tank contract with the Baldwin Locomotive was found to involve more than 2,000 subcontracts. Steps have already been taken to draw subcontractors into the negotiations with prime contractors where feasible. The extension of the uniform termination article put out by the Joint Contract Termination Board and the provisions for various loans to subcontractors to take care of settlements and terminations are further efforts in the direction of reducing difficulties of subcontractors. Fortunately, most manufacturers engaged on war work are in a financial position to continue with reconversion without the need of outside capital. Few requests are coming to the banks for financial aid in connection with terminations and reconversions.[1]

SURPLUS SUPPLIES

The point need not be burdened that it takes clairvoyance along with statistics to estimate the postwar surpluses while the war is undecided. The rate of use of munitions is decided in the last analysis by the varying fortunes of war. The progress reports of the armed forces, even when available, have obvious deficiencies with regard to units on the front. The best one can do is to apply apparently reasonable multipliers to the procurement data to which access may be had, achieving a rough reconciliation of the information and views of the agencies closest to the situation.

In the inventory of government surpluses at the end of World War I, approximately 250,000 different items were listed. In October, 1944, a report by the Surplus War Property Administration contained the comment that in the area of aircraft and component parts alone, "Army and Navy catalogs list between 500,000 and 600,000 different classifica-

---

to that time was between 6 and 8 months. He pointed out that it took the contractors an average of 4.2 months to present their claims, and that the War Department averaged 3½ months in completing settlements after the claims were in. Presumably the training of some 20,000 contract officers and associate staff members in the business of claims settlement since that time, coupled with the manuals of procedure issued by the agencies to the contractors, will bear fruitful results in having claims ready for prompter action when the bulk of terminations comes up at the end of the war. (Hearings before Committee on Military Affairs, on H. R. 3022, Pt. 2, pp. 169–170.)

[1] See Livingston and Weiler, "Can Business Finance the Transition?" *Survey of Current Business*, February, 1944, pp. 9–11.

tions."[1] The inventory of World War II ranges from small household gadgets, snapped up so eagerly that the Office of Price Administration must keep a sharp eye on the prices offered and paid, to millions of tons of combat matériel and specialized munitions which are disposable only as scrap, at a small fraction of their original cost. A general idea of the major areas of supply may be had from the breakdown of the procurement (excluding construction and industrial facilities) over the 4-year period ending June 30, 1944, shown in Table 1.

TABLE 1.—WAR PROCUREMENT, JULY 1, 1940–JUNE 30, 1944

	Billions	
Supplies:		
Aircraft:		
Combat aircraft	$39	
Transports	2	
Ships:		
Combat vessels	23	
Merchant shipping	9	
Guns and ammunition	21	
Trucks	5	
Clothing and equipage	7	
Food	7	
Other munitions and supplies	21	
Total		$134
War construction:		
Military installations	17.5	
Industrial plant and facilities	15.5	
Total		$ 33
Total, actual and scheduled		$167

With the peak of production apparently behind us and the grosser discrepancies between estimated and actual military requirements ironed out by the war experience, the procurement is tending to level off at established reserve requirements. On items that do not require a long production period, stabilization of the general run of supplies to maintain a reserve of from 4 to 8 months of requirements has become increasingly feasible. This program of maintenance as contrasted with the earlier drive for accumulation has already justified a reduction of earlier estimates of postwar surpluses which had run as high as $100 billion. From the available information, a prospective remainder above $60 billion of original cost is not visualized. A lower figure is more

---

[1] Surplus War Property Administration Report to Director of War Mobilization, "Activities under Executive Order No. 9425," October, 1944.

likely. The over-all figure of $60 billion would include, besides current reserves, ships and other capital items which have long production schedules and do not lend themselves to programing on a current reserve basis; the net stocks that will accrue to the government from contractors' inventories; and those items that already proved superfluous during the war.

Only a fraction of the over-all stock of supplies is destined for the merchandise markets. One-half of the value of all the war supplies has been devoted to the two categories of airplanes and ships. A quarter of the supply is accounted for by specialized combat material, such as guns, tanks, ammunition, and other highly technical military equipment. The remaining $15 billion of original cost, representing the merchantable surplus, will be partly abroad and partly in this country. In the last war, our expeditionary forces had been in the field only a few months; our surplus abroad was then roughly 40 per cent of the total. This time, considering the advanced stage of the war and global character of our participation, the ratios will probably be reversed, with 60 per cent or more of our surpluses abroad. In other words, the surplus supplies applicable to our domestic market will be covered by a figure of the general magnitude of $6 billion of original cost.

A broad classification would distribute the domestic stock about as follows: motor vehicles, parts and accessories, and other transport equipment, 25 per cent; foodstuffs, 10 per cent; clothing, equipage, textiles, and other soft goods, 20 per cent; government stockpiles of critical and other controlled raw materials, 10 per cent; machinery tools, hardware, and engineering equipment (including cranes, tractors, and structural steel), chemicals, and a great variety of portable communication apparatus, 35 per cent.

In the conglomerate, a few striking cases can readily be found—some very substantial, like machine tools; others, like surgical dressings, buried in the larger total—in which stocks will represent one or more years of peacetime production. But the domestic surpluses taken as a whole can be equivalent to only a few months of normal consumption. In the prewar year of 1940 retail sales averaged $3.9 billion per month. For 1943 the average of monthly retail sales, despite rationing, exceeded $5 billion.

Aircraft and shipping have already been noted as dominant in the war inventory. In the case of the former, production attained a peak of more than 9,000 military planes per month. There is a chance of our being left with 100,000 military planes and at least 10,000 more transport planes. Yet a total of 2,500 transport planes would suffice for substantially increased commercial air transportation on a global scale. The military aircraft is generally impracticable for civilian purposes, and obsolescence for security purposes will set in almost immediately after the war. The problem, then, looms as one of disposition for educational and training purposes and for scrapping rather than for sale of any appreciable fraction of the total.

Although the shipbuilding capacity of the United States is five times the prewar total and our merchant marine likewise will be several times its prewar size, the problem of ship disposal is not immediate. Transport requirements for demobilization of our armed forces and shipments for relief and reconstruction are likely to keep our shipping busy in the months following the end of the war, and so provide a breathing spell in which international agreements for the distribution of our excess shipping may be worked out.

INDUSTRIAL FACILITIES

Although the investment in industrial plant and equipment has been less than 10 per cent of the whole procurement program, it nevertheless represents the more acute and more prolonged problem of surplus disposal. The government's investment, obviously, was made to supplement that of private enterprise in those lines of war production which did not hold sufficient promise of profitable postwar use to justify private investment. This aspect of the war construction will be revealed in Table 2, showing the distribution of the war industrial facilities financed with public and private funds.

One-third of the government's facilities is seen to be in the category of ordnance. The scattered and often flimsy structures employed for explosives, ammunition assembling, and loading have little postwar value. The equipment therein appears at this time to be too highly specialized for ready conversion, except in the shops turning out guns.

Another third of the $15 billion investment is divided between aircraft and shipbuilding facilities. Wartime expansion of these two fields has been spectacularly high. The structures are very large, representing, in general, capacity beyond practicable postwar limits. These two industries together will be fortunate to hold 10 per cent of their wartime volume. The aircraft equipment is regarded as versatile, much more so than that in the shipyards, but in both instances the large units may

Table 2.—War Industrial Facilities Financed with Public and Private Funds
(In thousands of dollars)

Type of product	Estimated cost		
	Public	Private	Total
Manufacturing and mining facilities:			
Ordnance:			
1. Explosives, ammunition assembling, and loading..........................	$2,848,346	$20,651	$2,868,997
2. Ammunition, shells, bombs, guns, and combat vehicles.....................	2,318,508	355,811	2,674,319
Total: 1 and 2...................	$5,166,854	$376,462	$5,543,316
3. Aircraft—engines, parts, accessories....	3,113,768	282,089	3,395,857
4. Ship construction and repair...........	2,128,465	172,932	2,301,397
5. Iron and steel and its products........	1,068,866	881,097	1,949,963
6. Nonferrous metals and their products, total...............................	1,167,568	362,797	1,530,365
7. Machinery, metal-working, electrical, and miscellaneous manufacturing....	864,102	803,216	1,667,318
8. Chemicals, including synthetic rubber, petroleum, and coal................	1,400,044	1,008,254	2,408,298
9. Mining of metal ores and minerals.....	147,424	176,177	323,601
Total: 1 through 9	$15,057,091	$4,063,024	$19,120,115
Industrial-service facilities:			
10. Gas, light, heat, and power...........	$472,767	$794,655	$1,267,422
11. Transportation......................	191,309	1,188,885	1,380,194
12. Communication.....................	3,975	131,320	135,295
Total: 10 through 12..............	$668,051	$2,114,860	$2,782,911
Grand total	$15,725,142	$6,177,884	$21,903,026

have to be dismantled and made available to different branches of the mechanical industries.

The remaining $5 billion is the investment that comes closest to meeting peacetime requirements. Half of it is in the primary metals. In the nonferrous metals, the war has given the government the command of the industry, with more than 90 per cent of total capacity. In iron and steel, the government is responsible for wartime increase of capacity around 20 per cent. For aluminum and magnesium, war urgency indicated some construction in isolated areas in locations where power is too costly for peacetime continuation. This additional capacity in primary metals will obviously have to be fed into the national economy at a rate comparable with increases in postwar demand which may take more than a decade to attain. The promising area of the chemicals, in which high-octane gasoline and synthetic rubber are most prominent, will likewise have to await postwar market expansion in order to find buyers at prices comparable with replacement cost.

In the miscellaneous category of machine equipment, motor vehicles, electrical equipment, and general manufacturing, the plants are small enough and varied enough to justify the expectation of an early disposal to new owners who can employ the facilities for early postwar production. Included in the last category is a large part of the structures and equipment coming under the head of scrambled facilities—government facilities added to existing private plants or so closely integrated with them that the present owners will probably acquire them under existing option clauses.

Aside from this last miscellaneous group, the bulk of the government plant consists of units too large for visible utilization in their present form. Units costing more than $10 million account for 70 per cent of total government facilities. At least 10 of the plants are in the $100 to $200 million class.

Taking the plant-facilities picture as a whole, it is questionable whether more than one-third can be disposed of in the near future except for stand-by equipment or by scrapping or by waiting a rather extended period before uses emerge for them. What could be readily utilized would, therefore, constitute a minor fraction of the prewar industrial plants.[1]

Because of the prevailingly specialized character of the plant equipment acquired by the government, the war investment has failed to take care of a number of factors of industry in which plant facilities will require replenishment after the war. Moreover, the deferred war construction in these lines should be considered against the background of additions to manufacturing facilities during the decade before the war. That the accumulation of capital during the 1930's was substantially below the average of the last three decades may be seen from the accompanying chart.

The availability of the government surplus in war plants and equipment will not preclude the acquisition of a considerable amount of additional plants in the postwar period. The acquisitions will be not

---

[1] The Bureau of Internal Revenue in the Census of 1939 gave the aggregate value of the private industrial plant in 1939 as $39 billion. The replacement cost of that prewar plant is estimated at 40 per cent above this official figure, or better than $55 billion.

LIQUIDATING WAR PRODUCTION

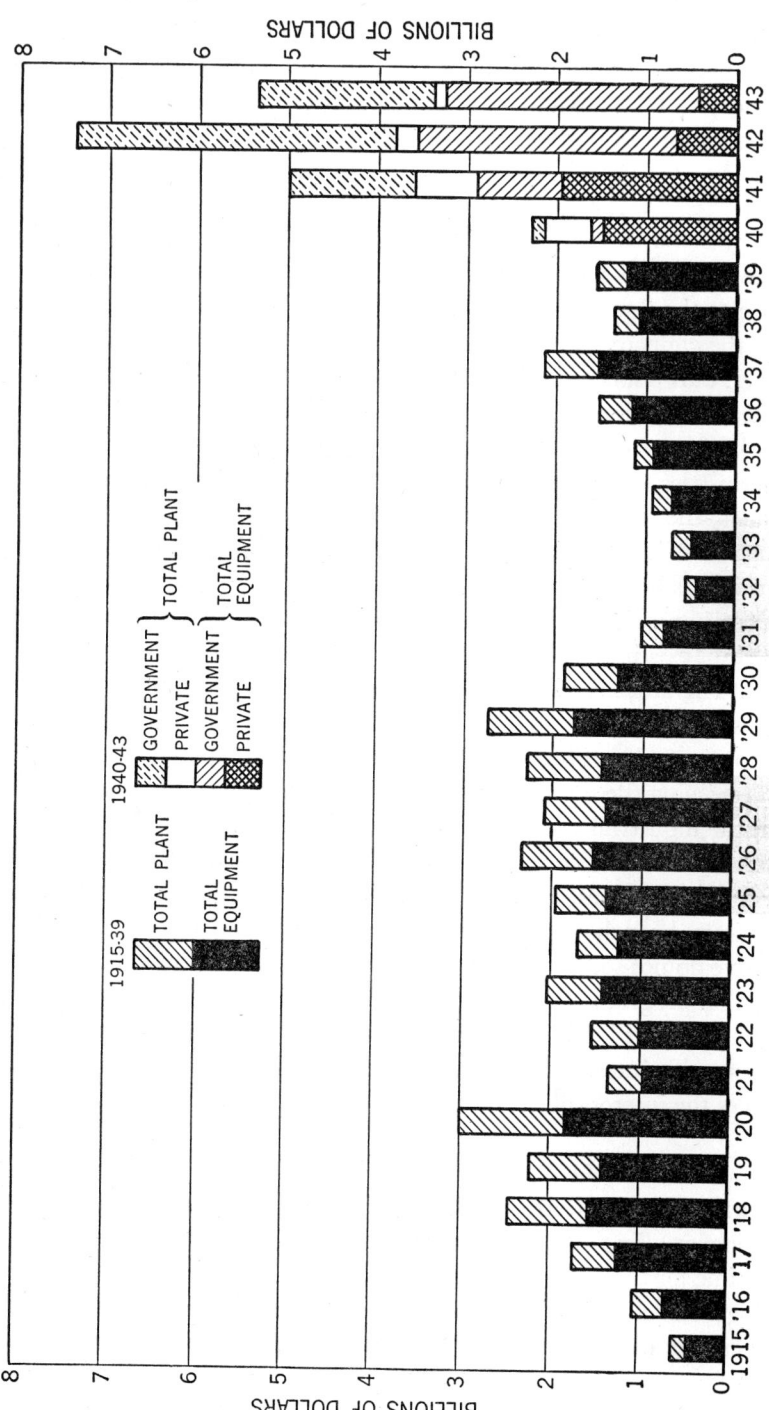

Estimated capital expenditures for plant and equipment for all manufacturing industries in the United States.

only in the soft lines and product development which were curtailed during the war, but also in more efficient and more highly specialized machinery to take advantage of opportunities for less costly, more efficient operations in postwar industry.

II. Policy and Administration

The discussion so far may suggest that the magnitudes actually entering into the liquidation of war contracts and war surpluses are easily within the capacity of our economy to absorb them. It does not follow, however, that a successful liquidation will be easy to administer.

The termination of prime contracts and subcontracts breaks into a network of sensitive relationships between competing and complementary industries, establishments, labor groups, and commodities. In specific lines, the ill-timed disposal of government surpluses can upset the production and sales programs of manufacturers and distributors. The government's holdings of plant facilities may change the prewar pattern of industry, particularly where government war plants now constitute the bulk of existing capacity, as in aircraft, aluminum, magnesium, and rubber. The administration can also influence the general distribution of industry within the country by the manner in which it encourages or discourages the utilization of its widely scattered plants.

In resolving these problems we must reckon with conflicts of interest within the industrial structure or between private industry and the government. We must also reckon with differences in emphasis among the government agencies, *e.g.*, between the War Production Board and the military branches and with those cases in which Congress and the Executive do not see eye to eye. It follows that the administration of the liquidation program requires oversight by a central agency to which the over-all policy of liquidation is entrusted: one which weighs the problems of specific interests and resolves them within an over-all policy that conserves the interest of the nation as a whole.

CANCELLATION POLICY

WARTIME CANCELLATION. A span between victory in Europe and total victory offers both advantages and complications. The interval allows time for the government to perfect the administrative machinery for a vigorous elimination of unneeded war contracts, cushioned by 50 to 60 per cent of wartime employment remaining in the production essential for the Pacific war. This period also provides a breathing spell for some industries which, while tapering off on war production, may move forward with the planning and organization of reconversion activities.

On the other hand, the military effort cannot be relaxed if the paramount objective of shortening the war is to be realized. In the furtherance of the military objective, many firms whose war contracts have been cut back or canceled will be estopped from resuming civilian output, because commodities essential to resumption will still be tied up in the pipe line of war production. Such inequalities are inevitable while the economy is doubly engaged, producing for both war and peace.

Granting that every other consideration must yield to the winning of the war, there remains a responsibility of which the military branches are not unaware, to gauge the war needs rationally, so that facilities which can safely be released for civilian production will be promptly released. It is especially desirable to make a moderate supply of strategic materials available for experimental purposes, for retooling, and for those preparations by which time will be gained for the resumption of employment when war contracts are over. There is also the area of useful small items, like razors, bobby pins, clocks, and electric irons, in which the quantity of raw material and labor is small compared with the value of restoring employment and supply.

During the war, the selection of contracts for cancellation will influence the competitive position of the war contractors. Those which have been cut back will want to resume civilian output. Those which are still on war work will want to start with the others. To serve both war requirements and home morale, the administrative agencies have tried to operate on the following principles:

That, in general, contractors who can readily reconvert to civilian production are to be released first, the balance of the contracts to be carried out by the government arsenals and the regular suppliers of military goods;

That contracts will be cut back earliest in the areas which have the tightest labor market, so as to free labor for other essential activities;

That essential contractors permitted to return to civilian production will hold a part of their establishments in readiness for a speedy return to war production, in case of emergency;

That as the war effort progresses and the more urgent military requirements have been met, increasing consideration be given to economic factors in the selection of firms for cutbacks; and

That the War Production Board and War Manpower Commission be consulted before decisions are made on cancellations which involve a choice of contractors.

POSTWAR CANCELLATION. During the war, the labor released through cutbacks of contracts has been absorbed into the areas of labor shortage for essential civilian needs. The pressure to prolong contracts has, therefore, not been as great as must be expected when cancellations rise to flood tide with the end of the war.

With the end of war, a vast pipe line of goods in process has to be cleared. Uncompleted parts in plant or shipyard must be removed; supplies are caught in transit. Goods in process will often be most economically liquidated by permitting their manufacture to be carried to completion. Demobilization of the armed forces and rehabilitation of occupied areas will add to the requirement of goods and services, engaging an estimated 5 million workers during the transition period.

To wind up the war, the nation must expect to supplement its wartime obligations and to keep a certain fraction of its labor force from the production of peacetime goods and services. But, beyond the constructive requirements of the war and the demobilization, the prolonging of war contracts to make work must be regarded as delaying conversion to a healthy peacetime economy.

During the immediate transition period, a certain amount of fluidity in the labor force is more essential to the restoration of peacetime prosperity than is an artificial maintenance of employment which does not contribute to sustained peacetime production. If artificial barriers are not to be placed on the prompt release of war contracts when they are no longer required, every effort must likewise be made to meet the impact of such cancellations. Notice should be given as far in advance as possible, so that the diversion of persons may be planned by the industry, so that opportunities for employment in other fields may be provided through the government employment services and through the release of materials by the War Production Board.

Measures for the amelioration of distress among the unemployed are necessary insurance against the slowing up of the liquidation. Adequate provision of unemployment benefits would make easier the necessary emigration of workers from congested areas and reduce the tendency to continue operations in war plants which have little or no economic value for the peace.

LIQUIDATING WAR PRODUCTION

CONTRACT SETTLEMENTS. There has been little dispute of the need for expeditious settlement of claims on terminated contracts to facilitate the reconversion. Under the Contract Settlement Act the determinations of the contracting agencies are final, except for fraud. Other features of contract-settlement policy reinforce the position that, while the speeding of settlements may involve some liberality in the treatment of claims, additional allowances are far less costly to the nation than are delays resulting in lost production and pay rolls. Along with the speeding of settlements go measures for advance payments and government-guaranteed credits, pending settlement of contracts, so that working capital for reconversion may be available.

SURPLUS-DISPOSAL POLICY

Obviously, the higher the general level of postwar business activity, the smaller the surplus will seem. Toward creating a climate of business confidence, with respect to the surplus, a first step is to eliminate uncertainty as to the size of the government's inventories. The substitution of fact for rumor in this field paves the way for definite policy with respect to the disposal of specific commodity groups. It would likewise clear the atmosphere of false emphases and undercurrent pressures if the Surplus Property Administration were to take the position from the start that disposal of the surplus is to be geared to the goal of an expanding economy rather than one of retrenchment and scarcity.

The cost of living rose 30 per cent during the year and a half following the Armistice of World War I. This time the potential war-deferred demand for war-curtailed products is incomparably greater. During the process of reconversion the release of some parts of the war surplus to relieve scarcities can be a factor in stabilizing the postwar market. This applies, in particular, to durable consumer goods. Such goods should be made speedily available to consumers on the widest possible scale.

If we repeat the mistake of November, 1918, of holding surpluses off the market when the consumer was in a buying mood and we allow prices to reach a level that meets buyer resistance, then we may likewise expect the jam of surplus stocks to be broken by a delayed flooding of the market with the surplus at exactly the wrong time as was done at the end of 1920. Even in the case of commodities which may prove relatively abundant, there is much to be said for eliminating the uncertainties of withheld stocks overhanging the market. If, for example, the supply of rayon hose purchased for the women in the armed forces proves unmarketable at prices near their original cost, there is good reason to make them readily available to low-income families, even as a 5-and-10-cent-store item, and clear the way for the nylon and other better grades coming into the postwar market. In many less obvious cases, the disposal of prewar brands to the lower income consumers will not seriously affect the desire of those who can afford newer and better models to acquire them. Indeed, such disposal may stimulate the emergence of newer models which will be attractive to those who already have the older ones.

The advantage of early disposal is applicable to producers' goods as well. It is clear, for example, that the production of machine tools in connection with the war was the equivalent of that of 15 prewar years. Nevertheless, the increased efficiency of specialized tools has already placed orders for them on the books, making available the older general-purpose tools for replacement of worn-out equipment and for disposal to countries which are in earlier stages of industrial development.

A general policy of disposal for the benefit of consumers is not inconsistent with the policy of timing disposal so as to prevent the dumping of goods into a receding market. Under bold policy in getting the wide distribution of goods, careful attention may be given, nonetheless, to the timing of disposals with changes in supply and demand and with the state of the business cycle. A product available in quantities beyond the absorbent capacity of the market may be offered in periodic sales, so spaced as to permit both the gauging of the market and the adjustment of minimum prices to the market behavior. In the final analysis, when a definite choice must be made between a prolonged market overhanging and a brief crisis, it is better to assume the latter. If business has to take a loss on surpluses, that loss should be taken in the earlier stages while there are still wartime profit reserves with which to meet it.

SURPLUS WAR PLANTS. Administering the disposal of the government war plant poses a problem for which we have no precedent in World War I, when private investment furnished the means of production and the government supported this investment chiefly through liberal prices paid for the product.[1] It is a problem, therefore, which calls for original solutions.

In the case of the war plant which is specialized for military purposes—as in the case of explosives and shell loading—the armed forces will naturally have first call on the facilities for stand-by purposes. This

---

[1] The total direct investment of the government in new plant construction in World War I did not exceed $600 million.

does not necessarily mean, however, that the Army and Navy must be loaded with a huge agglomeration of stand-by plant. The stand-by plant is hardly worth maintaining unless it undergoes continuous modernization, to keep up with the latest developments in military technology. Rather than acquire excessive plant, it may be more desirable to scrap what is not needed for experimental purposes and current upkeep of supplies, putting upkeep funds into experimental work and the maintenance of high efficiency in a fraction of the plant now available.

The fact that in particular instances facilities aggregating hundreds of millions of dollars can be most economically disposed of by scrapping does not make a case for indiscriminate scrapping of the war plant in general. In aircraft, for example, the war-built facilities have been increased about 4,000 per cent over prewar capacity. It may be a decade or more before peacetime demand in aircraft approaches a need for the existing capacity. Nonetheless, the time may come when the capacity now in aircraft will be highly useful. In any event, the machinery and general equipment are modern and versatile. A sound program, therefore, would avoid indiscriminate scrapping on the one hand or disposal at windfall prices of plant which may prove to be worth many times the disposal figure at a future date. The tools and other equipment of these plants may be redistributed for uses other than for aircraft. Where the size of the structure is such that no one firm could use it in peacetime production, consideration should be given to the division of it or joint operation by smaller firms which could gain mutual benefits from working in close proximity.

Outright sales have the obvious advantage of a definitive disposal. There is little question about the desirability of the outright sale where it can be concluded in accord with the terms of purchase options given the companies which built the plants for the government. Yet, to avoid sacrifice sales or to test the practicability of the plant for postwar operations, leasing may prove to be the only practicable means of putting the facilities into immediate useful operation. Leases may also be employed to keep in working order those plants which the armed forces could not afford to operate but would want to hold against future emergencies.

The terms of the leases, like the terms of sales, should be liberal enough to encourage the use of venture capital in new enterprise. At the same time there must be due regard for the position in which the transaction places a given plant within the industry as a whole; there is no net advantage in encouraging new production which merely destroys established companies.

The location of many plants within communities in new areas, where such production did not previously exist, raises the question of maintaining such industry after the war. The over-long subsidization of sub-marginal plants is suspect as tending to throw the affected industry out of balance and to discourage forward planning. Genuine community initiative to continue economically feasible production should be encouraged. The reality of such initiative can be exhibited best by the willingness of the community to make its own substantial investment of working capital and to share the risks of competitive operations.

The specter of monopoly has been brought into current discussion of war-plant disposal. Public policy will aim at wide distribution of facilities, on terms sufficiently liberal to give small business the opportunity to participate. Part of the urge to give small business greater prominence comes from the fear that large companies already enjoying dominant positions in an industry—aluminum is an oft-cited case—may strengthen their monopoly position by the acquisition of government plants, some of which they had already operated during the war. If it is the policy of the government to curtail monopoly or to encourage small business by withholding facilities from the largest operators, such a policy should be clearly enunciated lest confusion and uncertainty retard the given industry. Refusal of bids from the large operators should not be carried out indiscriminately to break up integrated facilities, that can be used for peacetime reemployment, merely because they are in the hands of large business.

Whereas the general policy with respect to surplus supplies should aim at a rapid clearance of stocks, the same haste is not called for in the disposal of or scrapping of war plants. The program there should be one of making the plants as widely useful as possible, but timing that use so that there may be a net addition to the national income. In the case of chemical plants and magnesium and similar facilities for which the pre-war demand did not exist, the encouragement of research which will cause demand to expand is a prerequisite to the final disposal of government plant and equipment for production that can be sustained.

LIQUIDATION AND DISPOSAL AGENCIES

ADMINISTRATIVE MACHINERY. Definite steps looking to the formulation of an over-all program for liquidating war production emerged from the executive departments with the issuance of the Baruch-Hancock report in January, 1944. Prior to that time, technical staffs had been quietly preparing memoranda and procurement agencies were acquiring some experience administering surplus disposals; but the official line in the Executive was that discussion of postwar economic plans must be sublimated lest it interfere with the all-out prosecution of the war. Congress, however, became sensitive to the complaints from contractors who were handicapped by delays in settlement in the removal and clearance of government war property and in isolated sales of surpluses which were allegedly inimical to their interests. Hearings held by various Congressional committees and reports issued by them undoubtedly stimulated the issuance of the Baruch-Hancock report on behalf of the Administration. Administrative proposals in the report were implemented early in 1944 by executive orders establishing (1) a Joint Contract Termination Board under John Hancock, coauthor of the Baruch-Hancock report; (2) a Surplus War Property Administration under W. L. Clayton, Assistant Secretary of Commerce and director in the various procurement programs of the Reconstruction Finance Corporation; and (3) a Retraining and Reemployment Administration under Brig. Gen. Frank T. Hines, the veteran administrator of veteran affairs. Legislative sanctions for these three programs and the establishment of an over-all organization for the reconversion were enacted by Congress in the Contract Settlement Act approved in July, 1944; the Surplus Property Act, of October, 1944; and the War Mobilization and Reconversion Act of 1944, also approved in October. The last supplanted the Office of War Mobilization under Justice Byrnes with an Office of War Mobilization and Reconversion. It confirmed the organization of the Retraining and Reemployment Administration; it also provided funds for liberalizing state unemployment insurance and encouraging the local planning of public works.

The Contract Settlement Act is, in the main, a confirmation of the organization set up under the executive order with a Director of Contract Settlement who is chairman of the Contract Settlement Advisory Board. The Board consists of representatives of all the procurement agencies and those which—like the War Production Board—have an immediate interest in the liquidation of war production. Under its administration a uniform contract-termination clause was made applicable to all prime contracts, to be supplemented by an extension of the uniform termination clauses to subcontractors whenever practicable.

By the end of 1944 some progress had been achieved toward predetermination of the amount of claims which would develop in connection with future cutbacks and cancellations. The Act provided for expeditious removal of government property and permitted contractors to remove such property at government expense when the government failed to do so within the time limits set for them. Other provisions of the Act included advance payments and loans to contractors and subcontractors, pending settlement; and machinery for appeals by contractors from the decisions by contracting agencies.

Substantial agreement was readily achieved on the Contract Settlement Act, in accord with the conduct of the Joint Contract Termination Board under the original executive order. The same may not be said of the Surplus War Property Administration. Here the pressures of various industries and of different sections of the country were powerful enough to modify the original administration in important respects. Instead of a Surplus War Property Administrator, empowered to act as a focal point who could make decisions with the advice of the Surplus War Property Board and Industry Advisory Councils, the administration of the surplus war property disposal was lodged in a Surplus War Property Board of three who were jointly to administer the program. It also provided for the indefinite freezing of stock piles of war minerals and prevented the disposal of government war plants costing $5 million or more until the proposals could be reviewed by the Congress. The Act embodied a number of compromises which allowed special terms for purchase of surplus property by local governments, public-welfare agencies, hospitals, and educational institutions. Consideration was also given to the intervention of the Smaller War Plants Corporation in the interest of small business, to facilitate the disposal of surplus property in small lots.

With the passage of the Surplus Property Act of October, 1944, Mr. Clayton resigned as Surplus War Property Administrator. The long-drawn-out negotiations in the conferences of Senate and House members who participated in reconciling the House and Senate versions of the Surplus Property bill called attention to the conflicts of interest between manufacturers and distributors, between producers and consumers, and between various sections of the country which will have to be reconciled before the Surplus War Property Disposal can be made to operate smoothly in the total public interest.

In this complex of competing interests, it is notoriously true that a single industry, concentrating on what looks like its own immediate advantage, may fail to see that it is thereby helping to forge the very instruments which may drag it down along with the whole economic structure. We should have learned from National Recovery Administration days that measures to restrict the flow of goods and services may often boomerang on the very interests which were most active in demanding the restrictions.

There is still a large program of economic education ahead to set our sights at postwar rather than prewar levels. Obviously, if we are going to look back to 1940 with its 9 million of unemployed as the top of the market and are planning in those terms, then the surplus is a major threat; but even in that event the efforts to prevent disposal are not likely to prevent heavy unemployment and depressed business conditions. If, on the other hand, we think and plan in terms of the latent purchasing power and expanding markets that are before us—of an economy adequate to support the productive output of 55 million employees and backed by $65 billion of accumulated war savings to catch up with deferred demand—then the surplus recedes to its proper place in the postwar perspective.

Chapter VIII

The Redistribution of the Labor Force

by CHARLES D. STEWART [1]

THE CESSATION of the war will have numerous, and obvious, *shock* effects upon the American economy. In terms of the redistribution of labor, the problems range from the much-discussed reabsorption into civilian life of 10 million of our military personnel, to the transfer of millions of civilian workers from the manufacture of munitions to the production of goods and services for civilian consumption. Without minimizing problems of this kind, it is the intention in this chapter to evaluate the possible *lasting* effects of certain of the important wartime developments upon the labor force and the structure of employment. These effects can only be anticipated at this time but will probably be greater and more varied than those of World War I or, perhaps, any other series of events in so short a period of time.

The shock effects constitute or will create the immediate problems of reconstruction involving large-scale changes in the industrial, geographic, and occupational distribution of labor. The magnitude and character of the problems are dependent upon a number of timing and economic factors which cannot be evaluated with any certainty—*e.g.*, the relative duration of the European and Asiatic phases of the war; industrial mobilization prior to and following victory in one phase of the war and military demobilization prior to complete cessation of hostilities; the degree to which the reduction of consumer incomes resulting from curtailment of war expenditures can be offset more or less simultaneously by increases in civilian expenditures. Eventually the economy

[1] The writer wishes to express appreciation for the assistance of Judith Grunfel, Leonard Eskin, Richard Lewis, and other members of the staff of the Bureau of Labor Statistics.

REDISTRIBUTION OF THE LABOR FORCE

must be transformed from one in which government war expenditures accounted for $85 billion of a gross national product of $195 billion to one in which such outlays will be relatively small. The details with respect to the shifts in the industrial composition of employment will depend at any time upon the total level of economic activity and the character of demand. To the extent that these changes are anticipated and measures designed to deal with them, their consequences may be moderated. In any event, however serious the shock effects may prove, they are obvious consequences of the transition from war and war production to peace.

The influence of World War II upon the number of people who will make up the working population—how they will work and where they will work—may be expected to be considerable for many years in the future. Following years of economic stagnation, the war made for striking increases in the number of people employed and their income, in marriage and birth rates, and in the occupational status and mobility of women, as well as a resurgence of vocational training and growth of occupational experience. Advances were made in ways of work and techniques of production under the pressure of demands for speed and with improvement in the nation's capital equipment. Large-scale migration occurred within the country in response to employment opportunities in expanding centers of production and economic activity. Not least important perhaps was the widespread realization of the meaning of this wartime experience for postwar economic objectives and policies.

SIZE OF THE LABOR FORCE

The total number of Americans employed in civilian jobs or in the armed forces increased from $45\frac{1}{2}$ million in the spring of 1940 to more than 62 million (excluding seasonal workers) in the autumn of 1944. This gain of $16\frac{1}{2}$ million in the actively employed labor force was made possible in part by the absorption of 7 million persons who were unemployed in 1940. But the most remarkable feature of wartime man-power mobilization was the addition of $9\frac{1}{2}$ million persons to the labor force as compared with an expected peacetime growth of only 3 million.

I

In much of the recent discussion of postwar problems there is an implicit, if not explicit, hope that a substantial part of the extra labor force of 6½ million will be self-liquidating. This attitude is understandable only within a framework of general pessimism about the prospects for high-level economic activity in this country after the war. Actually, large numbers of these workers will voluntarily withdraw when the special circumstances and motivations which brought them into the labor market no longer exist; others may reluctantly drop out under certain conditions. It would be surprising, however, if all the extra workers should disappear from the labor market. The fact that World War I apparently had no significant lasting effects in this connection is readily explicable because of its short duration for the United States and its relatively small impact, compared to this war, on either the number of civilian workers or the size of the armed forces.

The extent to which wartime developments will affect the size and character of the postwar labor force is dependent on a number of considerations, including the nature and level of job opportunities, social security policies, and the number of war casualties. But some indication of the relative permanence of the increases which have occurred can be obtained by an examination of the demographic characteristics of the 6½ million extra workers, who may be classified roughly into the following groups:

	Millions
Young persons under 25 from school and college	2½
Young women under 25 normally out of school but not working or seeking work	1
Women over 35	1½
Men over 25	1½
Total	6½

II

The 2½ million young persons (including 0.6 million girls) who would ordinarily be devoting full time to their schooling will cease to be extra workers when they reach the age at which they would normally have sought employment. The 1½ million of these youth who left school completely to take jobs or enter the armed forces will probably not return to school in large numbers except, perhaps, in the case of servicemen who did not quit school voluntarily. Yet, even if job opportunities prove to be plentiful, it is unlikely that there will be a reversal of the historic trend toward longer schooling except insofar as the trend might be affected by the possible adoption of compulsory peacetime military

REDISTRIBUTION OF THE LABOR FORCE 149

training. If such a program should be adopted, the total labor force of young men in their late teens and early twenties might exceed prewar levels by as much as 0.5 million, but the civilian labor force in this age group would undoubtedly be smaller than before the war.

III

In addition to the labor supplied by the half million girls and young women who would ordinarily be full-time students, other young women under 25, most of whom would normally be taking care of homes, have contributed about 1 million to the extra wartime labor supply. Although no net number of extra workers is shown from among young women twenty-five to thirty-four years of age, the effect of the war upon women workers in this age group has by no means been insignificant. The entire group of young women under thirty-five altered their normal work habits substantially. Many who would ordinarily have remained out of the labor force took jobs; many others who customarily would have quit upon marriage remained at work. This was especially true among service wives. On the other hand, marked wartime increases in marriage and birth rates tended to reduce labor-market participation,[1] as did increases in family income and other special factors, such as the dependency features of early Selective Service regulations which tended to induce wives to stay out of the labor force in order to protect their husbands from the draft. The rise in marriage and birth rates is particularly important in accounting for the absence of any net number of extra workers in the twenty-five to thirty-four years age group, because most women do not ordinarily continue to work outside the home after they are married and the great majority of those who do, do so only

[1] Marriage and birth rates per thousand of female population aged ten to fifty-four for selected recent years are as follows:

	Marriage rate	Birth rate
1929	30.1	56.0
1933	25.6	48.6
1939	30.5	50.3
1940	34.4	52.0
1941	36.7	54.9
1942	38.2	61.0
1943	34.1	63.5
1944 (forecast)	31.1	59.3

until they have children. In 1940, for example, the proportion of workers among single women in that age group was 79 per cent as compared with 33 per cent among married women with no young children and only 9 per cent for those with young children.

The rise in marriage and birth rates in 1940–1941 and their maintenance at relatively high levels throughout 3 years of war suggest that the increases resulted primarily from economic prosperity rather than from the psychological impact of the war itself. If prosperity is maintained after the war, the increased percentage of women married and with children would also be maintained for some time and exert a strong downward pull on the labor-market participation of young women. Moreover, it should be noted that one-half of the 3 million women with husbands in the armed forces were in the labor force as against one-fifth of the married women with husbands present. Many of the service wives as well as many of the young single women whose marriages have been delayed by the absence of millions of young men on duty with the armed forces will undoubtedly quit work after the men return to civilian life. Offsetting these two sets of factors pointing to reductions in the number of young women working or seeking work, perhaps below normal rates, will be the effect of casualties upon wives and those who remain unmarried because of the excess of women over men. These women will, to a large extent, replace the men who are taken from the labor force by wartime casualties. There is, in addition, the fact that a certain percentage of the young women who might not otherwise have entered the labor force will, because of their job experience during the war, constitute a permanent addition throughout the working life of the generation to which they belong.

IV

With respect to the 1½ million extra women workers thirty-five to sixty-five years of age, the same reasons which led to their entry may prove to be the reasons for large numbers remaining in the postwar labor force. As a group they were little affected by the rise in marriage and birth rates and are generally not responsible for the care of young children. Few of them were service wives forced to work because of the absence of their husbands. Whereas a substantial number of women over thirty-five may be expected to remain, postwar job prospects will influence their labor-market propensity to a large extent and in a manner quite different from that of younger married women. There will be less pressure upon them to return to the home, but they may in general be at a competitive disadvantage with younger women who may be forced to return to the labor market to supplement family incomes.

The 1½ million extra men over twenty-five years of age in the wartime labor force are approximately evenly divided between those aged twenty-five to fifty-four from the fringes of the labor market and men fifty-five and over who have either postponed retirement or reentered from retirement. Since very few able-bodied men twenty-five to fifty-four years of age are normally outside the labor force, the extra workers include men who before the war sought work only occasionally or intermittently and men on the border line of employability. The availability of steady jobs reduced significantly the number of occasional workers—*e.g.*, migratory, casual workers—who are outside the labor force at any one time. The physical or social handicaps of men in the border-line group, and their lack of seniority, will render them first to be dismissed. For all practical purposes they are unemployable during a period of large labor surplus. Recent experience has demonstrated that their services can be utilized, but special measures may be needed to prevent them from being squeezed out of the labor market or forming a "hard core" of unemployment. As to the older group of extra workers aged fifty-five and over, most of them will disappear soon after the close of the war unless unusual opportunities for their employment continue. The long-run trend has been toward earlier retirement, and this may be accelerated by extension of social-security legislation.

V

To summarize, wartime developments will probably have noticeable effects upon the size and composition of the American labor force during the next generation. Among men in the youngest and oldest age groups wartime additions to the labor force are likely to disappear very shortly because the youngsters will soon reach normal working age and the oldsters are already past normal retirement age. Surpluses over prewar levels among men and women in the middle age groups are likely to persist, however, unless job opportunities are so poor as to force these people out of the labor market. If opportunities are in fact unfavorable, many of the young women forced into the labor market by the war are likely to remain in order to supplement family incomes. Otherwise, the percentage of young women working or seeking work may actually fall below normal levels based on prewar trends. On balance, it would appear that the actual labor force in 1950 would exceed the estimated normal figure of 60 million for that year by approximately 1 or 2 million.

Changes in Industrial and Occupational Composition

Not only has the war resulted in a great expansion of the labor force; it has required and led to vast shifts of workers from one industry to another, from occupation to occupation, and a general upgrading of skills within industries. Altogether civilian employment expanded by more than 5 million while at the same time some 11½ million were added to the armed forces. The dominating influences were, of course, the unprecedented outlays for munitions, the resulting increases in income payments, and the restriction of activity in various segments of the economy in consequence of man-power, facilities, and materials limitations.

I

The industries which now comprise the munitions group employed 4.4 million workers in September, 1940, mostly on civilian production, as against a peak of 10.3 million workers in November, 1943, who were engaged almost exclusively in war production. Employment in Federal war agencies (exclusive of manufacturing arsenals and navy yards) increased from 100,000 to 1.6 million in the period 1940–1944. The only other broad industry group to show persistent gains in employment under the pressure of war needs was the transportation and public-utilities industries, which advanced from 3.1 to 3.8 million. Construction employment increased markedly during the early stages of mobilization and later declined to an abnormally low volume.

Contrary to common impressions, there was no substantial reduction in other major components of employment during 1940–1944 except for agriculture. In fact, all other nonagricultural employment remained unchanged in the aggregate at a level of about 28 million, with upward and downward deviations of approximately only 1 million over that period. Employment in trade and service establishments, for example, was virtually identical in point of numbers in September, 1940, and 1944. State, local, and nonwar Federal employment declined by only 100,000. The same general situation obtained with respect to the manufacturing industries not included in the munitions group; their total employment increased somewhat early in the war and has since receded to the level of September, 1940. There was apparently no marked decline in the self-employed except for domestic-service workers. In short, the expansion of the working population made unnecessary the curtailment of civilian employment to the degree widely anticipated in 1941–1942.

II

Except for man-power and other limitations, employment in all fields excluding perhaps agriculture would have expanded under the prevailing level of income payments induced by the war.[1] This situation underscores the importance of the level of economic activity that may prevail during and after the transition to peace, with respect to both the shock effects of transition and the long-run changes in the industrial allocation of employment. The fact that employment was not reduced, except in agriculture, means for one thing that there are no segments of the economy which will automatically absorb large numbers of released war workers and fighting men, unless the rate of income payments can be well sustained during reconversion.

The uncertainty with respect to interindustry shifts in employment —with all the resulting occupational, locational, and other ramifications— is illustrated by the wide range of possibilities as to the level and pattern of economic activity. Although it does not appear possible, for example, even with total employment at the unprecedented figure of 55 million after the war, that manufacturing would continue to employ 16 or 17 million, the number would decline to approximately 10 million if total employment fell to 1939 levels. Employment in the metal-producing or -using manufacturing industries as a whole will necessarily fall off with the elimination of upward to 3 million workers in aircraft and shipbuilding alone. The heavy industries other than aircraft and shipbuilding may conceivably maintain their wartime employment (on a 40-hour week) if capital-goods expenditures are high relative to total expenditures. A common presupposition, however, is that prosperity based upon an economic structure heavily weighted in this way is not likely to be sustained for long. But, even under conditions of full employ-

[1] The decline of approximately 1½ million in the level of agricultural employment exceeded the rate indicated by the downward prewar trend. But it is doubtful whether under optimum conditions of labor utilization the prewar volume of employment, or any more than the current volume, would be required in agriculture.

ment, it would appear probable that the numbers of wage earners in the iron and steel industry, for example, will decline from a peak of 1.1 million, which represented a 30 per cent increase from 1940, particularly if account is taken of probable changes in productivity. Only with full employment is there any great possibility for employment in transportation and public utilities, which increased over 20 per cent since 1940, to be held at wartime volumes.

If total civilian employment after reconversion should approximate the prewar maximum of 50 or 51 million prevailing immediately before Pearl Harbor, very few industries, except construction, would experience any substantial net increases in employment. Employment in manufacturing would probably decline to about 12 or 13 million. Where increases over wartime volumes would occur—presumably in trade and services—the changes would generally represent shifts to lower income industries. It would also mean the loss of wartime gains in skills and experience on the part of millions of workers, employed and unemployed; underutilization of the vast capital equipment built up in the past four years; reduced demand for many so-called "luxury" goods and services which can add so much qualitatively to the standard of living.

III

Whatever the aggregate volume of demand after the war, the allocation of workers as between industries is expected, as in the past, to be considerably influenced by changes in industrial techniques and improvements in capital equipment. Is it true, as generally supposed, that the war has accelerated the upward trend of productivity which has characterized manufacturing during the past two decades? The effect of the war upon long-term trends in output per man-hour has been so obscured by numerous conflicting forces of a temporary nature that it is impossible to draw more than general conclusions of a qualitative character. Spectacular gains in productivity have occurred in aircraft, shipbuilding, and munitions products largely as a result of the shift from small-scale custom production to large-scale mass production. Otherwise there are indications that productivity in the war industries has increased only moderately. For the industries which have continued producing civilian goods, there is evidence that the trend has been almost completely halted since 1941 in some industries and has declined in others to 1939–1941 levels.

These negative conclusions are supported by what we know of the factors affecting productivity of labor during the war years. New and more efficient plant facilities in the munitions industries, the reorganization of many old plants for greater efficiency, and the increased efforts of workers and management to meet schedules tended to make for gains in output per man-hour. These factors were offset by military inductions from the potentially most efficient age groups in the working force; replacements and additional personnel from less experienced and efficient workers; increased turnover and an abnormal proportion of newly hired workers in the plant at any time; labor hoarding attributable to man-power shortages and the absence of incentives to reduce labor costs; the effect of lengthened hours of work, extra shifts, etc. The net effect of these factors cannot be evaluated on the basis of available data, but it is not unreasonable to conclude that output per man-hour has not increased more rapidly than normally in the industries producing munitions. A premium was necessarily placed upon speed rather than on efficiency. The reversals in productivity trends in the industries producing civilian goods can be explained in part by similar considerations and in addition by the loss of workers to war industries, by deterioration of equipment, by their relative disadvantage in obtaining materials, transportation, and other business services.

The fact remains that a decade or more of experience and innovation has been crowded into a few years in the war industries. After the abnormal circumstances of war production disappear, productivity in the industries which now make munitions should be advanced by years, despite the fact that many of the apparent gains in productivity will be lost because they occurred in connection with products which will become relatively unimportant. It is impossible to predict the ultimate effects of wartime innovations, but the reduction in labor input per unit of product following reconversion will exert a positive influence upon the industrial and occupational demands for labor. The effects will naturally prove most significant in the metal-fabricating manufacturing industries, and in transportation and mining. This probable development, considered in conjunction with the proportionally greater demand for services as against manufactures, if national income is maintained substantially above prewar levels, suggests underlying tendencies with respect to the industrial and occupational redistribution of labor.

IV

Because the enrichment of the occupational skills and experience of the American working force came about in response to the special demands of a war-centered economy, a lack of balance from an occupational point of view will inevitably arise between labor supply and postwar job requirements. The particular demands of war production required larger proportions of workers as operatives, craftsmen, and foremen in the mechanical trades than will be usable in a civilian economy. In addition, military needs of the Army and Navy resulted in the training of large numbers of men in skills for which no demand, or relatively small demand, exists in civilian life. This is part of the problem of retraining and occupational readjustment. The war demonstrated, however, the occupational mobility of workers and the speed with which workers can be trained and retrained under conditions of effective demand. That particular skills may prove unwanted in a peacetime economy is relatively unimportant, even to the individual concerned, provided training facilities and alternative job opportunities are available. More significant from a long-time point of view has been the growing role of women in mechanical work which may alter social mores with respect to fields of activity for women workers. Less certain is the permanence of some of the occupational gains of Negroes.

In absolute as well as in relative numbers, the largest changes, occupationally, occurred among operatives, with an influx of 2.5 million women and about 1 million men. For the first time, women employed as operatives constituted the largest occupational group of women. Although now only the second largest group, the number of women in clerical jobs increased not much less rapidly than the number in operative jobs, and women more and more dominated the clerical field—almost doubling in number in the 4-year period while the number of men remained unchanged. Likewise in sales occupations, the number of women almost doubled, with the result for the first time that more women are so engaged than men. Percentagewise, the increase in women craftsmen and foremen was the largest gain shown in any of the occupational groups, but the total number involved was relatively small. In this connection it may be noted that among men a larger gain occurred in the number of craftsmen and foremen than in the number of operatives, as might naturally be expected as a result of upgrading of personnel in a period of rapid expansion accompanied by

REDISTRIBUTION OF THE LABOR FORCE 157

some measure of occupational deferment. The remarkable increase of males in upper job classifications points to effective mobilization of skills not previously utilized as well as to the success of training programs and upgrading. It also underscores the problem of equitable occupational readjustment as veterans are demobilized.

Unlike all other broad occupational groups, except domestic service, the professional occupations declined in numbers in the civilian population during the war. Whereas vast numbers of women, youths, and older workers more than replaced drafted men in most occupational groups, the withdrawals of professional men to the armed forces were not compensated for by sufficient numbers of women. This is explained in part by the length of training required in the professions and in part by the withdrawal of women teachers from elementary and secondary schools for higher paying jobs. Some 40 per cent of the women who left professional fields, for example, took jobs in manufacturing. This shift may be reversed during reconversion, but it appears evident that in professional occupations returning veterans will not be confronted with a war-expanded civilian labor force. The relatively high percentage of college graduates and professional men in the military services and the educational opportunities provided by the G.I. Bill of Rights point to a considerable increase in the supply of potential entrants to the professions after the war. Informed sources report a strong tendency, on the part of military personnel, to favor scientific and technical fields, whose numbers have expanded considerably during the war, at the expense of the liberal arts and nonengineering occupations which were not given preferential treatment under wartime educational policy.

V

Occupationally, Negroes experienced gains during the war comparable to those made by the population generally. Employment of Negroes increased somewhat more than average, with changes in the various occupational groups paralleling those shown for white workers with some exceptions. For example, the employment of white women in agriculture increased while, because of migration from the farms, the number of Negro women declined; the employment of white women in domestic service declined substantially while the number of Negro women remained about the same. With respect to service occupations, however, a smaller percentage of the total of employed Negro women was engaged in domestic service and a larger percentage in other services than in 1940. For both men and women, the most significant factor in the occupational redistribution of Negro workers was the exodus from the farm to the factory, where the war gave the Negro his first big chance in skilled and semiskilled jobs. The Negro made substantial gains in employment in various crafts and in sales and clerical occupations, but the numbers involved are still comparatively small. In a recent study, Seymour Wolfbein points out that the greatest gains in the employment of Negroes were in occupations and industries which will experience extensive cutbacks, and in congested production areas with heavy in-migration whose labor forces will experience considerable readjustment in the postwar period.[1]

Geographic Changes in Population and Employment

The expansion of nonagricultural employment, particularly in the metal-fabricating manufacturing industries and in centers of military activity, resulted in extensive internal migration of workers. This differential impact, geographically, of wartime man-power requirements created serious housing, transportation, and other community problems. With reference to the implications for postwar adjustment, it is important to note the factors which influenced the disproportionate increases in employment in the various states.[2]

I

The prewar industrial composition of areas and states was necessarily a leading factor in determining wartime growth. A large proportion of war contracts were awarded to metal-working companies which were in a position to convert and expand operations to meet demands for munitions. Military and man-power considerations resulted in the location of new plants in inland states or in labor markets where underutilized pools of labor were believed to exist. Among the other locational factors effective during the war was the increased demand for basic metals and metal components in areas where the production of military end products was expanding. Natural and physical characteristics of an

---

[1] See "War and Post-war Trends in the Negro Labor Force," *Monthly Labor Review*, January, 1945.
[2] *Cf.* Dr. McLaughlin's discussion in Ch. IX.

area determined in part at least the location of military facilities. California is an excellent example where all these factors were operative except that of inland security from potential attack. Contrariwise, North Carolina provides an interesting case of a state which before the war had been increasing its relative share of manufacturing employment but suffered a relative decline during the war both in total nonagricultural and in manufacturing employment because of the concentration of its output in industries which have not expanded during the war.

The changes in manufacturing employment in the various states varied more widely, of course, than nonagricultural employment in general. Variations in manufacturing employment from July, 1940, to July, 1944, ranged from small increases in South Dakota, Wyoming, and New Hampshire to increases of over 100 per cent in California, Oregon, Washington, Texas, Kansas, Oklahoma, Arizona, and Nevada. The rapid growth in employment in the various states frequently reflected even greater increases in certain metropolitan areas. Although important to the states involved, the changes that did occur affected the national distribution of factory employment only moderately. The most heavily industrialized regions—the Middle Atlantic and East North Central states—retained their predominance as centers of manufacturing employment. Of the nine census geographic divisions, only the Pacific Coast states experienced a change of more than 2 percentage points between July, 1940, and July, 1944, in their share of the nation's total of factory jobs. This simply reflects the fact that existing facilities were necessarily utilized to the greatest extent possible in meeting the demands of war production.

In many of the states with the largest relative increases in nonagricultural employment, nonmanufacturing activities accounted for a substantial proportion of the increase. Texas, for example, with the fifth largest gain in employment, derived only 50 per cent of the increase from expansion in manufacturing. Where manufacturing was not responsible for the bulk of the increase, a growth in Federal employment was usually a major factor, especially in those states with relatively small prewar nonagricultural employment. In Florida, for example, Federal employment increased sevenfold.

II

The prewar rate of growth of a state's industrial employment as shown by changes in its share of the national total is one of the important considerations bearing upon the prospects for maintaining its wartime growth. In many states the war-stimulated gains reflected acceleration of underlying locational shifts evident before the war. It is obvious, however, that if a state has been greatly affected by expansion of munitions production, its postwar expectations are dampened by an inevitable curtailment in the scale of operations in many industries. Unconvertibility of some of the new facilities to civilian-type products and the proportion of government-owned facilities are related factors that may exert considerable influence. Prewar trends are important in evaluating postwar prospects insofar as they reflect long-run factors determining industrial location. If industries were located in an area for extraeconomic reasons or could not be supported in the kind of industrial structure which might exist in the region following reconversion, there would appear to be small probability for a war center to survive the postwar competition of other areas.

III

On the supply side, changes in the geographical concentration of employment were made possible by new entries into the labor force and by extensive geographic migration. To the extent that industrial shifts simply accentuated prewar trends, migration also represented a continuation or exaggeration of long-run population movements. Between 1935 and 1940, for example, 6½ million persons—or 1 in every 20 of the population—moved across state lines, and 9 million additional moved across county lines within states. In the 3½ years between April, 1940, and November, 1943, the gross volume of migration probably approximated the figure for the previous 5-year period, with the difference that the movements were over longer distances and more in one direction. Between 1935 and 1940, for example, the net effect of population movements was an increment of only 1.4 million in the population of 20 states which gained through internal migration; the corresponding figure for 18 states in 1940–1943 was 3.4 million.

The two most striking population movements were those from farms to cities and from the interior of the country toward the sea coasts—particularly the Pacific Coast—and the Great Lakes. With but few exceptions these movements represent an acceleration of prewar tendencies. For this reason it would appear unlikely that any marked reversal in movement would take place after the war. Economic opportunities comparable to those induced by the war are not likely to arise in other parts of the country to cause large-scale back migration. Considering the relatively low levels of economic activity generally before the war, many of the expanded war centers can employ larger working forces in a wide range of activities than previously, provided the economy generally is at a higher level of operations. This, of course, glosses over the difficulties to be faced in greatly overexpanded local areas where there is no possibility for supporting the currently inflated labor force. But neither does it take into account the lasting effects of locational shifts in those states or areas where wartime developments may have established entirely new industries which can be utilized for peacetime production and continue as a source of employment after reconversion.

Summary

The lasting effect of wartime experience upon the size of the American labor force may not prove so striking a phenomenon as was the demonstration of the flexibility of the labor force under emergency conditions. By 1950 the number of workers in the labor force may not exceed the estimated normal figure for that year by more than 1 or 2 million. Probably more significant will be the effect of changes in labor-market participation among women in particular age groups upon family and social life after the war. The technical innovations stimulated by the war will inevitably have a considerable influence upon the economy, with effects upon labor utilization, costs and demand, the geographic distribution of employment, and upon occupational requirements, which we cannot now fully evaluate. Whether population movements of the war period will prove lasting will depend upon the degree to which wartime changes were in line, or out of line, with underlying and long-term tendencies affecting geographic location of industry. In quantitative terms, the actual redistribution of the labor force will depend upon the level of total economic activity, the pattern of expenditures and production, and whether the economy is stabilized at high levels or subject to large variations in level. In the reconversion period, the shock effects of the cessation of hostilities upon the labor force will be determined by the character of economic adjustments involved in the whole process of industrial and military demobilization. The significance for the future of the great gains made in occupational training and experience can be interpreted only in terms of the volume and the nature of the prospective demand for labor. Not all the skills acquired during the war in industry and in the armed services can be utilized in the postwar economy; but the gains can be largely dissipated within a decade if large-scale unemployment is not eliminated as a characteristic feature of the American economy.

Chapter IX

Regional Problems of Industrialization

by GLENN McLAUGHLIN

THE PRESENT war has brought forth the greatest expansion both in industrial output and in plant capacity ever achieved during a similar period in the history of the country. Without a reduction in the total volume of civilian goods—but with significant alterations in its composition—there has been a tremendous rise in finished munitions from $1.8 billion in the second half of 1940 to about $64 billion in 1944. During this period, the expenditures on plant and equipment have equaled the total investments of the 1920's. This great expansion of the economy is bound to have a significant effect on industrial readjustments after the war and on the future regional distribution of industry.

OVER-ALL WAR-INDUSTRY EXPANSION

The volume of finished manufactured goods is estimated to have increased from about $38 billion in 1939 to roughly $110 billion in 1944. Even after price adjustments, the expansion associated with war production has been unprecedented. For war manufacturing facilities, the cost of projects approved from mid-1940 through June, 1944, has amounted to roughly $20 billion. In addition, there has been an investment of several billion dollars in transportation, utilities, and other industrial services. Although at the end of 1944 the increased needs for certain items were still leading to projects for new facilities at a rate of about $100 million per month, the war facility program was apparently near completion.

The $20 billion in new war plant and equipment, including extensions to old plants, represents an increase of roughly one-third in the gross value of manufacturing facilities, which in terms of 1943 dollars

TABLE 1.—ESTIMATED VALUE OF MANUFACTURING FACILITIES, WAR AND NONWAR, AS OF MID-1944
(In billions of dollars)

Industry	Civilian manufacturing plant		War-plant expansions, ‡ July, 1940–June, 1944	Total plant on munitions production	Plant kept on nonmunitions production
	Replacement value, 1944 *	Value converted to munitions productions †			
Total............................	$60.0	$29.0	$20.0	$49.0	$31.0
Food and kindred...............	8.1	0.0	§	0.0	8.1
Tobacco........................	0.4	0.0	0.0	0.0	0.4
Textiles........................	4.4	2.0	§	2.0	2.4
Apparel........................	0.5	0.2	0.0	0.2	0.3
Leather and products...........	0.5	0.1	0.0	0.1	0.4
Rubber products................	0.9	0.7	§	0.7	0.2
Lumber and timber..............	2.3	1.2	0.0	1.2	1.1
Furniture......................	1.0	0.4	0.0	0.4	0.6
Paper and allied................	2.9	0.9	0.0	0.9	2.0
Printing and publishing.........	2.1	0.2	0.0	0.2	1.9
Stone, clay, and glass...........	2.8	0.4	0.0	0.4	2.4
Chemicals and allied............	4.0	2.8	4.3 ‖	7.1	1.2
Petroleum and coal products.....	10.5	4.6	1.1	5.7	5.9
Iron and steel and products......	8.8	6.6	3.6	10.2	2.2
Nonferrous metals and products..	1.4	1.1	2.1	3.2	0.3
Electric machinery and equipment	1.1	0.9	0.5	1.4	0.2
Other machinery................	3.3	2.6	1.0	3.6	0.7
Automobiles and equipment.....	2.6	2.4	0.7	3.1	0.2
Transportation equipment except automobiles..................	1.0	1.0	5.8	6.8	0.0
Other manufacturing............	1.4	0.9	0.9 §	1.8	0.5

* Replacement value estimated for manufacturing plant and equipment in place as of mid-1941, expressed in 1944 prices. Total apportioned among industries on basis of gross capital assets, as reported in *Statistics of Income*, 1939.

† Based on Department of Commerce estimates of percentage of industrial production devoted to war output.

‡ Based on data of the War Production Board, with estimated reclassification into census industry groups.

§ Other manufacturing includes some nonmunitions industries for which no amount is shown.

‖ Includes shell loading.

was probably in the neighborhood of $60 billion just before our entrance into the war (Table 1). This great expansion in new capacities to turn out munitions, however, appears to have been overshadowed by the prewar factories converted to war use. With the value of this converted capacity estimated at $29 billion, the value of all plants on war production at mid-1944 is set at $49 billion.

In the four years, mid-1940 to mid-1944, capital expenditures for manufacturing establishments were three or more times the usual rate in good business years. This expansion, however, was not evenly distributed. More than nine-tenths of all plant investment during the war has been in the metal and chemical groups of industries, which normally account for only about half the capital requirements of manufacturing. In these groups, therefore, the rate of investment has been roughly five times normal. Specifically, during these four years, metals and chemicals absorbed about $19 billion of new capital, whereas in an equal prewar period of good business they would have absorbed roughly $4 billion.

As Table 1 indicates, there has been a manyfold increase of the prewar plant in nonautomotive transportation, a doubling or more of capacity in nonferrous metals and chemicals. (This is of course without regard to the degree of peacetime use of the new, and often specialized, war plants.) On the other hand, there have been insignificant expansions in the civilian type of industries, although for many plants in these industries, maintenance needs have been liberally provided for.

The great bulk of wartime manufacturing facility investment has been financed by public funds, amounting to $16 billion out of the $20 billion. The flow of private funds—about $4 billion—into metal and chemical capacities has been about what would be expected in good business years. Thus, the entire excess of wartime demand for new capital has fallen on the government, a consequence of the size and special nature of the war needs for production capacity.

Private funds have gone mainly into basic metals, chemicals, and machinery (Table 2). In fact, in the machinery groups, petroleum products, and miscellaneous products, half the new capacities are privately financed.

The degree to which the war program has been concentrated in a few munitions products is clearly reflected in contract awards as well as in new plant investments. Of the total supply contracts of about $175 billion let through September, 1944, roughly half were for aircraft and ships—$58 and $27 billion, respectively. Guns, ammunition, explosives, and combat vehicles together account for another one-fourth of the total. In terms of new facilities, the importance of these industries is altered somewhat, although aircraft dominates (Table 2).

TABLE 2.—ESTIMATED COST OF WAR-MANUFACTURING FACILITIES, BY TYPE OF PRODUCT, APPROVED JULY, 1940–JUNE, 1944
(In billions of dollars)

Product	Total	Publicly financed	Privately financed	Percentage privately financed
Total............................	$20.0	$15.8	$4.2	21
Aircraft, engines and parts........	3.7	3.4	0.3	8
Explosives and shell loading.......	2.5	2.5	0.01	0.4
Shipbuilding and repair...........	2.4	2.2	0.2	7
Iron and steel....................	2.0	1.3	0.7	35
Chemicals........................	1.8	1.3	0.5	26
Nonferrous metals................	1.4	1.1	0.3	19
Ammunition, shells, bombs.......	1.3	1.1	0.2	14
Guns.............................	1.0	0.9	0.1	12
Machinery and electrical equipment........................	0.9	0.5	0.4	49
Petroleum and coal...............	1.1	0.5	0.6	56
Combat and motorized vehicles...	0.7	0.6	0.1	20
Metal-working machinery.........	0.3	0.2	0.1	51
Other products...................	0.9	0.2	0.7	73

GEOGRAPHIC DISTRIBUTION OF WAR PRODUCTION

Of the $168 billion in prime contracts awarded through September, 1944, and assignable by plant locations, nearly 60 per cent have been placed in the two leading manufacturing regions—the five Great Lakes states and the three Middle Atlantic states (Table 3). Next in importance are the West Coast states and New England. The remaining five regions account for only 17 per cent of the national total. This distribution applies only to direct government orders for finished munitions. It ignores subcontracts for materials, supplies, and parts. Nor does it take into account the continuing volume of civilian production which of course is concentrated mainly in the older producing areas.

In the main, there is a rough correspondence between the patterns of munitions production and the 1939 net output of civilian manufactures. A major change, however, has occurred in the importance of the Pacific region, which has obtained 13 per cent of prime munitions contracts or just double the region's share of 1939 net output. The only other region to improve its position materially was the West South Central, notably Texas. On the other hand, the Mountain region, the Southeastern

TABLE 3.—REGIONAL DISTRIBUTION OF PREWAR MANUFACTURING ACTIVITY, WAR PLANTS, AND WAR-SUPPLY CONTRACTS
(In per cent)

	Value added by manufacturing, 1939	War-supply contracts through August, 1944	Plant expenditures, 1939	War-plant expenditures approved July, 1940–June, 1944	Per cent of war plant privately financed
United States	100.0	100.0	100.0	100.0*	21
East North Central	31.5	33.9	32.9	30.0	22
Middle Atlantic	29.8	24.4	24.5	18.4	26
New England	9.8	9.2	8.4	4.7	29
South Atlantic	9.1	5.9	11.6	6.7	25
Pacific	6.5	13.3	6.8	8.9	26
West North Central	5.5	5.6	4.5	7.1	11
East South Central	3.4	2.1	4.0	6.0	19
West South Central	3.3	5.1	6.0	10.9	18
Mountain	1.1	0.5	1.3	3.8	12

* Includes 3.5 per cent undistributed.

states, and the Northern Plains states dropped far behind. The loss in importance of the Atlantic coastal regions is somewhat illusory, because the primary munitions effort of many manufacturing centers in these regions has been on subcontracts.

War manufacturing facilities have also been concentrated in the Great Lakes and Middle Atlantic regions. The former is far in the lead with nearly one-third of the $20 billion. In terms of new capacities, the West South Central region outranks the Pacific Coast. These four regions leave only about 30 per cent of the new plants for the other five regions. Among states, the heaviest investments have been in Pennsylvania, Ohio, Illinois, Michigan, New York, California, and Texas—each with over $1 billion, and together accounting for half of all war-plant expansions.

Although there has been general agreement between the geographic division of investments in war plant and equipment and the prewar distribution of manufacturing activity, there are some significant variations. Perhaps most notable is the trend away from the Eastern seaboard. The three regions there have obtained only 30 per cent of war-plant expenditures in comparison with 45 per cent of private funds going into manufacturing plants in 1939 and nearly 50 per cent of the net output in that year. With the exception of the Great Lakes states, all other regions have significantly increased their proportions of manufacturing investments. The West Gulf Coast is outstanding in this comparison. This more rapid growth in the center and western part of the country has resulted from the policy of the government to locate new facilities in the interior of the country for strategic reasons and from the effort to bring into war production the resources from nonmanufacturing activities.

Here it should be pointed out that privately financed war facilities, consisting principally of additions to existing factories, have been placed primarily in the older manufacturing areas and that the investment in war plants in the South and Central West have consisted in large measure of publicly financed projects (Table 3).

For each type of munitions product, the major share of new facilities has been located in two or three regions (Table 4). For aircraft, the Great Lakes and Middle Atlantic states account for two-thirds of an investment now approaching $4 billion. Ohio and Michigan make up about one-fourth of the total, whereas California, which leads in aircraft-supply contracts, has received only 6 per cent of new plant awards. In new shipbuilding facilities, East Coast yards far exceed those on the West Coast. For combat and motorized vehicles, Michigan alone takes up nearly half the total and three adjacent states another 30 per cent. For guns, Michigan, New York, and Ohio account for half the new facilities. In ammunition and shells, much of the new capacity has been located in Northern inland areas, whereas explosives and shell loading were heavily represented in South Central as well as in North Central states.

For the materials industries, there has been some increased emphasis on the West and the South. Thus, in the steel industry, plants of considerable size have been located in Utah, California, and Texas, although the bulk of new investments have been in the old Northern steel-producing centers. For nonferrous metals, there have been heavy investments in the Western and Southwestern states and also in the older production centers in Michigan, New York, and the Tennessee Valley. For chemicals, including synthetic rubber, there has been a high

TABLE 4.—COST AND REGIONAL DISTRIBUTION OF WAR-MANUFACTURING FACILITIES, APPROVED JULY, 1940–JUNE, 1944

(Dollar figures in millions)

	Total	Aircraft	Ship construction	Motorized vehicles	Guns and ammunition	Explosives and ammunition loading	Iron and steel	Nonferrous metals	Metalworking machinery	Machinery and electrical equipment and appliances	Petroleum products	Food process and other manufacturing
Grand total.........	$20,022	$3,710	$2,426	$634	$2,318	$2,511	$2,026	$1,427	$313	$863	$2,870	$924

Per cent distribution by regions

New England.........	4.7	3.3	11.8	0.3	8.7	0.2	1.9	1.9	21.7	13.3	0.8	5.4
Middle Atlantic.......	18.4	18.8	24.8	6.0	21.1	6.4	26.9	15.2	21.7	35.8	11.3	25.0
East North Central...	30.0	44.2	5.4	78.6	35.9	30.7	35.1	24.9	52.7	37.0	12.9	24.3
West North Central...	7.1	6.5	0.6	5.8	18.5	17.6	3.2	0.8	1.3	2.9	3.4	6.7
South Atlantic........	6.7	3.9	13.6	0.2	4.0	7.0	5.5	2.2	*	4.2	9.2	17.3
East South Central...	6.0	1.4	1.9	0.3	2.5	22.5	4.4	8.6	*	0.9	7.4	4.3
West South Central..	10.9	7.0	3.5	2.1	2.0	12.8	3.9	13.2	1.3	0.2	39.7	3.8
Mountain............	3.8	0.8	*	*	4.8	2.8	11.1	15.3	*	0.1	3.0	1.5
Pacific..............	8.9	7.3	25.3	0.9	1.9	*	8.0	16.1	1.3	2.8	11.1	10.9
Undistributed........	3.5	6.8	13.1	5.8	0.6	.....	*	1.8	.....	2.8	1.2	0.8

* Less than 0.05 per cent.

degree of concentration in the Gulf Coast area, with investments in West Virginia and Ohio also of importance.

On the other hand, for the machinery and parts industries, there has been little shift in geographic patterns. In a singularly basic industrial operation, the making of machine tools, production has remained concentrated in Northeastern production centers. Ship parts and components have also deviated little from the prewar pattern, although in this industry as well as in scientific instruments some representation has developed on the West Coast. In general, there has been some dispersion of plant capacities in each type of industry, but the older manufacturing states in the Northeast have usually obtained the larger shares of investments and have participated much more widely in the different parts of the program.

IMPACT ON LOCAL INDUSTRIAL STRUCTURE

Among the metropolitan areas of the country, there has been a wide variation in the rate of industrial expansion during the war. Some communities have experienced a rapid gain in industrial employment, whereas others have had a decrease. Even among cities of more than 100,000 population, there are several instances of a threefold expansion in manufacturing employment since 1939, whereas in a few there has been a decrease of 10 to 30 per cent. With few exceptions, the great increases have occurred outside the old manufacturing belt. In fact, of 15 instances of a tripling of industrial employment, only Evansville in southern Indiana is in the industrial Northeast—*i.e.*, east of the Mississippi or north of the Ohio-Potomac. The Southern and Western communities with the greatest industrial expansions were for the most part prewar distribution centers with less than the average proportion of employment in manufacturing. The new dominant industry in almost every case is either aircraft, shipbuilding, or ammunition. These specialized munitions industries are certain to shrink to a minor percentage of their present importance and to present the local community with severe postwar readjustments.

Although the bulk of war-plant capacity has been placed in established manufacturing communities, the local structure of industry has often remained essentially unchanged. This is especially true where the war boom in production has resulted in large measure from the heavy procurement of peacetime types of products for military needs. Several areas in the Northeast have thus participated in the war effort by expanding existing capacities and by a higher rate of operation. Pittsburgh and Youngstown have made more steel, Cincinnati has produced more machine tools, Massachusetts mill towns have manufactured more textiles, some Connecticut towns have finished more brass mill items, and Toledo has turned out more automotive products. Of course, in some of these cases there have been changes in the quality, shape, and size of products. Areas with war industries of this kind obviously have a good chance of converting to peacetime operations.

On the other hand, there is another group of areas in which new industries have materially changed the industrial composition of the community. For example, Buffalo has shifted relatively from heavy steel and machinery to aircraft. In Los Angeles the tremendous expansion in ships and airplanes has submerged a rather diversified prewar industrial structure. In some of these communities, the prewar industry has been closed down or converted to war production. In other instances the war industry has simply overshadowed prewar operations, as in Kansas City where aircraft now outranks meat packing.

In a third group of areas, the wartime expansion has for the first time brought important industrial operations to the community. A former trade or governmental center has obtained a very large industrial operation which now accounts for employment of a considerable proportion of its citizens. Notable examples are Atlanta, Oklahoma City, Denver, Omaha, Phoenix. In most instances where manufacturing operations have come to dominate a community during the war, a single plant or two account for the change. In fact, in several cities one plant now employs more workers than did all manufacturing in 1939. For this reason, the readjustment at the end of the war may be very difficult. Convertibility of the plant to peacetime production is unlikely, both because of the specialized nature of the new product and because of the size of the plant. Moreover, the introduction of large-scale government-supported manufacturing operations into nonindustrial districts, often far removed from sources of supply of materials and parts as well as from normal markets, furnishes no indication that conversion to peacetime output will be successful.

SURVIVAL OF NEW INDUSTRIAL ACTIVITY

After the war most metropolitan communities will possess, as a heritage of munitions production, additional industrial assets—new manufacturing facilities and often newly trained management and labor. Will these resources be used? The new war plants may be handled in three ways: either as stand-by units for a later emergency, or as useless units to be dismantled, or as facilities to be converted to peacetime use. The other newly developed resources can find a local outlet either through conversion of war plants or through the construction of new facilities after the war. In the long run, management experience and new labor skills may prove of greater value to the community than the physical investments. For both, a period of readjustment and redevelopment will usually be required.

STAND-BY NEEDS. As yet there is no indication of the postwar needs for stand-by manufacturing facilities for the services or of military appropriations for plant maintenance. It is clear, however, that most of their needs will be covered in government-owned plants. Here and there, arrangements may be made with private producers to keep their facilities in such condition that production on a munitions item could be immediately undertaken. These latter provisions, however, will not seriously restrict the potential civilian output of a facility. On the other hand, the designation of a large government plant as a stand-by facility probably will put an end to all possibility of civilian production and will mean very little, if any, employment on military items. In most instances, this is not a serious loss because the facilities involved are in the main special-purpose installations which have a low degree of convertibility. They include shipyards, explosives, plants, and ammunition-loading facilities.

No doubt, stand-by facilities will be selected with the aims of dispersion and protection. Very likely important naval and merchant ship facilities on the West Coast will be retained for limited operation. For ordnance stand-by facilities, in addition to the old arsenals, inland locations will be preferred. Some inland cities are likely to find that the possibility of employing workers from their one big war plant depends primarily on constructing new facilities.

PRESENT PRODUCTS. As already noted, some war facilities can produce for normal markets essentially their present items—notably, plants making basic materials, common components, standard machinery, and in a few cases airplanes and ships. The question is mainly one of demand.

Yet, even if the gross national product remains high, there will still be an excess of capacity for certain basic materials. In these instances, it is not at all unlikely that the new plants will supersede older, higher cost units. The volume of foreign trade will, of course, play an important part in the future of many facilities. For a few plants, the addition of finishing units may assure at least partial peacetime operation. Many of the new basic-materials facilities are located in the West and Southwest, where local markets are small even though growing at favorable rates. Possibilities of postwar operation appear to be much better for the new mills in the Northeast.

New establishments making common components such as castings and forgings have been concentrated mainly in the older Northeastern manufacturing communities. The same is true of plants manufacturing standard machinery. As far as postwar operations are concerned, plants in these groups face three possibilities: either substitution for older facilities, or partial operation in competition with the older plants, or shutdown because of high costs or inadequate markets. Even in the latter event, however, some of these facilities might be converted to making other products. These war industries are an added element of strength in the prospects for the older manufacturing belt.

Facilities possessing a reasonably good market for present products are also of dominant local importance in two younger industrial sections—the Mountain states, except Idaho and Colorado, and the Texas-Louisiana Gulf Coast. This group of plants are of only minor local importance in the Great Plains states, the Southeast, and indeed in all communities heavily dependent upon shipbuilding and aircraft.

ENGINEERING CONVERTIBILITY. For released plants with little or no market for their present products, the physical convertibility becomes an important consideration. Many of these specialized war plants are, nonetheless, similar to peacetime establishments as far as either equipment, processes, or final products are concerned. The technical adaptability of these new facilities to different uses will usually be more difficult for equipment than for buildings. Buildings are not always easily usable, however, either because the space has been divided into numerous separate units, as in shell-loading and explosives plants, or because plants are so large that postwar use can be achieved only after subdivision. Also, some of these factories are of temporary construction. Despite these difficulties, most war manufacturing buildings have been well laid out, some with peacetime uses in mind. Many of them are ideal industrial properties, built according to latest designs. Among the different regions of the country, the South and Central West contain an unusually high proportion of both large facilities and highly specialized plants not easily convertible. Very large factories are typical of war construction throughout the country but small facility expansions have been much more numerous in old manufacturing areas.

The problem of converting equipment applies primarily to special-purpose machinery. For general-purpose tools there is really no conversion problem unless they become obsolete as a result of rapid wartime technological changes. Disposition problems will of course arise, mainly because of the great oversupply for certain types of tools. On the other hand, much less can be salvaged from special-purpose equipment. Part will be junked and perhaps the most valuable units stored for another emergency. Even where adaptable to peacetime operations, these special machines may be discarded, because of the greater long-run economy in using more up-to-date models.

The war industries producing specialized munitions are of varying local importance, but in most parts of the country they account for more than half of the total war-plant investments. In many Southeastern and Great Plains states, the proportion is as high as nine-tenths of all war-plant investments. Even in the industrial states of Michigan, Indiana, Wisconsin, and New Jersey, the group makes up more than 70 per cent of the total.

Of these specialized war plants, the most valuable of course are those easily convertible to peacetime use. In the main, the specialized plants are estimated to be more frequently convertible in the Great Lakes district and in most of the Rocky Mountain area than in the rest of the country. Indeed, in Michigan, Connecticut, and some of the Mountain states, fully nine-tenths of the specialized facilities consist of plants for which there is a fair to good possibility of conversion. These include the following industries: guns, combat and motorized vehicles, ammunition, shells and bombs, aircraft, and aircraft parts. The proportion of convertibility in specialized war plants ranks unusually low in the Great Plains and in some of the Southern states.

It is clear that for most of the Northern manufacturing section, the new facilities are desirable either because they have a good chance of continuing production of present types of products or because of their adaptability to normal civilian products. Even in this manufacturing belt, however, there are places which possess an unusually high proportion of plants with poor markets for their product, or which are nonconvertible. These are the communities dominated by explosives, shell loading, or shipbuilding.

USE OF CONVERTED PLANTS. The actual possibility of manufacturing civilian products in a rehabilitated war plant will be determined by several factors. The ability of a plant to compete both with existing facilities and with facilities which can be constructed after the war obviously depends on the size of the gross national production, the cost position of the individual plant, and to some extent on government policy. If the new plant is based upon satisfactory local resources, average assembly costs, and modern equipment, it may still have to face the problem of reaching a satisfactory market. Some war plants are located in out-of-the-way places for which both assembly costs and distribution costs are high. Much depends, of course, on whether the peacetime operation is based upon a local or a national market. In some instances, foreign trade may furnish sufficient additional markets to ensure plant operations.

Western plants are probably in the worst position so far as markets are concerned, although many branches of the economy in that section could support additional capacity. If a sizable fraction of the new population remains on the West Coast, a great expansion in durable consumers' goods could develop. Converted plants there will, of course, face competition of outside facilities customarily supplying Western markets.

Many producers who plan a postwar expansion of capacities will pass over the available war plants, even when offered for sale at a great reduction in price. Construction of a new facility specially designed for the particular operation has many advantages. Moreover, for a new plant it is possible to resurvey the whole location problem and perhaps to select a site more ideally suited to the preferred sources of supply and the markets to be covered.

Government policy enters into the picture in determining the procedure for the disposal of plants. Much depends on when the plants become available, whether they will be for sale only or for sale or lease, and if for sale how the price will be determined. In England, it has apparently been decided that leasing is the more satisfactory procedure; the government will retain title and make leases for a 10-year period. In this country, a lease with an option to purchase may prove to be the best device to bring these plants into civilian production, particularly if the government is willing, directly or through an agent, to divide up some of the larger plants. Such arrangements may be of special assistance in new industrial areas.

LONG-RUN GEOGRAPHIC EFFECTS

The great expansion in war production realized through conversion and expansion of industrial capacity is well known. It is perhaps not so well recognized that this expansion has modified the comparative industrial importance of different regions and has drastically altered the structure of manufacturing. Among the major regional effects of the munitions program have been the following:

1. Assignment to the older manufacturing belt of the bulk of war orders and war facilities and, significantly, concentration of a high proportion of the more convertible plants to this Northeastern section.

2. Acceleration of the industrial development of three new manufacturing areas, which even before the war were growing rapidly: the Gulf Southwest, the Tennessee Valley, and California.

3. Rapid expansion of production in the Far West, resulting in a significant rise in its proportion of the national total. This growth, highly concentrated in ships, planes, and basic metals, represents the most important departure from the prewar geographic pattern of industry.

4. Introduction of large manufacturing operations into the agricultural areas of the Central West, with only limited possibilities for postwar operation of new facilities.

5. Restriction of new munitions capacity in most of the Southeast to specialized war products, notably shipbuilding and explosives, for which postwar prospects are poor.

6. Continuation of the industrialization of the Tennessee Valley, with considerable emphasis on basic metals and chemicals, a large proportion of power having been allocated to the aluminum industry.

7. Acceleration of industrial expansion in the Gulf Southwest, including the development of many new branches of production, such as certain chemicals, synthetic rubber, tin smelting, magnesium, and steel.

8. Location of a high proportion of war production in metropolitan areas. As a result, there has been in all regions a significant movement of population out of rural areas.

Many of these regional trends are related to the varied influence of the war on particular industries. The major industrial effects can be summarized as shift of the economy into metals and chemicals; more particularly, rapid growth in aircraft and ships; extensive additional capacity for producing industrial machinery and equipment; large quantity additions to basic metal capacity, both in steel and nonferrous metals; shifts in the nature and location of raw materials; and little or no new capacity in the light consumer industries.

The significance of new war plant and equipment in postwar industrial development can be overemphasized. Perhaps little more than half of the new investments can be economically adapted to peacetime use and that only under favorable conditions as to timing of release and terms of sale or lease. Very few of the new plants will be fully as satisfactory for operation under the new conditions prevailing after the war as would newly constructed factories. It is important to emphasize, consequently, that the prospects of a region for new peacetime industrial production are not entirely dependent on the utilization of these war plants. An effort to postpone the utilization of the government-owned facilities in any part of the country probably would not seriously handicap the economic future of that region, certainly not of the industrial Northeast. (It would more than likely turn the demand for new plant and equipment in the direction of new construction and simply make it more difficult for the government to dispose of its investments.) The recommendations along this line by the Senate Special Committee to Investigate Industrial Centralization are negative and constitute an ineffective method of stimulating the development of the newer industrial sections of the South and West. Undoubtedly more significant and positive government action could be taken in the direction of facilitating the establishment of new enterprises in these areas and of aiding existing producers.

Perhaps, as already indicated, the newly trained labor and management in the newer industrial sections of the country will make a greater contribution to postwar production than the new industrial facilities. Widespread knowledge of new products and new processes favors the successful conversion of many producing units outside the older manufacturing district. In many manufacturing industries, improvements of this type as well as experience in subcontracting have altered the economies of size and permit a greater dispersion of plants. Moreover, the war has forced many producers to reexamine their plant locations with respect to both assembly and distribution costs. As a result, many of the older concerns have already found that production can be profitably carried on at points other than the older centers in which they have been accustomed to operate.

These varied industrial developments of the wartime period make it difficult to estimate the postwar geographic structure of industry. It is possible, however, to point to several significant questions which arise out of this wartime experience:

1. Will the wartime spread of industrialization across the country continue, or will a wider differential in favor of the older manufacturing belt be reestablished?

2. Will the younger industrial areas that were growing rapidly before the war (the Gulf Southwest, the Tennessee Valley, and the Pacific Southwest) be able to shift successfully from specialized war products and continue their comparatively high rates of growth?

3. Will the South retain so little of its war manufacturing as to revert to its position as the nation's number one problem section?

4. Will the West Central sections of the country go back to the previous high dependence on agriculture? Will they continue to lose population to coastal areas?

5. Will the war-type industries return to coastal regions, or will inland producers of aircraft, basic chemicals, and other important potential munitions survive?

Naturally, the solutions of these postwar readjustment problems would be facilitated by common agreement on the desirable and feasible pattern of our postwar economic structure and on means for attaining it. Increased public discussion of the problem is desirable. But in the absence of a common goal it will be difficult to reconcile the many diverse regional and industrial interests. Certain objectives, however, are clear. Both government and private industry should mutually support conversion of all possible war industrial resources to peacetime use, both for the sake of the entire economy and for encouragement of industrial beginnings in newer sections of the country. Although the initiative in reconversion must come from private business, the government alone is responsible for the achievement of a strategically safer and economically more desirable distribution of industrial activity. Toward these ends, special limited assistance may be appropriate for the conversion of war plants in relatively safe inland areas, particularly those with stand-by importance and those in distressed or economically handicapped sections of the country. Cooperative planning by government and private industry will be needed in order to use our new resources and to continue the gains in production which have characterized all parts of the country during the war.

Part III

CONTROLS

Chapter X

Economic Controls in Postwar Transition

by JOHN M. CLARK

1. War Controls: Mechanisms and Objectives

FOR THIS country, the present conflict is much the nearest approach to "total war" we have ever experienced. It is still a long way from total, as we should soon learn if we were to change places with some of the other belligerents, but it has required us to put fully half of our economic system at the service of the nation—mostly for war. The entire economy is subject to an impressive list of special wartime controls.

War orders can be made compulsory, either directly or by limiting or prohibiting the production of civilian goods which the same facilities might turn out. Scarce materials have been conserved by limiting the amounts that can be used in civilian products; and even military specifications have been adjusted when they called for more than could be had of some limited materials. In these matters the government was rightly unwilling to let its procurement of tanks, for instance, depend on competing in the markets with civilian buyers whose pockets were bulging with the government's own dollars, paid to them for producing ships or planes.

Scarce materials were first subjected to priorities and then to outright allocation, with control of inventories as a logical corollary. There has been rationing of many foods and of automobiles, tires, and gasoline. Domestic transportation has been controlled. Exports and imports have been controlled, with an eye to the art of "economic warfare," and shipping space has been allocated. There has been international allocation of materials. As part of the campaign against inflation, there has been control of prices, of wages, and of consumer credit. In the field of man power, there has been no general service law, but a lesser degree of man-power control has been set up, with sanctions derived partly from the power over occupational draft deferment and partly from support by other agencies, such as the War Production Board (WPB), whose power of allocating materials can be used to enforce limitations on the number of workers employed in civilian industries.

These are temporary emergency controls and have been entrusted to temporary agencies, which would naturally go out of existence soon after the end of active hostilities. Not only are the kinds of controls foreign to our normal peacetime practice, but the procedures cut the corners in a way that would not satisfy peacetime conceptions of "due process," though necessary in wartime, when the situation imperatively demands quick and decisive action of unaccustomed sorts. The attempt has been made to adopt forms of procedure which would safeguard the minimum essentials of due process while still enabling the administrative agencies to do the things that have to be done.

Another feature of wartime controls which should not be continued unchanged in peacetime consists of the large extent to which agencies may in effect enlarge their powers by securing the support of other agencies, without such specific authorization as would be proper in peacetime. The agencies are under general instructions to cooperate and to further one another's assigned purposes. The objection is not to the correlation and mutual support between agencies; that is a necessity, not only for the war emergency but probably also for any economic policy sufficiently coherent to handle postwar economic problems. Along with this goes need for increased administrative initiative and leadership in the formulation of policy. But in peacetime it is not exactly desirable to have agencies using their powers for purposes for which they were not designed, at the behest of other agencies. On the positive side, this means that important policies should be formulated and implemented in regular and recognized ways, in a good strong light, and subject to legislative approval. The way in which powers are made available to the War Manpower Commission, already mentioned, may be taken as one example. It is necessary but is not a good model for peacetime procedure.

These war controls will presumably be taken off as soon as they are no longer needed, either for their original war purposes or for helping to avoid the pitfalls of reconversion to a successful working economy. The dominant objective of war controls is quick mobilization of all available resources, to turn out the largest and best organized war output of which they are capable. The combined demand for war goods and civilian supplies is unavoidably in excess of the utmost possible supply. If it were not, that would mean that the sights for the war program had been set too low. Therefore wartime economic policy is a matter of allocating supplies unavoidably scarce and combating the hoarding which, left to itself, would make the scarcities worse, and the accompanying inflation which aggravates the resulting hardships.

In reconversion, there will be both shortages and surpluses, and it is impossible to predict with certainty whether the prevailing trend will be toward inflation or deflation; hence it is necessary to be prepared for both. Violent price collapses and temporary shutdowns of essential industries are to be feared, just as inflation is. It is also necessary to be prepared for temporary surpluses followed by renewed shortages, as reconverted industry renews its demands for materials and fabricated components. To be clear of possible shortages, supply needs to be sufficient, not only for current withdrawals, but for the building of inventories and for assurance that overordering by some will not leave others short. The larger and stronger producers, who are best able to look out for their needs, may be willing to see allocations of materials and inventory controls dropped sooner than would be safe for smaller producers, especially for new enterprises. One of the objectives of reconversion policy is to see that those wishing to start new enterprises have access to the necessary means of production.

War policy must accept the dominant fact of inescapable shortages; reconversion policy looks toward a situation in which supply will match demand at reasonable prices. War policy focuses on increasing the kind of production for which the government is the buyer. It must have the goods at any price, but the price incentive does not act alone. It is reinforced by the patriotic motives of the producers and by the power of the government to issue compulsory orders if they are needed and to restrict alternative forms of production. Reconversion requires an increase, beyond all previous experience, in the kinds of production that depend on voluntary buying by many millions of private consumers who need not buy unless price and quality attract them. Success really depends on production in anticipation of such buying, by producers who will not produce unless they see a sufficient prospect of profit. The motive of profit is supplemented to a large but uncertain extent by the realization that it is crucially important for business, in its own interest, to make a good record in furnishing employment. The war problem will reverse itself as we pass from the problem of getting enough workers to the problem of furnishing enough jobs.

2. Stages of Reconversion

The outstanding feature of the present prospect of reconversion is the expectation that it will come in two major installments, the first after VE-day (victory in Europe) and the second after VJ-day (victory over Japan). The first, being nearer, bulks larger in present thinking and planning, tending to make people forget that the second will involve the release of many more war workers and servicemen—possibly about twice as many. After the final armistice, there will be an initial period of retooling for those industries which need it, reshuffling of inventories, and the other incidents of reconversion to civilian production. Then will come a period in which the whole economy will be stimulated by the work of making good deferred demands—chiefly, of course, for durables, with automobiles as the probable dominant factor in the domestic market. Rehabilitation work overseas may also still play a material part, though the most urgent work may have been done earlier. Finally will come the transition to the long-run necessity of getting on without this special and temporary stimulus.

3. The Example of 1919–1921

Reconversion after World War I affords an example of what may happen if economic controls are promptly and abruptly terminated, after the end of hostilities and while war expenditures are still large. Many of the conditions were similar to those we shall be experiencing in the coming reconversion, but with differences of quantity and timing which would naturally influence the outcome. Fighting ended suddenly, production dropped, and prices sagged slightly. Then came the boom during which wholesale prices and cost of living each rose approximately 29 per cent from the low of February, 1919, and wages were increased. There was vigorous consumer buying, probably aided by the large existing accumulations of war savings; and a scramble to build up inventories, resulting in the multiplication of orders.

ECONOMIC CONTROLS 185

During the 12 months following the armistice, some 3.7 million servicemen were discharged, representing a considerably smaller net addition to the civilian working force. Reabsorption went on with apparent success until the boom broke in June, 1920, after which total employment shrank by over 4 million from the third quarter of 1920 to the third quarter of 1921.[1] Shrinkage of employment due to the depression exceeded the number of servicemen discharged.

In the coming reconversion, all the quantities will be larger. There will be more retooling to be done and more chance to do part of it before the final armistice. Total production has increased more, leaving wider margins of capacity above probable demand, even at high levels of employment. But deferred demand for the major durables will take longer to make up, even working at capacity, and consumer buying must show a greater increase above prewar levels, if high levels of employment are to be realized.

4. The Period of Full War Effort

Until victory in Europe, there will probably be only a trickle of reconversion, plus planning and preparing for the larger reconversion that is to come. At the time of writing this paper, man power is still scarce, but a number of basic materials are plentiful, especially aluminum and magnesium. This suggests a shifting of man power from the production of the plentiful materials, after accumulating reasonable reserves. It also suggests using materials to economize man power, where this can be done. Where "M" orders have restricted the use of scarce materials to the point of deteriorating quality and reducing service value, a release of restrictions may enable a limited amount of man power to turn out more service value.

Then the substandard goods resulting from the restrictions could be disposed of on a war market, where they would make a minimum of trouble and difficulty; and dealers could face the peace with shelves stocked with goods of standard quality. One incidental awkwardness, from the standpoint of price control, would arise in some cases in which this would require an increase of price, converting into an open increase one that had previously been hidden under deterioration

---

[1] There was a further shrinkage of 0.9 million to the first quarter of 1922, but this may be reckoned as largely seasonal. *Cf.* W. I. King, *Employment, Hours, and Earnings in Prosperity and Depression*, p. 30.

of quality. Logically, however, orders conserving materials are about the earliest candidates for fairly widespread release.

Orders restricting the production of particular commodities present more complications, and limited release of such orders has a number of baffling aspects. Permission to produce a particular commodity means little unless the necessary man power, materials, components, and subassemblies are available and not tied up by war contracts or by other WPB orders. Therefore, one order cannot be considered by itself. The method of setting limits on such releases defies any simple formula.

The WPB answer to these difficulties consisted of a general order (the Spot Authorization Order), issued on Aug. 15, 1944. This permits the lifting of a long list of "L" and "M" orders (orders limiting or prohibiting the production of particular products, or conserving particular materials by limiting the manner in which, or the extent to which, they may be used). The lifting of the orders is not automatic; each producer wishing to take advantage of it must make special application which may be granted by the regional WPB offices if local man-power and other conditions permit it to be done without interfering with the war effort. The regional offices are also to give preference to more essential commodities.

It was not originally expected that a great volume of production would be released under this general order. The recent announcement that some 750 applications had been granted probably does not mean that large volumes of output and employment are involved. The possibility of prolonged war with Germany has led some to surmise that a great deal of our reconversion may take place under this general order. At present, this seems unlikely. Prolonged war with Germany would naturally mean much hard fighting and a stepping-up of various requirements for munitions. Mr. Byrnes has recently announced that reconversions may have to be stopped if important sections of the war-production program continue to lag behind schedule.

One complexity of limited reconversion arises from the natural desire of industrialists that all competitors should get an equal start. That is, it arises when this desire comes into conflict with the necessities of the emerging situation. It was urged that, when civilian production was resumed in an industry, all the members should be allowed to resume at once and that, if only partial resumption were possible, output should be allocated by quotas, prewar output being the obvious preferred basis. Strict adherence to this rule is out of the question.

In the first place, the government will want to keep some producers fully occupied on war work and to cancel the contracts of others. The models made by some producers will be discontinued and those made by others retained. As between makers of the same models, the government will often prefer to keep some at work and release others, rather than to make a uniformly distributed cutback. Where producers have some capacity capable of being used for civilian production, some will be in areas of special labor scarcity and others not. If quotas based on prewar output are practicable in some cases, they are likely not to be fair as between producers, some of whom have multiplied their total operations sevenfold or tenfold, while others in the same industry have expanded only moderately. The domestic laundry-appliance industry is a convincing case in point.

If reconversion by quotas is tried at a later stage of the war, new producers will have to be given an allowance on some basis or other. Inequities resulting from letting some producers get a head start over their competitors in reconversion will probably not be serious in the period of full war effort, since it is unlikely that large and formidable producers will be released to a sufficient extent to gain important advantages over their competitors.

As to price and wage controls, until VE-day it will be necessary to "hold the line" as stiffly as it has been held during 1944, if a cumulative inflationary spiral is to be avoided. Where costs have increased since production of certain civilian products was suspended, resumption of production will require adjustment of price ceilings in substantially the same way in which the Office of Price Administration has been adjusting ceilings on commodities which have not been out of production. The price administrator has announced that 1942 prices will be the basis for reconversion pricing and that, where wages and prices of materials have increased by a given percentage, past experience indicates that it is not likely to be necessary to increase these prices by an equally large percentage in order to enable the producers to make liberal earnings.

5. War in the Pacific Only

After victory in Europe, it is estimated that the war production program will shrink by 35 to 40 per cent overall, in perhaps 3 months' time, the shrinkage being greatest in ground-army munitions. This is a medium estimate—extreme forecasts show very wide variation. The Army will be reduced by releasing possibly as many as 2 million men, while the Navy will be maintained and possibly even slightly increased. But the repatriation of men no longer needed for overseas service may be delayed because so much of the shipping available in Europe will be needed to carry men and matériel to the Far Eastern theater. Of course no one can say how long this phase of the war will last. The typical estimate is about a year, but the most recent and authoritative place it at 18 months to 2 years. The amount of shrinkage in war production, and the particular industries in which it is located, will determine what kind of policy of economic control will be possible in this period; and the extent and duration of this shrinkage will go far to determine the character of the periods of adjustment that will follow.

A partial offset to the shrinkage of our production of war supplies will be the need for relief and reconstruction in Europe. This is a good investment for us on almost any financial terms. We cannot afford not to do it; and we cannot afford to do it on terms that are bound to acquire for us once more the title of "Uncle Shylock" among the nations. Other offsets are to be looked for in the reduction of overtime work and the departure of a considerable part of the workers who are only in the working force on account of the emergency. There are said to be some 6 million of these, and enough overtime to be equivalent to 5 million more. Get rid of half the overtime, let half the emergency workers go back to home or school, and this would very nearly offset the expected release of some 4 million war workers and possibly 2 million servicemen.

Of course, it will not work in just that way. There will be areas of unemployment and areas of tight labor supply, and we shall not succeed in moving the work or the workers so as to make the surpluses and shortages cancel. The tendency will be to release civilian production to take up the unemployment and hold onto the emergency workers and the overtime where labor is short. The main point is that the release of 6 million war workers and servicemen will not be anything like a clear addition to the working force and should not be. And the idea that every bit of reduction in the war program must be replaced with an equal amount of civilian production, so that our real or physical output shall remain at its war-peak level—this is at best an ill-considered idea, and at worst may be positively dangerous.

The VE-day crisis looks big because it looks near. But in terms of man power needing to be reabsorbed it is, by current estimates, only about half the magnitude of the VJ-day crisis to follow. And it would not be desirable to use all our economic ammunition in meeting the first crisis and have nothing left with which to meet the second. We shall want to begin producing some automobiles to replace those that cannot safely stay on the roads. But it is highly desirable that, when final victory comes, there should still be a great many more people than usual wanting new cars.

It is against this background that our post VE-day policy will be worked out. Depending partly on circumstances and partly on policy, there may be a general surplus of labor with particular shortages, or a general shortage with particular and local surpluses. There may be general inflationary pressures on prices with some weak spots, or general deflation with some tight areas. It is impossible to predict to just what extent war controls can be released in this period without bad results. Advance policies and programs, therefore, have need for flexibility.

The preelection program of the Federal government may be summed up as "holding the line" on prices and wages, with conservative price adjustments on resumed civilian products as necessitated by increased costs, while victory in Europe is to be followed by a sweeping relaxation of control of production and man power. Production controls are, according to this program, to be stripped down to allocation of a few specially scarce materials, a blanket priority for war work, a possible second priority for the most essential civilian products, and a watching of inventories. Rationing will presumably be continued wherever shortages persist.

All the compulsory features of man-power controls are to be dropped after victory in Europe. To induce workers not to desert war work for civilian production, any essential work that may be threatened in this way may offer its workers a 48-hour week and the overtime pay that goes with it, while normal civilian work will presumably be on a 40-hour basis. This would give the war work a 30 per cent advantage in weekly "take home." There are strong reasons for the judgment that it would be a mistaken policy to maintain a 48-hour week for this reason, if it is not needed for other reasons. And if this mistake is necessitated by the abandoning of man-power controls, then it would seem that this is a mistake also, unless these controls have become outright untenable.

The theory of this program is that although there will not be enough of all resources to meet all demands, there will be enough for all the essential needs, and enough over so that no serious harm would result if the nonessential demands were to take what each could get on a catch-as-catch-can basis. Or perhaps a more potent theory is that the alternative would be intolerable, from the standpoint of administrative practicability and of prompt and unhampered resumption of civilian production and employment. These considerations are serious.

Allocation of limited materials and man power, as between a multitude of competing products and producers of nonessential status, would be full of stubborn dilemmas, which could not be resolved by any simple general rules. Grappling with these difficulties would be calculated to produce wholesale nervous breakdowns among the administrative officials. Furthermore, allocation of the sort represented by the full-fledged "controlled materials plan" requires that production programs be geared to a definite output, and that this output be translated into definite requirements in terms of quantities of particular materials. The latter process is surprisingly difficult and would take time in the case of freshly resumed civilian products, while it might be impossible to forecast output with any approach to exactness. This kind of allocation would delay reconversion. This might be avoided, however, by a looser system of allocation, suited to a less stringent supply situation, in which the initial allotments are made with more margin for error, and the errors are subsequently corrected by inventory controls.

As to the termination of man-power controls, if this necessitates any considerable continuance of overtime which would otherwise be unnecessary, it seems clearly inappropriate to a situation in which the country is likely to be facing difficulty in finding enough jobs. This would be true, even if, as already suggested, the apparent general surplus of man power should be due, not to a true over-all surplus, but to the impossibility of fitting together perfectly the many pieces of the complex picture of supply of man power and demand for it in different industries and areas.

The order in which different industries and different producers will be released from war work will, under the present plan, be left to the procurement agencies in consultation with the WPB. Considerations which may be given weight include early release of the less efficient producers, the smaller producers, plants in areas of labor shortage, and plants which have been converted from civilian production as against those built fresh for war work. Simultaneous cutbacks for producers in general may also be considered, but only if it would not mean substantial sacrifice of efficiency. The advantage going to those who get the earliest start in resuming civilian production may be minimized if they start on prewar models, and especially if postwar models are not introduced until all can start even with them. Two kinds of release which should take high rank are release of ample materials for experimental development of new models and new products, especially the latter; and facilities for advance retooling of plants, even if full production in these plants is not yet practicable.

Rationing of petroleum products will presumably be needed until the end of fighting. Rationing of food will probably be needed for one year after VE-day if we do what should be done to meet the needs of war-torn Europe. Rationing of limited supplies of automobiles and other heavy durables presents a problem, since the kind of rationing required involves a certificate of individual need for every purchase and is the most burdensome form of rationing. This may be avoided, when a fair amount of production is resumed, by resort to some more informal system—possibly one of general rules as to use priorities. This would be a makeshift but might work well enough, for a limited period, to be a lesser evil.

As European supplies of food increase, there may be a weakening of our own food prices. On the other hand, as resumption of civilian production of suspended manufactures becomes increasingly important, it may become necessary to interpret price-ceiling policies more liberally in the manufactured-goods field. If agricultural prices decline, even to the limited extent permitted by present provisions for price supports, this may make room for some limited increases on resumed manufactured products, without bringing about a rise in the cost-of-living index. If this index should rise further, wage stabilization would be threatened, and a fresh inflationary spiral might be started.

This situation will be complicated by demands for wage increases to make up for reductions of weekly earnings due to shortened hours and loss of overtime pay. Downgrading and shifts to lower paid jobs will also reduce earnings but will not so easily afford a basis for wage demands. It may be objected that, when weekly earnings rose faster than wage rates and faster than the cost of living, it was the wage rates that labor claimed should keep pace with costs of living, while, when earnings shrink under stable wage rates, it is the earnings that must be stabilized. However, labor has not got all it asked for, and such objections to the valve-action nature of this proposal will not be particularly effective. Forgetting the past and thinking only of future effects, wage rates should be raised as high as possible without necessitating increased prices which would start the inflationary spiral and neutralize the workers' gains. But the high theoretical "real earnings" of war work in wartime may be impossible to maintain. They were theoretical in that, if the workers had insisted on converting them all into real current commodities, they would instead have dissipated them in inflation. These theoretical real weekly earnings may shrink and still be well above prewar levels, while personal incomes may still be large enough to buy all the civilian goods that will be available when the released workers are at work. More than this is not necessary, while the war lasts.

6. The Period of Initial Postwar Reconversion

The character of the initial postwar reconversion period will be affected in considerable measure by what goes before; especially by how abruptly or how gradually the fighting ends, how much or how little retooling, reconversion, and preparatory work has been done during the later phases of the fighting, and how much or how little effective demand there may be for American products for purposes of reconstruction abroad. In any case, there will be an abrupt and heavy transitional decline in income, output, and employment. Possibly 5 million war workers will be quickly released, and perhaps 7 million or more servicemen and women will be released more slowly, the average rate being probably in the neighborhood of 600,000 per month.

The dominant purpose of the country's economic policy will change. In the closing phases of the fighting we shall have been riding two horses: war and reconversion. Now reconversion will be supreme. We shall be striving to come through the transitional shrinkage without allowing it to cumulate into a runaway depression. As to controls, the aim will be to facilitate and promote the speediest possible transition to a situation in which the chief control will be ample civilian output under conditions of healthy competition. Determination of what goods are needed will pass from the military authorities to the market; *i.e.*, to the sum of the demands of millions of independent consumers who will exercise their own judgment as to what they wish to buy, and when. The main and proper purpose of such controls as may be continued in this period is to see that the resumption of civilian production is not hampered by inability of producers to secure the means of production or by violent disturbances of demand and supply, of prices and wages, which would tend to destroy confidence, interrupt the flow of spending, and delay resumption of production, employment, and income.

Among things to be sought, speed in reconversion is of the first importance; also maintenance of purchasing power and a mood of confidence leading to willingness to spend war savings as soon as goods are available on which to spend them without bringing on inflation. Things to be avoided include a drastic deflation, a runaway inflation of a sort that would lead to drastic deflation later or leave us with a price structure too high for healthy international trade relations, an undue pegging of prices and wages in the face of declining demand, or a contest in which producers try to build up inventories at an abnormal rate and thus create unnecessary and artificial scarcities.

Liberal unemployment benefits are clearly indicated, but they will be doing well if they make up for as much as one-fourth of the shrinkage in wage incomes. "Made work" should be avoided, at least during this first transition. Retraining is a better occupation. Normally useful public works should be resumed, but to take effect promptly enough, they will need not only to have been blueprinted during the preceding period; some actual initiatory work will need to have been done. Otherwise, major projects will not reach the stage of large employment soon enough to be of much help in this initial transition. A "large shelf of small projects" will be particularly appropriate.

In the labor market, the no-strike pledge will have ended and also presumably the possibility of setting compulsory wage ceilings. Wage-rate increases will be desirable to the extent that industry can absorb them without either raising prices or holding particular prices at a level which demand will not support without curtailing sales, or setting up noncompetitive disparities in the wage-price structure. Some reduction of business taxes might enable business to absorb some wage increases which would otherwise tend to curtail employment. Earnest thought should be given to the question whether a National Labor Board, operating on an altered basis, might carry on the standards of relative equity which the present board has developed and make them influential in promoting a more equitable wage structure than might otherwise come out of the postwar readjustment.

Controls of production and allocations of materials will be ended, with possibly a very few exceptions in which temporary scarcities may persist. But some temporary inventory controls of a modified sort may be appropriate so long as there remains any likelihood of an inventory-grabbing scramble in which prices might be inflated (as in 1919–1920) and some producers might be unable to secure materials needed for prompt resumption of production. Care should be taken not to employ any form of inventory control which could operate to restrict production of the controlled supplies.

In the field of prices, the agricultural price supports to which the country is already committed will have to be implemented. In other fields, price supports should be limited to orderly disposal of accumulated surpluses. This might involve some temporary stock-pile operations by the government, aimed mainly at averting disastrous and temporary shutdowns of production and resulting unemployment; but the dangers of abuse in such policies place them under a peculiarly heavy burden of proof.

As to price ceilings, this power should be retained as long as there is likelihood of a general inflationary movement. For this purpose the last danger point would be the point at which reviving employment revives confidence and a willingness to spend war savings, which might temporarily cause demand to run ahead of available supplies of many products. The one field in which postwar price ceilings will be definitely needed will be that of rentals and the major durables. In the case of rentals, care needs to be taken to allow ample incentive for repairs, improvements, and new construction. In the case of the major durables, a limited number of products, produced on a large scale by a limited number of companies, comprise the bulk of the output and employment. Most of these producers are likely to be ready to follow a farsighted price policy looking to large sales on small margins, and informal price controls have therefore a good chance of success. Dealers' margins may need closer watching than manufacturers' prices during the period before the backlog of deferred demand has been provided for. Formal rationing will probably be avoided, for reasons already mentioned.

Controls of consumers' credit should be released at a time when demand needs the stimulus which this release can afford and when supplies are available. This may mean releasing general charge accounts and installment selling at different times. Meanwhile, necessitous cases should be granted relief. Serious consideration should be given to retaining this type of control as a permanent part of a system for reducing the sharpness of business fluctuations.

7. The Sequel

The above is a brief, sketchy, and unduly dogmatic survey of reconversion problems and probabilities with respect to the main domestic wartime controls. It does not cover the whole field of domestic war controls and omits the entire area of international dealings. In that area some of the war controls may last longer or may have more direct lineal peacetime descendants. At home, we shall be facing a task for which there are no obvious and simple models: namely, to return to, and maintain, a system of private enterprise with the added requirement that it must furnish ample and reasonably stable employment or else expect powerful public intervention directed to that end. It is private enterprise, affected with a novel public interest which it has not yet demonstrated its ability to assimilate.

The problems involved in this undertaking are many, and any attempt to consider them would lead us too far afield. In particular, the place of competition in the future economy presents a welter of incongruities. It seems clear, however, that great importance will be attached to the maintenance of competition between business enterprises—with numerous probable exceptions. Perhaps the foremost single contribution which the reconversion period can make to the more enduring tasks of the postwar economy will be to resist tendencies to increased consolidation and to initiate or promote positive measures tending to make it more possible than it has been in the past for a healthy number of independent enterprises to develop and maintain enough efficiency to make them positive market factors rather than semidependent poor relations. The enforcement of antitrust laws is important, as long as we persist in the policy of a competitive system, but it is only the negative side of such a policy, and the positive side seems more important. It begins with the disposal of the government's war-plant facilities.

The acid test of the postwar economy will probably come when we have exhausted the temporary stimulus that will come from renewing our stocks of durable goods, catching up with our housing needs, and aiding in rehabilitation work abroad. There may be two crises: one when the supply of automobiles catches up with demand and the other when the postwar wave of housing construction slackens off. The way in which we come through these crises will go far toward telling whether we have developed a combination of peacetime economic incentives, plus peacetime economic controls, which will work.

Chapter XI

Development of Price Control and Transition Price Problems

by DONALD H. WALLACE [1]

I. Sketch of Development of Price Control

PRICE control began in the summer of 1940. For nearly two years, until the spring of 1942, a policy of selective price control was followed. Commodity after commodity was brought under ceiling price control as inflationary pressures spread from one field to another under the influence of the mounting defense program. Control was first instituted in the fields of metals, lumber, pulp, used machine tools, and other basic war materials. By the end of 1941 most raw materials, with the exception of farm products, were under control, and control had been extended to some manufactured goods where price pressures had developed. Scarcely any retail ceilings had been set.

Late in 1941 it became apparent that inflationary pressures had become general throughout the whole economy as a result of the great increase in expenditures on war goods and the consequent large increase in people's incomes. Accordingly, in April, 1942, the General Maximum Price Regulation (GMPR) was issued freezing all prices hitherto uncontrolled, with some exceptions, at March, 1942, levels. The principal exceptions to this general price freeze were farm and food products, whose prices had not yet reached the levels of the special pricing standards required for them by the Emergency Price Control Act of January, 1942, and finished combat equipment and some parts and subassemblies thereof.

---

[1] The views expressed herein are the personal views of the writer. They are not to be considered as representing the official position of the Office of Price Administration (OPA).

The Stabilization Act of October, 1942, directed that prices and wages affecting the cost of living be stabilized so far as practicable at the levels of Sept. 15, 1942. Thus effective wage stabilization was instituted. Changes in the special provisions of the law relating to price control in farm products and food were also made which, taken in conjunction with the price levels already reached by farm products, enabled OPA to begin the work of establishing effective price control in this field.

In the past 2½ years OPA has extended control over most of the farm-product and food areas, formulated special ceilings for a large part of the products initially frozen by GMPR, crystallized strict pricing standards and made their application more uniform throughout the various commodity fields, obtained the use of subsidies in limited amounts, developed the community dollar-and-cents retail ceilings, and improved compliance, especially through the price panel program and more vigorous enforcement. Most of these developments were aided by the "hold-the-line" executive order of April, 1943, issued because the rise in the cost of living had not been satisfactorily checked during the 6 months following passage of the Stabilization Act. As a result of policies and methods adopted earlier or instituted to implement the "hold-the-line" order, the cost of living has been effectively stabilized since the spring of 1943.

II. Pricing Methods and Policies of OPA

This section outlines briefly the pricing methods and policies used in the price-control program and notes some effects of price control and other wartime influences on the price structure.

The language and tone of the laws and the executive orders under which OPA operates show clearly that the main purpose is to prevent inflation. A second purpose is to aid in securing adequate supplies of essential war goods and essential civilian goods. The main responsibility for supply is lodged in the war supply agencies, the Army, the Navy, War Production Board, War Food Administration, etc., who employ direct controls over production and distribution. It is, of course, impossible to build a war economy, ensure essential civilian production, and avoid inflation by reliance primarily upon pricing in such a way as to make it profitable to produce some things and unprofitable to produce others. Only direct controls on production and distribution can be quick enough and precise enough. OPA pricing must not interfere with getting the things we need produced, but it is not its function to "steer" the economy by price regulations.

Three principal pricing methods have been used in setting price ceilings: (1) freezing the prevailing prices or in some cases the list prices of a given base period; (2) specifying dollar-and-cents ceilings; and (3) formula pricing. Formula pricing has been used chiefly, although not entirely, for the purpose of pricing new goods, including new varieties or styles of old goods.

Having once imposed price ceilings, the endeavor has been to hold these ceilings unchanged in the face of cost increases so long as they remain generally fair and equitable. If they cease to be generally fair and equitable, a price increase is required by law, unless the inequity can be corrected by some other means, such as reductions in prices of materials or subsidies.

This policy of forcing absorption of cost increases until a certain limit is reached contributes to stabilization in two vital ways: (1) prices are not allowed to increase until there is a real need for the increase; (2) a strong incentive is given to business to hold down its costs as effectively as possible. The latter point was especially important before initiation of wage control, but it is still very significant. Effective wage control is even more difficult than effective price control. If employers knew they could get price relief when they raised wages or otherwise pirated labor from other firms, it would be doubly difficult to control man power and hold wages reasonably in line. Similar considerations apply to cost of materials and, indeed, to matters of efficient management throughout the entire business operation. The cost-absorption requirement makes the businessman a partner of OPA in keeping costs down and thus keeping prices down.

An attempt has been made to secure the same cost absorption on new goods, priced by formula, as on old goods with dollar-and-cents ceilings or frozen prices. In general, the formula ceilings for new goods take one or another of the following two forms: (1) The direct labor and material cost of the new good is computed, not at the current cost but at what the cost would have been in a base period. This is done by using the wage rates and material prices paid by the firm in the base period. To this computed base-period direct cost is added the base-period gross margin between price and direct cost on that one of the old goods sold in the base period which is most nearly comparable to the new good. (2)

The current labor and material cost is used and to this is added the current gross margin between price and current direct cost of the most nearly comparable item. Although admittedly not wholly successful in forcing the same amount of cost absorption on new goods as on old goods with frozen prices or dollar-and-cents ceilings, nevertheless the results of new-goods pricing have been far less inflationary than straight-out cost-plus or escalator pricing would have been.

The most common criticism of OPA price policy is directed against this forced absorption of cost increases. There is hardly an industry in the land which has not maintained vehemently that every cost increase should be matched, dollar for dollar, with a price increase. It is plain, however, that economic stabilization cannot be achieved unless strict standards are used to define (1) the conditions under which a price increase is required by law and the amount of increase required, and (2) the conditions under which a price increase, above the minimum required by law, is needed to aid in securing essential supply and the amount of such increase. The real question is not whether to force cost absorption, but how far to carry it before a price increase is permitted.

The law requires that the maximum price of each commodity be "generally fair and equitable" to sellers and buyers. Two standards have ordinarily been used as criteria of general fairness to sellers of a commodity. The first is the "industry earnings standard." As long as an industry is receiving from all its operations a return on its investment which equals or exceeds the return received in a representative peacetime period, its maximum price or prices are generally fair and equitable to sellers in the industry. If, however, costs increase to such an extent that earnings fall below the peacetime return, a price increase is ordinarily required.[1] The basic philosophy of this standard is that an industry is not entitled, as a matter of law, to a *price increase* for the mere purpose of enabling it to earn a larger return than it obtained in peacetime. It can increase its return by larger output or lowered costs at stable prices, but it is not entitled to increased return by raising prices during the emergency. The period 1936–1939 is ordinarily used as the measure of the peacetime return. Special standards are employed for the few special cases where the peacetime return was exceptionally low or exceptionally high.

This is a standard for price *increases* only. It is not a standard by

[1] A price increase would not necessarily be required, however, if the fall of profits was due to a decline in volume of sales below the peacetime rate.

which ceiling prices are originally set. Most ceiling prices were originally set at levels prevailing at the time or in a near-by period. Most of these prices were above peacetime levels. Moreover, the industry earnings standard is not ordinarily a standard for *reductions* in maximum prices. It is used as a standard for price reductions only where reductions in prices of materials or supplies are made as a means of avoiding an increase in ceiling prices of the products made from such materials or supplies.

Thus the use of the industry earnings standard for price increases required by law does not mean that profits are held down to the prewar level in all or in most industries. In fact, in most industries return on investment is much above the prewar return.

In industries producing a number of different products, a second standard is needed to test the general fairness of the maximum price of a particular line or product. The maximum price for a particular line or product is considered to be generally fair and equitable as long as there is no cash or out-of-pocket loss on this product to the industry generally—*i.e.*, on the bulk of the output. Ceiling prices in these multiple-product industries must, of course, satisfy *both* the industry earnings *and* the particular product standards. If aggregate industry earnings on all products taken together are below the peacetime level, prices would have to be raised even if no out-of-pocket loss was being suffered on particular products.

During the Congressional hearings prior to enactment of the Stabilization Extension Act of 1944, the industry earnings standard and the product standard were described to Congressional committees by OPA officers. Although proposals to change the law so as to change these standards were made to Congress by many business groups, the law was enacted without modification of the statutory standard—"generally fair and equitable"—of which the industry earnings standard and the product standard are interpretations.

In a recent case the Emergency Court of Appeals, the special court dealing with price-control cases, upheld the validity of these standards after intensive examination of them. The Court said:

> We conclude that the use by the Administrator of the industry earnings standard in conjunction with the product standard to determine whether a maximum price previously set by him is no longer generally fair and equitable and such as will effectuate the purposes of the Emergency Price Control

Act is a reasonable exercise of the discretion conferred upon him in the administration of the act and is in consonance with its mandate.[1]

The standards outlined above apply to all commodities. The law contains also a set of special standards for agricultural commodities and commodities processed in whole or in substantial part from agricultural commodities. The ceiling for an agricultural commodity must reflect the *highest* of the following four legal minimums:

1. The parity or comparable price as determined by the Secretary of Agriculture and adjusted by him for grade, location, and seasonal differentials.

2. The highest price between Jan. 1, 1942, and Sept. 15, 1942.

3. A higher price, if that is necessary, to reflect increases in costs incurred by producers since Jan. 1, 1941, giving adequate weighting to farm labor.

4. A higher price, if that is necessary, to increase production of the commodity for war purposes.

The maximum prices for commodities processed from agricultural commodities are subject to two provisions:

1. They must reflect to producers of agricultural commodities the highest of the four minimum legal prices for that commodity. This means that the ceiling price for the processed agricultural commodity must not be such as to prevent the raw agricultural product from rising to its legal minimum or staying there. In the case of cotton textiles this provision must be applied separately to each major item made in whole or in major part from cotton or cotton yarn.

2. They must allow a generally fair and equitable margin for processing. This requirement repeats and emphasizes the requirement that maximum prices must be generally fair and equitable.

In some instances price increases above the levels required for general fairness and equity, or above some of the special standards for agricultural commodities and their products, may be needed to aid in securing essential supply. In single-line industries producing only one general type of commodity, such increases will usually be needed, if at all, only by some of the firms, since the industry earnings standard assures to the industry as a whole its peacetime earnings, and under these conditions the lower cost firms in the industry will ordinarily have costs well below the existing ceiling price. The attempt has been made

---

[1] *Gillespie-Rogers-Pyatt Co., Inc., et al. v. Chester Bowles*, 144 F. (2d) 361, Aug. 24, 1944.

to handle such cases by individual price adjustments confined to the firms which need them. Where individual price adjustments are made, the standard used is to bring the price up to manufacturing cost, total cost, or total cost plus a moderate profit, depending on the nature of the industry and the current profit position of the firm. Where technical factors require a uniform price for all sellers and individual adjustments above the ceiling therefore cannot be used, the ceiling price is raised to cover the cost of the highest cost firm whose supply is needed.[1] Cost here means direct cost or total cost or something between, depending on the circumstances.

The most difficult problem is posed where a multiple-product industry can shift its production from one line to another, depending upon the relative profitability. In a "sellers' market" an industry may drop not only lines which have become unprofitable but also the lower margin lines, unless it is prevented from doing so. The lower price merchandise has usually carried lower profit margins. Hence the shift to the more profitable lines is a shift to higher price merchandise which raises the cost of living. This process has been most evident in clothing, which is the only important field in the cost of living in which effective price stabilization was not achieved some time ago.

In reality there is no completely satisfactory solution to this problem of shifting production in accordance with relative profitability. To equalize profit margins on all products at the level of the highest margin on any of the products would be highly inflationary. To say, on the other hand, that the war-supply and war-procurement agencies must get what is needed at existing maximum prices so long as these equal or exceed the minimum requirements of law—the standards outlined above —would place a heavy burden on direct controls of production by these agencies. They might have to order firms to produce a good on which there was no profit at all and forbid production of another which was highly profitable. In fact, the war-procurement agencies are not often willing to take so much of the burden. To make an "even-Stephen" price readjustment, reducing prices on the higher price products and increasing prices on the lower price products, is often impossible because the pattern of relative production of the products differs greatly between the firms comprising the industry.

---

[1] In a number of instances subsidy or government purchase plans have been used to avoid the necessity of raising the price of the whole supply up to the price needed for the marginal increments.

The position has been that the war agencies should use their powers of direct control, provided price impediments are removed by raising the price to a level at which firms can reasonably be expected to produce. As OPA interprets it, this calls for a price increase on a particular product sold by multiple-line firms so as to cover at least manufacturing cost on that product, often total cost, or, if over-all earnings from all operations are not satisfactory, total cost plus a moderate profit.

Here, also, such cases are handled by individual price adjustments confined to the firms which need them, in order to minimize the total amount of price increase involved.

OPA's pricing methods and policies may be summarized as follows: Prices were taken approximately where found when controls were first instituted. The job of getting everything under control extended from the summer of 1940 to the end of 1943. Increases subsequent to initiation of control have been permitted on grounds of fairness, for which the test is peacetime earnings, or current cash loss, or the special standards for farm commodities; *and* on grounds of supply, for which the tests are stricter than would apply in a free market. OPA has used real incentive pricing rather little. The war-procurement agencies have, however, used incentive pricing to a larger extent in those areas into which OPA control has not been extended, chiefly finished combat equipment and many parts and subassemblies thereof.

The principal result of the application of these pricing standards is that severe inflation has been prevented and that the framework of general price stability has facilitated the remarkable expansion of production. When the results of wage control are brought into the picture, it can be said that a very satisfactory measure of general economic stabilization has been obtained. During the period of stabilization controls, profits, farm income, and labor income have reached unprecedented heights. Finally, it appears that the *general* relations of the levels of prices, wages, and profits in the economy as a whole are not a bad starting point for transition to a peacetime economy.

There is no reason to think, however, that the present relative cost-price-profit relationships between products and between industries are the particular set of relationships that would be most conducive to a rapid and smooth transition to a full-employment, full-production peacetime economy. These intercommodity and interindustry price-cost-profit relations have come into being as a result of a varied complex of wartime influences of which price control and wage control are only a part, albeit a very significant part. They have not been planned. They are obviously not the intercommodity, interindustry relationships which free market forces, if permitted to operate, would bring about under present wartime conditions. And they differ strikingly from the relationships existing in the past few peacetime years.

Price movements in different commodity fields have been quite diverse since prewar years. Using 1935–1939 prices as a base of 100, the indexes of several commodity groups in the Bureau of Labor Statistics wholesale index in October, 1944, were as shown in Table 1.

Table 1

All commodities.............	129	All chemicals and drugs.....	133
Iron and steel................	104	Tires and tubes.............	137
All fuel and lighting..........	110	Woolen and worsted goods...	138
Chemicals....................	110	All textile products..........	140
Cereal products..............	112	Dairy products..............	142
All metals and metal products.	113	Livestock and poultry........	153
Nonferrous metals............	113	Cotton goods................	156
Meats.......................	120	Grains......................	161
Shoes.......................	124	All farm products............	162
Furniture....................	125	Fats and oils................	170
Paper and pulp..............	128	Lumber.....................	171
All building materials........	130	Fruits and vegetables........	171
Clothing....................	130	Cattle feed.................	176
All foods....................	132		

The disparity in price movements since the war began is to be explained by a number of factors, among which are the following: (1) difference in movement before the fall of 1940 when price control began; (2) differences in movement between the fall of 1940 and the dates when control was imposed on different commodities; (3) the special statutory standards for farm prices; (4) some unevenness in application of OPA standards; (5) differences in supply problems, including wage problems, reflected in maximum prices. For example, some industries had abnormally low wages which had to be raised greatly in order to hold man power; some industries had more disparity in cost between the low- and high-cost producers and thus needed more increase in prices to assure needed supplies, etc.

The profit picture also shows substantial changes between industry groups, as indicated by Table 2.

TABLE 2.—Profits before Income Taxes of 1,910 Leading Industrial Corporations *
(1936–1939 Average and 1943)

No. of companies	Industrial groups	Indexes of aggregate dollar profits before income taxes in 1943 † (1936–1939 = 100)	Profits before income taxes as a percentage of			
			Sales		Net worth ‡	
			1936–1939 average, per cent	1943, per cent	1936–1939 average, per cent	1943, per cent
1,910	Total of all groups................	343	8.0	11.6	9.4	28.0
771	Durable-goods manufacturing.........	430	10.1	12.4	10.1	36.7
818	Nondurable-goods manufacturing.....	283	7.3	10.9	8.8	22.0
321	Nonmanufacturing..................	279	6.6	10.9	9.5	22.8
	Selected industrial groups §					
21	Aircraft and parts...................	4,109	11.5	9.2	17.1	129.1
80	Chemicals..........................	242	16.2	18.8	13.5	25.7
29	Crude petroleum and natural gas.....	199	17.1	21.7	8.6	17.4
218	Food and kindred products..........	291	4.3	6.7	9.2	24.9
139	Iron and steel and their products.....	438	7.4	11.6	5.7	22.6
55	Leather and leather products.........	481	3.3	9.4	7.0	29.5
80	Machinery—electrical...............	516	11.8	15.5	13.7	56.9
221	Machinery—nonelectrical............	454	12.0	17.4	11.7	42.4
18	Metal mining (exclusive gold and silver)............................	227	21.6	20.5	8.4	14.5
16	Motor vehicles......................	215	12.8	10.4	21.7	35.3
36	Motor-vehicle parts and accessories....	936	6.3	12.2	11.3	90.1
62	Nonferrous metals and their products..	325	6.9	11.7	8.3	30.7
88	Paper and allied products............	404	6.1	14.0	5.3	20.3
27	Petroleum refining..................	211	10.0	13.9	6.9	13.0
14	Railroad equipment.................	758	8.1	12.8	4.4	36.9
125	Retail trade........................	248	5.2	7.9	12.9	26.1
17	Rubber products....................	712	5.9	13.7	8.9	53.5
91	Stone, clay, and glass products........	204	11.9	13.5	9.9	19.5
210	Textile-mill products................	603	4.4	12.3	5.4	28.7
20	Tobacco products...................	136	11.1	9.3	15.7	20.2

NOTE: These figures have been prepared by the Division of Research of OPA from OPA *Financial Reports*, Moody's *Industrials*, and Standard & Poor's *Corporation Records*. Indexes and returns are based on profits before Minority Interest and Contingency Reserves which are deemed to be nonallowable appropriations from current income. Renegotiation reserves have been allowed as an expense, and deducted from profits in every case where the amount set aside was shown as an expense or was known to be included in the provision for income taxes.

* Includes only corporations with total assets of $250,000 or more.

† Profit indexes are based on all 1,910 corporations; returns on sales and net worth are based on only 1,676 of these corporations which reported complete financial data in all years. However, the reduction in coverage was fairly evenly distributed among the industrial groups and was not concentrated in a few.

‡ Net worth is the sum of the common and preferred stocks, surplus, and surplus reserves. The return has been calculated on the average of net worth at the beginning and end of each year.

§ Fifteen groups, totaling 343 companies, were omitted because of small coverage of the industries.

III. Transition Price Problems

In discussing transition problems it is necessary to make some broad assumptions about the future changes in the war-production program. Indeed, for a truly refined analysis, detailed assumptions would be needed on a host of factors, such as future changes in the man-power situation (apart from the direct effects of cutbacks in war production), fiscal policies, the propensities of individuals and of business to spend their incomes and invest their savings, the international situation, and the like. No detailed set of assumptions covering all these factors can be made here.

The following basic assumptions are made: (1) that the war in Europe will end before the close of the war in the East and that there will be no substantial cutback in war production until the European war is over or, at least, until the end is in sight; (2) that the intervening period between the first substantial cutback in war production and the end of the war in the East will be long enough—say, 8 to 15 months—to constitute a separate period with conditions substantially different from those of the periods preceding and following it; (3) that, in the period of the one-front war in the East, war production will be reduced enough to free a substantial quantity of resources for reconversion and present a problem of reemployment of several million workers; and (4) that, after the defeat of Japan, war production will be abruptly cut to very little.

Within wide limits it is impossible to predict the economic situation which will exist at various times during the transition period. It seems reasonably clear, however, that during much of that time both inflationary and deflationary forces will be at work side by side.

The danger of inflation will not disappear with victory in Europe. Serious inflation could occur thereafter, especially during the period while government expenditure on the war in the East is still large. Although the total of money incomes of individuals will be initially reduced in this period by the contraction of the war program, it will still remain quite high unless the cutbacks are much larger than has yet been indicated. Immense potential expenditure exists in the form of very large savings, bank deposits, some potential of credit expansion, substantial foreign dollar balances, and the like. There is a large accumulated backlog of demand for consumers' durable goods, industrial equipment, and construction. Inflationary pressure on prices of these

TRANSITION PRICE PROBLEMS

goods, as they become available, will be great if this accumulated demand expresses itself in a short space of time rather than spreading itself over several years.

Inflationary pressures from the cost side will diminish during the transition period as a result of such factors as a fall in the prices of some basic materials, improvement in the quality of the labor force, some reversal of the wartime upgrading of employees, and utilization of technological improvements. How soon and to what extent influences of this kind will make themselves felt is, however, conjectural. They may be counteracted in part by increases in straight-time labor rates after resumption of the 40-hour week.

The existence of this huge inflation potential signifies the danger of the same sort of scramble for inventories of materials and finished goods which characterized the speculative inventory price boom of 1919–1920. This danger could, of course, be accentuated if a wave of strikes should occur. Thus, inflation might come through failure to control the explosive force of a potential inventory boom. It might also come through failure to hold the cost of living and the consequent upset to the delicate balance between cost of living, wages, and farm prices.

On the other hand, there is danger of a serious depression at one stage or another of the transition. The government is now taking for war approximately half of the output of the economy. During the transition period this will be cut to a small figure. Unless reductions in government demand for war goods are offset in large measure by increased spending from consumers and business on civilian goods and services, reemployment and expansion of civilian production will lag and depression forces may grow. Some reduction in total money income of wage earners is probable, at least in the early part of the transition period, as a result of unemployment, reduction of hours worked, downgrading, and shifts from war jobs to lower paid civilian-goods jobs.

There cannot be a severe depression so long as the government is spending $40 to $60 billion per year, which might be the approximate range within which actual government expenditure would fall during the one-front war in the East. It is possible, however, that the high momentum of war economy might be lost in that period and that the initial unemployment coming from the cutbacks might grow, instead of declining as a result of speedy reconversion. This would put the economy in poor shape to withstand the additional shock of large cuts in war expenditure at the end of the Eastern war. The smaller the reductions in war spending prior to defeat of Japan and the slower the reemployment and reconversion in that period, the greater the task of avoiding depression after the final cutbacks at the end of the Japanese war.

Since it is impossible to predict within broad limits the economic situation which will exist at various times during the transition period, the policies and procedures of price control must be flexible to meet changing conditions.

The objectives of price control are, however, clear. Assurance of a sound, full-production, full-employment peacetime economy and assurance of a smooth and rapid transition to such an economy as well as assurance of adequate war production until Japan is defeated require, among other things, maintenance of general price stability and maintenance in large degree of the high economic momentum of the war economy. It follows that during the transition period price control should (1) continue to prevent inflation wherever and however it threatens and (2) help to promote smooth and rapid reemployment and expansion of civilian production.

Price policies appropriate to these objectives may be summarized in very general terms as follows: As long as inflationary pressures are general and severe, pricing standards must be tight. If the economy begins to lose momentum fast, more liberal pricing standards may be needed. Some changes in interindustry price relationships may be required as conditions change, in order to facilitate transition. Reconversion presents a special price problem since many civilian goods have been out of production for two years or more. Prices of these returning products should give an expectancy of good profits with large volume, taking into consideration elements in the situation which have continuing rather than temporary significance.

Ceiling price control can contribute greatly to an orderly transition to a sound, high-level peacetime economy by maintaining a facilitating price framework. It cannot, of course, itself supply the driving propulsion needed to obtain full employment and full production. Finally, price controls should be removed in one commodity field after another as the danger of inflation disappears here and there. A temporary hesitation with some softening of prices, due to a temporary fall in demand at the time of cutbacks in war production, should not be mistaken for a true balance of supply and demand.

Let us now discuss these policy problems.

1. PREVENTION OF INFLATION

As long as there exist serious general inflationary pressures in the economy—pressures from a general excess of demand over supply, pressures from cost increases actual and potential, and widespread pressures for wage increases—the principal responsibility of price control is to hold prices firmly in check. As long as these conditions continue, the balance of cost of living, wages, and farm prices, which is partly economic, partly political, will be a precarious balance. "Hold the line" means hold the balance.

The existing balance has been successfully held for over a year and a half. If it is once upset by a sharp advance in any of the three elements, a new balance could be established, if at all, only at much higher levels.

This means that until general inflationary pressures no longer threaten, the price-control agency must continue to use strict pricing standards, such as those outlined in part II of this chapter, which are adequate to prevent a break-through on the price line. It also means that in many instances direct controls on production and distribution, such as production directives and limitation orders, simplification and standardization orders, allocation and priority systems, and rationing controls will continue to be needed as supplementing controls. Such direct controls, instituted by war supply agencies, have been established with the primary purpose of assuring production and proper distribution of war goods and essential civilian goods. In many instances, however, these controls have also been a great aid to effective price stabilization by reducing the actual effective demand, limiting the shift from production of lower priced to higher priced articles, and restricting the production of new styles, varieties, or models of a commodity which, as we have seen above, often cannot be held exactly in line with prices of the items which they supersede.

Finally, continued cooperation and compliance by business and all other groups will be needed. Without continuation of the high degree of compliance by business and the fine cooperation shown in many different ways by the various groups, it is doubtful that price control could be as effective as it has been.

As noted earlier, there will be danger, some months after victory in Europe, of an inventory price boom such as occurred in 1919–1920. Inflationary potentialities will be far greater than they were in 1919. Continuance of effective price control should go far to give a general expectation in the business world that prices will not rise appreciably, and hence to remove in large part the motive for the scramble for inventories. To scotch this virus completely, however, control of inventories may also be needed.

Disposal of government surplus commodities presents a special pricing problem. Although much of this merchandise can command only low prices, many consumer goods could be sold at prices much above the ceilings on the same or comparable articles. Maximum prices for sale of government surplus goods should be in line with ceilings on the same or comparable merchandise sold by private industry. Otherwise consumers will be exploited and observance of ceilings by private industry will be weakened. Subject to this limitation the government should, as a rule, obtain the best prices possible for the surplus commodities.

2. RECONVERSION PRICING

The special problem of prices of the goods that return to production as the war plants reconvert to civilian output focuses sharply both objectives of price control during the transition period: to continue to prevent inflation and to facilitate the transition.

It is estimated that the metal-using consumer durable goods, which represent the largest part of the "reconversion goods," accounted for about 8.5 per cent of total consumer expenditures in 1941, a not inconsiderable part of the cost of living. Unnecessary price increases in this field would jeopardize stabilization of the cost of living.

Reconversion pricing is also important in relation to the objective of facilitating rapid and orderly transition. The problem of the relation between maximum prices and production, investment, and employment will be most clearly evident in this field.

The term "reconversion pricing" is used here to mean the pricing of goods which have been out of production for some time past as a result of government orders incident to the war-production program. Nearly all of these "reconversion goods," such as automobiles, refrigerators, egg beaters, and garden shears, have ceiling prices established before they left the market. Most of these ceiling prices are based on March, 1942, levels. Hence pricing of these goods means reappraisal of the last ceiling prices.

Ordinarily OPA makes an appraisal of established ceiling prices by application of the pricing standards outlined in part II. These pricing standards are applied by using recorded costs and earnings of the most current period for which such data are obtainable. Projections or estimates of change in costs or earnings are made only on the basis of known changes, the effect of which can be estimated with close approximation. In other words, appraisal of existing ceiling prices is made on the basis of the actual record without consideration of changes which are possible but not certain or changes the effect of which cannot be closely estimated. In reconversion pricing it is necessary, however, to appraise the last ceiling prices without benefit of an actual cost and earnings record of a current period. It would be inconsistent with the objectives of price control in the transition period to refuse to reappraise the last ceiling prices until a record of costs and earnings was available from actual operations over a period. Moreover, the actual costs in the earlier months of operation may be abnormally high on account of temporary influences.

Hence it seems necessary to use for this special problem of reconversion pricing a somewhat different kind of pricing standard which is in line with standards described in part II but takes account of the special characteristics of the reconversion problems. Chief among these special characteristics are various imponderables which render it impossible to estimate future costs and earnings with any assurance. Over a period, labor productivity in these industries will certainly show marked gains over that of 1941 or 1942. How soon after resumption of production these gains can be obtained will often be conjectural, however. Marked uncertainty may also be present with respect to the volume of output attainable in the first 6 months and the second 6 months of operations. It may be quite impossible to predict the extent to which key items of equipment must be held on war production, the rapidity with which replacements of worn-out or obsolete equipment can be obtained, the time at which shortages of particular materials or component parts will disappear.

Special reconversion expenses, such as reconditioning and reinstalling equipment, retraining labor, rebuilding distribution systems, constitute another special characteristic of the reconversion industries.

Finally, the unemployment problem will appear first and most acutely in these industries and in industries supplying basic materials for war goods whose production is cut.

Under these circumstances pricing standards are needed which will result in prices that are generally fair and equitable and which will facilitate reemployment and the largest volume of civilian production consistent with the needs of the war-production program. The pricing standards should not be such as to force deflation of wage rates in an industry. Unless high wage income is maintained, the danger of severe depression at some stage in the transition will be intensified.

In reappraising the last ceiling prices of the "reconversion goods," consideration should be given to increases in straight-time wage rates and in prices of materials and parts since the last normal period of production, which will in many cases be 1941. This does not mean, however, that the cost increases so computed should be added to the prices of that period. During the past three years most industries with products that have been in continuous production have absorbed some part at least of the increases in labor rates and/or material prices and have still enjoyed large profits. In other words, these industries have either had no increase in prices or an increase amounting to less than the simple per unit equivalent of wage-rate and material-price increases. Economies of large volume, reduction in selling expense, improved methods, and shifts to more profitable production patterns are some of the elements which have variously contributed to this result. It seems evident that producers of the reconversion goods will enjoy for some time a sellers' market. Hence it appears that they can, in some measure at least, obtain economies and cost reductions in the transition period similar to those experienced by other industries in the sellers' market of the past three years. The full amount of the increases in wage rates and material prices is thus not to be considered a true cost increase.

Owing to all the various uncertainties of the situation, it will not be possible to make precise estimates of ability to absorb increases in wage rates and prices of materials and parts. The most that can be done is to use the best available evidence, neglecting elements which are purely conjectural.

It is desirable for several reasons that a temporary upward bulge in prices of reconversion goods should not be permitted. First, this would mean a temporary increase in the cost of living for a few months to a year at a time when the balance between cost of living, wages, and farm prices may still be precarious. Second, the task of reducing these prices later would be difficult, especially as long as demand exceeds supply. Third, if prices were not reduced rapidly enough, consumption and production might not expand sufficiently when such expansion is badly needed for the health of the economy.

It follows that, in general, no consideration should be given in reappraising the last ceiling prices to artificial elements of high cost which may be expected to disappear in the near future, such as temporary labor inefficiency, bottlenecks, and misfits in the starting-up period, temporary low volume, and the like. Nor, as a rule, should lump-sum reconversion expenses themselves, including retraining of labor, be considered as requiring a price increase. Studies indicate that, in general, business has ample liquid reserves to defray lump-sum reconversion expenses without harm to its financial health.

The last ceiling prices of the reconversion goods at the manufacturing level should be reappraised from the standpoint of whether they will give an expectancy of good profit on large volume after temporary or artificial elements of high cost are eliminated, taking into account the considerations sketched above. On this test it appears from preliminary studies that, with few exceptions, the reconversion goods will not require substantial increases above the 1942 level of prices. It is further evident that most of such increases as may occur at the manufacturing level can easily be absorbed at distribution levels. Thus prices adequate to facilitate reconversion and expansion of employment and output in the reconversion area will not need to result in much increase in prices to consumers above 1942 levels.

After a period of actual production, the ceiling prices of the reconversion goods can be appraised on the basis of experience and appropriate adjustments made.

3. OTHER PROBLEMS OF FACILITATING TRANSITION

The most important contribution which price control can make to rapid and smooth transition is the maintenance of a general framework of price stability. Proper pricing of the reconversion goods is also imperative for this objective. There are, however, several additional problems relating to prices and transition.

The particular price-cost-profit relationships now existing in a particular industry, and as between industries, are the result of a complex of war influences including price control and wage control. As noted above, there is no reason to think that these relationships are those best suited to promote rapid transition to full peacetime employment and production.[1] In some industries the current price-cost-profit relations are probably well suited for this, in others not. During the transition

---

[1] The price-cost-profit relationships that would have occurred had inflationary pressures been unrestrained by price control would, of course, contain much greater divergencies from the relationships most appropriate to aid the transition.

period very considerable change in these relationships will probably be needed. One can envision a task of realigning prices so as to obtain in each industry the particular price-cost-profit relations which, when all added up together, would present an ideal, integrated pattern of all prices—an ideal integrated pattern in the sense that with these prices the amounts of production, employment, consumer spending, and business spending would be such that total demand and supply in the whole economy would balance at a high level of production and employment.[1] In the present state of knowledge of the relations between the structure of relative prices and incomes on the one hand and the total production and employment in the whole economy on the other hand, we cannot be optimistic concerning the ability to develop a complete picture of the particular interindustry price-cost-profit relations that are appropriate for full employment and full production.[2]

To a large extent, solution of this problem will have to be left to market forces, working under ceilings prior to their removal and without ceiling control thereafter. Price control should, however, undertake to iron out the more serious maladjustments in the price structure, if proper and appropriate standards can be developed.

Another problem, implied here and there above, concerns the relation between price ceilings and the amount of investment or business spending. Price control should be so administered during the transition period as to help encourage adequate investment.

Some persons question whether price control will exercise any significant effect on the rate of investment, one way or the other. Most business firms, it is argued, will make their investment plans on the basis of their expectations of profits *after* removal of price control, paying little attention to the immediate profit prospects while price control is still in the picture. To the price controller this is tempting doctrine, for ascertainment of the prices in various industries which will facilitate the

---

[1] One approach to this problem might be to work several different bills of consumer goods back through Prof. Leontief's *tableau économique*, simultaneously testing different price relations in the attempt to find a set of relations which would produce full employment and full production, on the basis of assumptions about saving, spending out of hoards, investment demands, man power seeking jobs, mobility of man power, and so on. Although it is questionable whether this could be successfully done on the grand scale, use of Leontief's *tableau* may be of aid in disclosing some interindustry price, income, and production relationships which would be far out of line with the relationships appropriate for a full-employment economy.

[2] *Cf.* J. M. Clark, "Educational Functions of Economics after the War," *American Economic Review Supplement*, March, 1944, pp. 65–66.

right amount of investment to maintain a high level of prosperity is a difficult problem. Although there may be some truth in this view as far as some of the large corporations are concerned, its general correctness is doubtful. The investment plans of most small and medium-sized firms, and of some large ones, are probably made on rather short-term expectations and will be considerably influenced by current prices. Also, it is possible that some firms will anticipate some resistance to price increases after price control is removed so that ruling prices will be considered important in their planning.

For these reasons, the price-control agency will have to keep well in mind the importance of permitting prices which will help to encourage investment. This does not imply, however, that price increases will be needed in many industries. Current profits in most industries are so large that there can be little question of their adequacy as an incentive to investment if prospective demand is satisfactory.

4. DECONTROL

Inflationary pressures may be expected to disappear at different times in different commodity fields. Surpluses may appear in some fields at the time of the defeat of Germany. Shortages may persist in others, such as some consumer durable goods, for a considerable time after the defeat of Japan. It would be dangerous to remove price control completely as long as there is danger of harmful price increases in particular fields. Yet it is needless to maintain universal price control when it is no longer needed in some fields. Selective removal of control in one field after another as inflationary dangers subside is the proper policy.

There are no precise criteria by which to decide that control is no longer needed in a particular field. This is a matter of judgment based on the best available estimate of supply and demand conditions during the rest of the transition period. Care should be taken to avoid an underestimate of the coming demand as the transition proceeds. Hesitation and softening of some prices in periods immediately following substantial cutbacks must not be mistaken for a condition of continuing surpluses or of true balance of supply and demand. Premature removal of price ceilings can do more harm than holding them in effect a little longer than necessary. Wherever the true situation is in doubt, suspension of the ceiling is wiser than outright revocation. Ceilings on many commodities of negligible importance in the cost of living can probably be safely removed, however, when man power and materials become abundant enough to preclude any further danger of diversion of resources from more essential to less essential uses.

There are many other important price problems of the transition period which I have not attempted to treat in this short chapter, such as import and export prices in relation to reopening world markets, policy on subsidies and their removal, and the question of whether government-maintained minimum prices might help to counteract ephemeral deflationary forces.

The brief discussion of major problems presented here suggests these conclusions: It has been demonstrated that prices can be successfully stabilized in the face of an enormous inflationary potential, without harm to production and without undue hardship. There is a serious danger of inflation in the transition period, but we can be confident that this can be prevented if there is no weakening of the law or its administration. The transition period will present some new and difficult price-control problems, but there is good reason to think that satisfactory solutions can be worked out with the result that price control can aid significantly in promoting a rapid and orderly transition from the war economy to a full-employment, full-production peacetime economy. Price controls should be removed, on a selective basis, as soon as conditions in one field after another make it safe to do so. It would be foolhardy to risk, by premature removal or relaxation, both the loss of the solid stabilization achievements up to this point and the additional contribution which price control can make in the transition period.

Chapter XII

International Commodity Controls; Cartels and Commodity Agreements[1]

by EDWARD S. MASON

THE WORD "cartel" is currently enjoying an extraordinary and somewhat curious vogue in the United States. Like many more or less technical words adapted for popular consumption, its meaning, while becoming more vague, has become more portentous. The overtones, moreover, are definitely sinister. If international finance is somehow more to be feared than that of the domestic variety, how much more is this true of international cartels! People are either for or against cartels, and very little of the recent literature is devoted to careful description or cool appraisal of cartel activities. Those opposed have relied on such words as "conspiracy," "monopoly," "Fascism," and "treason," while, on the other side, Lord McGowan of Imperial Chemical Industries describes cartels as a means of assuring orderly marketing, planned expansion of international trade, elimination of cutthroat practices, and all that is admirable and reasonable. It must be said that the anti-cartel people have been much more successful than the pro-cartel people in getting their favorite connotations accepted, at least in this country.

Cartels

Cartels, in the narrow—and proper—sense, are agreements between firms in the same branch of trade limiting the freedom of these firms

---

[1] This chapter is based for the most part on a paper ("The Future of International Cartels") published in *Foreign Affairs*, July, 1944. The editors of that journal have allowed us to republish it.

with respect to the production and marketing of their products. Typically, cartel agreements aim at the restriction of output or sales by the member firms, at an allocation of market territories between firms, and a fixing of the price of their products. Such restrictive agreements are, of course, illegal as between firms engaged in domestic trade in the United States, but American firms can form export associations which then, on occasion, have entered into international cartel arrangements with associations or firms in other countries. These American export associations are formed under the Webb-Pomerene law, which contains certain limitations now being tested in a series of antitrust cases. As stated by Wendell Berge, present Chief of the Antitrust Division of the Department of Justice, export associations are not permitted under the Webb law to enter into international agreements which,

(a) restrain trade within the United States; or
(b) restrain the export trade of any domestic competitor or association; or
(c) enhance or depress prices within the United States, substantially lessen competition within the United States, or otherwise restrain trade therein.

Despite these limitations, American firms have in a number of cases entered into full-fledged international cartels fixing prices and allocating markets and, unless the Webb-Pomerene law is more strictly interpreted, may be expected to enter such cartels still more extensively in the postwar period.

Although cartel in the strict sense of the word means a marketing agreement between private firms, in current usage its meaning has been greatly broadened. It is used to include patent and process exchange agreements between firms in different countries such as those which have been consummated with foreign interests by Du Pont, Standard Oil, and International General Electric. Frequently, patent-exchange arrangements contain marketing agreements; indeed, the market agreements may be the real reason for exchange of patents and processing knowledge. This type of cartel arrangement is, perhaps, the one which primarily concerns American firms. Since, however, the market-control features depend in the main on the patent rights which are exchanged, the nature and extent of the restrictions on international trade involved, and the means of avoiding or lessening these restrictions, become technical patent questions which it is not our purpose here to discuss. International cartels are also interpreted to include joint ownership by potential competitors of foreign affiliates, such as the Latin-American

Duperial companies jointly owned by Du Pont and Imperial Chemical Industries.

International cartels are sometimes formed under governmental auspices and with government participation; indeed, some of the best known—most notorious if you will—international cartels have been negotiated by governments. This was true of the prewar tin and rubber cartels. Government-owned enterprises may also—and frequently do—participate in what are, in other respects, private international cartels. As government participation increases—as it promises to do in the postwar period—the international cartel which, in its pure form, is an agreement between private firms, takes on the character of an international commodity agreement. The United States government has entered into commodity agreements respecting wheat and coffee, and agricultural interests are pressing for broader participation after the war. If other governments sponsor and participate in international cartels in industrial materials and manufactured products, not only will a considerable part of the international trade of the world be brought under a high degree of commodity control, but the distinction between cartels and commodity agreements will become progressively less meaningful. In any case, as the term "cartel" is now used, it suggests a much broader range of problems than those relating merely to international marketing agreements between private firms.

Before proceeding to a consideration of some of the problems which a policy with respect to cartels must take into account, two facts bearing on the formation of cartels should be emphasized:

1. Most of the important international cartels have arisen out of situations in which it could be plausibly argued that a serious lack of balance existed between productive capacity and current consumption of the products in question.

2. A functioning international cartel has usually required the effective prior "organization" of producers in the domestic market.

The formation of international cartels in rubber, tin, nitrates, steel, and many other important products was preceded by situations in the participating countries considered to be unsatisfactory by politically important producing interests. Productive capacity existed for outputs greater than could be absorbed on the world market at prices sufficient to maintain the owners of this capacity in the style to which they had become accustomed. In some cases, the number of workers employed was large and falling world-market prices had seriously influenced wage rates. In others, the exports in question were heavily relied on for government revenues and for foreign exchange. When producing groups are confronted with declining or inadequate markets, they turn naturally to methods of controlling output and price. If private action proves inadequate, appeal is made to the state and, if the groups in question are politically influential, the appeal is usually not made in vain.

Given excess capacity—either real or arguable—in politically important sectors of the economy, demands for relief will arise. Relief may be provided by limiting imports of the affected commodities, either directly or by protective tariff. Relief may be provided by export bounties, by production subsidies, and in many other ways. Among these other ways is the formation of an international cartel which will "adjust supply to demand" (*i.e.*, restrict output), which will provide for "orderly distribution" (*i.e.*, allocate market territories), and which will "stabilize prices" (*i.e.*, raise prices). In the postwar period, partly as a result of war-expanded output, we may expect to be confronted by excess-capacity situations in many countries, and on a large scale. The only successful remedies will be the maintenance of a high level of income in the principal countries of the world accompanied by a shift in resources out of war-expanded industries into other employment. Yet we may expect other remedies to be suggested which will take the form of restriction of imports, export subsidies, and international cartels with or without government participation. In many cases cartel agreements will appear to governments confronted by excess capacity or balance-of-payment difficulties to be preferable to other types of restrictive arrangements.

This will be particularly true in countries in which domestic industries are already well organized or, if one prefers a synonym, monopolized. The members of international cartels are ordinarily either very large firms controlling a predominant share of the export of the cartelized product from a given country or export associations including the principal exporters of such products. Restriction of output or exports, a typical cartel activity, frequently requires an allocation of shares in the restricted quantities as between the member firms. Such allocation, if it is to be effective, may require policing or control measures on the part of the export association. Unless export business is completely separated from domestic production, effective cartelization for exports is difficult without considerable control of the domestic market. English participation in the European steel cartel, for example, was impracticable as long as the tradition of competition between steel producers ruled the domestic market and, when English exporters were finally brought into the cartel, this action was accompanied by a substantial cartelization, at government insistence, of the domestic market.

Extensive American participation in cartels would likewise presumably require a considerable measure of cooperation between firms in the domestic market. Since, however, the United States is rather enthusiastically committed to an antitrust policy at home, such participation appears unlikely at least in those industries in which exporting firms are not only numerous but also engaged in production for the domestic market. Our antipathy to monopoly, however, is not shared by other countries. In many European countries international cartels will be favorably considered, along with import restrictions, export bounties, and other measures, as a means of coping with excess production in the postwar period. Industries are so organized domestically as to be able to take up with international cartels where they left off at the outbreak of war and to carry these arrangements to a bigger if not better future.

A discussion of the effects of international cartels may fairly center on the following three aspects of cartel practice:

1. TRADE-BARRIER ASPECTS. Cartels are said to involve privately imposed limitations on the free flow of commodities in international trade.

2. SECURITY ASPECTS. The participation of American firms in international cartel arrangements is alleged to have involved restriction by these firms of the production and development of products and processes necessary to the war effort, and the use of American connections for enemy espionage purposes.

3. POLITICAL ASPECTS. International cartels are said to promote a relationship between private enterprise and the state which may involve

   a. the use of the power of the state to further the purposes of private interests; and
   b. the use by the state of business enterprises as instrumentalities of public policy.

There are also various cartel problems which might be treated under the general heading "economic warfare." International cartel connections have posed certain difficulties for blacklisting and other economic-warfare policies by reason of ambiguities of ownership and the mobility of assets involved in such connections. These problems are not, however, limited to cartels nor will they be of much significance in the postwar period.

CARTELS AS TRADE BARRIERS

There can be little doubt that international cartels on balance restrict the total volume of world trade, divert to a considerable extent the channels of world trade, and affect, through price and output controls, a considerable proportion of world trade. The primary purpose of cartels is to restrict the freedom of participating firms and associations to compete on the world markets, and cartels would not long continue to exist if prices and outputs under cartelization were not more satisfactory to participating members than they would be with competition unrestrained. Instances are numerous in which tariff reductions have not produced an expected increase in imports because market allocations by cartels have restrained foreign producers from selling outside of allocated territory. On occasion, it is true, cartel restrictions may have increased the total volume of world trade. High cartel prices have frequently brought into the market productive capacity and a volume of exports greater than would have existed had the cartels in question not been forced. If an international cartel, by threatening to cut prices in a particular country, prevents the installation of domestic capacity, imports into that country may be maintained and, along with them, world trade. This result has been achieved on more than one occasion in Latin-American countries. Such expansion of trade, however, is not likely to be adduced as a merit of cartelization.

The influence of cartels on the diversion of trade from normal competitive channels is undoubtedly greater than is their influence on the total volume of trade. International cartelization tends to divide the world into spheres of commercial influence by allocating to the nationals of particular countries exclusive selling rights—apart from outsiders—in allocated territory. American firms, through cartel arrangements, are normally assigned the United States market, sometimes the whole of North America, and on occasion parts of South America. British firms have special claims to Empire territory and, in the period before the war, the growing strength of German participation in a number of cartels led to the assignment of increasing areas of European territory to German cartel participants. In the period between the wars mandated areas were frequently reserved by cartel agreement to the firms of the country holding the mandate and, as we shall see later, there is a clear tendency for cartel allocations to follow the lines of political influence.

Although, in general, international cartels tend to restrict the volume of world trade, it does not necessarily follow that restriction is in all cases undesirable nor that, under the competitive conditions facing American firms, American participation in such cartels would lessen our foreign trade.

Restriction of the exports of strategic materials to present aggressor nations may be one of the policies followed by an international security organization in the postwar period and, if so, fairly serious restraint of foreign trade will be involved. Unrestricted competition between the nationals of various countries may lead to the rapid exhaustion or the wasteful exploitation of irreplaceable resources; if so, the case for regulation and restriction is a strong one. In some branches of commerce, of a public-utility character, such as shipping, air transport, and international communications, competition between the nationals of the various countries concerned is not likely to produce desirable results and agreements limiting the freedom of the competing interests are probably necessary. The immediate postwar period will see a number of industries expanded beyond the needs of civilian consumption. Temporary control of international competition pending a conversion of facilities and a shift of man power into other employment is perhaps desirable.

All these areas of foreign trade in which a restriction of competition may serve broader interests than those of the producers immediately involved raise questions concerning the appropriateness of private cartels as the restricting and regulating agency. If an international agreement restricting trade is necessary to accomplish a purpose widely recognized to be within the public interest of several states, the agreement should presumably be consummated by public bodies rather than by private business enterprises. The word presumably is used advisedly since the intervention of the state in foreign trade introduces a possibility of political conflict which may be more dangerous to the maintenance of peace than are conflicts between private cartel interests. The other side of the picture is that a tradition of governmental agreements on specific and relatively minor matters is probably necessary to broader international agreements on the vital questions of war and peace.

It does not follow that because international cartels restrict foreign trade, American participation in cartels will restrict American trade.

With a goodly part of world trade already cartelized, it has been argued that American participation is necessary in order to maintain or increase our exports. It is said that by local price cutting, monopolization of distributing outlets, and other practices, fair and unfair, foreign cartels can effectively deny certain foreign markets to certain American products whereas, if American firms were members of the cartel, access to these markets would be secure. This argument is difficult to document and, on its face, not very plausible. High cartel prices abroad offer excellent competitive opportunities to American enterprise, and cartel practices have in all probability lost more business to American competition than they have ever gained from it.

A more serious danger to our exports rests in the influence which foreign cartels on occasion exert on the governments of their national participants. Through this influence tariff barriers may be raised against our products and our exports impeded by other forms of state action. Although American participation in international cartels might lessen these barriers, it would probably be at the expense of a smaller share of the foreign market than might be won by outright competition. Moreover, it is within the power of our government to deal with trade barriers raised against our products by the usual international bargaining processes. There is, however, truth in the contention that if the trade of the rest of the world is cartelized and our own exporters excluded from cartel participation, we shall purchase our imports at monopoly prices and sell our exports on world markets at competitive prices. The terms of trade, in technical language, may be turned against us by foreign cartel activities. Again, however, this is probably a matter to be handled through the bargaining powers of the American government rather than by permitting cartel participation to American export firms.

In general, it may be said that private cartel restrictions constitute a definite type of trade barrier, that the seriousness of this trade barrier is greatly increased by government support of cartel practices, and that neither world trade nor American trade is likely to increase through American participation in cartels, regardless of how widespread are cartel ramifications in other countries.

SECURITY ASPECTS OF CARTELS

The fierce light of Congressional investigation and antitrust prosecution has in recent years beaten on certain American firms which in the prewar years entered into patents and processing arrangements, mainly with German firms, involving, in a number of cases, market agreements extending considerably beyond legitimate patent rights. The committee hearings and the antitrust prosecutions have been surrounded by effective publicity on an absorbing subject, and the implications of the agreements have, in consequence, lost nothing in the telling. Out of the facts thereby revealed (of which the most complete compilation is in the Bone Committee reports) have grown various generalizations ranging from a description of the American participants as dupes and their firms as cogs in a "German master plan" to a characterization of international cartels as essentially Fascist institutions without differentiation between the Fascist potentialities of the various national participants. Whatever the generalization, there has been no doubt in the minds of the generalizers that American participation in international cartels is highly dangerous to American security.

Antitrust cases against American firms restrained by agreement with German firms in their freedom to develop or produce useful war materials were effective in the early stages of the war in eliminating these restraints and releasing, thereby, American production. The much publicized cases of magnesium, beryllium, military optical instruments, and synthetic rubber are too well known to require further comment. Whether the patents and processing agreements between American and German firms have, on balance, hampered American war production is, however, an open question. To answer that question we would need to know the value of the technical knowledge disclosed by both sides and the uses, considering the restrictions imposed in the contracts, to which this knowledge has been put. To date only one side of this story has been effectively told. There can be little doubt that the Nazi government exercised much more careful supervision of the disclosure by its nationals of technical knowledge having potential military usefulness than did the American government nor that, on occasion, the disclosure to American firms was accompanied by restrictions framed with an eye to the military ends of the Nazi state. It would be very difficult for the American government to exercise that degree of supervision without a pretty serious alteration of our political and economic traditions. No doubt the exchange of technical information by American firms holding important Army and Navy contracts will have to be scrutinized more carefully in the future, but it is more than doubtful whether the exclusion of these firms from an international exchange of patents and processing knowledge, even of the prewar type, would benefit this country either in war or in peace.

International cartel connections have been used by nationals of our present enemies for espionage purposes and, particularly in Latin America, for political propaganda and psychological warfare. It is hard to see, however, that these activities raise questions peculiar to cartels. Foreign affiliates and foreign agencies can and do serve much the same purpose. The intimate relations between nationals of different countries involved in the exchange of laboratory and processing information may be peculiarly suited to such purposes, but these arrangements do not necessarily involve participation in cartels.

There is, of course, a widely spread doctrine that the foreign economic interests of monopoly capitalists are a primary source of war and, since the interests of such capitalists are frequently served through international cartels, cartels are in some sense a menace to peace. "The internationalism of international cartels is the most dangerous type of internationalism." Insofar as cartel participants enlist the support of their respective governments, thus bringing the interests of the state into what would otherwise be the concern of private enterprise, there may be some truth in this thesis. The danger, however, lies primarily in substituting state conflict for the conflict of private interests, not in the attempt of business interests to lessen international competition by private agreements.

One of the most ominous attempts of organized business groups to secure state support for international restrictive arrangements, an attempt which, had it succeeded, would almost certainly have produced extreme international friction, was the Düsseldorf discussion undertaken shortly before the war by the leading British and German industrial associations. In a joint communiqué it was declared that:

> Both organizations are fully aware that the advantages of agreements between the industries of two countries or of two regions could be frustrated by the uneconomic competition of the industry of another country refusing to join the agreement. In such cases it might become necessary for the organization to ask for the *support of its government*. Both organizations agree to ask for such support if the need arises.

POLITICAL ASPECTS OF INTERNATIONAL CARTELS

Although examples are not lacking of the use of international cartel connections to avoid legitimate obligations to government such as the payment of customs duties, compliance with domestic legislation, administrative rulings, and the like, the important political questions have to do with state action in the interests of cartel participants and the use by the state of the cartel as an instrument of public policy.

The American government, in keeping with our strong antitrust tradition, has pursued a policy of arm's-length dealing with business associations both in domestic and foreign trade which is unique among industrial nations. The British government went very far in the prewar years in permitting and encouraging business control of output and prices in the domestic market and the participation, through export associations, of British industries in international cartels. State assistance in the formation of cartels and the policing of cartel regulations was a common feature of continental industry, and the enlisting of governmental support in international cartel negotiations had become almost standard practice.

The granting of tariff protection to increase the bargaining position of their nationals in cartel quota allocations was a policy followed by many European governments. As Sir Alfred Mond, organizer of the British Imperial Chemical Industries, observed:

> In negotiation, the man behind the tariff wall always has something with which to bargain, which the man in the Free Trade country has not. Any one who has had practical experience of bargaining with continental producers knows that the first thing they say is: "You cannot export to our country, because we have a tariff. How much of your market are you going to give us?"

Cartel participants have also solicited the help of their governments in enforcing domestic cartel regulations and in negotiating more effective international agreements. Private attempts to cartelize the production and export of tin and rubber were ineffectual, and it required the cooperation of the governments of the principal producing areas to make these attempts successful. Private cartel arrangements always run the risk of nonobservance by certain members of controls upon which the effectiveness of the cartel depends, and resort to government is frequently the only course of action which can assure satisfactory results.

For these reasons and because of increasing public awareness of the character of the trade barriers which cartel regulations impose, it is probable that, if the postwar period sees an expansion of international cartelization, it will be under the sponsorship and regulation of governments. Private interests would suffer thereby some infringement of their freedom of action, but cartel controls would be much more effectively enforced. Within this framework the term "regulation" should not be taken too seriously. The experience of European governments in the regulation of cartels is both extensive and unhappy. Government sponsorship of the participation by their nationals in international cartels would, no doubt, impose limitations on private action. Publicity might be required as well as the avoidance of the grosser forms of restrictive practice. But there is no reason to expect and, on the basis of experience, every reason not to expect, that effective regulation of cartel output and price policies in the interests of groups broader than those composed of cartel members would be accomplished. Governments will sponsor and regulate cartels with an eye mainly to the expansion of the exports of their nationals, and the more important foreign-trade interests are in the economy of a country, the more active will be government support and the less likely will be a consideration of anything other than export interests.

This view is further supported by the behavior of those government-owned firms which participated in essentially private international cartels in the period between the wars. Government-owned aluminum-, timber-, nitrogen-, potash-, and phosphate-producing or -exporting enterprises participated in all the restrictive practices pursued by the cartels of which they were members.

As governments penetrate into cartel activities, private controls are not only in part circumscribed, but cartel arrangements become available to the state as vehicles of foreign policy. In the mercantile period many foreign trading companies were semipolitical in character. The British government accomplished through the East India and the Levant companies tasks which, in the nineteenth century, were the sole prerogative of state officials. There is considerable evidence that semi-public cartels engaged in foreign trade may come to fulfill similar purposes: Mention has already been made of the use by the Nazis of German cartel connections to attain various military objectives. Cartels, moreover, have been one of the important instrumentalities in the integration, during the last four years, of European industry under German control.

If, in the postwar period, limited world supplies of strategic materials are to be produced and allocated by cartels with government participation, private interests are likely to be overshadowed by the security considerations of the government participants. Likewise spheres of political influence in Europe and elsewhere will have their effect upon the scope and function of cartel activities.

The interpenetration of government and business in foreign-trade activities creates problems which are likely to be of serious concern to this country. In the United States, more perhaps than in any other country, business has remained private, and public affairs have been carried on by public officials. Nor is our form of government well adapted to a flexible interrelationship of public and private interests in foreign affairs. It would be well for us to recognize that, abroad, the trend of events appears to be quite definitely in the direction of greater state participation in all forms of foreign economic activity.

Commodity Agreements

This interpenetration in other countries of government and business should be taken into account in the formulation of American policy toward intergovernmental commodity agreements. It is possible that the role of such agreements in postwar international trade will be large, and it is important that American interests with respect to such agreements be clearly perceived.

The traditional case for intergovernmental commodity controls rests upon certain characteristics of raw-material production; *viz.*, a tendency toward the emergence of chronic surpluses, excessive price instability, and wasteful methods of exploitation. Chronic surplus production is particularly prevalent in agricultural industries, especially foodstuffs. The consumption of foodstuffs increases slowly and is not very responsive to a decline in price. The rate of growth of agricultural output per worker has, within recent years, been rapid. Under these circumstances the prices of agricultural products—apart from government subsidy—could be maintained only by a large transfer of workers out of agriculture. The worker-owner character of agricultural production, however, and the lack of jobs in industry have hampered such transfer with the result that, in the interwar period, the terms of trade between agriculture and industry tended to move markedly against agriculture. In this sense agricultural products tend to be produced in chronic surplus, and there are strong reasons for believing that this situation will persist in the postwar period.

The prices both of foodstuffs and of industrial raw materials, moreover, are notoriously unstable. In the case of foodstuffs the unresponsiveness of demand to price changes together with large harvest variations and, in some cases, an inverse elasticity of supply with respect to price, makes for great price fluctuations. The consumption of industrial raw materials varies with industrial output and is complicated by large inventory accumulations and decumulations in anticipation of price changes. In the absence of output controls the prices of these materials tend to fluctuate wildly. It is argued, therefore, that intergovernmental commodity controls are advisable in the interest of maintaining raw-material price stability.

Finally, the unregulated overcropping of certain resources and the wasteful exploitation of irreplaceable deposits may be difficult to avoid without international commodity controls. Such controls have been applied with benefit to certain branches of the fishing industry and have an obvious potential utility in the field of metals and minerals.

This is the traditional case for intergovernmental commodity controls, and it is alleged that in the absence of such controls, countries, particularly the exporters of raw materials, will be inclined to take unilateral action which will hamper the flow of goods in international trade more seriously than would commodity agreements. In the postwar period, furthermore, the potential scope of commodity controls will probably be broadened to include intergovernmental action regarding strategic materials. Exports of strategic materials to potential aggressor nations may be subject to control. The competition of the great powers for control of existing sources of scarce materials may lead to some sort of intergovernmental agreement regulating the production and distribution of these materials.

Obviously, the area of possible intergovernmental commodity regulation is a large one. In formulating American policy in this area, however, it must be emphasized: (1) that American interests run very strongly in the direction of a relatively unimpeded flow of commodities in foreign trade, (2) that the United States is predominantly an importer and not an exporter of raw materials, and (3) that it is impossible to undertake extensive international commodity controls without a pretty thoroughgoing control, either by government or by private monopoly, of the domestic market.

As an industrial country with a rapidly growing output potential, we are becoming a continually larger importer of raw materials and will be adversely affected by restrictive raw-material controls.[1] As a creditor country the United States has a primary interest in a large volume of international trade and in the convertibility of foreign currencies which is dependent on that trade. The maintenance of a high level of domestic employment is significantly dependent on our finding export markets for an increasing volume of industrial products. Finally, and most important, we have a strong political interest in preventing a development of world trade in the direction of economic blocs and spheres of influence.

If foreign-trade statistics are compared with national-income data, a close correlation is evident between changes in the national income and the size of our raw-material import balance. The larger the national income, the greater the excess of imports of raw materials and unprocessed foodstuffs over exports from the United States. It is probable, with a postwar national income of from $130 to $140 billion, that imports of raw materials and unprocessed foodstuffs will exceed exports by an amount of the general order of $750 million. Under these circumstances, it would seem extremely unwise for the United States to promote a system of international controls which is bound to increase the value of our imports more than the value of our exports.

Finally, international commodity controls, whether governmental or private, are ineffective without a prior organization of a system of domestic commodity controls. We have already gone a long way in developing such controls in the field of agriculture. How far do we want to go in this direction in the field of industrial products? Unless we wish to undertake an extensive reorientation of the relation of business to government in the United States, it would appear wise in formulating our policy toward intergovernmental commodity controls to draw a sharp distinction between owner-worker industries, typically agricultural, and others. And with respect to the former, it would be also wise to remember that our import interests in the products of such industries are more important than our export interests.

Within the framework of a commercial policy favorable to American interests, it must, however, be recognized that intergovernmental commodity agreements will have a place. Even after a transition period, in which disposal of war surpluses will call for international commodity

[1] The next two pages are largely taken from a contribution by the author to the Proceedings of the Norman Wait Harris Foundation meeting, September, 1944, entitled, "The Future of Commodity Agreements."

action, intergovernmental controls will be necessary to meet a set of special situations. The export of strategic materials to potential aggressors may have to be limited; agreements regulating overcropping or wasteful methods of extracting irreplaceable national resources will inevitably increase in number and importance; unmanageable agricultural surpluses will exist in certain areas even on an optimistic forecast of world trade; in some commodity agreements, involving effective output controls, buffer-stock programs for evening out price fluctuations may be practicable.

However—and this is the central point—the use of intergovernmental commodity controls should be subordinated to the requirements of a commercial policy oriented in the direction of an expansion of world trade and a reduction of trade barriers. Such a policy will not bring about the elimination of all quantitative import restrictions, of all exchange rationing, or of all protective or preferential import duties. No more will it—nor should it—accomplish the elimination of commodity controls. What it should accomplish, however, is a recognition of commodity controls as an exceptional device whose use is strictly limited to exceptional situations.

Postwar Prospects

The prospects for a liberal foreign-trade policy in the postwar period, including a policy of reducing private as well as public trade barriers, depend primarily on two conditions: the emergence of effective security cooperation among the great powers, and the development of domestic economic policies oriented in the direction of full employment. Effective cooperation among, at least, the great powers is a necessary but not a sufficient condition. In the absence of such cooperation the world might well tend to split into spheres of influence which will have serious economic as well as political connotations. A competition for available supplies of strategic materials would ensue which in itself would be sufficient to blast any chances of a liberal economic solution.

Domestic economic policies, furthermore, designed to promote reasonably full employment of resources are a *sine qua non* for such a solution. It was the depression of the thirties which produced that array of protective tariffs, exchange controls, quantitative limitations, currency depreciation, export subsidies, commodity agreements, and cartel restrictions which had by the end of the decade succeeded in putting international economic relations in a strait jacket. Prolonged depression in the postwar period would maintain all the old restrictions and, no doubt, add new ones.

Since governmental policy respecting commodity controls, public and private, is part and parcel of foreign economic policy broadly conceived, what can be accomplished in the field of cartels and commodity agreements is largely dependent on what can be accomplished in other areas. If the postwar world sees the development of an effective international security organization and sensible domestic policies, it may be possible by international agreement to get rid of the more restrictive types of international commodity controls along with other barriers to foreign trade. There are also other possibilities, in the imposed terms of a peace settlement, of important alterations in the European cartel structure which centered in Germany. It must be recognized, however, that such measures are not likely to be successful unless they conform to the long-run economic interests of the countries affected.

The interests of the United States, both political and economic, run so strongly, at this stage of affairs, in the direction of a liberal foreign policy that the appropriate attitude toward international commodity controls may be said to be predetermined. The fact that this attitude also conforms to a long-established antimonopoly tradition gives assurance that this aspect of a liberal foreign policy will probably have stronger domestic support than some others. It should be recognized, however, that if international events and domestic policies make the possibilities of a liberal international-trade world illusory, we may be confronted with the necessity of a rather drastic change in our attitude toward commodity controls both public and private.

Part IV

MONETARY AND FISCAL PROBLEMS

Chapter XIII

Central and Commercial Banking in Postwar Finance

by HOWARD S. ELLIS

1. MONETARY CONTROL BY THE TREASURY OR BY THE FEDERAL RESERVE?

AS A consequence of the excess reserves of the thirties, and as a consequence of the requirements of war finance more recently, monetary control in the United States has very largely rested in the hands of the Treasury. There are those who believe that the restoration of a peacetime economy will raise the profound question as to whether central banking will continue to exist, at least in a form recognizable under our traditional concepts. Closely allied to this is the question as to whether commercial banking is not "on its way out." The present essay does not attempt to predict the future of central and commercial banking, but it does venture to point out the ways in which the kind of economic order that we have conditions the character of monetary controls and, conversely, the ways in which our money and credit institutions contribute to the general economic evolution.

Of these two undertakings, the first is the easier. It is possible to state with reasonable certainty that a less than full-employment economy would see the continuance of Treasury dominance over money and finance. If *ex ante* savings tend to outstrip *ex ante* investment, the state would exercise the marginally significant purchasing power— whether through the creation of new money by deficit financing or through the activation of existing money balances by taxing and spending. Commercial banking would largely be supplanted—such indeed was the tendency of the thirties—by "cloakroom" banking. These institutions would simply exchange the excess savings of the public for government securities and derive their income from the yield of these securities and from charges for their services as a "chequeries." Central banking—again with the exception of sundry service functions—would disappear. Fiscal policy would have completely absorbed monetary policy. Thus a setting of depression or "secular stagnation" would bring to pass the ideal of the "100 per cent reserve" school of monetary reformers, complete centralization of control of the quantity of money in the hands of a government authority.

Sustained prosperity or cyclical alternations of depression and prosperity would probably, by contrast, perpetuate commercial banking and the central-banking monetary controls with which it has traditionally been associated. On the one hand, the active demand for bank credit which good times produce would provide, either continuously or on the average, a profit inducement to the extension of bank loans. Indeed, some of the advocates of 100 per cent money eventually concluded that in these circumstances it would be difficult to suppress the creation of credit by extragovernmental undertakings. If the multiple expansion of credit were forbidden to the banks, it would spring up with all manner of black-market lenders. On the other hand, paralleling the inability of the banking system to control a general movement toward liquidity, the Treasury does not possess very effective instruments against inflation. Taxation moves slowly, since it awaits Congressional action. Furthermore, the explicit use of taxation to curb inflationary developments in peacetimes would require a degree of illumination of the public and of legislators considerably beyond its present state. Prospectively it will not be possible to dispense with central bank controls, which are administrative and hence available immediately and which can be made to effect all new loans immediately.

In "normal" peacetimes there might seem to be a presumption in favor of a division of labor, the Congress and the Treasury determining the structure of taxation and the Federal Reserve the quantity of credit. Actually, however, this presumption is overridden by the consideration that peacetimes are never normal by an inherent stability of private enterprise, but only as the result of authoritarian controls. It so happens that the Treasury is equipped with legal powers and institutional devices which are relatively powerful and varied on the side of monetary expansion but slow and clumsy on the side of restraining inflation, whereas the reverse prevails for the Central Bank. It is not easy to imagine a rearrangement of powers and prerogatives which would change this much without converting the Treasury to a central bank and the Central Bank to a Treasury. Recent years do not afford many distressing instances of these two institutions working at cross purposes, and the chief financial problems are questions of general policy, not a clash of these monetary institutions.

The conclusion that the state of employment effectively determines the roles of commercial and central banking relatively to the Treasury does not deny that these institutions themselves play a part in determining the character of the economy and the magnitude of its output. It is to this more difficult problem that the present chapter is chiefly addressed. More particularly, what contributions can commercial and central banking make to the attainment of full employment under a predominantly free-enterprise economy?

2. Central Bank Action in the Transition to Peace [1]

The concluding months of war and the one or two years of initial reformation to a peace economy may witness any one of a number of economic sequences. It is argued plausibly in some quarters that we have already passed the peak of activity and that henceforth, uninterrupted by any postwar boom, production will decline gradually throughout the months of war in the Orient, and more rapidly thereafter. Still more probable is a short period of frictional unemployment at the end of European hostilities and then a substantial boom based on deferred demand and the high liquidity of business and public. Adroit public policy might convert this boom into sustained prosperity; or a lack of timely measures may permit it to run off into speculative excesses to which depression would be the inevitable sequel. By the time these pages are printed we shall possibly be well launched upon one of these courses. It is clear that the central banking authorities must be prepared for all contingencies.

Whereas the major problems will eventually be "monetary" in the sense of general inflation and deflation, the intervening months may confront the Federal Reserve System with the more specifically banking problems of supplying the necessary supplements to available resources for industrial reconversion, and of securing sufficient Reserve Bank re-

[1] I am indebted at various points throughout this paper to my associates at the Board of Governors of the Federal Reserve System, including Messrs. Robinson, Thomas, and Parry.

serves to meet the demand for currency if gross national product continues to be high.

a. FEDERAL RESERVE LOANS AND GUARANTEES IN RECONVERSION

The Securities and Exchange Commission has recently concluded that the financial position of United States corporations is sufficiently strong to permit a considerable, and perhaps adequate, expansion of private production into the segments vacated by government, without recourse to outside funds.[1] On its part the business community points to the possibility of a rapid sapping away of liquid resources in meeting pay rolls if hitches in contract termination, in the orderly flow of supplies, in moving government equipment, etc., interrupt the change-over to new production. Such losses, combined with outlays in reordering physical plant, could produce a demand for outside financing, to which of course the commercial banking system would contribute directly or indirectly.

Whether such a general demand should develop or not, the special credit risk of small business would in itself warrant the proposal, incorporated in identical bills introduced by Senator Wagner and Representative Spence, to authorize Federal Reserve bank guarantees or purchases of bank loans to small and medium-size enterprises. This legislation would offset the rigorous limitations set upon Federal Reserve bank loans to small industries under Section 13b of the Federal Reserve Act—the restriction to maturities of five years, to "established" businesses, and to working-capital needs only. In addition to the mere availability of credit, however, small businesses might well be accorded the support of an agency similar to the Smaller War Plants Corporation, which would offer facts and advice concerning managerial techniques, technological processes, and marketing to this crucial portion of a competitive economy.

b. CENTRAL BANK CONTROLS AND A POSSIBLE POSTWAR INFLATION

It is altogether possible that the shrinkage of Federal expenditures within three or four years from $100 billion annually to a fifth of this sum or less may overweigh any expansion in private industry. But it is also possible, during the remaining months of war or shortly thereafter when Federal expenditures are still large, that public sentiment and

---

[1] Securities and Exchange Commission (Philadelphia), *Statistical Release 739* for morning papers of Friday, June 9, 1944.

Congressional action may prematurely force the abandonment of direct controls upon spending, the only absolute hedge against inflation. Many unsatisfied demands will appear as simple physical needs (housing, clothing, scarce food items) and many others will appear as a part of a "decent American standard of living" (automobiles, household appliances, etc.). If, as might be hoped, the income-tax rates are not too rapidly revised downward, inflation could be held in check; but here, again, public sentiment may not tolerate the restraint. In the absence of fiscal limitation, a strong spending movement after the removal of price ceilings, rationing, and production priorities could be held in check only by central bank action, if even by it.

The first great obstacle to effective control by the usual "monetary" devices is, of course, the enormous liquidity of the public. As the accompanying figures reveal, the total "public" holdings of money including time and demand deposits and currency has increased by twofold since the end of 1939 ($53.8 to $116.9 billion) and the total liquid assets of the "public" have increased by nearly three times, to $193.6 billion. The "public" in these figures excludes those sectors, state and local governments, insurance companies, building and loan associations, and foreigners, which spend at rates independent of their liquid-asset position or which merely reflect the decisions of ultimate owners. The inclusion of government securities in the total of liquid assets is justified by the necessity which the Treasury faces of keeping its securities virtually interchangeable with money during the postwar refunding operations. What appears clearly from the table is that if private individuals and businesses are disposed to draw upon their enormous liquid assets, they can drive an inflation without recourse to borrowing.

The second great obstacle to central bank control of inflation is that the same situation obtains with respect to the commercial banks as prevails for the public. On Jan. 31, 1945, commercial banks held $72.6 billion in U. S. government marketable securities; of this total only 1.4 per cent had maturities over 20 years, 4.7 per cent from 10 to 20 years, 28.4 per cent from 5 to 10 years, 29.1 per cent from 1 to 5 years, and 36.3 per cent within one year. With so large a volume of short-term assets and without higher rates of interest on the part of the Treasury and Federal Reserve, the banks could expand their reserves and loans simply by holding the securities to maturity.

Because of the importance of maintaining government securities at par through the refunding period, the Treasury would obviously be loath to move toward higher rates unless inflation became a serious threat. If this policy became necessary, however, it would not, at least formally, break faith with investors, since they would be paid full values at maturity dates. Paramount to other considerations would be the aim

TABLE 1.—LIQUID ASSETS OF BUSINESS AND INDIVIDUALS *

(In billions of dollars)

	End of year					
	1939	1940	1941	1942	1943	1944
Corporations: total	13.0	14.9	17.5	27.0	38.1	47.1
Demand deposits	9.8	11.9	12.7	16.0	20.6	22.4
Time deposits	0.7	0.7	0.7	0.7	0.7	0.7
Currency	0.4	0.5	0.6	0.7	0.8	0.9
U. S. government securities	2.1	1.8	3.5	9.6	16.0	23.1
Unincorporated business: total	4.5	5.4	6.7	10.0	13.5	18.9
Demand deposits	3.0	3.9	4.6	6.3	7.9	9.1
Time deposits	0.2	0.2	0.2	0.2	0.2	0.2
Currency	0.2	0.2	0.3	0.4	0.4	0.6
U. S. government securities	1.1	1.1	1.6	3.1	5.0	9.0
Nonentrepreneurial individuals: total	48.4	51.3	57.9	75.7	101.4	127.6
Demand deposits	8.5	9.3	11.0	14.9	19.8	23.2
Time deposits	25.4	26.0	26.0	26.8	31.1	38.0
Currency	5.6	6.4	8.5	12.6	17.4	21.8
U. S. government securities	8.9	9.6	12.4	21.4	33.1	44.6
Totals, all categories of holders	65.9	71.6	82.1	112.7	153.0	193.6
Demand deposits	21.3	25.1	28.3	37.2	48.3	54.7
Time deposits	26.3	26.9	26.9	27.7	32.0	38.9
Currency	6.2	7.1	9.4	13.7	18.6	23.3
U. S. government securities	12.1	12.5	17.5	34.1	54.1	76.7

* This table summarizes a detailed analysis by Mr. Roland I. Robinson (at the Board of Governors of the Federal Reserve System) of each component item.

to induce or permit only a mild decline such as to persuade the banks and public—through the penalty otherwise of taking a loss—to hold the securities, without a panicky dumping on the market and sharp collapse in price. Undoubtedly this is chiefly a "psychological" matter. Almost *any* departure from the antecedent policy of complete support *might* dislodge the avalanche, with disastrous consequences not merely to the relatively weak or poor holders of securities and to Treasury financing, but also to bank credit, entrepreneurial expectations, and employment.

In the background several elements distinguish the present from the Liberty bond situation of the twenties. Both banks and businesses are relatively much more liquid to begin with and would therefore seem to have less reason for moving from securities to money. For both, average maturities are much shorter, and the inducement to hold to maturity to escape depreciation correspondingly stronger. Furthermore, banks are allowed to carry governments on their books at par whatever the market price; and they are more accustomed than formerly to hold their earning assets in investments as against loans. Finally, banks would rather quickly recoup the capital loss on outstanding issues through increased interest income if the Treasury moved toward higher rates.[1] On the other hand, banks have become habituated in the past few years to selling governments as a method of adjusting reserve positions; and in a boom they might move with alacrity from government to commercial bonds or loans if the effective yield on governments declined even slightly. In comparison with the twenties, the holdings of bonds are certainly more democratic. In wartime this contributes substantially to financing from savings but in the postwar period may prove the small holders to be "weak hands." Estimates made at the Federal Reserve Board indicate that persons with less than $5,000 annual income may have purchased as much as $22 billion in government securities (largely Series E savings bonds) since 1939. If on balance these considerations do not indicate an inherently weaker position for government securities now than in the twenties, it must be conceded that their wider distribution and larger volume make it more difficult to check inflation without abrupt reversal into depression.

As the Treasury moved toward longer maturities and higher rates, the Federal Reserve would abandon its unlimited offer to purchase Treasury bills at the posted buying rate and would terminate the repurchase option accorded to banks. The selective credit controls administered by the Federal Reserve authorities for consumer buying under Regulation W could be extended toward complete elimination of credit buying; and margin requirements for security purchases under Regulations T and U could be progressively increased. In the sectors of urban real estate and farm land, inflation is probably impotent without credit and the Federal Housing Administration has powers

[1] According to Dr. Arthur Upgren's estimates, based upon certain assumptions as to the asset distribution of commercial banks as of June 30, 1945, the commercial banks could recoup losses entailed by a horizontal 1 per cent increase of interest on all securities, in 3 or 4 years.

to curb mortgage credit in the sphere of housing. Special legislation to reduce the fraction of purchase price coverable by mortgage on agricultural land would be superior to attempting to devise an *ad hoc* tax on speculative gains, as proposed in a recent bill,[1] since differential taxation of "unearned" income or gains is dangerous and inequitable unless carried through to *all* sources including unearned wages or personal rents. In the aggregate such selective controls might eliminate some spending altogether; but if the inflationary movement proved to be strong, they would merely deflect the flow of money to other markets.

If a movement from securities to cash were not restrained by a moderate decline in the price of government bonds and if the use also of selective controls did not check the price inflation, it would be necessary to resort to additional general credit controls. Higher discount rates would of course not prevent security, commodity, or real-estate speculation, but the higher bond yields would cut off some long-range planned investments. The instrument of higher reserve requirements should be held until last because it falls with uneven severity upon individual banks. To avoid these difficulties, banks could be required to provide 100 per cent reserves for all *additional* deposits above a certain amount.[2] But so far as concerns old deposits, the existing fractional reserves would, at least for the time being, remain unchanged. The new "ceiling reserve" requirement would not cause any bank to be short on reserves and thus be forced to sell securities or borrow; but credit expansion would be definitely stopped.[3]

Since it is unfortunately impossible to count with certainty on other devices against a possible postwar inflation, central bank controls over the aggregate supply and availability of credit must be retained. The fact that the English and Canadian authorities seem to have committed themselves definitely for an unlimited time to the present low rates [4] does not argue for a similar course in the United States. Cyclical and

---

[1] E. C. Johnson, "The Farm Real Estate Market," *Federal Reserve Bulletin*, March, 1944, p. 232.

[2] In the United States this proposal was inaugurated by Dr. E. A. Goldenweiser of the Federal Reserve Board. It was suggested earlier by Fritz Machlup in the German edition (1931) of *The Stock Market, Credit, and Capital Formation*, p. 240.

[3] A plan by Lawrence H. Seltzer ("The Problem of Our Excessive Banking Reserves," *Journal of the American Statistical Association*, Vol. 35, pp. 24–36, March, 1940) to require a reserve in special "Reserve privilege" bonds issued by the Treasury would also effectively establish an absolute limit for bank credit, but with considerably more apparatus than the ceiling reserve plan would involve.

[4] *Cf.* the White Paper on *Employment Policy*, Sec. 59, and Bank of Canada, *Annual Report to the Minister of Finance and Statement of Accounts*, statement by Governor Towers, p. 5.

CENTRAL AND COMMERCIAL BANKING

episodic variations in economic activity have always been more violent here, and the controls must consequently be more severe. Furthermore, the diversity of our population elements and the lack of sophistication and rationality about financial matters in our Congress make our monetary policies volatile and unpredictable. If the direct controls over inflation stand in jeopardy from the very character of democratic government, it is important to preserve the defenses which do not depend upon popular caprice. The Federal Reserve should keep its own counsels, continue for the present to give complete support to the market for government securities, but not commit itself irrevocably for the future.

3. INFLATION CONTROLS AFTER THE TRANSITION PERIOD

Despite demagogic phrases about perpetual prosperity and an economy of abundance and despite a categoric imperative to avoid recession and unemployment, the monetary authorities will have in the future to cope with cyclical inflation. Indeed, this will continue to be an absolute prerequisite for avoiding downturns. What are the prospects for effective monetary control and what have we learned from our current experiences?

Margin requirements for security purchases will certainly be retained; and other existing "selective" controls, augmented by some device to curb speculative prices for agricultural land, might well be held in abeyance after the termination of postwar inflationary pressure but available for future contingencies. These methods are less extreme than a drastic raising of discount rates against speculative profits; they impinge at the proper places; and they do not need to be *selective* in any very great degree.

Whether the selective credit controls should be extended in scope to include for future use the bulk of staple commodities, as sometimes proposed, is more than questionable. It would involve the danger that the apparatus become *genuinely* selective, *i.e.*, discriminating through its distortion of relative prices from their structure in a free market. The temptation to utilize discriminating credit requirements for various "ulterior" designs, *i.e.*, for adjusting relative prices to fiscal, welfare, foreign-trade-strategy purposes, makes this variety of selectivity unsuitable to a private-enterprise economy. On the other hand, if the selectivity pertains not to particular *commodities* but to particular *types* of consumer credit, there would be every reason for its use against really inflationary developments. Service credit, single-payment loans, and charge accounts follow no cyclical pattern; but installment credit is distinctly cyclical. For the purpose of contributing to full employment through economic stability, "selective" controls—aside from margin requirements for securities—should therefore be restricted to installment credit in any renewed application after the transition period; and within this field it should be limited to the quantitatively important installment-credit commodities, such as automobiles. Power to extend the controls to other types of consumer credit might, however, be retained as precaution against evasions of installment regulation.

If American export surpluses persist and if the Treasury continues to buy gold, we may again witness the piling up of excess reserves. The best solutions to this problem would be a downward revision of our tariffs, the maintenance of employment and incomes, and the granting of loans within and outside an international stabilization fund and investment bank. If these fundamental corrective measures are not pressed with sufficient zeal, the Treasury may again need to sterilize gold as it did in 1936–1937. Nothing prevents sterilization even of existing gold stocks by the Treasury's purchase from the Federal Reserve banks of gold certificates out of the proceeds of taxation. Approximately the same results follow from a mere transfer of Treasury deposits from member banks to Federal Reserve banks, and one writer has emphasized this as an unexploited device available in the future to help manage excess reserves.[1]

The Board of Governors of the Federal Reserve System possesses more flexible powers than the Treasury for the restraint of price inflation, since fiscal action—aside from two examples just cited—depends upon the typically slow-moving action of Congress. Excess reserves of sufficient magnitude can, of course, render all but the "selective" controls inoperative; and upon these grounds larger discretionary powers ought to be vested in the Board with respect to member-bank reserves. I will not now venture upon an appraisal of a number of proposals from one quarter or another for implementing this added power.[2] In brief

---

[1] E. C. Simmons, "Treasury Deposits and Excess Reserves," *Journal of Political Economy*, Vol. 48, No. 3, pp. 325–343, June, 1940.

[2] These include debentures to be issued by the Federal Reserve banks in order to augment the resources of the Open Market Committee (Goldsborough Bill, H.R. 10517); "100 per cent reserves"; reserve bonds (Seltzer); velocity reserves; and capital-deposit ratio stipulation (*cf.* Mead Bill, S. 3867; so far as capital regulation influences bank-loan and

compass, the simplest and most effective reforms would be Congressional enactments widening the zone of discretionary authority for the Board over fractional reserves, and legalizing the use of ceiling reserve requirements. To avoid hardships for a growing member bank and general deflation through the failure of some banks to utilize all their reserves while others pressed upon the limit, it would be necessary to provide for periodic reallocation of ceilings. Since the ceiling reserve puts an absolute limit to credit expansion, it is superior to fractional requirements—even very high ones—in checking strong inflationary movements. By the same token, the device would presumably not be utilized in more normal times.

4. Long-run Prospects of Commercial Banking

a. COMMERCIAL BANKING AND COMPETITION

If we are interested in preserving and perfecting the price system and increasing competition and if we want to nurture institutions which articulate smoothly with such an economic society, we shall be concerned, I am confident, to maintain a flourishing commercial banking system and to restore some of its significant functions. Despite limited local monopoly, particularly in the West and South,[1] commercial banking is probably a satisfactory example of "workable" competition.

Specifically what is needed is to encourage the shifting of the risk on capital from the state toward less universal institutions and toward the individual. This implies two things: (1) that the state eliminate the risk of a great depression, since the character of such a risk is intolerable to private enterprise and fatal to venture capital, and (2) that all uses of

---

investment policies, the subject is touched upon later, pp. 250–251 below). I am indebted to Major Victor M. Longstreet for permission to use unpublished material regarding "Proposals to Control Bank Reserves," and to Dr. E. A. Goldenweiser similarly with regard to his Ceiling Reserve Plan.

[1] This fact is illustrated by an analysis, for the year 1938, of the earnings of 6,256 banks throughout the country. Classified by the ratio of total interest income on loans to the total of each bank's loans, the largest number of banks lay within the limits of 5.0 to 5.9 per cent in the region characterized most generally by several banks in a community (the Boston, New York, Philadelphia, and Cleveland Federal Reserve Districts). In the region characterized by one or two or relatively few banks in a community (the Kansas City and Dallas districts) the largest number of banks was found in the bracket 8.0 to 9.9 per cent interest earnings on loans relative to total loans. A *part* but not the larger part of the difference in these ratios is explained by the diseconomies of small-scale banking, since the statistical evidence shows largest net earnings relative to capital invested in the middle-sized banks ($1 to 5 million capital). Observe further that differences in risk of default on interest are already reflected in the ratios as given. *Cf.* Releases of the Federal Reserve banks of Kansas City and Dallas.

capital be characterized by "free entry," *i.e.*, that profits shall not be skimmed off through private monopoly in the most attractive investments. These requirements are stated in a categoric way, not to imply that categoric solutions or panaceas lie ready at hand to meet them, but rather to make dramatic the commonplace truth that the most important reforms for banking lie outside rather than within this institution. The history of the preceding decade should afford sufficient evidence that, of all businesses, banking is most intimately touched by depression, and that, of all businesses, it is most dependent upon an open competitive field for investment.

b. BANKS AND OTHER LENDING INSTITUTIONS

Commercial banking has been adversely affected by an excessive channeling of savings into life insurance companies. Insurance companies have the disposition over outside funds equaling the total of savings accounts in commercial and mutual savings banks, as the figures in Table 2 reveal. I shall not dwell upon the progressive concen-

TABLE 2.—SIZE OF RESERVOIRS OF MONEY SAVINGS, 1938 *

	Billions
Life insurance assets (including fraternal organizations)	$28,775
Commercial bank time deposits	14,359
Mutual savings bank assets	11,572
Building loan	5,712
Government pension and trust funds	6,169
Postal savings	1,252
Baby bonds	1,238
Total	$69,077

* Hearings before the Temporary National Economic Committee, Part 9, Appendix, Exhibit 601, p. 4052. These figures pertain to savings entrusted to institutions but exclude securities owned directly by individuals or held by corporate and individual trustees.

tration of economic power, which has attended the remarkable growth of life insurance, to a point where 54 per cent of the total assets of the legal reserve companies belong to five firms.[1] What is relevant to the present theme is the artificial extension of the demand for riskless investment (including government securities) and the inappropriateness of life insurance companies as the chief middlemen for savings.

That life insurance companies have the disposition over such vast accumulations is chiefly explained by the sale of "fancy" policies (endowment, educational, etc.) having very little to do with term insur-

[1] Temporary National Economic Committee, Monograph 37, *Saving, Investment, and National Income*, p. 34.

ance, the essence of real insurance. This admixture of true insurance reserves and mere accumulation extends the gilt-edge requirement—undoubtedly appropriate to *insurance*—to the whole mass of savings disposed over by life insurance companies. They have been able to reply to critics, who would combat stagnation of investment by persuading them to buy equities, that what people want in insurance is as near absolute safety as possible. But unless they were to establish as numerous local offices as there are now commercial banks, the insurance companies must continue to miss the small fellow, the local venture, and even sizable regional enterprises. The alternatives might appear to be a pointless reduplication of existing facilities, or the continuance of institutions with disproportionate masses of capital for their real function, inevitably biased toward big businesses, monopolies, and the state,—all for the sake of safety.

The escape from this dilemma is the conversion of the "life insurance" companies to life insurance proper through a legal limitation of new policies to that character. Such a change would be slow working; but the main thing is the disposition of *new* savings, of which a substantial part would immediately be directed toward the stock exchanges, investment trusts, and banks.

Another long-range undertaking should be the simplifying and reordering of the numerous Federal loan agencies to articulate with commerical banking more effectively. The proliferation of these agencies was a by-product of the last depression, and undoubtedly their aggregate effect was to prevent further deflation and even to expand bank credit.[1] Where these agencies clearly reduplicate facilities offered by the banks, the interests of a private-enterprise economy now require withdrawal by the government. By and large, however, the onus rests upon commercial banking to demonstrate its adequacy; and if this comes to pass, we may expect to see an almost automatic shrinkage of government-agency banking. A step in this direction is the extension of Federal Reserve bank powers to guarantee industrial loans by commercial banks, as contemplated in the Wagner-Spence bills.

c. COMMERCIAL BANKING AND ACTIVE ENTREPRENEURSHIP

Commercial banking can contribute significantly to the shifting of active risk taking and entrepreneurship from the state—to itself, to

[1] N. H. Jacoby, "Government Loan Agencies and Commercial Banking," *American Economic Review*, Vol. XXXII, No. 1, part 2, pp. 250–260, March, 1942.

businesses, and to individuals. This requires a reversal of characteristic tendencies, as shown in the asset and liability position of banks during the past decade and a half: the growth of deposits from mere hoarding by the public, the decline of "other securities" and loans in favor of government securities, and the reduction of capital relatively to total liabilities.

Bankers cannot be expected by spontaneous resolution or from exhortation to launch into more risky investments and loans. Consequently, the point of departure in the present analysis is the *demand* for bank credit and its activation through anti-restrictionist measures in the economic scene generally, through government policies to sustain employment, through taxes favorable to equity financing, and through limitation of insurance companies to the insurance function. As a result of these general forces and specific policies, bank profits would increase. Increased earnings are not desired because of a present inadequacy,[1] but in order to permit two fundamental reforms—the requirement of higher ratios of capital to total assets, and of reserves to deposits. The increase of these two ratios in conjunction with continued higher absolute dollar earnings would permit and induce the assumption of higher risks without sacrifice of safety for the depositor or bank.[2]

The ratio of capital to total assets fell from 14.1 per cent to 9.2 per cent from 1929 to 1942, that is, by one-third. This thinning of the owners' equity lessens the pressure on banks to seek an asset distribution bringing high yields. The process can be reversed by expanded earnings, increased investment by banks in their own business, and a turn toward loans and securities which afford higher returns for higher risks. Spread over a broader capital base, these greater risks imply no sacrifice of traditional banking standards. Explicit legal requirement would be necessary to raise the capital-assets ratio, and this should be complemented by differentiation of the requirement according to the risk

---

[1] Net profits, as a ratio to total capital accounts, for member banks moved in the range of 10.4 per cent to 7.1 per cent from 1919–1929, fell to minus 7.3 per cent in 1933, but equaled 6.3 per cent in 1939, 6.2 per cent in 1940, 6.7 per cent in 1941, 6.4 per cent in 1942, rose to 8.8 per cent in 1943, and to 9.7 per cent in 1944. *Cf.* Board of Governors of the Federal Reserve System, *Banking and Monetary Statistics*, pp. 264–265; and *Federal Reserve Bulletin*.

[2] The reforms imply a revision of standards of bank examination favorable to more risky loans and investments; but the increase of the two ratios would prevent a deterioration of liquidity and solvency. It cannot be gainsaid that at the present the individual banks showing the highest capital-assets ratios are not the leading venturers into new fields for commercial bank credit. Existing differences seem to rest, however, upon contrasting regional traditions, *e.g.*, as between New England and the West.

category of assets.[1] Putting the measure into effect *now* during a period of credit expansion and high profits in the banking business would appear to be reasonable; and, if the capital requirement were based upon types of assets, it would not limit the capacity of banks to absorb government securities.

An increase of the required minimum ratio of reserves to deposits would bring two substantial gains from a social angle: Without impairing bank liquidity, it would augment the power of increased capital requirements to force the banks to seek more venturesome and profitable loans and investments. In the second place, economic recession could not cause so large a deflation through the contraction of bank credit. A flight into currency would of course still be possible, but the bankers' own desire for liquidity could no longer play so large a role. In other words, we approach closer to government control of the volume of money, which is, I believe, one of the essential conditions for full employment in a liberal economy.

Another reform which would induce banks to riskier loans and investments without sacrifice of safety would be the extension of both deposit insurance and loan insurance. Deposit insurance now covers 97 per cent of *depositors;* but the $5,000 limit and the refusal of some banks to insure restricts it to less than 50 per cent of total *deposits*. The principal shortcoming is not so much the vulnerability of large depositors as it is the risk of destruction of purchasing power in depression. Since the activities of supervisory agencies, such as the Federal Deposit Insurance Corporation, tend to diminish the number of failures, and since an actuarial basis converts risks of failure to calculable losses, deposit insurance signifies to a very large degree the elimination of risk, rather than a transference of risk to the government.

Much the same analysis is applicable to loan insurance. It simply is not true, as some people have maintained, that the insuring banks are "relieved of all loss absorption." [2] For the uninsurable fraction of loans, the bank bears the risk of loss absorption; and for the insurable fraction, the bank absorbs a small certain cost in preference to the risk of a large loss. For neither portion does the government assume risk. But the commercial banking system can pursue more venturesome loan and investment policies without increasing risk over its magnitude before insurance.

---

[1] R. I. Robinson, "Capital-deposit Ratio in Bank Supervision," *Journal of Political Economy*, Vol. 49, No. 1, pp. 41–57, February, 1941.
[2] J. B. Willis, *The Functions of the Commercial Banking System*, p. 185.

5. Conclusion

Those persons who believe that a private enterprise system has sung its swan song and who look to state investment as the great and inevitable wave of the future will, of course, expect the gradual atrophy of commercial and central banking. There are others who, recognizing the possibility of protracted periods of investment stagnation and unemployment in our present mixed economy, would nevertheless believe that institutional reforms are possible which would bring about sustained high levels of national income without the actual conduct of production by the state. Such a program would aim at economic governance by a competitive price system in place of economic governance by master planners and other less benevolent despots. But this program would be a far cry from *laissez faire*, since it would recognize that active intervention by government is necessary to provide an open field for competitive production and to offset the tendency of a monetary economy to violent swings of boom and depression.

Important agenda in a liberal economic program would be a compensatory fiscal policy, the shifting of taxation from business to personal incomes, a general attack upon monopoly restriction whether by industry, labor, or agriculture, a freeing of international trade from protectionist trammels, and the whole gamut of policies designed to provide for equality of economic opportunity for the individual. But it is essential that the institutions most directly concerned with the passage of the planned savings of individuals and businesses to investment answer to the character of a free-enterprise economy. In a future demonstration of the employment possibilities of a liberal economic order, commercial and central banking can play an important and aggressive role.

Chapter XIV

Fiscal Policy in Economic Reconstruction[1]

by GERHARD COLM [2]

The Problem

ALTHOUGH the idea that fiscal policy should be regarded as a major constituent of broad economic policy is of recent origin, it has already been widely accepted.[3] It is no longer necessary to argue that the level of income and employment can be affected by policies of government expenditures, revenues, borrowing, and debt redemption. The unsolved questions lie, first of all, in the institutional field. What government legislative and administrative arrangements must be made in order to use fiscal policies effectively? A second group of problems has to do with the relative significance of fiscal policies. There are those who believe that fiscal policy can serve as the master key for almost all problems of government control—for preventing inflation and overexpansion on the one hand, deflation and contraction on the other hand. In their opinion, balanced economic expansion and full and steady employment can be assured by an appropriate manipu-

---

[1] The writer is particularly grateful to Arthur Smithies and L. H. Bean for helpful suggestions.

[2] The views expressed herein are those of the writer and do not necessarily reflect the official views of the Bureau of the Budget.

[3] *Cf.*, for example, writers coming from such different camps as Beardsley Ruml (see his speech, "Fiscal Policy and the Taxation of Business," before the American Bar Association in Chicago, Sept. 11, 1944); and Raymond Walsh (address on "Taxation and Fiscal Policy in the Postwar," before the National Tax Association conference in St. Louis, September, 1944). In an editorial in *Fortune* magazine of November, 1944, p. 101, it is said, "Social security and the use of a fiscal policy aimed to prevent the waste of boom and depression are fortunately no longer minority notions. They are English-speaking common sense."

lation of fiscal policy. There are also those who believe that the task of assuring "jobs for all" is of such a magnitude that fiscal policy is only one among many tools of government policies which must be used for a postwar reconstruction policy. In appraising the relative significance of fiscal policy, it is necessary to visualize the magnitude and character of the job of economic reconstruction.

The wide acceptance of fiscal policy as an instrument of economic policy can be attributed to a combination of two factors. The first is a deeply rooted skepticism about the ability of the free-enterprise system to assure automatically, without the support of government, full and steady employment of all available resources. The second factor is an equally deeply rooted aversion to direct government regulation of economic activities. Fiscal policy appears to be the ideal instrument of government. It promises to influence private economic activities by a stabilization of aggregate markets with a minimum of direct government control of individual industries.

In this respect fiscal policy has an appeal similar to that of the neo-classical idea of use of central bank policy to steer a free competitive economy. The discount policy of the central bank was regarded as an effective instrument of over-all control at a time when regulation of the rhythm of business expansion was the main problem of economic policy. This concept of economic policy was in accord with the general economic conditions prevailing in the decade before and the decade after World War I. Variation in the discount rate was thought to work like applying and releasing the brakes of a vehicle moving downhill. It was no problem to make the vehicle move; the problem was to regulate its speed. When the vehicle has to climb uphill, however, the brakes can no longer regulate the movement; speed must then be regulated by feeding the engine with the proper amount and mixture of fuel. Markets are the fuel that makes the engines of business run. An assurance of markets becomes essential when business expansion is threatened by lack of markets. Thus it is certainly not an accident that the concept of fiscal policy was developed on the basis of the experience of the Great Depression.

Is the current acceptance of fiscal policy as a tool for postwar reconstruction then perhaps another example of "cultural lag"? Is a tool derived from the unique experience of the thirties being recommended for a basically different postwar situation? What evidence do we have that the postwar world will be characterized by a lack of markets? The belief that there might be not only a temporary lack of markets, but also the possibility of continuing unemployment, is by past standards truly unorthodox. It is a negation of the basic traditional notion of capitalistic expansion. According to classical doctrine, if there are unused resources of labor or capital, wage rates (the price of labor) and the interest rate (the price of capital) will decline more than commodity prices, so that profits induce additional use of labor and capital (in proportion to their relative abundance) for new investments. The outlays for new investments create additional markets for goods and services so that the expanded production can then be sold. Unless the increase in capital equipment and the subsequent increase in consumers' demand fail to match each other in detail, there can never be a continuing lack of markets and job opportunities.

These patterns of classical economic dynamics are questioned among other factors on the ground that business expansion is largely guided by *existing* markets rather than by the confident anticipation that expansion will itself create *new* markets. Under such conditions, a decline in wage rates will not induce additional investments by improving profit expectation; it will deter investments because of the depressing effect of wage reductions on the markets for consumers' goods. Unless business actually expands more than is justified by *present* markets and unless business anticipates *future* markets, there is little chance that all savings will be absorbed by business investments at a high level of national income.

The essence of the so-called "mature" economy is not "saturation" of demand, or technological "stagnation," or decline in population increase, but the fact that the patterns of development differ in the earlier stages of industrialization from the patterns of growth in the later stages of industrial and institutional development.[1] If this interpretation is valid, then the great depression of the thirties was not merely another depression. It revealed a change in the structure of our economic institutions. Then it must be expected that the same fundamental problems will occur again—and possibly on a larger scale—sooner or later. The problem is one of adjusting our economic institutions, including government policies, to the requisites of balanced economic expansion at our stage of industrial development. Economic reconstruction, which is the

---

[1] By pointing out one factor which I believe is of importance for the discussion of fiscal policy in a "mature" economy, I do not deny that other factors—particularly changes in the *character* of technological developments—are of equal or even greater importance.

subject of this book, is thus interpreted here to include adjustment to present-day patterns of economic dynamics. The general objectives of economic reconstruction, understood in that broad way, might be formulated as follows:

1. Liquidation of certain distortions and maladjustments which the postwar period will inherit from the war period. Examples are maldistribution of labor in relation to peacetime location of industry (involving a migration either of labor or of peacetime industries, or both); concentration (due to special war advantages of large corporations); lag in technical equipment in certain farm regions and nonwar industries; disproportionate development of certain wartime prices and wage rates.

2. Assurance that the sum total of the demand of consumers, business, and government will equal the potential production of goods and services at a level of full employment.

3. A composition of total production, particularly a relationship between business expansion and consumption, which will be in such balance as to facilitate *sustained* expansion with a minimum of fluctuation.

4. A composition and distribution of work and product that will give a maximum of social benefit compatible with that inequality in the distribution of incomes that is necessary to give adequate production incentives. We are interested not only in a high-speed, full-employment economy but also in an economy which serves the people and provides them with the goods and services most needed. This objective includes a proper proportion of years devoted by each individual to schooling, training, household work, gainful employment, retirement, and of work and leisure.

These four objectives are not all of the same immediate importance. A full-employment demand can probably not be assured unless certain wartime distortions are eliminated at the same time. The second objective, however, is of primary immediate importance. In pursuing it, the third and fourth objectives should be kept in mind, although they are guideposts rather than directly attainable goals.

What is the role that fiscal policies can play in the achievement of these objectives of economic reconstruction? I do not intend to give here the full answer to this question. I shall present only a few thoughts which may help in the development of an answer.

Fiscal Policy in the Period of Partial Reconversion

War curtailments have resulted in a considerable amount of deferred demand. Some part of war restrictions results simply in a loss of individual satisfaction which cannot or will not be deferred. The steak we did not eat during the war we shall never eat. There is, however, on the other end of the scale a category of deferred demand which is very likely to be made up. Certain household necessities, repairs of buildings and business equipment, certain public works, and refilling the pipe lines of trade for peacetime consumers' goods belong in this category. In between these extremes is that deferred demand which will become active demand if jobs appear pretty safe but which may be further, and perhaps indefinitely, deferred under conditions of postwar insecurity.

When victory in Europe makes possible partial resumption of production of civilian durable goods, while war production is still continued on a considerable scale, it is likely that demand will run high. Even if a cut in overtime should reduce current earnings, it can be expected that additional demand may be financed by accumulated wartime savings and that foreign demand will be high, offsetting a part of the decline in purchases from current domestic income. In that period markets for nondurable goods and services may decline while markets for durable goods may be under inflationary pressure.

Simultaneous inflationary and deflationary developments might well characterize that period of transition. Fiscal policy can make only a limited contribution at that time. Tax rates can be reduced to a considerable extent only when goods become plentiful again, presumably not before final victory, and particularly if some upward adjustment in wage rates should take place in this interim period. Proper timing of removal of direct controls and appropriate industrial reconversion policies will be of greater importance than variations in fiscal policies in the transition period.

Fiscal Policies in the Postwar Period

POSSIBLE PATTERNS OF A PEACETIME FULL-EMPLOYMENT ECONOMY

It is difficult to say how long the extraordinary demand for consumers' and producers' goods will sustain a high level of employment when war production is curtailed and finally reduced to a peacetime level.

It might be useful to demonstrate the order of magnitude of the problem. When the wartime rise of the labor force and the size of the armed forces has been reduced to a new peacetime "normal," we can expect a civilian postwar labor force, say, by 1950, of somewhat less than 60 million [1] as compared with a civilian labor force of 53 million during the year 1944. Under conditions of full peacetime employment in 1950, the gross national product should be not much less than the wartime gross national product—assuming no substantial change in the price level.[2] Full peacetime employment requires that demand for nonwar goods and services must increase by about the same amount by which war production and war services are reduced. In other words, the sum total of demand for consumers' goods and services plus producers' goods plus nonwar government purchases of goods and services must increase by between $70 and $80 billion in order to assure full employment in future years.

Such an increase in demand may occur in a variety of ways, depending on the proportionate share of consumers', business, and nonwar government activities. Economists [3] have developed possible patterns of a full-employment postwar economy which aid greatly in visualizing the magnitude and character of the job to be accomplished.

These 1950 projections have been proposed by Hagen as a basis for his analysis. There are, however, a number of consistent patterns of a full-employment economy. The National Planning Association has published a number of models of full-employment budgets for the nation.[4] These projections are expressed in dollars of the 1941 price level, which explains most of the difference in totals with Hagen's figures which are expressed in approximately 1944 prices. I am selecting only three of the

---

[1] Everett Hagen and Nora Kirkpatrick, "National Output and Full Employment in 1950," *American Economic Review*, September, 1944, estimate a labor force of 60 million, including 2 million in the armed forces. Hagen informs me that his revised estimate is ½ million higher.

[2] It is assumed that the shift of workers from war industries implies in general a shift from higher to lower dollar output per man-hour. (This assumption has been challenged by J. L. Mosak—see Ch. V in this volume. I believe that more work remains to be done on this issue.) It is assumed further that productivity in each industry will continue its prewar increase and that wartime innovations in war production will be applied gradually in peacetime industries.

[3] See, among others, Department of Commerce, *Markets after the War;* Grover Ensley, "A Budget for the Nation," *Social Research*, September, 1943; an address by H. C. Sonne, "A Preview of National Budgets for Full Employment, 'Model T,' " June 8, 1944; and a paper by Everett Hagen (unpublished) on "Postwar Prospects: Inflation, Depression, or Stable Full Employment." See also the National Planning Association's forthcoming report, *National Budgets for Full Employment*. After this article was completed, the bold and significant book by Sir William Beveridge, *Full Employment in a Free Society*, appeared.

[4] Sonne, *ibid.*

TABLE 1.—THE NATION'S FULL-EMPLOYMENT BUDGET IN WAR AND PEACE
(In billions of current dollars)

Expenditures of	1944 *	1950 †
Consumers..........................	$97	$131–135
Business (gross investment)..........	3	37– 33
Government......................	98	27 ‡
Total gross national product.......	$198	$195

* Estimated annual rate July–December, 1944.
† The 1950 projections are Hagen's. They are expressed in prices 30 per cent above the 1939 price level.
‡ Twenty-seven billion dollars for government purchases of goods and services corresponds, according to Hagen, to total budgetary expenditures of about $30 billion. In his estimate, interest payments are treated entirely as "purchase of goods and services"; $3 billion for veterans' benefits and social-security payments as "transfer" expenditures. Disbursements from social-security trust funds are not included in these estimates. The $30 billion Federal, state, and local expenditure estimate is meant to be a rock-bottom figure but is probably too low even for a rock-bottom estimate. A low government expenditure estimate is consistent with the other data in the projection because government outlays can be kept to a minimum when consumption and business investments are assumed to run high.

seven National Planning Association models. These three models all show the same full-employment total gross national product. They differ, however, in the way in which the full-employment level is sustained.

TABLE 2.—THREE NATIONAL PLANNING ASSOCIATION Models * OF THE NATION'S FULL-EMPLOYMENT BUDGET IN 1950 (COMPARED WITH 1941)
(In billions of 1941 dollars)

Expenditures of	Model 1	Model 2	Model 3	1941
Consumers.....................	**$120**	$112	$99	$75
Business (gross investment)........	21	**29**	14	19
Government....................	29	29	**57**	26
Total gross national product....	$170	$170	$170	$120

* The National Planning Association publication gives considerable details of the flow of incomes and expenditures for each of these models. Boldface figures indicate items in which an extraordinary increase is assumed.

The full-employment level of gross national product is achieved in model 1 by extraordinarily high expenditures of consumers; in model 2 by extraordinarily high business investments; in model 3 by heavy government spending. These various models can be of great help in an analysis of the various ways in which a high-level peacetime economy can be sustained. They demonstrate that consumers' expenditures, or business investments, or government outlays, or a combination of the three, must be raised to an extraordinary (extraordinary, as compared with prewar patterns) level. How can fiscal policy affect consumers' expenditures, or business investments, or government outlays?

These projections present consistent patterns of a full-employment economy. In each case, the probable magnitude of two of the main components is estimated on the basis of past experience, and then it is asked, how large must the third component be in order to fill the "gap"? A realistic target should probably aim at a combination of the three with shifting emphasis in the component parts. The Hagen estimate assumes a minimum of aggregate Federal, state, and local budgets balanced at $30 billion under conditions of full employment. The National Planning Association estimates of rock-bottom government expenditures are slightly higher, considering the difference between the 1941 and 1944 dollars. Whether or not balanced budgets at rock-bottom levels are consistent with the objective of reaching and maintaining a full-employment economy depends on the likelihood that consumers' expenditures and business investments will reach the figures predicated in these same models (Hagen's model and models 1 and 2 of the National Planning Association projections).

There is considerable doubt that consumption—given the expected distribution of income—would increase by about $35 billion above present levels, even if a restocking boom should lift total production and income to the full-employment level in the transition period. This is true even if during that period a part of consumers' savings is offset by some liquidation of the extraordinary wartime savings. An increase in consumers' demand to the level required to sustain a high-level income would necessitate specific efforts by government policy. Otherwise, a high level of income reached, say, through extraordinarily high business investments during a postwar restocking boom would be bound to drop. If, however, an increase in demand is expected not only to *support* a high-level income but to help bring it about—in other words, if a high-level demand should be necessary to induce large investments and thereby cause the increase in incomes—the policy task becomes still larger.[1]

If balanced government budgets on minimum levels and a level of consumers' demand in accord with past experience are assumed, business investments must serve as the pivotal component to assure that a

---

[1] I emphasize this point of dynamics because the "models" indicate only the magnitudes needed to sustain a certain level of income and employment. They are "static" models. What we need, in addition, are dynamic models which outline the ways in which we can make the transition from a low- to a high-level economy or can sustain a high level if one or more components (*e.g.*, business investments) change.

full-employment income can be sustained. The models indicate that in this case business investments must amount to about $35 billion (present prices).

It is very difficult to estimate what business investments are likely to occur after the restocking activities of the transition period have spent themselves. Although the required business investments are about $35 billion (present prices) according to the models, the highest amounts realized in the period between the wars were $19 billion in the year 1920, and $18 billion in 1929. These were 22 and 18 per cent of the gross national product of these years. Gross investment was 17 per cent of gross national income in the decade 1920–1929, 10 per cent in the decade 1930–1939.[1]

For a gross national product of $195 billion, the ratio of the twenties would suggest business investments of about $33 billion. This, however, is questionable in several respects. First, there are in the category of business investments component parts such as residential construction and net exports (or net capital investments abroad) which may move independently and differently from the gross national product. Second, the ratio of investment in plant and equipment to gross national product may be different in a period of heavy fluctuations from a level that can be sustained over a longer period of time.[2] Third, granted for argument's sake that there will be investments of $33 billion *if* we have a full-employment income, it still would not follow that that level of investments will precede the high level of income so that these high investments will aid us in reaching a full-employment income. This leads us back to the statement made in the introductory section that business investments may fail in *anticipating* the full-employment level of markets.

An analysis of the various full-employment models in the light of past experience, with respect to the propensity to consume and the propensity to save and invest, indicates that a sizable amount [3] must be added to consumption, investments, or government outlays above what they would be without any special policy, in order to sustain a

[1] Derived from tables in the Appendix of the National Planning Association publication quoted above.

[2] A historical relationship for business investment, particularly plant and equipment, should be computed by possibly including, among other determining factors: (1) level of disposable income, (2) change in disposable income as compared with preceding year, and (3) the capital value (depreciable assets) of industry. However, the determining influence of investments on national income appears to have been so strong that the statistical measurement of the influence of income on investments is hazardous.

[3] The National Planning Association, *op. cit.*, estimates that the initial full-employment "gap" would be $20.8 billion under present wartime taxes or $8.5 billion under revised taxes and other modifications in the assumptions, expressed in 1941 prices.

high-level income and employment. There can be much argument about the size of full-employment income and employment and about the appropriate conclusions from past experience concerning consumption and investments, but I do believe that the general order of magnitude cannot be very different unless one expects a drastic change in behavior of business or consumers.

FULL-EMPLOYMENT POLICIES IN GENERAL

Full-employment policies can be classified on the basis of these considerations as follows:

1. Policies affecting the size of the full-employment income by influencing, for example:
   a. Hours of work.
   b. School age.
   c. Retirement age.
   d. Productivity of labor.
   e. Social hygiene measures.

2. Policies affecting consumers' demand by influencing, for example:
   a. Minimum wages.
   b. Propensity to save.
   c. Social-security measures.
   d. Tax policies, affecting size and distribution of disposable income.

3. Policies affecting business investments by influencing, for example:
   a. Replacement of worn-out or obsolete machinery in industry and agriculture.
   b. Stimulation of low-cost housing.
   c. Promotion of foreign investments and exports.
   d. Promotion of technological research.
   e. Development of power resources.
   f. Promotion of competitive investments.
   g. Tax policies designed to stimulate investments.
   h. Government underwriting of business investments (particularly for small business and investments not financed by private sources [1] because of the risk involved).

4. Public expenditures and debt operations.

[1] It will be of interest to observe the operations of the Industrial Development Bank in Canada.

The job of sustaining a full-employment economy is of such a size that it cannot be expected to be accomplished by any single device, certainly not by fiscal policy alone. On the other hand, it cannot be assumed that employment can be stabilized on a high level in a free-enterprice economy without the use of fiscal policies. It is difficult to sketch a blueprint of a future full-employment program in detail. It appears more important that the various types of policy be appraised regarding their potential contribution to a consistent and comprehensive full-employment policy program.

REDUCTION IN WARTIME TAX RATES

In the Hagen illustration above, it is assumed that the Federal, state, and local tax systems of the postwar period will permit balancing all budgets at a minimum rock-bottom level of expenditures and a high level of incomes. This tax objective requires tax rates well above peacetime rates but substantially below wartime rates. Let us assume, for instance, that this tax target permits a reduction of tax rates equivalent to a yield of $10 billion on the present tax basis. In deciding what kinds of taxes should be reduced, a number of factors will be considered, such as equity and costs of administration. From a fiscal aspect that combination of postwar tax reduction is best which will give the greatest increase [1] in the national product and employment.

Tax reduction (leaving other factors unchanged) affects income and employment either through its effect on business investments or consumers' purchasing power. Pay-roll taxes, excise taxes, and the individual income tax are the taxes which—in that sequence—affect purchasing power most directly. Wartime taxes on corporate profits are much more drastic than those on individual incomes. Therefore, if only a limited reduction in taxes from the wartime level is possible, the reduction should aim first at removing wartime impediments to investment. If we could reduce taxes only by the equivalent of, say, $2.5 billion, the most desirable reduction would probably be a reduction in taxes on corporate profits. Wartime rates not only impair the incentives to economical management but also tend to restrict, and were designed to restrict, nonwar investments. When corporate taxes are reduced, however, to the point where investment incentives are restored, then each further

[1] The increase is measured by comparison with the gross national product as it would be under continuing wartime tax rates. It is possible, for instance, that this "increase" in reality may be a lesser decrease in gross national product than would occur without the tax revision.

reduction in rates will result only in a smaller increase in gross national product and employment. If a further reduction becomes possible, excise taxes and individual income taxes should be reduced too.

In the accompanying chart, an attempt is made to illustrate the comparative effect of two groups of taxes: taxes on corporate profits and taxes on individual incomes.[1] The chart is so constructed that it shows

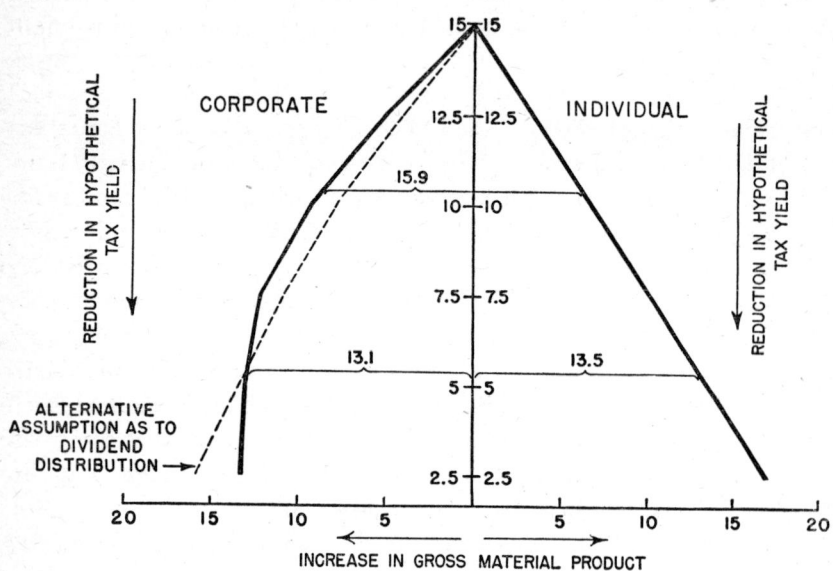

what I believe are reasonable assumptions as to the effect of the reduction of wartime tax rates. A reduction in taxes on corporate profits equivalent, for instance, to a yield of $10 billion results in an increase in the gross national product of $13 billion, according to the major assumption [2] of the chart. A corresponding reduction in the standard rate of the individual income tax shows an increase of $13.5 billion in the gross national product. If, however, the $10 billion reduction is divided equally between corporate and individual taxes, the resulting increase in gross national product, shown on the chart, is $15.9 billion.

Once taxes have been reduced from their wartime level, each further

---

[1] Richard Goode has provided the estimates on which the chart is based and has prepared the Appendix, p. 272.

[2] The estimates vary, of course, according to specific assumptions with respect to the specific provisions of the tax reduction. The effect also differs in the case of large and small corporations. Many other factors should be taken into consideration which cannot be discussed here. Some details are given in the Appendix.

reduction has a diminishing effect on investments and consumers' demand.[1] Tax reductions from lower levels result to an increasing extent in an increase in savings rather than in an increase in active demand.

The income- and employment-creating effect of tax reduction could be greatly increased if it were possible to discriminate between profits or incomes used for actual purchases or investments, and profits or incomes left idle. Also a liberal allowance for carry-over of losses may be more effective in stimulating investments than a small reduction in rates—once the rates are reduced from the prohibitive wartime level. Expenditures financed by a tax on idle funds [2] do not affect income and employment very differently from expenditures financed by bank borrowing, the latter not resulting in an increase in the national debt.

Tax reductions or tax abatements will be effective as incentives for investment only if there are prospects for sufficient markets. However, even with satisfactory market prospects, there may be certain factors hindering investment. Some of these impediments may well be offset by tax incentives. This whole question requires further exploration.

If reduction of Federal taxes were the only means available for increasing consumers' demand, it might be concluded that most Federal taxes should be at least temporarily discontinued. A. P. Lerner believes that taxes are justified only as a means to absorb purchasing power in the case of inflationary pressure of excessive demand. Sales taxes may then appear to be the most suitable taxes. If there is a lack of demand, taxes should be reduced or even transformed into "negative taxes" or tax bonuses until demand has reached the level required for a full-employment economy.[3] Beardsley Ruml, though acknowledging the other purposes of taxation, follows Lerner at least in the emphasis on the various purposes of taxation.[4]

The most important among the purposes of taxation, in my judgment, is to allocate relative contributions to the costs of government. This is not incompatible with the requirement to take into account economic considerations in revision of the tax system. Also the feasibility of

---

[1] The statement in the text refers to tax reductions in general. One can think, of course, of a specific sequence in tax reduction in which later reductions would have a greater economic effect than previous reductions.

[2] For the possibility of devising such a tax, see Gerhard Colm, "Full Employment through Tax Policy?" *Social Research*, November, 1940.

[3] A. P. Lerner, *The Economics of Control*, and *Principles of Welfare Economics*, pp. 307ff.

[4] "By all odds, the most important single purpose to be served by the imposition of federal taxes is the maintenance of a dollar which has stable purchasing power over the years. Sometimes this purpose is stated as 'the avoidance of inflation' . . ." Ruml, *op. cit.*

varying certain tax rates within the limits of the basic tax structure should be explored and carefully weighed against the disadvantages resulting from tax-rate changes.

Reliance on tax reductions or tax bonuses as the major or sole device for regulating demand, as Lerner suggests, would violate all the other purposes of taxation. Such policy would distribute the primary addition to disposable purchasing power in accord with what happens to be the distribution of the tax burden. Furthermore, it would give windfall gains not justified by economic results to those individual or corporate taxpayers who use the tax reduction for an increase in savings rather than an increase in actual consumption or direct investment.

It seems a fair conclusion that tax policy can contribute to increasing consumers' demand and business investments above wartime levels, but it can be only a moderate contribution to reaching the levels of consumption and investment required for a sustained full-employment level.[1]

INCREASE IN GOVERNMENT EXPENDITURES (FOR OTHER THAN WAR PURPOSES)

The high standard of living that is possible with present-day productivity includes also a high standard of government services. A high standard of government services in turn makes the accomplishment of a continuously high level of employment and incomes more feasible. A high standard of government services means enlarged government budgets (*i.e.*, larger than the rock-bottom figures of the models), but it does not mean waste of public money or make-work expenditures. Enlarged government functions must be discharged with even greater economy than expenditures on a smaller scale. The same instinct that revolts against spending money in an uneconomical fashion also revolts against letting national resources remain idle when there are such urgent needs to be served. (See the fourth general objective listed above, page 256.)

Various types of expenditure programs differ in their fiscal effectiveness just as various types of tax reductions have a different effect on income and employment.

There are, first, social-security programs with an automatically anticyclical effect. They provide a cushion which mitigates the spiraling effect of a reduction in employment and incomes.

[1] This discussion is not intended to deal adequately with all desirable revisions in the tax system.

Second, there are expenditures with a high leverage effect. The railroad grants of the last century are an outstanding example of the past. These grants made possible and stimulated investments of large private funds in railroads and railroad-equipment industries and opened up the development of entirely new industries and regions. Today there are still opportunities for developmental programs with a considerable leverage effect, such as programs for river development, urban rehabilitation and housing, and air transport facilities. Regional programs are among the most effective means of stimulating private business investments. There are also government programs possible which may have a negative leverage effect, namely, those which deter business investments. In many fields desirable investments can be stimulated by government underwriting and guarantee. In such cases no directly corresponding budget expenditure is implied. It is quite possible that there will be in the future a growing amount of such quasi-private or quasi-public investments. We are only at the beginning in developing an adequate machinery for that type of government-business cooperation.

Besides the leverage effect, there is, of course, the secondary effect of government expenditures, the effect on consumers' demand, and the tertiary effect on investments working indirectly through the increase in consumers' demand. The secondary effect of government expenditures on consumers' demand during the thirties occurred to the extent expected, in accordance with economic theory.

There is more doubt as to the tertiary effects on investments in that period. One important factor may have been the uncertainty that existed about the continuation of a determined recovery policy. The fact that the need for a full-employment policy is so generally recognized now is an important condition for making the objective more easily attainable. I feel, however, that we should not rely too much on policy declarations alone. Business will have confidence in sustained demand only when it sees that policy declarations are implemented by provisions for an adequate legislative and administrative machinery.

Deficit Spending and Economic Reconstruction

It is very unfortunate that an active fiscal policy is frequently identified in the public mind with simple "deficit spending." The concept, deficit spending, is misleading because it suggests that it is the deficit—

or the surplus—that is the essence of the income-creating or income-absorbing effect of fiscal policy. That is an unwarranted oversimplification. As far as the size of the deficit is concerned, it makes no difference whether taxes are reduced or expenditures increased. As to the effect on actual demand and employment, there is a considerable difference, however, between a tax reduction of $1 billion and an increase in expenditures of the same amount. With respect to tax reductions or tax increases, the effect depends on the type of taxes; and the same holds true in regard to various types of expenditures. There is the possibility of income-creating expenditures financed by taxation, provided that the right kind of expenditures and the right kind of taxes are selected.

An increase in government expenditures contributes most to aggregate demand, of course, if it is financed by methods of taxation or borrowing which curtail consumers' demand and business investments only by a minimum. Considering the limits of progressive taxation and of taxing "idle funds," it is probably true that an effective fiscal policy does imply in practice that a portion of government outlays must be financed by borrowing at times when a contracting tendency prevails in the economy. Surpluses and debt redemption can be expected in periods of excessive demand. The "deficit" or the "surplus," however, is not the essence of an effective fiscal policy.

The "models" demonstrate that the nation's budget is in balance only when an excess of private incomes over expenditures is offset by an excess of expenditures over revenue in the government sector, or when an excess of outlays over income in the private sector is offset by an excess of revenue in the government sector. The presentation of the "models" in the form developed by Grover Ensley and the National Planning Association demonstrates this relationship very clearly. The presentation above gave only the expenditure side of the nation's budgets. As an example, two of the National Planning Association's models are given in more detail in order to demonstrate the income-expenditure relationship in case (A) of a Federal surplus, (B) of a Federal deficit.

This presentation should not detract from the fact that fiscal operations do affect not only these government surpluses and deficits but also consumers' spending and savings and business investments and accumulation of business funds. Fiscal policy truly affects each component part of the nation's budget.

TABLE 3.—THE NATION'S BUDGET *
(In billions of 1941 dollars)

	A	B
Consumers:		
Disposable incomes	$120	$129
Expenditures	106	113
Net savings	$+14	$+16
Business:		
Accrual of funds (undistributed profits and depreciation and other reserves)	13	10
Gross investments (including residential construction and net exports)	32	14
Use of additional funds (equity capital or borrowing)	−19	−4
State and local government:		
Income	11	10
Expenditures	10	10
Surplus	+1	0
Federal government:		
Income	26	21
Expenditures	22	33
Surplus or deficit	+4	−12
Total:		
Funds disposable for expenditures	$170	$170
Expenditures	170	170
Surplus or deficit	0	0

* Cf. H. C. Sonne, "A Preview of National Budgets for Full Employment, 'Model T,'" June 8, 1944.

Fiscal policy does imply an influence on consumers' demand, but it requires more than simply opening and closing a faucet to regulate the flow of purchasing power by deficit spending. It is true that each disturbance in economic relations that results in contraction of production and incomes *can* be offset by creating additional purchasing power. An economic disturbance is not eliminated, however, by overcompensating its contracting effect. Economic and fiscal measures as part of a policy of economic reconstruction must aim at creating conditions for *sustained* and *balanced* expansion. (See the third of the basic objectives listed above, page 256.)

An example may illustrate this point. Assume that technological cost reduction has taken place but that wage rates have not been increased or prices not reduced correspondingly. Business keeps an enlarged amount of profits in idle reserves (neither distributed nor invested); a deflationary contraction ensues. According to Lerner's "functional finance," the government should reduce taxes and print money in such a situation until demand reaches the full-employment level. If tax reductions are large enough or even supplemented, according to Lerner, by tax refunds, the objective will be accomplished. The additional purchasing power would be distributed quite differently from the distribution which would have resulted from a wage increase or price decline. Considering that we want not only full employment but an economy of balanced expansion and maximum social benefits, it is obvious that in such a case price and wage policies recommend themselves as the most appropriate measures, possibly in conjunction with such fiscal policies as may be necessary to overcome the contraction that has occurred.

A policy of sustained and balanced expansion may require changing emphasis on various aspects of a full-employment policy. Such a policy can be outlined only on the basis of a detailed analysis of expected economic development over a number of years. Here I can only allude to the possible changes in emphasis that may be required during the postwar decade.

In the period of transition from a war to a peace economy, it will probably be of paramount importance first to facilitate business investments which were delayed during the war and which will be necessary for a high-level peacetime economy, in addition to those outlays abroad which may be necessary in the interest of international reconstruction. At the same time, it will be necessary to strengthen the income cushions which protect the system against the shock of contraction in case the restocking boom should come to an abrupt end.

As an objective of a more long-run policy, all measures, including fiscal policies, will be essential which assure a permanently high-level consumers' demand and an increase in the average time which an individual spends in school and training or retirement. A shortening of working hours also belongs in this category.

All these efforts may fall short of the objective, either because they are not sufficiently effective or because they are subject to cyclical variation. Variation in expenditure and tax policies appears to be the most appropriate policy to deal with such situations. Fiscal policies are involved in each of these phases of a policy of economic reconstruction, but the fiscal policies must be integrated with a variety of other measures into dynamic patterns of economic policy.

Institutional Arrangements

This outline of a dynamic economic policy may be regarded as aiming at an unattainable ideal. It might be questioned whether our government institutions and our knowledge of economic facts are adequate for the task. That is certainly a valid question. Such an admission should not discourage a movement in the direction of a necessary policy. We learn to swim only in the water. We shall develop an improved machinery for a comprehensive and consistent policy only by embarking on such a policy.

The Budget Director, Harold D. Smith, has outlined in various speeches [1] the need for provisions that make possible a flexible policy of developmental expenditures.

It is encouraging that Representative Doughton, Chairman of the Joint Committee on Internal Revenue Taxation, requested estimates of future budgets, national income, and other pertinent economic data as a basis for the deliberation of a postwar tax program.[2] From such a request to the determination of fiscal policies in the light of economic necessities is still a long way. But it is proof that the problem is being recognized.

It is interesting that the British White Paper on *Employment Policy* concludes that the development of an adequate economic reporting service, including projections into the future of expected business investments, is a necessary prerequisite of an effective employment policy.[3]

Projections may be needed not only of the broad outlines of the nation's budget, but also of the demand for specific categories of consumers' and producers' goods which can be expected to be forthcoming on an anticipated level of national income. A projection of future current demand in turn should make possible estimates of needed increase in capital equipment. Statistical projections of this character will be useful as a guide for government policies (for instance, with respect to stimulation and underwriting of business investments). They will also aid in raising the sights of business. If business determines its investment policies in the light of expected, and not only existing, markets, the task of

---

[1] *Cf.* paper by H. D. Smith, "Fiscal Policy and Budget Operations in War and Peace," presented at the Tenth Chilean Scientific Congress, January, 1944, and an address by H. D. Smith, "The Budget as an Instrument of Legislative Control and Executive Management," given in Cleveland, Ohio, June 9, 1944, *Public Administration Review*, summer, 1944.

[2] *Congressional Record*, June 23, 1944.

[3] See the section which has the significant heading, "The Policy in Practice," in *Employment Policy*.

government policies to assure full employment will become more manageable.

APPENDIX [1]

The chart on page 264 is based on the figures shown in the following table:

TABLE 4.—EFFECTS OF TAX REDUCTIONS
Increases in Gross National Product Associated with Reductions in Corporate and Individual Income Taxes
(In billions of dollars)

Tax reduction (corporate or individual)	Cumulative increase in gross national product		
	Corporate tax reduction		Individual tax reduction
	Assumption I *	Assumption II †	
$ 2.5	$ 5.0	$ 4.0	$ 3.3
5.0	9.3	7.8	6.6
7.5	12.2	10.8	10.0
10.0	13.1	13.3	13.5
12.5	13.3	15.7	17.0

* First assumption as to dividend distribution. (See Table 5.)
† Alternative assumption as to dividend distribution. (See Table 5.)

GENERAL NOTES

1. The effects of the two kinds of tax reduction are shown as if they were independent of each other, although actually they would be interrelated. This means that the increases in gross national product shown in Table 4 to be associated with given reductions of the corporate tax are based on the assumption that individual tax rates are maintained, and vice versa.

2. The tax reductions are initial reductions only. The "hypothetical yields" shown in the chart give effect solely to these initial reductions. The reduction in net yield in each case would be smaller than the initial reduction because additional tax liabilities would be associated with the resulting increase in gross national product. Moreover, a given initial reduction of corporate taxes does not reduce government revenues by the full amount, because a part of additional dividends, if any, associated with the decrease in corporate tax liability would be taxable to recipients. These qualifications are taken into account in estimating the secondary effects of the tax reduction on gross national product.

3. The tax reductions are assumed to have no effect on government expenditures (excluding debt retirement).

DETAILED NOTES ON ASSUMPTIONS AND PROCEDURE

1. INVESTMENT AND CORPORATE SAVING. The effects of tax reductions on corporate investment and dividend payments were arbitrarily assumed to be as

[1] By Richard Goode.

shown in Table 5 (starting with profits before taxes of $21.5 billion and corporate taxes of $15 billion).

TABLE 5.—ASSUMED EFFECTS OF CORPORATE TAX REDUCTIONS ON DIVIDENDS AND INVESTMENTS

(In billions of dollars)

Reductions in corporation taxes		Increase in		
		Dividends		Investment
From	To	First assumption	Alternative assumption	
$15.0	$12.5	$1.0	$0.0	$2.5
12.5	10.0	1.2	0.5	2.0
10.0	7.5	1.3	1.5	1.0
7.5	5.0	0.5	2.2	0.3
5.0	2.5	0.0	2.4	0.1

Some confidence is felt about the realism of the general character, but not the exact amount, of the assumed effects of corporate tax reductions on investment. It was difficult to choose even a general pattern for dividend payments and corporate saving. Therefore, two different assumptions were made: In the first, dividends were assumed to rise at a slightly increasing rate with the first reductions in corporate taxes but to increase little, if any, with still further tax reductions. In the alternative assumption, corporate saving and investment were taken to be equal with all funds freed by tax reductions used either for investment or for dividends. The first assumption is likely to be more characteristic of the behavior of large public corporations, the second of smaller corporations which do not use the securities market to any great extent.

Reductions in individual income taxes were assumed to have no primary effect on investment. It is recognized that lower individual taxes might well stimulate some additional investment by both corporations and unincorporated businesses. It is believed, however, that these increases would be much smaller than the increases in corporate investment stimulated by reduction in corporate taxes. For present purposes, the possible primary effects on investment resulting from reduction of individual taxes are not taken into account.

2. INCIDENCE OF CORPORATE TAX. The reductions in corporate taxes were assumed to have no effect on prices or wages.

3. CONSUMPTION AND SAVING; SECONDARY EFFECTS. No account was taken of differences among saving-consumption habits of dividend recipients, individual income-tax payers, and gainfully occupied persons generally. The probable effect of such an allowance would be to reduce the increases in gross national product associated with the tax reductions, especially the reductions of corporate taxes, insofar as these effects depend on increased consumption. Moreover, no allowance was made for a decrease in the propensity to consume associated with a rise in disposable income. Such an allowance would cut down the

increases in gross national product associated with the larger tax reductions. Probably the adjustment would be more significant for increases in dividend incomes than for other kinds of income. In the chart, the adjustment would make the curves, especially the two for corporate taxes, slope downward to the base more sharply.

Increases in dividends paid to individuals were assumed to be subject to a 30 per cent effective individual income-tax rate.[1] This means that a given increase in dividends was assumed to result in an increase in disposable income of 70 per cent of the increase in dividends.

Increases in consumption associated with increases in disposable income of individuals were estimated on the basis of the following formula:[2]

$$\text{Consumption} = K + ft + 0.806 \text{ disposable income}$$

where K is a constant and ft represents a time trend.

The relation between disposable income and gross national product at present tax rates was given by the following:[3]

$$\text{Disposable income} = M + 0.475 \text{ GNP}$$

where M is a constant.

From these two formulas a multiplier was computed to relate given primary increases in investment or consumption with the total increase in gross national product, associated therewith.

For the initial $2.5 billion tax reductions the multiplier was derived as follows:

$$\text{Increase in GNP} = \frac{1}{1 - (0.475 \times 0.806)}, \text{ primary increase in investment and consumption}$$

$$= 1.62, \text{ primary increase in investment and consumption}$$

This multiplier was increased for successive tax reductions to reflect the assumption that with lower taxes disposable income becomes an increasing fraction of gross national product. (The initial level of gross national product was assumed to be $170 billion.)

---

[1] The effective individual income-tax rate on dividends (excluding intercorporate dividends) in 1942 was approximately 25 per cent. Computations based on *Statistics of Income for 1942*, Part 1 (preliminary) and *Survey of Current Business*, April, 1944.

[2] Based on data for 1929–1940, inclusive.

[3] Based on a hypothetical projection of income flows, with present tax rates. The method is developed by Arthur Smithies in "Forecasting Postwar Demand," *Econometrica*, January, 1945.

Chapter XV

Postwar Tax Structure

by ROY BLOUGH

Wartime Changes in Tax Structure

EACH major war in United States history has left a permanent imprint on the Federal tax structure. The Civil War provided experience in income and estate taxation and added liquor and tobacco excise taxes as a permanent element in the tax system—an element that rivaled in yield the customs duties which had been the sole revenue source for many years before that war. World War I generated the excess-profits tax and left the income tax on individuals and corporations as the major revenue source. World War II has introduced no important untried taxes but will undoubtedly leave a tax structure differing sharply from the prewar system.

In the fiscal year ended June 30, 1940, internal revenue collections totaled $5,340 million.[1] The net budget deficit in that year was $3,611 million.[2] The budget estimates for the fiscal year ended June 30, 1945, anticipate internal revenue collections of $43,229 million [3] and a net budget deficit of $52,741 million.[3]

In part, the eightfold increase in tax collections represents unprecedented increases in tax rates. In part, it reflects the growth in gross national product, under the stimulus of huge war expenditures, from $88.6 billion [4] in 1939 to an estimated $198.7 billion [5] in 1944,[6] and the accompanying growth in income payments.

[1] *Annual Report of the Commissioner of Internal Revenue, Fiscal Year Ended June 30, 1943*, Table 6, p. 113.
[2] *The Budget of the United States Government for the Fiscal Year Ending June 30, 1942*, p. 1046.
[3] U. S. Treasury Department, *Bulletin*, November, 1944, p. 2.
[4] U. S. Department of Commerce, *Survey of Current Business*, April, 1944, Table 10, p. 13.
[5] *Ibid.*, February, 1945, Table 2, p. 5.
[6] The calendar years most comparable to fiscal years of collection 1940 and 1945.

The operative tax structure has changed radically in the five years from 1939 to 1944. The corporation standard income-tax rate has risen from 19 per cent for 1939 to 40 per cent combined normal tax and surtax for 1944. An excess-profits tax with a gross rate of 95 per cent and a net rate of 85½ per cent is now in force. Individual surtax exemptions for a married couple with two children have declined from $3,300 to $2,000 [1] and a 3 per cent normal tax applies to incomes above $500, with no additional exemption for dependent wife or children. The combined normal and surtax rates applicable to the first bracket of income subject to surtax have risen from 8 to 23 per cent. The former top rate of 79 per cent, which was reached at $5 million, has become 94 per cent, reached at $200,000, although its effect is somewhat ameliorated by a 90 per cent limit on the total effective rate. The tax on distilled spirits has risen from $2.25 to $9 per proof gallon, the tax on cigarettes, from 6 to 7 cents per package of 20. Most other taxes have gone up at least 10 per cent. Estate and gift taxes were increased by at least 10 per cent in each bracket, with much heavier increases at the lower end of the rate scale. Pay-roll taxes have remained stationary, the increases scheduled for Jan. 1, 1940, and Jan. 1, 1943, having been postponed by Congressional action.

The combination of tax changes and national income changes makes the anticipated internal revenue statement for the fiscal year 1945 something quite different from the statement for the fiscal year 1940, as is shown in Table 1.

Significant changes in other aspects of taxation have accompanied the sharp wartime increases in tax rates and bases. The individual income tax has been modernized by the shift from delayed to current collection, by the introduction of withholding, and by drastic simplification. In recognition of the impact of high wartime rates, many tax reliefs to avoid inequity or hardship have been introduced in both corporate and individual income taxes. The introduction of a 2-year carry-back of business losses has lengthened the period over which business income may be averaged for tax purposes. These and similar changes will inevitably leave their imprint on the postwar tax system.

The political conflicts which accompanied the relatively minor increases of the Revenue Act of 1943, passed over the President's veto in February, 1944, convinced most people that wartime taxes were at their peak. With the war going well and reconversion problems in the air,

[1] Other variations in the law make this comparison not precisely valid for most taxpayers.

TABLE 1.—INTERNAL REVENUE COLLECTIONS

Tax	Fiscal 1940 *		Fiscal 1945 †	
	Amount, millions	Per cent to total	Amount, millions	Per cent to total
Corporation taxes:				
Excess-profits tax.................	......	.....	$11,524	26.6
Income tax.....................	$1,121	21.0	4,991	11.5
Capital-stock tax...............	133	2.5	373	0.9
Declared-value excess-profits tax..	18	0.3	155	0.4
Total.......................	$1,272	23.8	$17,043	39.3
Individual income tax............	982	18.4	18,386	42.4
Estate and gift taxes.............	360	6.7	515	1.2
Excises:				
Liquor.......................	624	11.7	2,064	4.8
Tobacco......................	609	11.4	921	2.1
Other........................	660	12.4	2,679	6.2
Total.......................	$1,893	35.5	$5,664	13.1
Employment taxes.................	834	15.6	1,794	4.1
Total internal revenue...........	$5,340	100.0	$43,401	100.0

NOTE: Because of rounding, detail will not necessarily add to totals.

* *Annual Report of the Commissioner of Internal Revenue, Fiscal Year Ended June 30, 1940*, Table 5, pp. 100 and 101.

† Estimates based on *The Budget of the United States Government for the Fiscal Year Ending June 30, 1946*, Table 4, pp. A6ff.

various businessmen and other organizations prepared postwar tax plans, while many organizations and persons with no plans of their own prepared and published comparisons of the most publicized plans. In June, 1944, the Congressional Joint Committee on Internal Revenue Taxation passed a resolution calling on its staff and the Treasury tax staff to make a study of postwar tax problems. One effect of the publicity given to postwar taxes in 1944 undoubtedly has been to strengthen the general belief that no additional wartime taxes would be imposed.

The fear that the high wartime corporate and individual tax rates would be left in force after the war, presumably to help retire the debt, has given strong impetus to postwar tax planning. The various plans emphasize the restrictive effects that wartime taxes would have on peacetime industry and have succeeded in concentrating attention as never before on the relation of taxation to production, income, and employment.

If the postwar tax planners [1] had reached a general agreement on just what tax changes would minimize the restrictive effects of taxes on production, income, and employment, a clear outline of the most desirable postwar tax structure might have emerged. But, whereas there is a surprising amount of agreement on many points, differences of opinion on several basic issues have been revealed. An examination of competing points of view with respect to these issues may be helpful in advancing an understanding of the problems involved in adapting the tax structure to postwar conditions.

General Aspects of the Postwar Tax Structure

Before turning to the specific taxes which constitute the Federal tax structure, let us consider some issues which relate to taxation generally.

On the face of things, the differences of opinion and analysis appear to be predominantly differences in understanding of the economics of taxation rather than differences in objectives. The relative effects on economic activity of taxes that reduce consumption and of taxes that reduce "business incentives" are analyzed with great apparent objectivity. But the disagreement on economic forces, and hence on tax policy, which is reflected in such analyses probably springs from a more fundamental source than normal intellectual variation. To a considerable degree it probably grows out of an inevitable conflict of interests. If there were agreement on how the economy operates, a more intelligent effort to reconcile conflicting interests would be possible. Agreement in economic theory might so clarify the implications for governmental policy of a given economic situation as to modify political decisions. If economic theory remains in a constant state of intellectual confusion, special-interest groups will have a better tool of political conflict than if harmony in economic analysis is achieved.

There is the usual argument that taxation should be for revenue only. The "maximum revenue" test is used to make this argument consistent with simultaneous emphasis on the economic effects of tax changes. According to this test, concern over the economic effects of taxation is merely concern over the removal of restrictions to maximum revenue. Although it would be improper to seek through tax changes

---

[1] The plethora of postwar tax plans and discussions makes it appropriate to set up the genus, "tax planners," for convenience of reference.

such economic goals as maximum production, income, and employment per se, they become proper objectives of tax policy if they are identified with achievement of maximum revenue. Thus stimulus to business incentives becomes a legitimate goal on the grounds that increased business activity produces higher tax yields. The argument is a handy one, since, through it, desired changes can be defended as promoting maximum revenue and undesired changes condemned as interfering with maximum revenue.

In current discussions there seems to be great awareness of the inevitable repercussions of taxes on economic life and of the importance of producing the least undesirable, *i.e.*, the most desirable, repercussions. Recognition that tax rates should not be raised in periods of declining business activity—a view not widely held a decade or so ago—is now fairly general. This recognition does not necessarily represent a conversion to the economic tenets of compensatory fiscal policy. In some cases recognition has been forced by the logic that if low tax rates are necessary to maintain and encourage business activity after the war, an increase in rates can hardly be justified in a period of declining business activity. The intellectual and emotional clash between budget balancing and the logic of compensatory fiscal policy is probably severe for some people. The view that budgets should be balanced annually rarely appears, but there is some cleavage as to longer periods. The most prevalent view seems to be that, over the business cycle, expenditures should be matched by revenues and at least token progress should be made toward reducing the accumulated debt.

A few planners advocate flexible tax rates which rise in boom times and decline with the approach of depression. In view of the political and practical difficulty of applying flexibility, however, this proposal has in this country thus far remained largely in the academic realm.

The postwar tax plans and accompanying discussions have created a general awareness that government expenditures in the postwar years will be several times as high as before the war and that, notwithstanding a much higher national income than in prewar years, taxes will not revert to prewar levels. Some reduction from wartime rates is demanded and expected. However, failure to distinguish whether "cutting taxes" means cutting rates or reducing yields has led to some confusion. A reduction in yield, of course, involves the combined results of lower rates and lower national income.

The economic theories developed over the past decade or two are being used by some tax planners to eliminate a conflict that has appeared to exist between the equity of tax distribution and the effects of taxes on the level of production. The orthodox emphasis on a large volume of saving and investment as the basic requirement of expansion casts an economic doubt on progressive taxation because of its alleged dampening effect on saving. The new emphasis on the maintenance of consumption as the foundation of investment and maximum production points to progressive taxation as both equitably and economically sound. Maintenance of consumption is thus deemed to overshadow direct incentives to invest as a means of stimulating business activity. Needless to say, this view does not meet universal acceptance, especially among spokesmen for the business community.

Little support has developed for the use of special tax incentives to stimulate economic activity. Specific tax concessions for such economically desirable activities as expansion of investment or employment have gained few advocates. In part this is merely an extension of the principle of using taxation for revenue alone. But it goes beyond this. Some people oppose such incentives because they fear that in practice the incentives would become special privileges and tax loopholes far removed from the underlying purpose of economic stimulation. For example, special tax treatment of new businesses is frequently opposed on the ground that such an incentive device might be perverted to result in tax reduction for old businesses for which it was never intended.

Simplification receives a share of attention in the formal tax plans, but less than might be expected in view of the public pressure for simplification in the winter of 1943–1944. That pressure, of course, was primarily for individual income-tax simplification and was heightened by the fact that great numbers of new taxpayers faced the complexities of the 1943 return which stemmed from the Victory tax and the Current Tax Payment Act of 1943. Most of the postwar tax plans proposed would add new complexities to the law while removing some of the old ones.

Specific Taxes in the Postwar Tax Structure

In the postwar tax plans under discussion, modifications have been proposed for every important tax that was changed during the war. Some of the more important issues involved in these proposals are discussed in the following paragraphs.

EXCESS-PROFITS TAX

In the minds of people who are considering the postwar tax structure the problem of what to do with the excess-profits tax seems to command first attention. The name "excess-profits tax" does not describe the tax accurately, for it is more nearly a war-profits tax. However "excessive" in relation to invested capital, profits are not subject to excess-profits tax unless they are above the prewar earnings level, which is measured as 95 per cent of the average earnings in a base period of prewar years, 1936–1939. On the other hand, even though profits exceed the prewar earnings level, they are not subject to excess-profits tax unless they also exceed a percentage of invested capital varying from 8 to 5 per cent, according to the size of invested capital. In both cases only the amount of the excess is taxed as excess profits. A series of provisions has been placed in the law to relieve hardships which might arise from an abnormal element in current income or from an abnormally low earnings record in the base period years. Excess profits are not subject to the corporate normal income tax and surtax.

The excess-profits tax was brought into the tax structure in 1940 partly to raise revenue but chiefly to prevent profiteering from the war. The postwar tax planners with rare exceptions have approved or accepted the excess-profits tax as a wartime measure. The view is sometimes expressed that the high rates have probably operated to restrict production in some areas during the war but have not significantly impeded our total productive effort in view of the strong counterbalancing impact of patriotism and governmental war powers. Limiting civilian production during the war is probably desirable in that it releases labor and resources for war production. But the consensus is that the restrictions of the excess-profits tax on business reconversion and expansion would be unreservedly bad in the postwar period. Prompt repeal at the close of hostilities is generally urged, although there is some sentiment for retaining the tax at a lower rate until controls on wages and prices can be safely abandoned and perhaps even until war-caused high profits cease to exist.

Quite apart from the understandable desire of those subject to the excess-profits tax to get rid of it, the reasons for discarding this tax in peacetime are persuasive. A rough, although by no means fully achieved, effect of the tax is to maintain during the war a relative position among corporations similar to that which existed before the war. This tie to the prewar period makes the excess-profits tax unsuitable in any event after war excess profits have come to an end. For example, in the postwar period it is desirable that small corporations and new corporations be in position, unfettered by tax disadvantages, to grow and compete with established corporations. The present form of excess-profits tax would interfere with that competition.

It has been strongly urged that if, despite the objections, the excess-profits tax is retained for a year or so in the reconversion period, the rates should be substantially lowered. Proposals have been made to increase the excess-profits credits and, as an aid to small corporations, to increase the present specific exemption of $10,000.

The excess-profits tax presents many complications to the taxpayer and to the administrator. But suggested changes to simplify it are, in general, opposed by postwar tax planners. At this point, change itself constitutes a complication, since it would introduce a new set of rules applicable to some years, while the old rules would continue to apply to other years still under consideration.

A few voices advocate retention of some sort of excess-profits tax in the postwar period. They justify such a tax on the grounds that the higher ranges of profits relative to investment are less necessary to achieve a high level of production than are moderate profits and that consistently high profits commonly flow from monopoly control. They agree, however, that the existing excess-profits tax, because of its emphasis on the excess over prewar profits, is not fitted to play such a role. The difficulties of devising an excess-profits tax capable of reaching the desired profits in a peacetime system are impressive and have thus far seemed conceptually and practically insurmountable. Among the problems are the determination of invested capital; the treatment of intangibles, which may or may not reflect an investment of capital (even where they do, it is often impossible to measure the amount of the investment); allowances for risk appropriate to different industries; and the treatment of income which is essentially derived from personal services rather than from capital.

Although calling for early repeal of the excess-profits tax, a large majority of the postwar tax planners believe that the carry-back of unused excess-profits credits and of losses should remain effective until corporations have had the tax benefits of the expenses and losses which are caused by the war but not incurred until after the war. There is some difference of opinion as to how long a period will be necessary to achieve this end, but in general, a full two years after the repeal of the tax has been urged, and an even longer period has occasionally been suggested.

Some have pointed out, however, that the longer the carry-backs are maintained, the greater will be the offsets against wartime income of losses and expenses not connected with the war as contrasted with those that are war-connected. This not only operates to nullify the effectiveness of the excess-profits tax in taxing high war profits but will also necessitate higher tax rates than would be required if there were no carry-back refunds to finance.

Sentiment appears unanimously in favor of speeding up the use of the carry-backs by allowing them to be credited currently against income taxes due the government.

CORPORATION INCOME TAX

For the post-transition period the corporation income tax succeeds the excess-profits tax as the measure of greatest interest to the postwar tax planners. Perhaps the predominance of businessmen and their spokesmen in the planners' ranks accounts for this interest. What to do about the so-called "double" taxation of corporate profits is the chief problem raised in connection with the corporation income tax. At the present time corporate profits are taxed first to the corporations, then again to the stockholders when they are distributed as dividends. This means that distributed corporate earnings are subject to two taxes, while other kinds of income are subject to only one.

Is this double taxation of corporate profits real or only apparent? The answer turns on whether the corporation tax is borne by stockholders or is shifted to the consumers in higher prices or, alternatively, to workers in lower wages, creditors in lower interest rates, and so on. If the tax is shifted, it is not borne by the stockholder, and he is not doubly taxed.[1]

Economists have traditionally taken the view that general corporation taxes which are measured by net income or profits are not shifted but fall on the stockholders. But many other people, most businessmen included, view corporation income and profits taxes as a cost of production to be recouped through price. For example, public-utility-regulating commissions in general allow Federal income taxes as an expense in determining a reasonable rate.

---

[1] However, the stockholder may be affected adversely by the tax in other ways even though it is shifted.

It is also argued that, even if the corporate tax does rest on the stockholders, its burden has by this time been largely removed by the process of capitalization as reflected in the prices of securities. Accordingly, a substantial tax decrease would give a windfall to present stockholders. If high levels of national income are maintained, corporate profits after taxes may rise to unprecedented heights, thus enlarging the windfall. Moreover, it is urged, this situation might lead to an unfortunate stock-market boom. To a lesser degree the windfall point may be made even though the taxes are eventually shifted, provided that the shifting takes place gradually over a period of years. However, this point applies neither to new businesses nor to new investment in old businesses. In any event, its significance appears to be temporary.

Whether double taxation should continue permanently on the ground that the corporate entity should be taxed as such without regard to the stockholders is another question. Some tax planners have maintained that the double tax system should be retained both because a corporate franchise is valuable and because corporate business receives a large volume of costly service from the Federal government.

Whatever views they hold on the questions of tax shifting and of taxing the corporate entity, the postwar tax planners are virtually unanimous in maintaining that a large part of the corporation tax falls on the stockholder and that there is undesirable double taxation of distributed corporate profits. No method of eliminating double taxation, however, has gained common acceptance. Several competing plans are proposed. The advocates of each present strong arguments against the others.

One proposed method of eliminating double taxation of corporate profits is to treat corporations like partnerships. The partnership is not taxed as such, but partnership income is attributed to the partners and taxed to them when earned, whether or not they have actually received it. Similarly, this method would impose no tax on the corporation but would tax the stockholders on their allocable share of the corporate profits when earned, whether or not distributed in dividends. In behalf of this method it is urged that there is minimum tax interference with corporate management and maximum equity among different businesses. However, the proposal is strenuously opposed on the ground that a stockholder frequently is not in position to secure control over the income on which he must pay taxes and in fact may never receive it. A share of stock might turn out to be more of a liability than an asset.

Moreover, the technical problems and complications involved are generally agreed to be exceedingly great.

Some planners have proposed to meet the difficulties of the partnership method by requiring instead that corporations make their profits available to stockholders each year for dividends or reinvestment. They urge that this would promote tax equity among stockholders and a sounder relationship between corporation and stockholder. The proposal has been strenuously opposed on the grounds that it is a measure of corporate reform rather than a tax measure and that it would destroy corporate growth and expansion.

Unlike these two methods of eliminating double taxation, other proposed methods make it advantageous taxwise to retain earnings rather than to distribute them as dividends. This is also true of existing law.

Repeal of the corporate income tax, leaving only the individual income tax on the dividends received by the stockholder, is another method of eliminating double taxation. It is universally recognized that this procedure, in the absence of other measures, would make the corporation a tax-free haven for the accumulation of income by stockholders who did not need the income for current expenditure. Strengthening of the present tax on the unreasonable accumulation of earnings has been urged as a method of meeting this problem, but there is little faith in its efficacy and it does not go to the heart of the problem of tax-free accumulation of income.

The imposition of a tax on undistributed profits has also been urged. A rate of less than 20 per cent has been suggested as sufficient to prevent accumulation of earnings in the corporation without unduly penalizing corporations which had to rely on earnings as a source of capital for expansion.

A somewhat similar proposal is to continue a tax on corporate profits but to allow the corporation a deduction for dividends paid similar to the deduction now allowed for interest paid. This method would eliminate the preferential tax treatment which existing law grants to bond financing over stock financing. Because it is in the form of a reduction of present taxes on distributed profits, this deduction is considered by many to be more acceptable than a reduction in corporate tax rates accompanied by a special tax on undistributed profits.

All the arguments of earlier years have been leveled against the proposals which involve heavier taxes on undistributed profits than on distributed profits. It has been urged that such taxes would coerce corporate management into undesirable distribution of profits and would penalize growing corporations. The carry-over of a given year's profits for distribution over a period of several years is one of the measures suggested to meet this type of objection.

Another method of eliminating double taxation is to apply a withholding tax to the corporation profits at the time they are earned and to grant the stockholder credit for this tax at the time the dividends are distributed. The dividend to be included in the stockholder's tax return would exceed the cash received by him by the amount of tax withheld by the corporation, just as at the present time the individual is taxed on his gross wage or salary without allowance for the tax withheld at source. However, the stockholder would be allowed a tax credit for the amount of tax paid at source by the corporation and, if this credit were in excess of his tax liability, he would be granted a refund. This method has long been used in Great Britain.

An objection which has been made to the withholding method is that individuals with low incomes and tax-exempt organizations would receive refunds of tax. This would involve administrative difficulties. Moreover, some people would like to reach tax-exempt organizations indirectly through the corporate tax.

Still another method of eliminating double taxation is to allow the individual stockholder an exemption from the normal individual tax with respect to dividends received by him. The normal tax would be imposed at the rate necessary to reduce double taxation to the extent desired. This method was in operation prior to 1936, although double taxation was only partly eliminated. The dividend credit is supported as giving investment incentives to individuals by reducing the rate of tax on dividends below the level possible under other methods of eliminating double taxation.

A disadvantage of this method is that its effective operation requires a fixed relationship between the corporation tax and the individual normal tax. Flexibility and adaptability of the taxes is thus impaired. Moreover, this method eliminates double taxation more completely for stockholders subject to high income tax rates than for those subject to lower rates, and offers no relief at all to stockholders not subject to individual income tax.

This method is criticized also on the ground that it envisages a high rate of corporate tax, which would have a restrictive impact on corporate managers. It is pointed out also that, if the corporate tax were shifted entirely to consumers, the dividends received by the stockholder would be subject to less taxes than any other form of income, thus discriminating in favor of income earned through corporations.

A variant of the method of allowing an exemption from part of the individual tax would be to allow dividends to be included in individual income at some fraction, such as 60 per cent, of the amount of the dividend. Although this method has the advantage of simplicity, the relief it grants from double taxation is much more strongly weighted in favor of the higher income brackets than the other methods of reducing double taxation.

In addition to proposals regarding double taxation, the postwar tax planners have made recommendations regarding rates and exemptions of the corporation income tax. Spokesmen for small business urge that a lower-than-standard rate be continued for corporations with incomes of less than $50,000, with an even greater rate differential than exists at present. Some sentiment has developed for a reintroduction of an exemption of $2,000 or more to eliminate the smallest corporations entirely. Proposals have been made also to combine the normal tax and surtax in order to simplify the tax structure.

There is almost unanimous agreement that a long period of loss carry-over should be provided for businesses generally. Such a period might extend for about 5 years and would take the place of the present combination of a 2-year carry-back and a 2-year carry-forward of losses. The carry-backs have introduced complications, and their permanent retention has not generally been favored.

Some emphasis has been placed on relaxing the rules regarding depreciation. Two points of view are reflected. The first would relax the administration of the depreciation provisions so that the taxpayer might have more flexibility in determining the rates to be charged. The second would provide greater flexibility and, in addition, would accelerate depreciation in the early years of the life of the asset. An extreme example of such acceleration would be the continuation of the 5-year amortization provision employed during the war to encourage the construction of plants and equipment for war production. A more flexible depreciation policy is unanimously favored, but some questions have arisen as to the desirability of the departures from standard accounting procedures which would be involved in an acceleration of depreciation.

CAPITAL-STOCK AND DECLARED-VALUE EXCESS-PROFITS TAXES

Minor elements in the corporation tax structure are the declared-value capital-stock tax and the declared-value excess-profits tax; the latter is not to be confused with the wartime excess-profits tax. An earlier capital-stock tax based on the "fair" value of capital stock was repealed in 1926, in part because of difficulties of valuation. In the search for revenues during the depression of the thirties a capital-stock tax was again imposed in 1933, but to avoid the necessity for valuation, the taxpayer was permitted to declare once and for all any value he desired. To prevent undervaluation a declared-value excess-profits tax was imposed on all profits in excess of 10 per cent of the declared value of the capital stock. The taxes did not stand as originally passed; taxpayers who had made unfortunate declarations prevailed upon Congress to grant a succession of new options to redeclare. Existing law permits annual redeclarations.

The combined amount of the two taxes is at a minimum when the declared value is ten times the profits which are realized during the year. Corporations with unpredictable earnings will pay more than the minimum, either through a higher-than-necessary declaration of capital stock or through payment of the declared-value excess-profits tax. The taxes are thus a sort of guessing game bearing most heavily on corporations which cannot accurately forecast their earnings. This group is likely to include a disproportionate number of small companies, new companies, and companies in fields of relatively great risk.

The capital-stock tax has been defended as a method of taxing deficit corporations for benefits received. Although some other form of capital-stock tax might have achieved this result, the present tax does not. The deficit corporation pays only when it has failed to anticipate the deficit.

That the capital-stock and declared-value excess-profits taxes should be repealed as soon as possible is unanimously agreed. Since these taxes are deductible from income subject to income and excess-profits taxes, the loss of revenue under present rates would be largely offset by higher income and excess-profits taxes.

INDIVIDUAL INCOME TAX

It is almost a tax axiom that, since taxes must generally be paid from income, they should, insofar as possible, be imposed directly on income. This principle is supported by the fact that, although not perfect, income is the best single measure of taxable capacity which has thus far been developed. With few exceptions the postwar tax planners are assigning the individual income tax the most important role in the postwar tax structure. Necessarily, this role involves rates far above the prewar levels.

Few basic changes are proposed in the individual income tax. Some people have urged the introduction of averaging, but their proposals involve very substantial complications. Retention of the withholding and current-payment features is generally assumed, and discussion centers mostly around rates and exemptions. There is growing recognition that much heavier taxes on the bulk of the population will be necessary after the war than before, and that an income tax with low exemptions and a relatively high starting rate is preferable to heavy reliance on sales and excise taxes. However, it is being extensively debated whether reductions at the bottom to protect consumption, or reductions in the brackets above about $5,000 to encourage investment and risk taking, are more important to the health of the postwar economy.

Those who would introduce flexibility into the tax structure by increasing taxes in boom periods and reducing them in depression periods consider the individual income tax, especially in the lower brackets, the best place to apply the technique. Some would accomplish the result through raising and lowering personal exemptions, others by adjusting tax rates.

CAPITAL-GAINS TAX

The treatment of capital gains has long been a source of controversy in Federal taxation. It is worthy of note that tax planners generally have recommended that the present treatment of capital gains and losses be retained until there is an opportunity for more thorough study or until other postwar tax adjustments have been made. The view that the present law is not too bad a compromise of the various viewpoints is generally supported.

However, a few planners call for substantial revision of capital-gains taxation. Some would tax capital gains at full income-tax rates, although averaging the gains over a period of years, and would tax accrued gains at the time of making a gift or passing property at death. At the other extreme are those who would eliminate completely the capital-gains tax and the deduction of capital losses.

ESTATE AND GIFT TAXES

The estate tax and its companion gift tax are minor revenue sources, yielding less than alcoholic beverages or tobacco. Yet throughout the years there has been widespread interest in these taxes, indicating that much more important matters are at stake than the mere amount of revenue involved. The estate and gift taxes apply in only about 1 per cent of the adult deaths in the United States, and a relatively small fraction of the estates involved pay a large part of the total yield. Although top rates are high, reaching 77 per cent, the tax base contains numerous avenues of tax reduction and avoidance through such devices as life estates and trusts.

Wartime adjustments in estate and gift taxes have been less sweeping than in the case of any other important tax. This is not inappropriate since the estate tax is not well adapted to emergency modification. However, if other taxes remain at permanently higher levels, recommendations to enlarge the yield of the estate tax and its accompanying gift tax might be expected. In general, however, the estate and gift taxes have commanded little attention in plans for the immediate postwar period. The planners appear to consider these taxes a long-range problem to be taken up when other more pressing postwar adjustments are completed. However, technical committees have given considerable attention to the coordination of the estate, gift, and income taxes.

EXCISE AND SALES TAXES

The functions which excise taxes are generally believed to perform in the Federal tax structure are to keep down the rates of income tax and to reach classes of taxpayers not touched by the income tax. The principal objections voiced to excises are that they burden consumption, fall inequitably on lower income groups, and discriminate against the industries producing the taxed goods and services. The excises in use by the Federal government are imposed largely on items of optional expenditure. Thus the taxes are somewhat less objectionable than a general sales tax would be because, to the extent that they fall on the poor, they fall in an optional way and thereby mitigate the sting of the tax burden.

Postwar tax plans would in general continue use of some of the excises. Liquor, tobacco, and gasoline are the most frequently mentioned commodities recommended for continued excise taxation. However, some plans propose a large excise-tax program. Many of the programs condemn a general sales tax because of its adverse effect on consumption and its regressive incidence, but a few recommend its adoption.

PAY-ROLL TAXES

Postwar tax planners have generally avoided the subjects of social-security and pay-roll taxation on the premise that they are outside the regular tax structure. However, a strong sentiment to hold down the pay-roll taxes is shared by groups which desire to limit social-security expansion and by groups which maintain that the social-security program should be financed by general rather than by pay-roll taxation.

Conclusion

No one will deny that the Federal tax structure is an intricate one. Obviously, in a short space it is impossible to set down all the issues and problems involved in postwar tax readjustment. Some of those which appear uppermost in the minds of postwar tax planners have been briefly discussed. If undue emphasis appears to have been placed on corporation taxes, that emphasis is but a reflection of the fact that the postwar tax planners have concentrated most of their proposals for modification in this area.

An over-all view leads to the conclusion that the problems of postwar tax adjustment will be more difficult to solve than any tax problems heretofore faced by the Federal government. More emphasis than ever before has been placed on the difficult problem of the effects of taxation on the operation of the economy. Despite this fact, it appears that current differences of opinion over tax policy in the main follow the lines which are familiar to students and observers of tax history.

Chapter XVI

A Postwar Tax Program

by ALVIN H. HANSEN [1]

IN DISCUSSING a postwar tax program—Federal, state, and local—it would seem desirable first of all to consider the probable magnitude of postwar governmental budgets and the role they will play in the functioning of the economy.

I believe it to be true that the prevailing view among economists and fiscal authorities in England, the Scandinavian countries, Canada, and the United States is that the government budget should, on its expenditure side (and as far as feasible on the tax side) serve as a compensatory device to offset fluctuations in the private sector of the economy.

A high sense of social responsibility and prudence in public finance demands that government expenditures, taxation, and borrowing be managed so as to promote economic stability and high levels of income and employment. Fiscal policy is, of course, only one of many measures which can contribute to this end. Labor relations and wage and price policies are no less important. Moreover, we must work incessantly to achieve efficiency in government administration. True economy does not mean blind slashing of expenditures; it does mean efficient use of public funds, careful administration to eliminate waste, and thorough planning so that public expenditures may be made on useful and productive projects of a character which will increase the efficiency and well-being of our population and raise the productivity of the nation as a whole.

The first thing that needs to be said about a postwar Federal budget is that it should be a flexible one. One cannot talk intelligently, I feel,

[1] Adapted from an article for the *Commercial and Financial Chronicle*. Reprinted by permission.

about the magnitude of postwar public expenditures or the volume of taxes that needs to be raised, without regard to the business cycle or without regard to the then prevailing level of private capital outlays.

In my book on *State and Local Finance in the National Economy*, I have set forth four models of a postwar Federal budget varying according to different phases of the business cycle. At the one extreme, it is assumed that a strong private investment boom is under way, with inflationary tendencies. Under these conditions Federal taxes should exceed expenditures; my model for this situation provides a substantial budget surplus. At the other extreme, that of serious depression, useful and productive public expenditures, not wholly covered by taxes, should be made; in my proposed budget under these conditions a substantial Treasury deficit is assumed. Intermediate are two models: one provides for a balanced budget and the other a moderate deficit.

In this chapter I shall consider only these intermediate budgets since they are probably more useful for the purpose of introducing discussion about a postwar tax program. I assume in these two intermediate models a Federal budget (exclusive of the social-security program) ranging from $19 to $21 billion roughly around $20 billion.[1] I am interested to note that my budget is very closely similar to that proposed by Senator Taft last March. He proposes a Federal budget of $18 billion, social security excluded. His item for military expenditures is $5 billion, while mine is $6 billion. Possibly $5 billion is sufficient for this purpose, in which case his budget and mine come still closer together. We both suggest $6 billion for interest on the public debt, $2 billion for veterans, and are not so very far apart on the other expenditures which include government administration, public improvements and public works, social services (other than social security proper), and grants-in-aid to the localities. In point of fact, the main explanation for the difference between our budgets is that I suggest substantial Federal aid to the localities for urban redevelopment and for raising the level of public-school education. The war once again has disclosed in an impressive way the educational deficiency of millions of our citizens. It is intolerable that so many American citizens should be functional illiterates. This is a national problem. Some states and localities do not have the fiscal capacity to provide the required necessary standard of education. Their outlays

---

[1] In a period of threatened large-scale unemployment, the budget might need to be increased to perhaps $25 billion ($30 billion including social security). These figures are highly tentative. Long-range planning and research and continued adaptation to changing needs must determine the appropriate magnitudes.

for education are intolerably low, yet it is a fact that they tax their people, in proportion to income, more heavily in support of education than do the richer states. They have not the financial means to provide the educational opportunities to which every American citizen is entitled.

But the subject matter of this chapter is taxes not expenditures. As I said above, in one of my intermediate models the budget ($19 billion) is assumed to be balanced, and in the other ($21 billion) there is a deficit of $3 billion. In accordance with these models, the postwar tax structure should yield $18 to $19 billion. How shall we raise this money?

Let me say that I am not discussing taxes in the transition period. It may well be that in the interim transition period, wartime taxes should in large part be retained. I am here addressing myself to more normal peace conditions.

It should first emphatically be said that we must have a drastic reduction in taxes from the wartime level. Excess-profits taxes should be completely repealed and other tax rates should be reduced.

Omitting the pay-roll taxes (social security), which are here excluded, Federal taxes may broadly be classified in three categories: (1) direct personal taxes (income, estate, and gift taxes); (2) corporate income taxes, and (3) excises and miscellaneous revenues.

The first problem relates to the relative merits of excises (selective sales taxes) on the one side, and income (corporate and individual) taxes on the other. There is, I think, growing agreement that consumption taxes are bad for business since they curtail the volume of mass purchasing power. On these grounds, general sales taxes ought to be excluded altogether under peacetime conditions. The same holds for the whole mess of selective excises, on all manner of products, which are currently on the statute books. These have decided merit in wartime but should be completely eliminated in peacetime. How far we should go in reducing the excise taxes on alcoholic beverages, tobacco, and gasoline is a matter that will require much further study and should in part be determined by future developments. I would suggest, however, that we begin with a retention of these taxes, though with rates substantially lower than the wartime rates. Gasoline taxes ought, I think, to be entirely reserved for the states. There would remain for Federal taxation alcoholic beverages and tobacco. At substantially lower rates than the present, $2 billion may be raised from these sources. Another billion can be raised from customs duties and miscellaneous revenues combined. We account thus far, then, for $3 billion of the $18 or $19 billion desired.

Under this proposal, then, $15 to $16 billion would need to be raised from income taxes (personal and corporate) and from estate and gift taxes.

Should relatively greater reliance be placed on personal income taxes or on corporate income taxes? My answer is to go relatively light on business and corporate taxation and to rely mainly upon personal income taxation. It is my view that such a tax structure will be less restrictive on private investment and business expansion than one which weighs heavily on business and corporate income.

It cannot be denied that both corporate income taxes and the personal income tax (with graduated surtax rates) tend to restrict investment in new ventures. This unfavorable effect upon risk taking can, however, be very materially ameliorated by the provision for loss carryback for 2 years and loss carry-forward for 5 years. I would urge generous loss-offset provisions in order to minimize to the utmost extent the unfavorable effect of high tax rates upon risk taking and new investment. This argument applies to taxes both on corporate and personal incomes.

I would suggest that the current double taxation of dividends be eliminated. The plan which I suggest is an adaptation of the British method. The British method has sometimes been described as a tax exclusively on stockholders with no tax on the corporation at all. So described, it means that all stockholders pay the standard rate on the earnings retained by the corporation, regardless of their income status, while they pay according to their income status (taking account of exemptions and the surtax rates) on that part of the corporate income distributed in dividends. In point of fact, the standard rate (applied to the entire corporate income) is deducted at the source and paid over by the corporation to the national Treasury. The individual stockholder is credited with the deduction at the source on the distributed part. If he is a low-income person, he may, owing to exemptions, be entitled to a refund. If he is a high-income person, he will have additional taxes to pay on the distributed dividends, according to the surtax rate.

Now the British system may equally well be described as a corporate tax, at the standard rate, on the undistributed earnings and an individual income tax on the distributed part of the corporate income. The deduction at the source is, of course, only an administrative feature and has nothing to do with the final distribution of the tax burden.

In England, the standard individual income-tax rate (which applies to all taxable income in excess of the first £165) is very high—50 per cent; with us it is low, the "basic" tax (which applies to all taxable individual income) being only 23 per cent—3 per cent so-called "normal," and 20 per cent for the first bracket applicable to all taxpayers. In view of our low "basic" rate, it is not possible to apply the basic tax to that part of the corporate income which is retained. To do so would give a grossly unfair advantage to corporations as compared with partnerships. Moreover, it would give a strong inducement to tax evasion via retention of corporate earnings.

I would suggest, therefore, (Plan A) a rate of 45 per cent on the retained part of corporate income with no corporate tax whatever on the distributed part, the individual stockholder alone being taxed on this portion. As a convenient method of collection there could be deducted at the source the corporate tax on the retained earnings plus the "basic" individual rate on the distributed earnings, such deduction, however, being credited to the individual stockholder. Small corporations might be accorded a somewhat more favorable treatment.

Plan A (eliminating double taxation) would in fact prove to be a lighter tax on corporations in general than a 30 per cent corporate tax (Plan B) of the type we have been familiar with. Assuming—the statistical and analytical basis for this figure I cannot here explain—net corporate profits, prior to taxes, of $15 billion, after the war, Plan A (eliminating double taxation) could be expected to yield $4 billion of corporate taxes, while Plan B (30 per cent of all corporate income) would yield $4.5 billion corporate income taxes.

Personal income taxes, designed to raise $10 billion, would permit a very substantial reduction from the present tax rates. The effective rate on a $5,000 income in my schedule would be virtually cut in two from the current wartime rates. I would suggest raising exemptions to $800 for a single person and $1,600 for a married person, and a "basic" rate of 15 per cent. I assume postwar income payments to individuals at around $135 billion. The net income of individuals after Federal taxes would, therefore, be $125 billion or very substantially higher than in any former peacetime year. I believe gift and estate taxes might well be made to yield $1 billion.

To sum up, then, personal direct taxes (income, death, and gift) would yield $11 billion, corporation net income taxes $4 to $4.5 billion,

A POSTWAR TAX PROGRAM

and excises and miscellaneous revenues $3 billion. The main features of the program include:

1. Generous loss offsets carried back and forward in order to induce risk taking and new investment.
2. Major reliance on individual income tax.
3. Complete elimination of excess-profits tax.
4. A sharp reduction in corporate income taxes along one of two lines, whichever is preferred:

   a. Elimination of double taxation with a 45 per cent tax on the retained earnings and no corporate tax on the distributed earnings, or

   b. The type of corporate income tax with which we are familiar, with a 30 per cent tax on the whole corporate income.

5. Elimination of all Federal excises except alcoholic beverages, tobacco, and customs duties.

What about state and local taxes? These I am compelled to discuss very briefly. I would suggest that state taxes be simplified along the following lines: complete elimination of the chaotic mess of business taxes now common among the states. State taxes would then consist of the individual income tax, corporate income tax, inheritance tax, excises on alcoholic beverages, tobacco, gasoline, and motor vehicles, and miscellaneous revenues. The states would need to raise in my proposed model about $4 billion. This could be distributed as follows:

	Billions
Individual income tax	$0.5
Corporate income tax	0.6
Death duties	0.3
Alcoholic beverages	0.4
Tobacco	0.3
Gasoline	0.9
Motor vehicles	0.4
Miscellaneous revenue	0.5
	$3.9

The localities in my schedule would need to raise a little over $5 billion. This might consist of the following:

	Billions
Property taxes	$4.1
Gasoline	0.4
Motor vehicles	0.2
Miscellaneous revenue	0.6
	$5.3

The gasoline and motor-vehicle taxes referred to above would be collected by the states and shared with the local communities in the manner indicated in the state and local schedules as given.

Some intergovernmental transfers would, of course, be necessary. These I cannot go into in detail here.

This, then, broadly is, it seems to me, the program that we ought to work toward. The reform of state taxation cannot quickly or easily be achieved. The whole problem of a properly integrated tax structure, Federal, state, and local, is tremendously complicated and the study of it should be undertaken at an early date by a competent and broadly representative national tax commission.

The tax program which I have suggested, it will at once be recognized, is very different from that proposed by Prof. Lutz [1] in his article in the *Commercial and Financial Chronicle* of Feb. 10, 1944. For Federal revenues he relies heavily upon consumption taxes which I regard as undesirable. He, moreover, suggests the elimination of the graduated Federal income tax and proposes instead a flat 5 per cent rate on all individual incomes, collected at the source without exemption. The latter proposal runs counter to the well-nigh universal judgment of students of public finance over the last 30 or 40 years. It is, moreover, a proposal that I think would not be advanced by any responsible statesman in either of our major political parties nor would it be proposed in the platforms of either of our major parties. It violates the principles of equity and ability to pay. Moreover, it overlooks (what seems to me to be axiomatic) that personal income derived from great national corporations enjoying a *national* market should make its fair contribution to the support of national functions and national services. Professor Lutz does reserve the progressive income tax for states. However, since the more well-to-do reside mainly in a few states, though deriving their income from national corporations enjoying a national market, the net effect would be that progressive taxation could be used to support governmental functions only at the state level and not the governmental functions of the nation as a whole from which, in fact, their incomes are derived. This, it seems to me, is clearly inequitable and could be calculated to arouse violent opposition and regional conflict.

Professor Lutz has one element of flexibility in his program. He

---

[1] Professor Lutz's views are seriously considered by a large section of the business community and therefore deserve consideration.

wishes to adjust from year to year his proportional Federal tax on individual incomes. I have also suggested that the "basic" Federal income-tax rate be adjusted according to economic conditions. The difference between our proposals is that he wishes in depression periods to raise his rate in order to assure a balanced budget, whereas in depression I would wish to lower the rate in order to increase consumer purchasing power and sustain business activity. Professor Lutz is completely opposed to a compensatory fiscal program. As to what he proposes to do to meet a depression such as that which struck this country in 1929 and which caused the national income to fall to half its former level inside of 3 years, I am not at all clear. Experience reveals that a fiscal program (such as he suggests) which balances the budget and retires the debt at the rate of $1 billion a year, *regardless of fluctuations in the cycle, may lead to disaster.*

It is, I think, a fair statement to say that both theoretical and practical students of the problem of business instability have come to believe that a compensatory fiscal policy is the most hopeful measure yet proposed to cope with depression. Other measures can and should supplement it. And can it seriously be doubted that governments will in fact be compelled to use, more or less, a compensatory fiscal program? I do not think that any administration will in the future permit the national income to fall in 3 years to half its former level without engaging in large expenditures. Unfortunately, it may be done clumsily and tardily, owing to inadequate planning. Such expenditures would in large measure not be covered by current taxation. At other periods it will be necessary to exercise restraint, to balance or overbalance the budget. I find comfort in the self-discipline during the war. Imperfect as the record is, we have achieved substantial stability of prices, and we have supported a heavy program of taxation. This indicates that it is not unreasonable to suppose that, also in peacetime, in the event of inflationary tendencies, democratic governments can prevent inflation. In wartime, such restraint must take the form of increased taxes, rationing, and price control. Expenditures cannot be reduced, because the war must go on. In peacetime such restraint should take the form of a sharp curtailment in public works and capital expenditures, an increase in taxes, and indirect measures (such as Federal Housing Administration restraints on housing, consumer credit control, and the like).

The argument, sometimes made, that democratic countries cannot manage a compensatory fiscal policy, and therefore we should not undertake it, will not do. Whether we like it or not, governmental expenditures, borrowing, and taxes, on a large scale, *will* exercise a profound influence on our economic life. The only question is: Shall we permit their influence to be haphazard and chaotic, or shall we control them with a view to achieving a stable purchasing power of money and high levels of income and employment? I believe we cannot escape this task. And it *is* the task of a rational and responsible fiscal program.

Chapter XVII

Postwar Financing of Business Enterprise

by S. MORRIS LIVINGSTON

I. Wartime Liquid-asset Accumulation

DURING the immediate postwar period business enterprise will face unusual capital requirements. There will be a large deferred demand for equipment which cannot be obtained and structures which cannot be built during the war: delayed replacements, postponed expansion of growing industries, the adaptation to nonwar industries of war-born advances in technology.

Working inventories of civilian goods whose production has been curtailed will need to be replaced. Conversion of war plants to civilian use will be an expensive process. There is also the necessary plant expansion, including all the nonmanufacturing enterprises, in order to achieve a level of productive employment well above the best prewar year.

To meet these and other postwar requirements, business, as a whole, is building up large reserves of liquid assets during the war. The available data indicate that between the end of 1941 and the end of 1944 business enterprises, exclusive of banks, insurance companies, and other financial and eleemosynary institutions, have increased their holdings of currency, bank deposits, and government bonds by roughly $40 billion.

This figure is necessarily a rough approximation. A precise reconciliation of the Securities and Exchange Commission data on corporate and individual holdings of cash and government bonds with the Federal

Reserve Board survey of business and nonbusiness bank deposits may well be left to the specialists in this field. Since there is not room here to analyze these and other sources in detail, it will suffice to say that there is general agreement as to the magnitude of the wartime accumulations.

TABLE 1.*—ESTIMATED SOURCES AND USES OF FUNDS FOR ALL BUSINESS, 1939–1940

(For all businesses except banks, insurance corporations, and eleemosynary institutions)

(In billions of dollars)

	Sources	1939 uses	Net sources (+) or uses (−)	Sources	1940 uses	Net sources (+) or uses (−)	Sources	1939–1940 uses	Net sources (+) or uses (−)
A. Gross business savings:									
1. Corporate undistributed profits	0.4	...	...	1.8	...	...	2.2	...	...
2. Retained earnings of unincorporated business	0.5	...	...	0.7	...	...	1.2	...	...
3. Depreciation and depletion	4.7	...	...	4.9	...	...	9.6	...	...
4. Other business reserves and capital outlays charged to current expense	1.5	...	...	1.6	...	...	3.1	...	...
Total	7.1	...	+7.1	9.0	...	+9.0	16.1	...	+16.1
B. Gross business investment:									
5. Construction:									
a. Residential	...	0.8	...	...	0.9	...	...	1.7	...
b. Other	...	1.0	...	...	1.4	...	...	2.4	...
6. Equipment	...	5.1	...	...	6.5	...	...	11.6	...
7. Inventories	...	0.9	...	...	1.8	...	...	2.7	...
Total	...	7.8	−7.8	...	10.6	−10.6	...	18.4	−18.4
C. Net change in receivable-payable position:									
8. Net change in consumer debt	...	0.8	...	...	1.0	...	...	1.8	...
9. Government purchase debt	...	...	...	0.2	...	...	0.2	...	...
10. Net tax accruals:									
a. Corporate	0.3	...	...	1.3	...	...	1.6	...	...
b. Noncorporate	...	...	...	0.1	...	...	0.1	...	...
Total	0.3	0.8	−0.5	1.6	1.0	+0.6	1.9	1.8	+0.1
D. Net change in debt position:									
11. Net change in long-term debt	...	0.2	...	0.6	...	...	0.6	0.2	...
12. Net change in short-term debt	0.5	...	...	1.1	...	...	1.6	...	...
Total	0.5	0.2	+0.3	1.7	...	+1.7	2.2	0.2	+2.0
Net available for increases in currency, bank deposits, and U. S. government bonds	...	...	−0.9	...	...	+0.7	...	...	−0.2

* Except where otherwise noted the data in Tables 1 and 2 are from the Department of Commerce national-income and product estimates as published in the April and September, 1944, *Survey of Current Business*. Data for the second half of 1944 are tentative estimates derived from the same general sources.

After careful consideration of alternative methods, the following procedure was used in deriving a rough approximation of the retained earnings of unincorporated business. Proprietors in 1939 were assumed to have saved the same proportion of their income as all individuals. Changes in the number of self-employed, excluding farmers, since 1939 were derived from unpublished census data. Probable average consumption expenditures were derived by assuming that these expenditures moved in the same way as the average for all individuals. The total thus derived was reduced by 25 per cent on the ground that some self-employed are not businessmen in the generally accepted sense.

Depreciation and depletion excludes depreciation on farm productive facilities amounting to $0.9 billion from 1939 to 1940 and $1 billion thereafter. Depreciation on nonbusiness holdings of residential property amounting to $0.6 billion per year was also excluded. Similarly, the expenditures for farm equipment and two-thirds of the outlays for residential construction were excluded from gross business investment. Thirty per cent of the nonresidential construction was excluded as being of a nonbusiness character.

The estimates of changes in consumer and business debt are from the article by Alvin Slater in the July, 1944, *Survey of Current Business*. Tentative estimates for the last half of 1944 are the result of informal conversations with the author. The change in government purchase debt through 1943 is from a Securities and Exchange Commission release of Aug. 27, 1944. No change was assumed for the year 1944.

Estimates of noncorporate tax accruals take into consideration the partial forgiveness of 1944 taxes and the shift to a "pay-as-you-go" basis. It was assumed that the accruals of proprietors were proportionate to their share of total income of individuals for each year.

The figure must necessarily be rough and approximate because the concept itself is not clear-cut. The distinction between the liquid assets held by unincorporated businessmen for business purposes and the holdings of these same individuals as consumer reserves is necessarily rather tenuous. Frequently funds will be held in the same bank account with no clear distinction on the part of the owner as to the purpose for which they are being accumulated. Business enterprise, as used in this chapter, includes unincorporated business but excludes farmers. It also excludes the individual ownership of residential property.

In order to see how this accumulation has been built up and why it has been possible, it will be worth while to review briefly the process by which business enterprise was financed before the war. Table 1 summarizes this flow of funds for the 2-year period, 1939–1940.

During that period all business enterprises except financial and eleemosynary institutions spent a little over $18 billion for construction, equipment, and net additions to inventories. To finance these capital outlays they had almost $13 billion of depreciation and other reserves from current operations plus over $3 billion of retained earnings. They increased their ownership of consumer receivables by almost $2 billion, but this was approximately offset by increased tax accruals, leaving their net receivable-payable position substantially unchanged. This left only $2 billion to be obtained from outside sources, as reflected in the net change in debt position.

Table 2 presents a similar picture for the war years. During that period the gross capital outlays by business were in the neighborhood of $13 to $14 billion. Since this covers 3 years, it is at an annual rate substantially less than during the prewar period in spite of a much larger volume of business. It reflects the wartime restrictions on the purchase of many items.

Depreciation and other reserves from current operations amount to close to $25 billion, the accelerated rate reflecting the wartime need for more rapid amortization of these assets. Because dividends and the entrepreneurial withdrawals of unincorporated businessmen have not kept pace with increased earnings, the retained earnings for the 3-year period amount to another $24 billion.

The retirement of consumer debt, particularly installment debt, is only partly offset by increased amounts owed to business by the Federal government. Substantial amounts of cash have had to be set aside out of current operations to meet increased tax liabilities accrued but not yet

TABLE 2.*—ESTIMATED SOURCES AND USES OF FUNDS FOR ALL BUSINESS, 1942–1944

(For all businesses except banks, insurance corporations, and eleemosynary institutions)

(In billions of dollars)

	Sources	1942 uses	Net Sources (+) or uses (−)	Sources	1943 uses	Net sources (+) or uses (−)	Sources	1944 uses	Net sources (+) or uses (−)	Sources	1942–1944 uses	Net sources (+) or uses (−)
A. Gross business savings:												
1. Corporate undistributed profits	4.4	...		4.9	...		5.0	...		14.3	...	
2. Retained earnings of unincorporated business	2.7	...		3.5	...		3.9	...		10.1	...	
3. Depreciation and depletion	6.1	...		6.6	...		6.8	...		19.5	...	
4. Other business reserves and capital outlays charged to current expense	1.9	...		1.6	...		1.6	...		5.1	...	
Total	15.1	...	+15.1	16.6	...	+16.6	17.3	...	+17.3	49.0	...	+49.0
B. Gross business investment:												
5. Construction:												
a. Residential	...	0.5		...	0.3		...	0.3		...	1.1	
b. Other	...	1.1		...	0.6		...	0.7		...	2.4	
6. Equipment	...	4.6		...	2.9		...	3.8		...	11.3	
7. Inventories	0.5	...		0.5	...		0.3	...		1.3	...	
Total	0.5	6.2	−5.7	0.5	3.8	−3.3	0.3	4.8	−4.5	1.3	14.8	−13.5
C. Net change in receivable-payable position:												
8. Net change in consumer debt	3.0	...		0.9	...		...	...		3.9	...	
9. Government purchase debt	...	1.3		...	0.6		...	...		...	1.9	
10. Net tax accruals:												
a. Corporate	4.6	...		2.8	...		...	...		7.4	...	
b. Noncorporate	1.0	...		...	...		...	0.3		1.0	0.3	
Total	8.6	1.3	+7.3	3.7	0.6	+3.1	...	0.3	−0.3	12.3	2.2	+10.1
D. Net change in debt position:												
11. Net change in long-term debt	0.1	...		...	1.3		...	1.5		...	2.7	
12. Net change in short-term debt	...	1.7		0.4	...		...	...		...	1.3	
Total	0.1	1.7	−1.6	0.4	1.3	−0.9	...	1.5	−1.5	...	4.0	−4.0
Net available for increases in currency, bank deposits, and U.S. government bonds	...	...	+15.1	...	...	+15.5	...	...	+11.0	...	...	+41.6

* Cf. footnote to Table 1, p. 302.

payable. The net effect of these changes in the receivable-payable position of business as a whole has been to increase the holdings of liquid assets by roughly $10 billion.

Part of these funds has been used to reduce short- and long-term business debt by approximately $4 billion, but there is left a sum of over $40 billion available for increases in currency, bank deposits, and U. S. government bonds.

Comparing the two statements, it is apparent that, on balance, the bulk of the prewar capital requirements were met by depreciation and other reserves from current operations and by retained earnings. The huge wartime accumulation of liquid assets reflects (1) the inability of business to spend depreciation and other reserves for the purposes for which they were intended; (2) the conscious retention of a larger share of current earnings to meet postwar contingencies; (3) the accrued taxes which have been charged to current expenses but have not yet been paid over to the government; and (4) the liquidation of consumer purchase debt.

In appraising the significance of this accumulation of liquid assets, it is important to remember that it is not a measure of the profitability of business enterprise during the war. Profits after taxes have been large but not excessive relative to the volume of business transacted. Neither is it synonymous with business savings. A large part of the accumulation reflects the liquidation of other assets. Finally, a part of the accumulation is earmarked for other than postwar capital requirements. It must also cover tax accruals and rebuilding of consumer installment debt.

II. Postwar Sources of Business Funds

Any appraisal of the amounts available for postwar financing of business enterprise must take into consideration several other sources of funds in addition to the accumulation during the 3 years 1942 through 1944.

There will be further wartime accumulations beyond the end of 1944, depending on how long the war lasts before the postwar requirements have to be met. The annual rate of such accumulations during this period will depend on how war production has tapered off and on any relaxation of restrictions affecting the volume of private capital outlays.

There will be the net amount due business enterprise, after extinguishing prepayment liabilities, for output already delivered to the

Federal government. This balance of amounts owed by the Federal government to business minus government prepayments on war contracts amounted to roughly $2 to $3 billion at the end of 1943.

There will also be the claims arising out of the termination of war contracts as these contracts are closed. The magnitude of this item depends again on how war production is curtailed. Some impression of its size can be given by indicating what would have happened if contracts had been terminated abruptly on Dec. 1, 1943.

At that time the total book value of inventories held by war industries was in the neighborhood of $10 billion. For termination purposes these inventories plus related claims would be valued at a higher figure, possibly around $11 to $13 billion. The reason for this is that under the uniform termination procedures laid down by the Director of War Mobilization on Jan. 8, 1943, fixed-price supply contractors are entitled to compensation for costs incurred in connection with the uncompleted portion of their contracts plus profits. Costs are construed to include more than the direct costs usually considered in the establishment of the book value of inventories.

A small part of this total inventory was finished goods awaiting delivery to the Federal government. A large but indefinite part was already processed to the point where it would have been of comparatively little value in the production of civilian goods. Deducting the realizable value of unspecialized inventories of raw materials and those specialized inventories which would have some civilian use, the net amount which would have been taken over and paid for by the Federal government would be somewhere between $7 and $11 billion.

This was the situation as of the end of 1943. If, or as, war production is gradually curtailed, the claims arising out of the uncompleted portions of terminated contracts will be reduced.

Finally, there are the funds which will become available from current reserves and undistributed profits after the war. Regardless of the immediate urgency of the capital requirements, the gross business investment to meet those requirements will necessarily be spread over an appreciable period of time. The wartime accumulation of liquid assets will be needed to finance those outlays only to the extent that the outlays exceed the then current rate of reserves and retained earnings.

Merely as a means of visualizing the possibilities, let us assume arbitrarily that 1945 is a year of continuing but substantially reduced war production; that depreciation and other business reserves are charged against current operations in the same amount as in 1944; that, because of the decline in the total volume of business, retained earnings are reduced to less than two-thirds of the 1944 rate; that relaxation of restrictions will make it possible to spend twice as much as in 1944 on construction and equipment; that a partial termination of war contracts and the taking over of partly completed war goods by the government will provide business with $3 billion of additional funds; that the corresponding increase in inventories of civilian goods as production and distribution of these items are resumed will amount to $2.4 billion; that with declining earnings net tax accrual will be reduced by $3 billion; that as durable goods become available, consumer installment debt will be expanded by $2 billion.

TABLE 3.—SOURCES AND USES OF FUNDS IN HYPOTHETICAL YEAR 1945

(In billions of dollars)

	Sources	Uses
Depreciation and other reserves, including capital outlays charged to current expense..................	$8.4	
Retained earnings, corporate and noncorporate....................	5.6	
Construction and equipment expenditures...........................	...	$9.6
Partial liquidation of claims arising out of termination of war contracts.	3.0	
Increased inventories of civilian goods in process.......................	...	2.4
Net reduction in tax accruals........	...	3.0
Net increase in consumer debt.......	...	2.0
Total.......................	$17.0	$17.0

These assumptions are necessarily crude and quite probably wide of the mark. Certainly there will be no such exact balancing of the sources and uses of funds, leaving the liquid, asset position unchanged. It is evident, however, that only a very unusual combination of circumstances in 1945 could require the use of any substantial part of the liquid assets accumulated during the war.

Actual developments will depend, of course, on the timing of the curtailment of war production and the corresponding shift to civilian output. Since we are not concerned with business forecasting, it will suffice to continue the hypothetical picture by assuming that 1946 is a full transition year in which the adequacy of business funds is tested.

A major source of funds to meet capital requirements during the years 1945 and 1946 will be the depreciation and other reserves set aside out of current operations plus the charges directly to current expense where, as a matter of accounting practice, purchases of certain types of equipment are not charged to a capital account. Allowing for some reduction in depreciation and other reserves with a decline in business activity, possibly $13 to $15 billion could be obtained from this source.

The amount of retained earnings during these 2 years is necessarily quite problematical. Conceivably it could be a negative quantity but, since we are concerned with the adequacy of total funds relative to total requirements, it should be pointed out that the actual use of a large part of the wartime accumulation of liquid assets to finance the transition would, in itself, prevent as low a level of business activity as would be necessary if profits are to fail to cover dividends and entrepreneurial withdrawals. A range of $0 to $5 billion is not wide enough to cover all contingencies but is adequate for the immediate purpose.

The net claims on terminated contracts are also problematical, but it is doubtful whether even gradual termination would prevent substantial claims. Perhaps $5 to $10 billion is as good a guess as can be made at this time.

Table 4.—Sources of Business Funds, 1942–1946

	Billions
Accumulated during 3 years, 1942–1944	$41.6
Additional sources of funds during the 2 transition years, 1945–1946:	
Depreciation	13–15
Retained earnings	0– 5
Net claims on terminated contracts	5–10
Total	$59.6–$71.6

These funds, added to the 3-year wartime accumulation of over $40 billion, provide $60 to $70 billion to meet gross capital requirements. This amount is in addition to the liquid assets already held by business on Dec. 31, 1941, when presumably the current position was not seriously out of line with the volume of business being transacted at that time.

III. Postwar Uses of Business Funds

This $60 to $70 billion increase in liquid assets has been accumulated for a variety of purposes. In part it reflects the need to restore productive facilities, inventories, and receivables to their prewar condition and to meet increased tax accruals. In part it anticipates postwar expansion above the prewar level. In part it is a cushion against postwar business losses.

The third purpose is not properly a part of the present discussion. Furthermore, it can be argued that a postwar depression so great as to cause all business in the aggregate to earn a net loss would not be a period in which capital outlays would be so large as to make their financing any problem.

It will simplify the analysis if we also postpone consideration of the second purpose and cover first of all only those appropriate charges against the wartime accumulations necessary to restore business to its prewar position. Since the estimates are necessarily crude, it will be useful to indicate the *maximum* which might appropriately be charged to this account.

During the war years 1942 through 1944, the increase in business tax accruals, or the amount by which business tax liabilities have exceeded business tax payments, is approximately $8 billion. The retirement of these tax liabilities constitutes a charge against the wartime accumulations of cash and government bonds. Accordingly, $8 billion of the total amount should be earmarked for this purpose.[1]

The carry-back provision of corporate-income and excess-profits tax laws will offset some part of this increase in tax accruals. The Revenue Act of 1942 provides that a net loss during any taxable year may be set against the net profits of the two preceding years to reduce the income subject to taxation and thus provide the basis for a refund. The act also provides that the unused portion of an excess-profits tax credit for any one year may be carried back and added to the excess-profits tax credit of the two preceding years to reduce the income subject to excess-profits taxation and thus provide the basis for a refund.

The actual amount of tax refund depends, of course, upon the inter-

[1] The actual amount by which tax payments would exceed tax accruals depends upon (*a*) the postwar level of business earnings and (*b*) the level of tax rates. The excess of tax payments over accruals may be larger or smaller than $8 billion. However, the maximum amount which can be charged to the 3-year accumulation of cash and government bonds and war-contract settlement receipts, is $8 billion.

company distribution of postwar losses or declines in earnings as well as upon their magnitude. Some indication of the possibilities is given by the fact that total corporate income and excess-profits taxes on 1942, 1943, and 1944 income amount to between $40 and $45 billion. For our immediate purpose it is only necessary to indicate that $8 billion is the maximum which can be charged against the 3-year accumulation of cash and government bonds.

Another of the costs of liquidating the war program is the cost of reconversion. Unfortunately the term "reconversion" does not have a commonly accepted meaning. For example, the term is used to refer to the shifting of all war facilities to civilian-goods production, including those especially constructed for war production. It may also refer only to the restoration of civilian-production facilities which had previously been converted to war production. This second more restricted and more accurate meaning is used here. Conversion of newly constructed war plants involves not a restoration of prewar productive facilities but an expansion above that level.

Defined in this way, reconversion costs are limited. Only those prewar plants producing a markedly different product during the war are involved. The preponderance of prewar manufacturing facilities are being used to produce normal peacetime products or products so closely related to normal products that no significant reconversion of plant and equipment will be necessary at the end of the war.

The out-of-pocket costs of reconversion are limited chiefly to (1) the cost of purchasing new or rearranging old equipment; (2) payment of various overhead expenses during the period intervening between the cutback of war production and the receipt of cash from civilian-goods production; and (3) payment of special marketing costs involved in rebuilding sales organizations.

It is difficult to see how the outlays required under these three categories could total more than $4 billion. The replacement costs of the entire prewar equipment of converted plants did not exceed $4 billion. Much of this equipment has been stored or is being used in war production.[1] Some of it will be replaced by the purchase of war-production equipment from other firms, thereby involving only a shift in liquid assets from one enterprise to another. Altogether it is doubtful that the equipment costs, including the expense of rearrangement involved in

---

[1] *Cf.*, for example, the testimony of C. E. Wilson, President of General Motors Corporation, before the Truman Committee.

reconverting prewar plants to civilian use, would be more than $2 billion. Similarly, if past experience is any criterion, it is difficult to see how overhead, including special selling expenses, could total more than $2 billion before the firms now engaged in war production begin to receive funds from the sale of civilian goods.

All told, therefore, the out-of-pocket outlays required for the major categories of reconversion expenditure probably would not exceed $4 billion. Of course, if the conversion of new war-production facilities were also included, the amount would be much larger.

Another legitimate charge against the wartime accumulation of liquid assets is the cost of replenishing the inventories of civilian goods. The book value of total business inventories of both war and nonwar goods will be approximately the same at the end of 1944 as at the end of 1941. Stocks of war goods have increased while those of civilian goods have declined.

Of the total at the end of 1944 it is estimated that some $5 to $8 billion of war goods would have no commercial value and would, in effect, disappear from business inventories when war production stops. Since the proceeds of this liquidation are included in the total accumulation of liquid assets as part of the claims on termination of war contracts, the cost of the corresponding replenishment of civilian-goods inventories is properly chargeable to that accumulation.[1]

This cost of replenishment includes not only the cost of purchased materials but also the other direct manufacturing costs such as wages, power, etc., which would have to be advanced by business enterprises during the process of building up inventories of civilian goods.

Another of the charges against the total amount of funds accumulated by business during the war and to become available in the immediate postwar period is the cost of making up deferred replacements and deferred maintenance. Both concepts are rather nebulous.

One possible criterion of the underreplacement of capital assets during the war years is the average outlay by business enterprise for construction and equipment during the 4 prewar years, 1937 through 1940. This probably results in an overstatement of these deferrals rather than an understatement. On the one hand, the equipment was used intensively during the war years, thereby increasing the theoretical "deficit"

---

[1] It can be argued that inventories at the end of 1941 were already unnecessarily large or, contrariwise, that the increase in prices since that time increases the cost of replenishing them. Both points are immaterial for the immediate purpose since we are concerned only with the amount properly chargeable to the accumulation of liquid assets.

of equipment purchases. This deficit is also increased by the rise in equipment prices since 1940. On the other hand there is some evidence that the 1937 to 1940 equipment purchases exceeded replacement requirements. Also a portion of the underreplacement would be eliminated by the reconversion purchases already considered above, and another portion would be eliminated by adaptation of secondhand war-production equipment.

With regard to structures rather than equipment, the concept is even more difficult. It can be argued, however, that as buildings grow older a certain amount of new construction is necessary in order to prevent a net over-all deterioration of the nation's productive facilities and that again the prewar rate of such construction is a very rough measure of this requirement.

In both instances it should be noted that the actual depreciation charges for accounting purposes are not necessarily an accurate measure of the need for replacement outlays. In fact it can be argued that such depreciation charges are typically conservative in that they overstate the rate of deterioration of facilities.

Business outlays for construction and equipment in the war years 1942 through 1944 fell short of the prewar rate by a total of some $7 to $8 billion. With due regard to all the uncertainties, the maximum that can be charged to the wartime accumulation of liquid assets is no more than $10 billion.

Using the same criterion, a maximum of $15 billion may be required for normal replacements of structures and equipment in the two transition years. Since the total accumulation of business funds considered above includes the depreciation and other reserves during these transition years, these replacements are properly chargeable against this total.

It is doubtful that the net amount of undermaintenance, which would be left after making good the underreplacement of equipment, would be more than $2 billion. The amount may, in fact, be considerably less. This is not to deny that considerable undermaintenance may have accumulated in specialized areas in the economy. However, despite shortages of man power and materials, the available evidence suggests that undermaintenance is not widespread.[1] Because of wartime tax

---

[1] *Cf.*, for example, U. S. Treasury Department, *Postwar Expenses Related to Wartime Incomes*, reprinted in Hearings before the Committee on Ways and Means, House of Representatives, on Revenue Revision of 1943.

rates many companies have, in fact, found it profitable to overmaintain rather than undermaintain their facilities.

Finally, slightly more than $3 billion of the wartime accumulation of liquid assets by business should be earmarked to finance a reextension of consumer credit in the postwar period. This is the amount which has been received by business enterprise, exclusive of banks, in repayment of consumer debt since 1941.

Summarizing these calculations, it appears that a *maximum* of $50 billion might be required to restore the prewar plant, inventories, and receivables of American business and to liquidate the increase in tax accruals since 1941.[1] Since the estimates have been intentionally on the high side where they lacked any precise basis, this tends to be an overstatement of these charges.

TABLE 5.—SUMMARY OF MAXIMUM CHARGES AGAINST BUSINESS ACCUMULATION

	Billions
Retire wartime tax accruals	$ 8
"Reconversion"	4
Replenish civilian-goods inventory	8
Deferred plus current replacements of structures and equipment	25
Deferred maintenance (net)	2
Reextension of consumer credit	3
Total	$50

It is evident that the total of $60 to $70 billion, including accumulations during three war years plus the funds which will become available during the two transition years, is more than ample to cover all these items and leave a substantial margin for expansion above the 1941 level.

This is an aggregate picture. It tends to imply a pooling of resources as between individual enterprises which, of course, does not take place. The question may quite properly be raised whether important segments of business enterprise will be in a much less favorable position.

The available evidence suggests that there are comparatively few exceptions to the generalization that all sizes of firms in all types of business have improved their working-capital position during the war. The extent of the improvement varies substantially, however. The Monthly Letter of the National City Bank for July, 1944, gives one such

[1] If the postwar price level were significantly higher than at the end of 1944, the maximum amounts required might be higher than $50 billion.

comparison for the larger companies in various manufacturing industries.

As between the larger and smaller companies the *Federal Reserve Bulletin* for the same month concludes that the smaller companies in both manufacturing and trade have shown considerably greater increases in liquid assets. Comparisons are made between small, medium, and large firms in eight different manufacturing industries.

Regardless of the over-all picture, it is undoubtedly true that many individual enterprises will find their wartime accumulations insufficient to restore their business to its prewar condition. To this extent the aggregates are misleading.

Another qualification is in order. The foregoing calculations necessarily relate only to established businesses. They do not cover the capital requirements of new enterprises which will be started after the war. Because of the normal turnover of small businesses, these new enterprises will be only in part an expansion above the 1941 level.

To meet these latter requirements there is the enormous accumulation of consumer as distinguished from business savings. Some of these consumer savings are already earmarked to provide self-employment for returning soldiers and war workers. Other amounts will directly or indirectly find their way into capital investment. The process is not automatic, however, and leaves the question as to how readily available the funds will be to meet the capital requirements of new businesses.

IV. BUSINESS FUNDS FOR EXPANSION

A return to no more than the 1941 volume of business would leave a substantial part of the postwar labor force without productive jobs.[1] Many workers today are engaged in aircraft, shipbuilding, and other industries which have expanded greatly during the war. The conversion of these new war facilities is not concerned with the restoration of prewar plant, inventories, and receivables, but with the expansion of the civilian economy above the prewar level. Nevertheless, some of the most serious problems of transition lie in these fields. The question may be raised whether the funds accumulated since 1941 are adequate for the expansion necessary to provide peacetime jobs for these workers, either in converted war plants or elsewhere. There are two reasons why no satisfactory answer can be given.

[1] S. Morris Livingston, "Post-war Manpower and Its Capacity to Produce," *Survey of Current Business*, April, 1944, pp. 10*ff*.

In the first place the additions to productive facilities and working capital necessary to achieve such full utilization are extremely indefinite.

There is no way of determining how much, if any, increase in cash holdings business management would consider necessary or desirable with an increase in total business volume. There is no practical way of distinguishing between the cash necessary to facilitate business payments and the usually substantial sums held by business for precautionary purposes. The latter bear no necessary relationship to the volume of business and are more likely to be determined by business confidence in the future.

Similarly, it is not possible to determine what increase in inventories would be associated with a higher than prewar volume of sales. Inventories in 1941 were already large, and it is technically possible that a higher volume of business could be serviced with little or no increase. The actual amount of the increase would depend more on management's appraisal of the price outlook and on all the intangible factors affecting inventory policy.

The same uncertainties exist with regard to outlays for physical plant. Additional production could be achieved by adding more capacity or by making more intensive use of existing capacity through overtime, multiple shift operations, and utilization of marginal facilities. The decisions again depend not only on the current volume of business but also on management's appraisal of the future. Similar uncertainties arise with regard to the expansion of facilities in the important distributive and service fields commensurate with a larger volume of business.

In the second place, this accumulation is not the only source of funds for expansion. Business will continue to retain funds out of operations in subsequent years, and it also has access to outside sources of funds such as banks, institutions, and private investors.

Some idea of the relative magnitude of the minimum of $10 to $20 billion available from wartime accumulations for expansion purposes may be gained from a comparison with the net private outlays of very roughly $10 billion for expansion of productive facilities and inventories in 1941. This was the largest expansion in any one year during the past two decades.

Summary

Depreciation and other reserves from current operations, plus retained earnings, are normally the major sources of funds to meet business capital requirements. The use of consumer savings obtained either directly or indirectly through the machinery of the capital market has been an important but relatively minor factor.

The forced curtailment of private capital outlays during the war, the partial liquidation of nonwar inventories and receivables since 1941, and the extraordinary expenses involved in shifting back to civilian production add up to unusually large capital requirements in the immediate postwar years. The same curtailment and liquidation, plus the retention of a large share of earnings against postwar contingencies, have created a reserve of liquid assets to meet these requirements.

The large amounts of cash and government bonds accumulated by business during the war, together with the funds which will become available through liquidation of war contracts and from operations during the immediate postwar years, are sufficient, *when taken in the aggregate*, to meet all the charges which are in any way related to the transition from war production to the prewar level of peacetime output and leave a substantial balance for expansion above the prewar level. Since both the magnitude and timing of the expansion requirements cannot be predicted, no satisfactory conclusion can be reached as to the need for other sources of funds.

It should be remembered that there will be individual firms in a less advantageous financial position. It can be said, however, that the lack of funds will be localized rather than general and that, typically, the uncertainty of the adequacy of business funds has to do with the requirements for expansion rather than with the requirements for reestablishing the prewar volume of business.

Part V

INTERNATIONAL ECONOMIC RELATIONS

Chapter XVIII

Some Factors Affecting the Future of International Trade and International Economic Policy

by GOTTFRIED HABERLER

I

THE FUTURE volume and intensity of world trade, the extent to which international division of labor and specialization between countries will contribute to the output of goods and services of the world community of nations, will depend on numerous, complex, and partly interrelated factors. We may group them in the following manner: First, we have the fundamental technological factors relating to the methods of production, transportation, and communication. These factors determine to what extent the trading nations can, if they choose, benefit from international trade and division of labor, and how much countries will lose if they exclude themselves wholly or partly from participation in world trade, as a consequence either of a premeditated policy or of bungling. Second, we may list as a determining factor the volume of employment and economic activity, especially in the leading industrial countries. If these countries, particularly the United States, are able to maintain a high and stable level of employment, the volume of international trade will be higher, other things being equal, than if violent fluctuations were allowed to develop or if a depressed or semidepressed situation were allowed to persist.

The third complex of determining factors, which probably will be the most crucial and strategic one, is the political factor. To what extent will the leading countries be willing to specialize and rely on imports for the satisfaction of their needs? To what extent will international economic policies be an adjunct of military and power politics? Will it be possible to build up an international monetary system which permits a high volume of international trade? Will international investment be resumed to a sufficient degree? Will the leading countries be able to extricate themselves from the shackles of the planned war economy, or to what extent will central planning be carried over into the peace economy? If a high degree of central planning is continued, will it be possible technically, politically, and psychologically to integrate and adjust the various national plans internationally so as to take advantage of the potentialities of increasing output by international division of labor to an extent comparable to the degree to which this can be achieved under a comparatively free, competitive price economy?

The general tendency of the international economic policies, their liberal and expansive or restrictive, protective and autarchic spirit will depend to some extent upon the first two factors mentioned. The greater the benefits of international division of labor, which the basic technological factors permit, the greater the inducement to use them. The higher the level of economic activity and employment, the less insistent the demand for protection on the part of underemployed producers and the weaker the temptation to increase employment by shutting out foreign competition. The drift toward protectionist and autarchic policies of the past sixty or seventy years has been sharply accelerated by each depression. The movement away from free trade exhibits not only a secular trend, but also cyclical oscillations. Depressions and wars bring an outburst of protectionism—higher tariffs and other impediments to trade, which are only incompletely removed during the following peace or prosperity period.

To a large extent, however, the spirit of international economic policy is independent of the two factors mentioned. To a large extent it is a function of the general attitude toward state intervention and planning, administrative potentialities, and all the spiritual and material forces behind these factors. Some importance may also be attributed to the teaching of economists and the prevailing economic theories.

In the following pages some of these factors and recent changes that they may have undergone will be examined.

II

Let us first consider briefly the technological factor. Have there been any fundamental changes in the technique of production or transportation tending to bring about a radical change in the importance of international trade for many countries? The answer seems to be that there have been, of course, great changes, but not large enough to change the picture radically. For most countries, international division of labor could still make a substantial contribution to their economic well-being —a contribution which would hardly be less than it was twenty or thirty years ago.

There may be a few real—and there are certainly many apparent— exceptions to that generalization. Many countries have learned to do without certain things they used to get from abroad. For other things, they have developed expensive substitutes. Industrially backward countries, to be sure, have made great strides on the road toward industrialization and diversification. But the highly industrialized countries have not stood still either. The distance between the leading industrial nations and the raw-material-producing countries, in the tropical and temperate zones, is probably as great if not greater than it was thirty years ago.

It has been said (*e.g.*, by Keynes) that the modern development of the chemical industry has reduced the scope for profitable international division of labor. It is now possible to produce out of local dust and dirt (as Prof. Robertson once put it) all sorts of things which formerly had to be imported. This development probably more than offset the countervailing effect of the exhaustion of scarce natural resources in certain countries. Thus it has reduced the dependence of certain countries on international trade for minimum civilian and military requirements. In other words, the standard of living which could be maintained with no trade or little trade is higher than it was thirty years ago. But it does not follow that the improvement in that standard, which can be secured by utilizing to the full international division of labor, is less than it was. If the national income which can be produced without the help of foreign trade has been raised by the advance in the "synthetics industries," the volume of production which can be obtained with the help of trade has also been pushed up. The tremendous progress in the field of transportation (air transport, etc.) and the improved methods of mass production, presupposing as they do large markets, have contributed to making trade more profitable.

III

That the volume of international trade should rise and fall together with the rise and fall in national income and output of the trading countries is self-evident and has never been denied. It is true in the secular as well as in the cyclical sense. The upward trend in output and income the world over has been reflected in a rising trend in the volume of world trade. And the cyclical ups and downs in output and employment are closely paralleled by cyclical fluctuations in the volume of trade. Of course the rate of growth and decline in the two series need not be and is not the same. But the parallelism, especially with regard to recent short-term cyclical fluctuations, is very striking.[1] The reason is obvious: A part of the increased national expenditure is directed toward imported goods. Demand for foreign raw materials as well as for foreign finished goods increases (falls off) with a rise (fall) in national income.

In the case of cyclical fluctuations in national income which are due to fluctuations in employment and unemployment, the mechanical influence on imports is strengthened by influences via policy. In depressions the demand for protection from competing imports becomes irresistible. Moreover, in depressions disturbances in the balance of payments of many countries are apt to occur, which in turn lead to the imposition of exchange control and other impediments to trade. The experience of the Great Depression in the thirties has made a deep impression on economists, businessmen, and politicians, especially in Great Britain. The fear that the United States will not be able to avoid severe depressions [2] is the chief professed reason for the reluctance of the British to play ball with the United States in setting up a stable exchange system and a liberal and multilateral trading system.

[1] *Cf.*, for example, August Maffry, "Foreign Trade in the Post-war Economy," *Survey of Current Business*, November, 1944; and Randall Hinshaw, "American Prosperity and the British Balance-of-payments Problem," *Review of Economic Statistics*, February, 1945. See also Imre De Vegh, "Imports and Income in the United States and Canada," *Review of Economic Statistics*, 1941, p. 130.

[2] The explicit or implicit assumption that the severity of world depression of the thirties was due almost entirely to the instability of the American economy and economic mismanagement in the United States is greatly exaggerated. The depression had several important focuses outside the United States, one of them, for example, in Germany.

IV

The most important determining factor of postwar international trade will be international economic policy—international monetary as well as commercial policy. Commercial policy is, of course, no longer confined to tariff policy but has a most formidable armory of weapons at its disposal ranging from quotas, licenses, exchange control, informal pressure upon, or directives to, users of foreign goods, to partial or comprehensive government import monopolies.

In the capitalistic world the general tone of international trade policy, its degree of liberalism or restrictiveness, is (as explained before) strongly influenced by the state of business activity. But it is by no means uniquely determined thereby. Some of the other independent or semi-independent factors we shall discuss in the following pages.

The general outlook is profoundly different today from what it was at the close of World War I, and the probability of a speedy return to more liberal practices much smaller than it was in 1919. The economic ravages of the war are infinitely greater than they were twenty-five years ago. The objective chance of a durable peace based on a tolerably reasonable settlement following the present war seems to be decidedly less bright than it was after World War I; at any rate, the confidence of the world in the durability of the coming peace is likely to be less. This does not create an atmosphere favorable for the adoption of more liberal trade policies. But there are other factors pointing in the same direction on which the economist is more competent to pass judgment.

There is first the fact that economic planning and state interference in the economic process are much more widespread over the world than they were twenty-five years ago. The world has rapidly moved toward socialism between the two wars and had even before the present war reached the stage of collectivism in such important countries as Russia and Germany.[1] There can be no doubt that even without war and occupation the surrounding countries in eastern and southeastern Europe

---

[1] The difference between the German and Russian planned economy is hardly greater than one would expect in view of the cultural differences between the two countries and in view of the fact that Germany was rich and industrially highly developed, while Russia was poor and industrially backward. In Russia the middle and entrepreneurial classes were wiped out and the new economic system built from scratch to the accompaniment of incredible suffering and bloodletting. In Germany the transition was comparatively orderly, efficient, and somewhat more gradual; and the middle and entrepreneurial classes (excepting the Jews) were not wiped out but tamed and utilized by the Nazi state for its purposes.

and Asia would have been rapidly assimilated to the economic system of the two collectivist giants. In western Europe and in the Western Hemisphere the movement toward central planning has been slower and the resistance greater; at any rate it has not yet gone so far as in central and eastern Europe. But the trend is unmistakably in the same direction.

Now it is clear that national planning and government direction of production and prices of the type and intensity now practiced almost everywhere require regulation of international trade. It is true that theoretically it may be a different type of regulation from the old-fashioned restrictive protectionism. The theorists of socialism like Dickinson, Lange, and Lerner are fully alive to the advantages of international division of labor, and in their Utopias there is planned but "free" trade along the lines of comparative cost.[1] Unfortunately, international socialism is not likely to spring out of Mr. Lange's or Mr. Lerner's head as Pallas Athene sprang out of the head of Zeus. Whatever the final outcome, there will certainly be a long transition, a lot of muddling, with different countries advancing at a different pace (or even in different directions). This stage of development is obviously not conducive to bringing about a large volume of international trade.

To this should be added the fact that administrative skill and efficiency have increased greatly during the past twenty-five years. Today in many countries administrative tasks can be undertaken with a degree of efficiency which twenty years ago would have been entirely out of the question.

Parallel with these changes in institutions and policies has gone a change in economic thinking. We need not decide here which is cause and which effect, whether the chicken or the egg comes first. Probably economic thinking and economic ideas are led by economic events as much as they lead them.[2]

This change in economic thinking away from liberalism and free trade toward planning and protection has been especially marked in Great Britain, not so much in the United States. What holds of Great Britain holds also of Germany and other European countries, even of some of the smaller ones (*e.g.*, the Netherlands), although economists in smaller countries are more likely to have a vivid appreciation of the

---

[1] *Cf.*, for example, Lerner's *Economics of Control*, Chs. 26–29.

[2] Witness the fact that the Great Depression has made a large part of economics "depression economics." If the Supreme Court follows the election, is it surprising that economists move with the business cycle?

advantages of freer trade.[1] In the following pages we shall discuss the most important issues involved in this ideological evolution.

V

The new British protectionism and imperial economic nationalism —whose most vocal publicists and theorists are Thomas Balogh, E. F. Schumacher,[2] and Paul Einzig—admit, of course, the theoretical validity of the classical argument for free, multilateral trade.[3] Only the crudest protectionists have ever failed to preface their arguments in favor of protectionist policies by an expression of respect to the free-trade doctrine in the abstract. But the "new" doctrine is more refined than old-fashioned protectionism although almost every single element in the argument can be traced far back in the history of the theory of international trade.

Let us discuss now the most important cases of which it is said that drastic regulation of exports and imports cannot be dispensed with. It should be clearly understood from the beginning that the practical issue is never the retention or abolition (or even sharp reduction) of the existing tariff walls. Virtually everybody admits that a sudden elimination of existing tariffs is out of the question, although it may not be too much to hope for gradual reduction over a period of years, if wars and serious depressions could be avoided. The practical issues are whether the more drastic impediments to trade such as quotas, exchange control, clearing and payment agreements, bulk purchases, and discriminatory tariffs can and should be eliminated or in some cases

---

[1] Not much economic literature has come out of Germany since the outbreak of the war, and it has probably dried up progressively as the war went on. But so long as it was possible to follow German thinking and writing somewhat, the tenor in the field under consideration here was surprisingly similar to that in recent British writings. Even under the Nazis, German economics was strongly influenced by British literature, just as many of the younger Keynesians have undoubtedly been deeply impressed by the apparent success of Nazi economic policies, especially in the field of international trade. This influence is, for example, strongly in evidence in the essays on *The Economics of Full Employment: Six Studies in Applied Economics*, prepared at the Oxford University Institute of Statistics, Oxford, 1944. These essays were written by the theoretical mentors and coaches of Sir William Beveridge and contain the ideas on which his *Full Employment* program is based.

[2] It is a pity that the great majority of British economists has been silenced for the time being—at least as far as the public is concerned—by the fact that they are engaged in war work for the government. For a brief but incisive discussion of the change in the British views, see R. Schüller, "Great Britain's Trade Policy," *Social Research*, September, 1944.

[3] *Cf.*, for example, the opening article in the series "Principles of Trade," *The Economist*, Jan. 1, 1944.

replaced by uniform nondiscriminatory duties—not immediately after the end of hostilities, but during a period of transition of, say, 4 to 5 years. Today a free trader is an individual who believes that tariff protection is sufficient and that duties should be fairly stable and should be subject to the most-favored-nation principle, *i.e.*, should be nondiscriminatory.[1]

Let us begin with the case of the chronically scarce dollar. The fear of "the overwhelming competitive power of American industry" and "the irrepressible tendency of the American balance of payments to be active" and "to suck in gold," is a strong motive for the reluctance in influential British quarters to accept the Bretton Woods agreements and to renounce the utilization of drastic trade regulations. This theory has been accepted by the London *Economist* in a surprisingly extreme form. In the second of two articles on "The Dollar Problem" (Dec. 4, 1943, pages 750–751), which were devoted to a discussion of the well-known Department of Commerce study, *The United States in the World Economy*, *The Economist* came to the following conclusion:

> Indeed, it may very well be that the much-abused American tariff is more of an irritant than a real obstruction to the flow of trade. It is almost certainly true that any reduction in the tariff that is at all likely to be politically practicable would be wholly inadequate to solve the problem of the dollar. It may be, in fact, that the problem should not be regarded as the fruit of aberrations of policy . . . , but that it should be looked upon as the result of a set of economic circumstances never contemplated by the textbooks—namely, the existence of a country which, all policy apart, needs so little from the rest of the world, while the rest of the world requires so much from it, that an equilibrium of accounts can be brought about by no means available to a free, or even a tolerably free, market.

This is indeed an amazing statement and it is a sad experience to find it in the columns of *The Economist*. When writing the quoted passage the author of the article seems to have completely forgotten the most elementary principles of international trade.[2] It is on the same level as the view which used to be so popular in the United States, that America needs high protection, for otherwise she would be flooded by

---

[1] It should go without saying that a prohibitive or a very high duty can be more restrictive than a large quota or a mild exchange control. This, however, does not alter the fact that quotas and exchange control are much more disturbing elements in the price mechanism of a capitalist economy than duties. *Cf.* J. Viner, *Trade Relations between Free Market and Controlled Economies* and G. Haberler and Martin Hill, *Quantitative Trade Controls*.

[2] One wonders whether it was the same person who wrote the previously quoted series, "The Principles of Trade" which appeared in *The Economist* of Jan. 1 to Feb. 19, 1944.

imports because of the incomparably high living standard of American labor and the consequential high cost of production of the American economy. The lack of synchronization of policy and public opinion in the field of international trade in the United States and England is deplorable. When American industry and public opinion become ready to apply the elementary principles of trade, important circles in Great Britain seem to have all but forgotten them.[1]

There are, however, more refined versions of the theory of the chronic dollar scarcity. A well-known one can be found in Mr. Kindleberger's article, "International Monetary Stabilization," in *Postwar Economic Problems*.[2] It runs in terms of low price and income elasticity of American demand for imports, coupled with a high income elasticity of demand abroad for American exports and an absolute superiority of American industry in the production of durable goods over foreign competitors. The theory is not stated in precise terms and the exposition is marred by formal blemishes.[3] This makes it difficult to give a detailed criticism. It is certainly possible to make assumptions with respect to these elasticities which would preclude the existence of a stable or perhaps even any exchange equilibrium between two countries. Nevertheless, it is safe to say that, for countries with many actual and potential competing export and import goods (such as the great industrial countries), the assumption of the nonexistence of a stable equilibrium is entirely unrealistic. The question of the price elasticities will be taken up below.

VI

The next case must be taken more seriously. It is the case of the cyclical dollar scarcity or of the disturbing influence of American

---

[1] The following sentence, two paragraphs farther down in the quoted article, cannot fail to heighten one's amazement: "It would be a mistake to reach a conclusion of hopelessness. There may be hitherto unrevealed factors that will help to solve the problem—for example, an inflationary rise in costs in the United States unaccompanied by any fall of the dollar or any enhancement of tariffs." The writer seems to be entirely unaware of the fact that what he calls a "hitherto unrevealed factor" is nothing but the textbook case and he does not suspect that there may be a mechanism or a rule of the game to bring about that result; nor does he mention that for "inflationary rise in costs" he could substitute "appreciation of the dollar" or "depreciation of sterling." He even missed the terms of trade argument which he could have used with advantage for his case at that point; that is, he failed to point out that an "inflationary rise in cost" in the United States, although it would correct the balance of payments, would imply a deterioration in the terms of trade for Britain and other countries.

[2] Edited by Seymour E. Harris, pp. 375*ff*.

[3] *E.g.*, the author identifies marginal propensity to import and income elasticity of demand for imports; *op. cit.*, p. 380.

slumps. The American economy, so the argument goes, is subject to specially violent cyclical fluctuations. Whenever there is a depression in the United States, American import demand drops precipitously and American producers attempt to push exports in order to find some offset for the contracting home market, thus spreading the depression to other countries. Owing to the economic weight of the United States and the comparatively large marginal propensity to import, the disturbance wrought abroad is very serious.

It is intimated that the United States will not be able in the future to stabilize its economy with any greater success than in the past. On the other hand, it is assumed with implicit confidence that Great Britain, the members of the British Empire, and the countries in western Europe which are expected and invited to join the sterling bloc, will succeed in maintaining full employment all the time. Hence it will be essential for Britain and "like-minded countries," *i.e.*, for "full-employment countries," to keep their hands free to use all the trade weapons necessary to ward off deflationary influences from outside, *i.e.*, from the United States. In order to accomplish that purpose, discriminatory trade policies against the prospective mischief-maker are indispensable, while it is quite safe to practice multilateral trading methods within the "full-employment bloc." Therefore the "full-employment bloc" must reserve the right to use quotas, exchange control, bilateral (or intra-empire) clearing and payment agreements. The Bretton Woods agreements (and still more so the proposed commercial policy convention) would limit the freedom of action far too much and should therefore not be ratified.[1]

Now the idea that unregulated international trade and a regime of stable exchanges have the disadvantage of exposing a country to deflationary influences from abroad (inflationary influences are easier to ward off) is a very old one. But while it was formerly possible to reply that (apart from the long-run benefits of international division of labor) occasional expansionary influences from abroad were at least a partial offset to the disadvantage of being occasionally exposed to deflationary influences, that argument does not carry weight any more against the

---

[1] It has also been proposed that ratification should be contingent upon a formal declaration by the big powers, especially the United States, in which they "pledge themselves to stabilize national income at full-employment levels." It is not quite clear whether the political naïvety of these proposals is genuine or simulated. In any case it should be clear that there is no government which would not promise, in all sincerity, to do all in its power to maximize employment and national income.

conviction that full employment will be maintained anyway by domestic measures and that, therefore, expansionary influences from abroad are not needed.

It does not seem very useful to speculate which countries are likely to succeed best in maintaining economic stability.[1] It is probably true that in the past economic fluctuations in the United States were more violent than in Great Britain, and fluctuations in Britain were more violent than fluctuations in France, etc. But there are plenty of cases in which foreign countries managed to produce their own depressions without American help!

It will be more fruitful to consider what could be done if a big country, say, the United States, in fact experiences a slump. What could other countries do to insulate themselves as far as possible against deflationary influences from America? We exclude domestic deflation because it would spell unemployment, which is precisely what we wish to avoid.[2] With this limitation the first rule is that credit must not be tightened in the face of an unfavorable balance of payments and an outflow of international reserves (including gold and international credit facilities of all kinds). This alone will, however, not be sufficient to maintain activity. It will offset the secondary effects of a deterioration in the current balance.[3] The primary effect, the decline of activity in the export industries themselves (and in industries suffering from intensified competition on the part of the industries in the depressed country) is not yet eliminated. To offset the primary effect too, it would be necessary to stimulate domestic expenditures by about the amount

[1] In passing it may be mentioned that stability as such is important, not necessarily stability at full or a very high level of employment. Instability at a higher average level would be more disturbing than stability at a somewhat lower level.

[2] In case somebody answered that monetary deflation need not involve unemployment, if only prices and wages were sufficiently flexible downward, the answer is twofold: First, it is very doubtful whether a sufficient flexibility of prices and wages is politically possible and, if it were enforced, it would have many undesirable consequences. Second, waiving the difficulties just mentioned, it could work only if the same elasticity conditions are fulfilled which are required to make a policy of devaluation a success. *Cf.* now *Economic Stability in the Post-war World*, League of Nations, 1945, where the whole problem is discussed in considerable detail. See especially Ch. XVII of that report.

[3] By "secondary effects" is meant here effects via credit policy, not effects on consumption expenditures by way of the multiplier. It should be observed that champions of a gold standard with a broad gold base, like Prof. Hayek, recommend the elimination of the secondary effect. (*Cf.* his *Monetary Nationalism and International Stability, passim.*) This effect constitutes for him an "unneutral" behavior of money due to the erection of a multiple credit structure upon the gold base. Professor Hayek would, however, not approve of a policy of offsetting the primary effect and its multiplier consequences.

that aggregate expenditures have fallen in consequence of the deteriorated trade balance.[1]

If and when these offsetting policies are successful in preventing the spread of the depression, they intensify the outflow of reserves. What can be done about that? The ideal solution (apart from a domestic expansion policy in the depressed country which would effectively eliminate the trouble at its root) would be the existence of international reserves sufficiently large to enable the countries concerned to outride the storm. International monetary cooperation should, and through credit extension always could, make reserves large enough to achieve that end. How much would be required depends on numerous circumstances: on the comparative size of the countries involved; on the rapidity with which an export surplus in the depressed country makes its expansionary influence felt; on the severity and length of the depression. There is no space here to attempt a quantitative analysis, but it would seem that the depression of 1937–1938 could have been handled that way, while the depression of 1929–1932 would have required very large sums.[2]

If international reserves (including credit facilities provided by the Bretton Woods International Monetary Fund) prove insufficient to fill the gap, the adverse balance must be corrected by one method or another. This calls for important policy decisions which give rise to divergent opinions. Still excluding deflation, the choice is between an alteration in the exchange rate,[3] exchange control of different types, and import restriction by tariffs, quotas, etc.

There can be hardly a doubt that from the liberal point of view, which wishes to minimize government interference in the international

---

[1] It is, of course, misleading to discuss the problem entirely in terms of broad aggregates. In many cases it will be difficult to direct offsetting expenditures sufficiently in the direction required, *i.e.*, toward the export industries. Obviously highly specialized raw-material-producing countries will be in an unfavorable position in this respect. Lack of space prevents a more thorough discussion of the problem in the present chapter, but it is obvious that multiplier effects on consumption can be more easily offset by appropriate spending policies or tax remissions. (For further details see the above-mentioned League of Nations report.)

[2] The earlier depression was, of course, complicated by the disturbing upward revision of the American tariff of 1930. Such a policy would always wreck international cooperation. It should not be forgotten, however, that other countries raised their tariffs too and did worse things. Not all of these steps can be condoned as having been forced by prior balance of payments troubles.

[3] Assuming a *tertium comparationis* (gold or currencies of "third" countries), this may take the form either of a depreciation of the currency of the deficit (full-employment) countries or an appreciation of the currency of the depressed surplus country.

division of labor, devaluation would be the best solution. The question is, will it work?

VII

The attitude of many theoretical and practical economists toward exchange depreciation has undergone remarkable changes in the past 25 years. The traditional gold-standard position of the twenties gave way to an attitude favorable for exchange depreciation in the early thirties. Largely under the influence of Keynes, many economists and publicists, especially in England, regarded exchange depreciation as an easy cure for many different ills.[1] Now the pendulum has swung again in the opposite direction, not quite so far as under the gold standard, but almost as far and too far, in the writer's opinion.

The reasons for that latest reaction are manifold: During the first depression the currency depreciation was abused and overplayed; it will not work if all or many countries are ready to follow or to retaliate if any one country tries to steal a march on the others by depreciating its currency; all countries now have more powerful weapons of control at their disposal. Consequently, conservative as well as radical economists have become skeptical. The conservative frequently rejects exchange depreciation in the illusion that an immutable gold standard is a practical alternative; the radical rejects it because he prefers quotas and exchange control.

The conditions under which a change in the exchange rate is an efficient method for correcting disequilibriums in the balance of payments are as follows:

1. Competitive exchange depreciation must be avoided and the depreciation should not be greater than is necessary to equilibrate the balance of payments. This is generally accepted and it is to be hoped that the proposed international monetary fund will effectively eliminate the danger of competitive depreciation.

2. Much more important is the danger of speculative capital movements being induced by expected changes in the exchange rate. Especially for smaller countries this is a very serious matter. Even if frequent changes are avoided, the mere fact that rates are no longer sacrosanct

---

[1] For a well-balanced discussion see S. E. Harris, *Exchange Depreciation*, 1936. The extreme recommendation to leave exchanges entirely free to the forces of the market and to refrain from any attempt to keep them stable was made by only a few. See, *i.e.*, C. R. Whittlesey, *International Monetary Issues*. Why a system of free exchanges did not and could not work is well explained in Nurkse, *International Currency Experience*, p. 117.

as under the gold standard may be sufficient to create a disposition to capital flight which would necessitate indefinite maintenance or reimposition of exchange control for the purpose of regulating capital movements. However, if and so long as such controls are maintained anyway, which may well be the case, the matter loses much[1] of its importance.

3. The third condition is that demand of the countries concerned for each other's exports should be sufficiently elastic with respect to price.[2] This matter of elasticity of international demand is of great importance, not only for the problem under discussion, but for many others as well. We discuss it in the next and final section of this paper.[3]

VIII

If a country reduces its export prices by depreciation (or deflation), the value of its exports will rise the more elastic the foreign demand for its export goods in general; the value of its imports will fall the more elastic its own demand for foreign goods. It follows that the more elastic the demand, the easier it will be to correct the balance. If the elasticity were less than unity, a depreciation would increase the deficit, but in that case an appreciation would improve it. The situation would be most difficult to handle, if the relevant elasticities were in the neighborhood of unity. For in that case a correction either cannot be brought about at all through price changes or can be brought about only at the expense of disturbingly sharp changes in the terms of trade.

It is clear that it is a matter of utmost importance to know what the relevant elasticities actually are. This is important not only for the numerous questions connected with the balance-of-payments mechanism, such as the transfer of capital, reparations, etc., but also for commercial policy: If the elasticities are small, it becomes possible for countries to influence their terms of trade by export and import duties and other devices; in other words, to exploit other countries monopolistically or monopsonistically. Of course, what matters in these cases is

---

[1] Not all, because controls must be tightened if the propensity to move capital is strong.

[2] The elasticity with respect to income is also important. If it is high, a mild depression will be sufficient to correct an adverse balance. Since we rule out depression (unemployment) as a means of correcting a balance of payments deficit, income elasticity is not so important for us in the present context. But it is of some importance because, even without unemployment, real income will change with the terms of trade. In large industrial countries this is likely to be a negligible factor—a fraction of a fraction—but for small and internationally highly specialized countries it may be of some importance.

[3] As we remarked above, these elasticity conditions are also relevant for the case of a deflation with flexible factor prices, *i.e.*, deflation without unemployment.

not so much the total or average elasticities, but the elasticities of demand of individual countries and for individual commodities and the opportunity of dealing separately with single countries and commodities by means of the numerous discriminatory devices of commercial policy, currency manipulation, and exchange control. In the present chapter we shall, however, confine ourselves to making some remarks on the question of the over-all elasticities.

Until recently it was fairly generally assumed that the elasticities of international demand are great. This assumption was made in many cases implicitly or possibly without clear realization that it might be otherwise; Marshall, however, took a strong position, fully conscious of the complexity of the problem and its important implication. In a famous passage he said:

> It is practically certain that the demand of each of Ricardo's two countries for the goods in general of the other would have considerable elasticity *under modern industrial conditions*,[1] even if E and G were single countries whose sole trade was with one another. And if we take E to be a large and rich commercial country, while G stands for all foreign countries, this certainly becomes absolute.[2]

Nowadays the opposite assumption has become popular.[3] My impression is, however, that many or most of those who make it fail to realize sufficiently all factors involved. They argue as if the elasticity of reciprocal demand of countries for each other's products depends only on the elasticity of consumers' demand. In fact, it depends also on the supply conditions. The import-demand curve for each commodity can be derived by deducting, for each price, domestic supply from domestic demand.[4] Hence, even if the final consumers' demand for an imported article were entirely unresponsive to price changes, the import-demand curve of the country would have some elasticity, so long as there is domestic supply which is not absolutely inelastic. Moreover, the existence of potential export and import goods increases the elasticity of the aggregate curve.[5]

It follows that the time factor is of importance. In the short run, the elasticities will be less than if we allow time for supply to adjust

---

[1] Italics in the original.
[2] *Money, Credit and Commerce*, p. 171. *Cf.* also F. D. Graham, "The Theory of International Values," *Quarterly Journal of Economics*, Vol. 46, 1932.
[3] *Cf.*, for example, Kindleberger, *op. cit.*
[4] For prices at which the former exceeds the latter the curve becomes, of course, an export-supply curve.
[5] Of course, all that has been explained by Marshall, *op. cit.*

itself. Moreover, tariffs and other impediments to trade reduce the elasticities of international demand, by reducing the number of potential export and import goods. What is, however, more important than the existence of tariffs at, say, prewar levels, is the imposition of new duties to prevent increases in imports and the existence of quantitative import controls. These practices are calculated to make imports and exports very inelastic with respect to price.

But apart from the last two complications (widespread quota protection and *ad hoc* imposition of duties whenever imports rise), I am inclined to believe that Marshall's statement is still correct for all the larger countries with a great variety of actual and potential exports and imports.

Only recently attempts have been made to measure statistically elasticities of demand for imports.[1] These studies seem to lend support to the now fashionable assumption of low elasticities or even to point in the direction of these elasticities being in the neighborhood of one. These investigations are very ingenious and constitute a promising beginning. But for various reasons which cannot be discussed at this point, they are not yet sufficiently refined and trustworthy to upset the theoretical presumption that, except perhaps in a very short run, the elasticity of reciprocal international demand is likely to be great.

The only question which, it seems to us, can be seriously asked, is whether in a depression the elasticity of demand may be temporarily lower than usual. There are reasons for believing that this might be so.[2] But it is probably only a question of waiting somewhat longer for an appreciable effect.[3] This only underlines the desirability of large inter-

[1] See especially the excellent pioneering study by Randall Hinshaw, "American Prosperity and the British Balance-of-payments Problem," *Review of Economic Statistics*, February, 1945. Other papers on the same subject are in process of publication by various journals.

[2] See my notes "Currency Depreciation and the International Monetary Fund," in *Review of Economic Statistics*, November, 1944, pp. 178 and 191. Thomas Balogh believes that demand elasticities for imports are low in depressions. (See his paper "The International Aspects of Full Employment" in *The Economics of Full Employment*, p. 142.) He concludes that currency depreciation is no suitable weapon to ward off deflationary effects from abroad, if they are due to slump conditions in foreign countries. However, a few pages later (p. 163) he says that an appreciation of the currency of the depressed country (which is assumed to have an active balance) "could, in fact, work. [It] could largely neutralize the effects of a slump in one country on the world, or would at least reduce or wipe out the surplus resulting from the reduction of effective home demand on the balance of payments." Why an appreciation would work, but a depreciation would be ineffective, is not explained.

[3] Another more serious matter is that a depressed country is likely to interfere with the process of adjustment by imposing import restrictions. But that has nothing to do with the elasticity of demand, although Thomas Balogh mentions it as the chief reason for the elasticity being low (*op. cit.*, p. 142), thereby admitting that apart from this extraneous political factor they may not be so low after all.

national reserves with the help of which countries can wait for the forces of adjustment to correct the situation.[1]

IX

The allotted space is running out and leaves room for only a few concluding remarks. Clearly quantitative studies are needed. But I think it could be shown that, given moderately skillful management, the large liquid resources now available to most countries, supplemented by the lending facilities of the proposed international agencies, should be sufficient, after the lapse of a transitional period of a few years, to operate a multilateral trading system without recourse, except in rare cases, to exchange control, quotas, bilateral clearings, and the like. Of course, such a system can be mismanaged and misused.[2] Large liquid resources may tempt countries to go on a spending spree or simply keep them from taking the necessary corrective measures in time. It would be too much to expect that this will not happen. But if it happens only occasionally and not to the leading countries, the world system should be able to absorb such shocks. That wholehearted cooperation, at least by the leading capitalistic countries, a minimum of political security, and the absence of acute fear of war are indispensable conditions should be self-evident. Nobody can tell now whether these conditions eventually will be fulfilled. But it is certainly worth trying.

[1] Balogh (*op. cit.*, p. 161) argues that the full-employment countries will not wish to accumulate indefinitely debit balances with the country or countries that are unable to avoid cyclical depressions. But there is no reason why the balances should not be reduced during the years between depressions, in other words why the value of the currency of the full-employment countries should not be kept at an average level low enough to assure *long-run* equilibrium in the balance of payments.

[2] But surely the only practical alternative (which is not the gold standard but Schachtianism at least of the mild kind now proposed in Great Britain) would be also misused for other than its avowed purposes.

Chapter XIX

Monetary Stabilization: The United Nations Program

by E. M. BERNSTEIN

1. INTERNATIONAL ECONOMIC RELATIONS AND NATIONAL ECONOMIC POLICY

THE WAR has shown how great is the capacity of the economic system to utilize its resources in production. After the war, the public everywhere will be impatient with economic inefficiency and economic waste. They will want to know why it is not possible to have jobs in time of peace as in time of war, to divert the enormous production for war purposes to civilian uses, and to continue the industrial expansion which takes place so rapidly during war. In all countries, the people are insistent on, and governments are committed to, an economic policy that will assure high levels of employment, rising standards of living, and economic development.

The measures that must be taken to carry out this policy are principally domestic in character. Nevertheless, the success of domestic economic measures will depend in large part on harmonious and constructive international economic relations. A large volume of international trade and investment can contribute directly to strengthen domestic economic policies. Beyond this, with an appropriate pattern of international payments, countries can be sure that the measures they take to attain domestic economic objectives will not be offset by conflicting measures in other countries. For these reasons, it is in the interest of all countries to cooperate to encourage international trade and investment and to facilitate the maintenance of balance in international payments.

Consider what such a policy would mean to the United States. If our exports of goods and services could reach $10 billion a year during the postwar decade, it would mean nearly 3 million jobs in industry and a foreign market for the agricultural output of about 1 million people. To attain such a level of exports, it would be necessary for this country to import about $8 billion a year in goods and services and to undertake about $2 billion a year in international investment during the postwar decade. Our imports would provide us with raw materials for industry and a more varied collection of goods and services for consumers. At the same time, our international investment would facilitate economic development in countries which cannot provide for all of their investment needs out of their own current savings.

Such a balance of payments for the United States during the postwar decade would require for the entire world an aggregate volume of trade considerably larger than in the 1930's. Otherwise the pattern of international payments of other countries would become even more sensitive to fluctuations in our balance of payments and the danger of instability would be increased. Furthermore, in considering our balance of payments during the postwar decade we should bear in mind its proper relationship to subsequent periods. If international investment is to be of continuing importance in the world economy, there must be assurance that creditor countries will maintain a balance of payments which will make it possible for debtor countries to meet their obligations. These observations do not contradict the conclusion that an expansion of international trade and investment is desirable. They indicate that this expansion must be of a balanced character as between countries and in each country as between the present and the future.

The expansion of international trade and investment and the maintenance of balanced international accounts will be facilitated if the great trading countries adopt a common international monetary policy. Such a policy must be directed toward securing and maintaining orderly and stable exchange arrangements and freedom in exchange transactions. The experience of the 1930's shows clearly that the use of exchange depreciation and discriminatory currency practices to secure trade advantages inevitably encourages restrictive measures that diminish the volume of international trade and investment and distort the pattern of international payments. Only through international cooperation will it be possible to avoid such restrictive measures which adversely affect all countries.

2. International Monetary and Financial Cooperation

A common international monetary policy must be directed toward securing a pattern of international payments which will facilitate in each country domestic measures for high levels of employment, rising standards of living, and economic development, without the necessity for making adjustments to offset inflation or deflation originating in other countries and without imposing such adjustments on other countries. Such a pattern of international payments will involve a large and growing volume of international trade, and an amount of international investment related to the capacity of some countries to export capital and the need of other countries to import capital. There is general agreement that a common international monetary policy can be carried out only under orderly and stable exchange arrangements. The question is how to secure such an international policy.

The traditional basis for a common international monetary policy is the gold standard. The gold standard would provide orderly, stable, and free exchanges if the great industrial countries could maintain high levels of national income under the gold standard. Apparently, the modern economy does not have sufficient flexibility under the gold standard to adjust itself to an adverse change in the relative international economic position of a country without severe pressure on domestic prices and wages and prolonged unemployment. Twice within this generation most countries have thought it necessary to abandon the gold standard, and few countries are prepared to return to it in the postwar period. Speaking in the House of Commons in May, 1944, the Chancellor of the Exchequer said: "Certainly, the attitude of His Majesty's present government would be one of the most vehement opposition to any suggestion that we should go back on the gold standard." Since international acceptance of the gold standard cannot be secured, those who believe in it must seek through international cooperation the advantages it provides without imposing on other countries the hardships it may entail.

The difficulty of adjusting postwar balances of payments has led important sectors of public opinion in England and other countries to advocate the use of direct controls for this purpose. The proponents of this policy believe that, as the largest importer of staple commodities, Britain could make advantageous long-term agreements with raw-materials-producing countries for bulk purchases by the government, with payment made in British exports under bilateral clearing arrangements. The dangers of such a policy are obvious. Even enlightened bilateralism must involve the loss of many advantages of multilateral trade and affect adversely the standard of living. It would inevitably result in a system of economic blocs; and countries unable or unwilling to organize their international trade along such lines would be compelled to revert to economic isolation. Despite these objections, there would be wide public support in Britain for such a program if the alternative were the gold standard. As compared with international cooperation, it may be hoped that Britain would choose the latter.

By their nature, balance-of-payments problems are international in character and require mutual adjustment. For this reason the policy of the United States and other countries has been directed toward securing international monetary cooperation. Through its exchange stabilization fund, the United States has made bilateral agreements with a number of countries to help maintain exchange stability. Similar agreements were entered into by the Netherlands and Belgium in 1943, and recently by England with France, Sweden, Belgium, and the Netherlands. An attempt at multilateral cooperation was made by the United States, England, and France in the Tripartite declaration of 1936, to which Belgium, the Netherlands, and Switzerland became adherents.

On the basis of this experience, it was generally agreed in England and the United States that international monetary cooperation must be multilateral in character and broader in scope. In England, Lord Keynes prepared a plan for an International Clearing Union which was later submitted to the ministers of finance of the United Nations. In 1941, Mr. H. D. White prepared a memorandum of a plan for an International Stabilization Fund and a Bank for Reconstruction and Development. In April and November, 1943, tentative proposals for the Fund and the Bank were submitted to the Ministers of Finance of the United Nations. After extended technical discussions among 30 countries, a Joint Statement by experts was issued in April, 1944, recommending establishment of an International Monetary Fund. In July, 1944, the Monetary and Financial Conference at Bretton Woods prepared Articles of Agreement for the International Monetary Fund and the International Bank for Reconstruction and Development.

The Bretton Woods Agreements are the United Nations program for monetary and financial cooperation. The Fund recognizes the need for cooperation to maintain an orderly and stable pattern of exchange rates and freedom in exchange transactions, and it would have resources subscribed by the United Nations to help countries carry out these policies. The Bank recognizes the need for cooperation to secure adequate international investment, and it would have resources subscribed by the United Nations to encourage productive international investment. Cooperation among the United Nations through the Fund and the Bank will facilitate the expansion of international trade and investment and contribute to the attainment of high levels of employment, rising standards of living, and economic development in all countries.

3. An Orderly and Stable Pattern of Exchange Rates

The task of establishing initial exchange rates after the war, although difficult, is not overwhelming. Most of the allied countries have been able to maintain a considerable degree of order and stability in prices and wages, and present exchange rates in most countries will prove a satisfactory basis for initial parities in the postwar period. The Fund agreement provides that the initial par value of each member's currency, expressed in terms of gold, should be based on exchange rates prevailing 2 months before the Fund comes into force. If the member or the Fund believes this par value is unsatisfactory and cannot be maintained without excessive use of the Fund's resources, the member and the Fund must agree upon a suitable par value. For countries occupied by the enemy, the period during which an initial par value is to be determined may be extended by agreement between the Fund and the member country. In the meantime, the Fund may engage in limited exchange transactions with such countries at a tentative parity under conditions and in amounts the Fund may prescribe.

After initial parities have been established, member countries must maintain their currencies stable within a range 1 per cent above or below parity. A change in parity can be made only on the proposal of a member after consultation with the Fund and only for the purpose of correcting a fundamental disequilibrium.[1] Because the war has brought great economic changes to which adjustment can be made only gradually in the postwar period, a method must be provided to adjust

---

[1] A uniform change in the par values of all currencies may be made by a majority vote of the Fund with the approval of each country having 10 per cent or more of the total quotas. Any country that does not wish to have the parity of its currency changed as a result of such action may notify the Fund of its decision to retain the same parity.

promptly any errors in initial parities. Such adjustment is clearly preferable to allowing a persistent overvaluation or undervaluation of a currency, as happened with sterling and the French franc in the 1920's, merely for the sake of rigidity. To assure prompt adjustment of minor errors in initial parities, the Fund cannot object to a proposed change which, together with all previous increases or decreases, does not exceed 10 per cent of the initial par value. On all other changes in parity the Fund may concur or object.

Although the Fund has every reason to object to exchange depreciation where equilibrium could be better restored in other ways, it is not to the advantage of its members to force upon a country a rigid exchange that can be maintained only by a sharp reduction of wage rates and domestic prices. Exchange stability is for the purpose of encouraging international trade and investment. It would defeat these purposes to insist on exchange rigidity at the cost of a severe deflation which would reduce international trade and investment and spread depression from country to country. Nor can it be expected that countries will cut their social-security programs, as was done in the sterling crisis of 1931, or forego other social measures because they might affect stability of exchange rates. For these reasons, the Fund agreement provides that, if a change in parity is necessary to correct a fundamental disequilibrium, the Fund cannot object because of the domestic social or political policies of the country.

The Fund agreement forbids multiple currency practices, except as approved by it, and countries that now follow such practices must consult with the Fund as to their progressive removal. A distinction should be made between multiple exchange rates applied to exports, which are export bounties, and multiple exchange rates applied to imports, which are additional tariffs collected at the time the exchange is sold. In a number of American republics such multiple exchange rates are an important part of the tax structure and their removal must be undertaken gradually as other measures can be adopted to raise the needed revenues.

With these provisions, the Fund in practice will provide greater assurance of orderly and stable exchange arrangements than would be achieved under a gold standard in which each country regards exchange policies as its exclusive concern. The Fund proposal recognizes that exchange policies are an international responsibility, and it puts the sanction of international agreement on orderly and stable exchange arrangements. If any change in the parity of a currency is made after the Fund has expressed its objection, the member becomes ineligible to use the resources of the Fund, and if the difference between the member and the Fund continues, the member may be compelled to withdraw from the Fund.

4. Freedom of Exchange Transactions

In general, exchange controls restrict and divert international trade and investment into uneconomic channels by limiting the amount of foreign exchange made available to pay for imports and to meet service requirements on foreign investments. To eliminate such practices, the Fund agreement establishes the principle that no restrictions may be imposed on payments and transfers for current international transactions, including interest and dividends on foreign investment and moderate amortization and depreciation payments.

To avoid capital flights, member countries are authorized to control international capital movements, and the Fund may require a member to exercise controls to prevent use of the Fund's resources for large or sustained outflows of capital. None of these provisions is intended to interfere with capital transactions required in the ordinary course of trade, banking, or other business, or to prevent capital investment for productive purposes when it is made out of a member's own resources. When capital controls are imposed, they may not be used to restrict payments for current transactions or to delay unduly the transfer of funds in settlement of commitments. Their sole purpose is to prevent international monetary instability originating in a currency flight.

Countries like the United States, with large resources, would be perfectly free to allow all capital movements, and no country could be required to introduce controls to prevent small and intermittent movements of capital. In cases where controls are necessary, supervision or reports might be sufficient. Experience with foreign-funds control in this country has shown that without detailed control banks can be relied upon to see that transactions are not carried out contrary to regulations. Supervision of a similar character would probably be adequate in countries like England and Canada. There are countries in which complete control of payments may be needed to prevent an unauthorized outflow of capital. But the Fund would not cause such controls; by giving confidence, it would tend to minimize capital flights.

MONETARY STABILIZATION

Countries that now have exchange controls on current transactions must consult with the Fund as to their progressive removal and could retain them only with its approval. Countries whose international payments must cover relief and reconstruction are permitted to continue exchange controls during the postwar transition; but they must withdraw such restrictions as soon as they are able to balance their international payments without excessive use of the Fund. In exceptional circumstances, the Fund may make representations to any country that conditions are favorable for withdrawal or abandonment of restrictions; and, if a country persists in maintaining restrictions inconsistent with the Fund, it may be declared ineligible to use the resources of the Fund and may be required to withdraw from membership.

In all other cases, exchange controls on current transactions require the approval of the Fund. The Fund would probably authorize a country temporarily to impose such controls if an adverse balance of payments could not be corrected promptly by other measures. In some instances, the temporary use of exchange controls, while corrective measures are put into effect, can be advantageous both to the country employing the controls and to other members of the Fund.

If any country should have a persistently large favorable balance of payments, other countries might find difficulty in supplying enough of its currency to maintain exchange stability. The Fund provides a means of dealing with such a scarce-currency problem without a general revision of parities. First, the Fund would report on the causes of the scarcity and the measures necessary to correct it. The scarcity of a currency could be due to inadequate imports by that country or to excessive imports by other countries, and the appropriate remedies would depend on the facts in the particular case. Then, if its own holdings became inadequate, the Fund could apportion its sales of the scarce currency with due regard to relative need of members and other pertinent considerations. The Fund would, of course, never exhaust its supply of any currency, for it would acquire gold and the scarce currency from its other transactions.

When a currency is generally scarce, countries are bound to take steps to limit the demand for the currency. Without the Fund, there would be no restraint on the restrictions that could be imposed. Under the Fund agreement, the limitations on exchange operations with respect to a scarce currency may be imposed only after consultation with the Fund; they may be no more restrictive than is necessary to limit the demand for the scarce currency; and the limitations must be removed as rapidly as conditions permit. In the meantime, the Fund would use its resources to relieve the scarcity and it would press for corrective measures.

5. Use of the Resources of the Fund

Exchange stability and freedom of exchange transactions are possible only if countries have resources with which to meet an adverse balance of payments. Otherwise, they are compelled to force a prompt adjustment in their accounts through exchange depreciation or exchange control. Either policy might restrict the volume of trade and have a depressing effect on business in all countries. If other adjustments are preferable, a country should have help in avoiding extreme measures whose principal merit is their prompt, though harsh, effect.

The Fund will have resources of $8.8 billion in gold and in national currencies, subscribed by 44 countries on the basis of appropriate quotas, to help members maintain the exchange policies of the Fund. Although these resources are not exceptionally large, they are extremely important. After urgent postwar needs are met, gold and dollar reserves outside the United States may amount to $18 billion. It cannot be assumed, however, that these reserves will all be available for use in maintaining free and stable exchanges. Except for most of the Latin-American republics and two or three others, all countries will have far smaller reserves than they need. Even if these resources were better distributed, foreign countries as a group would not reduce their exchange reserves below $10 billion to maintain the Fund's exchange policies. By making its resources available to member countries, the Fund will give them confidence to use their own reserves, and the aggregate resources that can be used to maintain stable and free exchanges will be considerably increased.

A member country may purchase foreign exchange in limited amounts from the Fund for its own currency without special action by the Fund. It should be noted that the Fund's holdings of currency are guaranteed against depreciation in terms of gold. This is substantially the technique used in our stabilization agreements, and in the monetary agreements recently made by England, in which each country undertakes to acquire the currency of the other to a specified amount to help meet an adverse balance of payments. Subject to quantitative and qualitative limitations, the Fund gives each member a conditional right to purchase foreign exchange for local currency; but the Fund can terminate this right for any country that is not carrying out the purposes of the Fund.

On the quantitative side, unless the Fund expressly waives these limits, a country may not acquire foreign exchange from the Fund for its own currency in a net amount in excess of 25 per cent of its quota in any 12-month period; nor can it purchase foreign exchange from the Fund for its own currency if the Fund's holdings of its currency exceed its quota by 100 per cent. If a country has monetary reserves in excess of its quota, it must use its own reserves to the same extent that it draws upon the resources of the Fund; and, when its reserves increase, a country must use one-half of the increase in its monetary reserves, if they exceed its quota, to repurchase its currency from the Fund. On the qualitative side, the Fund does not permit use of its resources to support an untenable exchange rate. The Fund would not accept an initial parity that would cause excessive use of its resources; nor would it begin exchange transactions with a country that is not in a position to maintain balance in its payments without excessive use of the Fund. A country using the Fund is expected to take steps to correct any continuing maladjustments in its international accounts. For violation of the purposes or provisions of the Fund a member may be suspended from using the Fund's resources; and if the violation persists, it may be required to withdraw from the Fund.

The Fund's resources are a revolving fund available to member countries to meet an adverse balance of payments while they adopt measures to adjust their international accounts. The usefulness of the Fund would obviously be limited if its resources were not in a form in which they could be readily used by all countries. To discourage unnecessary use of the Fund, a charge of three-fourths of 1 per cent will be imposed on all exchange transactions with the Fund. To encourage restoration of the Fund's assets to their ideal combination (25 per cent in gold and 75 per cent in members' currencies in proportion to quotas), charges are levied on members whose currencies are held by the Fund in an amount in excess of their quotas. These charges increase with the amount and the duration of the period the currency is held by the Fund. When any charge reaches 4 per cent, the Fund and the member must consider means of reducing the Fund's holdings of that member's currency and, if agreement is not reached, the charge continues to rise to 5 per cent and thereafter the Fund may levy such charges as it deems appropriate.

Some critics have expressed doubt that in practice these safeguards will be adequate. In effect, they doubt the good faith of members of the Fund. It is quite clear to all countries that use of the Fund's resources is conditioned upon maintaining policies in accord with the purposes of the Fund. Nor is there any reason to assume that management of the Fund will be in the hands of debtor countries. The United States has 28 per cent and the five largest countries 57 per cent of the total voting power in the Fund. There is nothing that can prevent these countries from seeing that the Fund is used properly. Furthermore, special consideration is given to the position of creditor countries. The two largest creditor countries are entitled to name executive directors if they do not already do so. And on all voting on use of the Fund's resources, the voting power of creditor countries is increased while that of debtor countries is decreased.

6. The Role of International Investment

Unless there is an adequate volume of international investment, it will be extremely difficult to establish a pattern of international payments under which stable exchange rates and freedom of exchange transactions can be maintained. The policies of the Fund will to some extent encourage international investment. The Fund would regard the blocking of the proceeds of international investment, including reasonable amortization and depreciation payments, a violation of the Fund agreement. But it is doubtful whether this indirect encouragement will be enough in the postwar period. Although the losses from international investment in the 1920's have been exaggerated in the public mind, investors will hesitate to lend abroad during the immediate postwar period when loans will be most urgently needed. In order to give direct encouragement to international investment, the Bretton Woods Conference proposed the establishment of the International Bank for Reconstruction and Development with a capital of $9.1 billion subscribed by 44 countries. Because the benefits of international investment are general, the risks should be shared by all countries. This would be done through the Bank.

The Bank is designed to encourage international investment by guaranteeing securities sold to private investors for approved projects of reconstruction and development. Where the market is not prepared to make a loan on reasonable terms, the Bank would make the loan directly out of its own capital or from funds raised by issuing its own securities. Loans will be made or guaranteed by the Bank only after a committee investigates the proposed project and reports that it will contribute to the productivity of the country and that it is within the capacity of the borrowing country to service. Each loan must be guaranteed by the government of the country in which the project is located or by its central bank. Provision is made to assure the use of loans for the purposes for which they are made.

The Bank will guarantee loans for approved projects in return for a commission of 1 to 1½ per cent of the outstanding principal. A similar commission will be charged on direct loans, as the Bank will offer the securities to the public if the market becomes favorable. The commissions collected by the Bank must be held as a special reserve to meet its obligations in case of default. With a commission of 1½ per cent, this reserve would probably be sufficient to meet all losses on loans without impairing the Bank's capital even if one issue out of five were completely defaulted.[1] If the accumulated reserves are inadequate to meet defaults, the Bank may call upon its capital, of which 80 per cent is set aside as a surety fund for this purpose. Calls on capital are payable in gold or United States dollars or in the currency needed to meet the Bank's obligations. To give added security to investors, outstanding loans made or guaranteed by the Bank may not exceed the unimpaired capital and reserves of the Bank.

The Bank can be an important factor in placing international investment on a constructive basis. With full knowledge of the international economic position of a borrowing country, the Bank could prevent it from undertaking excessive obligations to service loans. Furthermore, by maintaining reasonable interest rates, the Bank places the greatest possible moral obligation on borrowers. In periods of exchange crisis, the Bank could also utilize its resources to permit for a time the servicing of international investment in local currency under a guarantee of repurchase, thus avoiding defaults because of temporary conditions.

---

[1] On the basis of loans liquidated in 30 equal annual payments, 4 per cent interest to the market, 1½ per cent commission to the Bank, and 2 per cent earnings on reserves, the Bank's special reserve would be more than sufficient to meet complete default of one issue out of five.

7. What the Bretton Woods Program Can Do

In evaluating the Bretton Woods program it should be borne in mind that the Fund and the Bank cannot of themselves assure either an appropriate pattern of international payments or national prosperity. They can, however, provide a favorable environment in which international trade and investment can be maintained at a high level. In such an environment, countries can adopt national policies for maintaining high levels of employment, rising standards of living, and economic development, with assurance of cooperation in maintaining international balance and without fear of conflicting policies in other countries.

After the experience of the 1930's, it is quite obvious that orderly international arrangements, as well as national prosperity, cannot be based on the prewar volume of international trade and investment. Unless measures are taken, national and international, to raise the real volume of international trade by at least 50 per cent above the prewar level, direct control of the balance of payments in some countries cannot be avoided. With $80 billion of international trade a year during the postwar decade, it will be possible for the countries that must increase their prewar level of exports to secure the necessary expansion without a deterioration in the terms of trade and to pass from the postwar transition into a period of stability, order, and freedom in exchange relations.

The expansion of international trade depends largely on whether the great industrial countries adopt measures to maintain employment. Otherwise, they will not purchase adequate quantities of raw materials and consumption goods from other countries, pressure will be exerted on the balance of payments of many countries, and the structure of exchange rates will be weakened. The greatest disturbances in international payments occur during periods of depression, for some countries have a very urgent demand for import goods, and when trade falls off there is a serious distortion in their balance of payments. If business depression can be avoided, international balance will be maintained with less difficulty. The primary responsibility for high levels of employment must be with the United States, because it is the greatest industrial country and its imports are extremely sensitive to business conditions.

Measures must also be taken to lower the barriers to international trade. If high levels of employment were maintained, the pressure to impose trade restrictions would be considerably reduced. The Fund, by assuring orderly and stable exchange arrangements, will facilitate the progressive removal of the barriers to international trade. It should not be overlooked that competitive exchange depreciation is in effect a device for increasing tariffs and for giving bounties on exports; and exchange control is another method of placing quotas on imports. With the Fund, competitive exchange depreciation and exchange controls will be avoided, and positive measures can be taken to remove other barriers to international trade.

Until the world has been restored to economic health, it will be difficult to secure adequate expansion of international trade and investment. The occupied areas in Europe and Asia are important factors in the world economy, and they must be restored and reconstructed promptly. Similarly, countries that have not had the opportunity for economic development should have access on reasonable terms to the foreign capital they need. The volume of international trade is certain to rise as productivity is increased in all countries. The trade of the United States has always been largest with such countries as Canada and the United Kingdom, which are highly industrialized and have high standards of living. There is no reason why this should not be equally true in other areas as they are developed. The measures that must be taken in each country for restoration of the national economy and for its reconstruction and development are in large part of a domestic character. But sound international investment for productive purposes will facilitate reconstruction and development, and international monetary cooperation will give countries the confidence they need in proceeding with the task of economic restoration.

The Fund and the Bank can make important contributions to the establishment of a balanced and growing world economy. They can help and encourage those countries whose economies have been disrupted by war and which must go through a period of transition or reconstruction to restore their position in the world economy. The Fund and the Bank can set standards for international monetary and investment policy. Together they can provide the means for constant and broad cooperation on international monetary and financial problems and contribute in this way to attaining the primary objectives of economic policy.

8. Is There an Alternative?

There are some critics who say that the United Nations program, specifically the Fund, is novel and complex. They prefer an agreement to stabilize the key currencies widely used in international payments, particularly the dollar and sterling. No formal organization would be established to help countries in maintaining such policies, although a loan of $5 billion to England has been suggested. At some future time, international monetary cooperation might be broadened to include other countries, and in the meantime any country could stabilize its currency by attaching it to the dollar or to sterling. In essence, this is a new version of the Tripartite declaration of 1936. Our own experience proves that no agreement on exchanges can mean much unless it includes nearly all countries and unless they help each other in maintaining a common exchange policy.

This preoccupation with key currencies misses the real exchange problem. All currencies are important in the world economy to the extent that their exchange policies affect international trade and investment. The dollar and the pound are obviously the most important. But 75 per cent of the world's trade before the war was of countries other than the United States and England, and of our trade only $11\frac{1}{2}$ per cent was with Britain and 23 per cent with the British Empire other than Canada. It is important to us to have orderly exchanges in the countries with whom we do more than 75 per cent of our trade. We are interested in the exchange policies of all countries because they are our customers, suppliers, or competitors. The American cotton exporter, for example, is interested in exchange rates for the currencies of England, Japan, India, Egypt, Brazil, Mexico, and other countries. When exchanges depreciated in these countries in 1931, the spot price of cotton in New Orleans fell from 9.08 cents in May, 1931, to 6.06 cents in October, 1931.

Exchange depreciation and exchange control need not originate in the countries with key currencies. A considerable number of countries depreciated their currencies long before England and the United States and adopted exchange control before Germany. Some countries may need flexibility in exchange rates and at times even exchange control. It would seem, nevertheless, that such policies should be adopted in cooperation with other countries after consultation with the Fund. The great trading countries have special responsibilities in maintaining a balanced international economy; but all countries must share in the responsibility for international monetary policy. The Fund recognizes this in the constitution of its Executive Directorate on which the five countries with the largest quotas have permanent representation.

The same critics suggest that the Fund be postponed until after the postwar transition is complete, although exchange and payments problems will be most acute during the transition and international monetary policy will be definitely determined then. The postwar pattern of exchange rates should be established by consultation between the Fund and member countries, and whatever adjustments become necessary should be made through and with the Fund. The same critics also suggest that the Fund be dropped and the Bank be authorized to make stabilization loans. The Fund's primary function is to maintain order, stability, and freedom in exchange transactions, and it holds resources only to help countries in carrying out such policies. Long-term stabilization loans are not a substitute for constant, continued, and general cooperation on exchange policies.

The world is in desperate danger of reverting after the war to economic isolation that will inevitably breed political isolation. Those who talk of waiting, of bilateral agreements with one or two countries, are in fact proposing that we do nothing, that we allow the world to drift back to the restrictions and the disorders of the prewar decade. This is a risk the world cannot afford. The Bretton Woods Agreements provide us with the opportunity to put into effect the fundamental principle that international economic problems are an international responsibility that can be met only through international cooperation. They offer the best hope of restoring and maintaining stability and order in international economic relations without which all countries will find greater difficulty in securing high levels of employment, rising standards of living, and economic development.

9. Summary

The Bretton Woods Conference has proposed the establishment of the Fund and the Bank to facilitate the restoration of an orderly pattern of international payments and to encourage international trade and investment through international cooperation. The Fund would help countries to maintain stable exchange rates and freedom of exchange transactions and thus facilitate international trade. The Bank would encourage international investment by private investors for approved projects of reconstruction and development. Other measures will also be necessary to assure adequate international trade and investment. It is especially important for the great industrial countries to maintain high levels of employment and lower the barriers to international trade. The Fund and the Bank will facilitate the adoption of such policies through international cooperation on monetary and investment problems. Unless the Bretton Woods Agreements are approved, there is real danger that the world will revert to economic isolation. With the Fund and the Bank, countries can proceed with domestic measures for their economic well-being without fear of conflicting international monetary policies.

Chapter XX

International Capital Financing

by ARTHUR R. UPGREN

1. REASONS FOR FOREIGN INVESTMENT

INTERNATIONAL capital financing in the postwar period can become one of the most important means to rebuilding and to advancing world economic recovery. To this there is wide agreement because there is such extensive realization of its advantages. Moreover, this agreement rests on the solid contrast in *capital* position between a creditor country such as the United States and a debtor (or economically "new") country such as China. In our country, annual gross capital formation after the war will probably exceed $40 billion; net savings will probably approach $20 billion. In China investment is keenly wanted; its volume has been so fantastically small that calculations are frequently made of cost-reducing investments that could show annual returns approaching the contemplated investment.

Such differences in capital resources and capital needs are widely convincing as to the basic advantages of reviving international capital financing on a substantial scale after the war.

What are the prospects that it can be revived? If revival seems likely, what are the prospects and what is required to realize most fully on them to the end that the outcome of revived international capital financing will be satisfactory to borrower and lender alike?

2. RECORD OF FOREIGN INVESTMENT

International capital financing or foreign investment is not a new phenomenon, but the period over which it has been conducted on a quantitatively substantial scale has been extremely limited. In the seventeenth and eighteenth centuries, there was scattered foreign investment with such concentration as did prevail centered in Antwerp and Amsterdam. From the end of the Napoleonic Wars to the 1860's, Britain was the important center. Prior to 1914 Britain lent at an annual rate of $1 billion a year, and total world lending before 1914 was at an annual rate of more than $2 billion. Allowing for the lower price level and rate of capital formation, these are indeed substantial figures. They have not been even closely approached since 1914.

The foreign loans outstanding of the four countries granting currently the greatest amount of foreign loans together with a rough estimate for the "little four" were as shown in Table 1 for 1914:[1]

TABLE 1

	Billions
Great Britain	$20.0
France	8.7
Germany	6.0
United States (net debtor country)	2.5
Netherlands, Belgium, Switzerland, and Sweden	2.8
World total international investment, 1914	$40.0

Though this total for world foreign investment had been built up over many decades, by far the largest part, perhaps $30 billion, had been lent in the three decades from 1884 to 1914.

These figures, $30 and $40 billion, are indeed sizable figures for a world that was much smaller, as it was at least economically, in 1914. Never since have the pre-1914 foreign lending rates been equaled. Prices, national incomes, gross capital formation, and net savings for many countries have far surpassed their 1914 levels. But not foreign investment!

In the short period of revival of interwar international capital financing, 1924 to 1930, a lending rate of two-thirds of the earlier rates was built up. But, if allowance is made for higher price levels, enlarged output, and the practically complete cessation of foreign lending in 1930, the record simply expired after that date.

This then is a brief description of the phenomena that helped so greatly to build the modern world. Capital is saved either at home or abroad. In the past, say a century ago, saving at home was at the cost

[1] Adapted from data contained in an article "Foreign Investment," by M. Palyi in *Encyclopedia of the Social Sciences*.

of uneconomic working conditions (child labor, female labor, long hours in the coal industry, unsatisfactory factory conditions of work, etc.) by means of which the capital supply was enlarged because current spending upon consumption was reduced. This was substantially the case in England. Alternatively, after western Europe's initial capital supply was secured, capital was borrowed in relatively larger proportion by countries which came later upon the industrial scene. It would perhaps be not far wide of the mark to say that the combination of several things for the United States, (1) our later industrialization, (2) our great borrowing from abroad, and (3) our free land, collectively eased greatly the problem of *our* capital supply accumulation.[1]

We as a country were probably in a sense "directly subsidized" by having foreign lending advance, with great bursts forward, our material welfare much faster than would have been possible without such lending. It was this advance in the last century that subsidized the generation that has lived in this century. In addition, the great industrial development of the United States has been fed upon imported raw materials such as rubber, tin, jute burlap, vegetable oils, manila fiber, and tung oil. To add to such a list the imported foods—tea, cocoa, spices, and sugar—supplies part of a total list of items that the present generation in our country has enjoyed only because capital was saved by an earlier generation and used in the economically new lands which are the source of these goods to develop the necessary production of them. Except for a very small amount of rubber, possibly manila fiber, and of course sugar, American capital had very little to do with the making of the investments necessary to produce these supplies. We profited greatly by them. We in turn accumulated capital and produced goods that were bought by other countries in part out of the proceeds of foreign loans which we granted. Are such processes to be considered ended?

The process, of course, is not ended. What is difficult, however, is to find the means for its revival in a way that can be satisfactory to modern lenders whose supply of capital is seeking many outlets, and to borrowers as well.

[1] Most of our deprivation incurred in national capital accumulation appears to have been suffered in connection with the exploitation of the land—getting to it and winning a living, ultimately good, from it.

3. Future Difficulties for Foreign Investment

Perhaps the difficulties can be made clearer by the use of an illustration in the field of domestic industrial bonds that presents in a parallel way the difficulties of foreign investment. The purchase of industrial bonds is frequently cautioned against by the old adage that "for industrial concerns the business cycle all too frequently has a duration (8 years) shorter than the customary life of their bond issues (say, 15 years)." There is a parallel double danger in the field of international investment. It is that in addition to the prior well-known risk of the *international* business cycle, we now have wars that seem to occur in a term that too appears to be shorter than the probable life of an "average" foreign bond issue.

In addition to the business cycle and now the "war cycle" risk for international investment, there is a still further risk that is represented by the lack of any set of rules, in the field of international capital financing, to govern behavior of debtors as we have rules of equity and publicity that apply in securing fair treatment to investors in the domestic field.

Investors have been long habituated to the assumption of credit risks—the risk that the debtor will not pay. That long risks here too were taken in the period after 1918 is evidenced by the fact that many loans were for 7 and 8 per cent coupon rates of interest. In contrast, 5 per cent was a rate much more frequently encountered prior to 1914.

But now a new risk—the exchange risk, to wit, that the currency of the creditor country cannot be secured though the debtor is making his contractual payments in his own currency—has become an important factor that has caused deterioration of foreign investments. This exchange risk has bulked large since 1929. The problem has been handled by improvisation that has had to resort to such things as blocked balances, standstill agreements, differential currency depreciation, barter agreements, and clearing agreements (not to mention outright credit default in lieu of solution of the exchange problem). Clearly what is needed is a common set of rules that will provide for international creditors some degree of equity. If this is achieved, it will prevent some of the past inequities that occurred when losses on long-term securities approached 75 cents on the dollar in a given period in which short-term obligations were being liquidated to recover as much as 75 cents on the dollar.[1] In addition, if fair rules are devised, the prospect *to debtors* of far less discontinuity in foreign borrowing may strengthen their experience and thereby their conviction that such borrowing can have more continuously beneficial outcomes. In this way it should be possible to strengthen their efforts at maintenance of constant debt service, thus avoiding the default that may occur because no future advantage is threatened by such default.

4. Recent Action for the Future

As is well known, the question of how to revive international capital financing was, together with proposals for international currency stabilization, the subject of the Bretton Woods International Monetary Conference held in July, 1944. At that conference was produced the charter for an International Bank for Reconstruction and Redevelopment.

What are the prospects that the sum total of action taken and to be taken (the latter along the lines of presently anticipated action) will be adequate to revive foreign lending with a satisfactory outcome to borrowers and lenders alike?

To answer this question requires (1) definition of the minimum requirements that must be met if the outcome of future international capital financing is to be satisfactory; (2) a review of the institution proposed (the Bank) to determine whether it contains promise of effective loan supervision and service both before and after default; (3) an estimate of the likelihood that other international economic cooperation will serve to reinforce action to be taken in the field of foreign investment.

Turning to the first of these three questions, it is generally agreed that, starting from a condition of balance in the trade and service accounts, foreign lending should be productive, to the borrowing countries, of the means whereby the debt can be serviced. There is good reason to be dubious about foreign lending. Some assert, since foreign bonds mature in a time period that is longer than the trade cycle, that such borrowing is unlikely to be repaid. This they assert is because national economies simply do not subject themselves, in time of deep

---

[1] The figures are probably rather close to actual experience with German investments to United States holders in the first half of the 1930's. There appeared no way to distribute to *all* creditors of Germany the limited supplies of dollar exchange that in one way or another became available for German debt service in the United States.

depression, to the pressure which then proves to be necessary fully to service such external debt. Those who hold this view are able to cite the fact that there are two countries (these are included among those to which the United States rather generally has lent in the past) that have never fulfilled the terms of a *single* international loan contract.

The answer to this pessimistic view of foreign lending is threefold: first, every country initially does fully observe the terms of its international loans. As a result a better outcome can be expected provided foreign lending is not made at the crest of the trade cycle and provided, on the other hand, means are adopted at the trough of the cycle for temporary extensions both of principal that then may happen to fall due and of interest payments that are currently due.

But the more satisfactory answer perhaps is had only when it is made certain that all loans are made for productive purposes with the term having two requirements as to its meaning. The term "productive" when so used shall mean that the operation financed shall bring about (1) an increase in the borrowing nation's productivity and (2) an increase in the borrowing country's exports or a decrease in its imports. Only if the funds are used productively in this way

. . . to enlarge output at home and, concurrently, to do so in a way that is productive over the life of the loan, of the necessary foreign currencies which must also require either reducing the volume of foreign imports or increasing exports . . .

can there be preponderance of prospects that both *ability to pay and willingness to pay* can safely be maintained over the life of the loan.

The second form of answer to the pessimistic view of foreign lending is that the disparities in supplies of capital as between different countries continue to be so wide that, given a fair degree of success in diversification of risk assumed by lenders, their losses should be covered, and the loans should yield a satisfactory return. Even in the interwar period, 1920–1940, the outcome of United States foreign investment was not perhaps so unsatisfactory as many suppose. This is indicated in Table 2 which supplies a summary of figures recently provided by the Department of Commerce covering the foreign-investment experience of United States investors.[1]

The outcome of United States foreign investments, up to the outbreak of World War II, was not unsatisfactory either as to "total" or as

---

[1] August Maffry, "Foreign Trade in the Post-war Economy," *Survey of Current Business*, November, 1944, p. 11.

to "average." But that investors in securities of countries which fully avoided default (Canada) were unscathed was of little comfort to the investor in securities upon which there has been a record of default of 10 years or more duration (Germany).

TABLE 2

	Billions
Lent abroad by U. S. investors:	
U. S. investments abroad at the end of 1919....	$6.5
Net new investments, 1920–1940..............	6.9
Total................................	$13.4
Credits applicable to loans made by U. S. investors:	
Value of investments at the end of 1940........ $ 9.8	
Income received on investments, 1920–1940.... 13.9	$23.7
Excess of credits.........................	$10.3

The third answer to the pessimistic view about foreign investment lies in the fact that a sound program of foreign lending can be of assistance in helping perhaps to avoid *some* of the principal causes of war. It is not so much differences in the standard of life between various countries that may tend to cause war as it is the failure of each and every group in the world community to make the hoped-for steady economic progress. It is such persistent, if not spectacular, progress that can yield to them adequate satisfaction in the ways of peace (even though such progress may fail to reduce the standard-of-life differences that have continuously prevailed between themselves and other countries). The inhabitants of many newer countries realize that progress for them, too, should be possible. Countries most friendly to the United States include some whose inhabitants work hard and over long hours to produce goods of which we are the world's greatest importers. These goods they, however, are glad to produce, because along that way lies their opportunity to climb up the ladder of economic progress. This advance, they believe, can be accelerated by foreign lending which, therefore, can serve the purpose of enlarging the numbers who come to have greater interests in peace than in war.

5. International Bank for Reconstruction and Development

To meet the needs of the future there has been now advanced, along with the proposal of an international monetary fund for currency stabilization and adjustment, the plan for the International Bank for Reconstruction and Development. The Bank is proposed specifically as the means to revive international capital financing.

A review of the specific purposes, organizational form, and contemplated operations of this new institution is particularly important at this time. This is doubly so: (1) because the Bank plan represents the unanimous agreement of the representatives of 44 united and associated nations; (2) because of the wide range of approval with which the plan has been received in our own country. This favorable accord is no doubt in part due to the fact that the objectives of the Bank are widely understood and, as understood, are generally deemed reasonably possible of achievement.

The purposes of the Bank are

1. To assist in reconstruction and development by facilitating the international investment of capital.

2. To promote private foreign investment by means of guarantees or participations.

3. To promote international equilibrium by promoting long-range balanced growth of international trade.

4. To arrange its assistance in such relation to loans through other channels that more *useful* projects, large and small alike, will be dealt with first.

5. To assist in a smooth transition from a wartime to a peacetime economy.

More briefly, the purpose could be stated as follows: Through the Bank (and encouraged private lending) to promote economic progress for its members over the transition period into a long-range enlarged trade-account position that permits debt repayment.

The form of organization results in the creation of a bank that can best be described as one of "subscription and guarantee." Commercial banks have commonly been termed institutions of "discount and deposit" because their two vital functions have been those of making advances to borrowers and holding deposits for the order of their customers. In a parallel way the important functions of the Bank for Reconstruction and Development are "subscription and guarantee" because the Bank holds subscriptions to $9.1 billion of its capital stock (of which only 20 per cent is to be paid in) and it issues its own, *i.e.*, guaranteed, obligations or guarantees international loans to a limit that has been placed at 100 per cent of its subscribed capital, namely, $9.1 billion.

The Bank in addition may make loans out of the currencies received in payment of the 20 per cent of its capital stock initially to be paid in. But its major operation will be embraced by the issue of its own guaranteed obligations or the guaranteeing of obligations issued by others. It is under these two arrangements that the Bank may lend funds for international investment—funds that are secured by the credit of the bank which derives from the subscriptions it holds from its members. In fact, when it is said that the securities issued by the Bank bear the joint and several guarantees of its members up to the amount of their several subscriptions, what is meant is that the Bank, through its ability to call subscriptions, is able to implement what proves to be the equivalent of such a guarantee. The subscription of the United States government is $3.175 billion or 35 per cent of the total subscriptions. The Bank will deal with members only through their treasuries or other appropriate fiscal agencies to make loans or give guarantees. Through the agency used, the Bank may make advances to political subdivisions or to specific enterprises.

All guarantees, loans, or participations must be made to finance *specific projects* of reconstruction or development. Special committees are to be appointed to review each such specific project and the committee must recommend the project and the advance in a written report. These committees are to include an expert representing the country in whose territory the project is located. Assistance of the Bank is to be given only if the borrower is unable to secure the loan on reasonable terms in private markets. Whenever loans are not made directly to the member government, that government is, however, required to guarantee the loan in an appropriate way. Except for loans made out of currencies initially paid in, the Bank is not to specify in what country funds it advances are to be spent. Loans made out of funds received from the paid-in subscriptions are not to be made without the approval of the country whose currency is being so used. In this way member countries do have the right to pass upon projects that are to be financed with their particular currencies. In the case of loans representing borrowings made directly by the Bank in one currency which are to be advanced to a country having a different currency, the consent of the country whose currency is being borrowed by the Bank must be first obtained. Although the Bank is intended to make advances only to finance the borrower's requirements outside its borders, loans may include, under special conditions, advances for the purchase of domestic supplies and labor (where these tend to reduce foreign-currency supplies because they are "bid away" from export industries, for example). The primary test is whether or not the project directly or indirectly leads to needs for foreign exchange by the borrowing country.

Charges covering interest, amortization, maturity, and commission are to be made by the Bank. They must be appropriate to the project being financed and vice versa. The rate of commission shall be between 1 and 1½ per cent per annum for a first 10-year period. The collection of this commission fund can serve to make it possible for the Bank to accumulate reserves to assist in meeting losses. For periods not exceeding 3 years the Bank may make special arrangements avoiding requiring payments in certain currencies and accepting in lieu the domestic currency of the borrower. The Bank has further discretion in being able to modify arrangements for amortization and, in fact, the term of the loan itself. The purpose in giving these discretionary powers is to avoid needless deterioration of loans where a rigid rule might result in inability temporarily to accept domestic currency. In this way what has been defined as the "exchange risk" would not be allowed to develop so as to cause deterioration in the "credit risk" (inability and unwillingness to pay).

The management of the Bank is vested in a Board of Governors and Executive Directors. Powers of operation are lodged in the Executive Directors and the administration is vested in a president as chief executive. The Bank also will have an advisory council of seven members representing bank, commercial, industrial, labor, and agricultural interests. The principal office will be located in the United States. The distribution of voting power, in part, is indicated in Table 3.

TABLE 3

Country	Percentage of Total Votes
United States	31.4
United Kingdom	13.0
Other British Empire	12.3
Russia	12.0
China	6.1
France	4.6
Latin America	8.2
All others	12.4
Total	100.0

There are many other special provisions covering settlement of accounts, withdrawals, suspension, interpretations, privileges, and arrangements for entry into forced and final liquidation. These, however, are only of technical interest.[1]

6. The Bank and Future International Capital Financing

Foreign investment in the future, from the point of view of the United States, might be left as a private matter; alternatively, it might be arranged with a full guarantee and coverage (100 per cent) provided by the United States government or some agency thereof; finally, it may be undertaken with a partial guarantee provided by an international agency created for the purpose. There seems to be wide agreement that the difficulties during the late 1920's and the complete cessation of foreign lending in the 1930's would make it extremely hard to revive any substantial amount of international capital financing on a private basis after the war. Separate unilateral lending by the United States has the disadvantage of not securing for American creditors the participation and partial guarantee by all other United Nations that is available in lending through the proposed International Bank for Reconstruction and Development. It is probably this reason, joint participation in the responsibility and joint participation in recommendations leading to loans, that carries a widespread appeal as a desirable way in which international capital financing may be revived after the war. It is clear that the risk of failure to set "the rules of the game for foreign investment after the war" would be obviated. The mutual determination of such rules and subscription to them by both creditors and debtors represents an immense step forward toward more satisfactory

---

[1] The "Final Act and Related Documents" (which include the charter for the Bank) are contained in a booklet entitled *United Nations Monetary and Financial Conference, Bretton Woods, New Hampshire, July 1–22, 1944*. The booklet is issued by the Government Printing Office.

Reference should also be made to an article entitled "Bretton Woods Agreements" reprinted from the *Federal Reserve Bulletin*, September, 1944, and freely available from the Board of Governors of the Federal Reserve System, Washington, 25, D. C. This article is by E. A. Goldenweiser and Alice Bourneuf.

Most writers on the subject of the international monetary plans have limited themselves to discussion of the stabilization proposals, *e.g.*, an excellent article, "Two Plans for International Monetary Stabilization," by Jacob Viner, *Yale Review*, Summer, 1943. Another excellent article, "International Monetary Plans: After Bretton Woods," by John H. Williams was published in *Foreign Affairs* in October, 1944. This article is primarily on international monetary stabilization, but in it Williams expresses his "growing appreciation of these advantages in the Bank" and raises the question of the possibility of "expanding the Bank's functions to include some part of what is desired from the Fund."

banking practices after the war. It is possible to take this step because the nature of the Bank is such that it could continually hold the promise of funds being available in appropriate situations. This freedom to act in an emergency is of great importance.

The degree of credit risk is reduced because of the fact that loans can be made only to finance projects that demonstrably possess "self-liquidating qualities" in contrast to the intangible kind of financing of the past that has been represented by advances to make good budget deficits.

The foreign-exchange risk is reduced for two reasons: (1) the Bank itself would be able to advance the current income called for in behalf of the investor and at the same time continue, in time of an exchange stringency, to see that the debt was serviced in the domestic currency of the borrowing country; (2) the Bank is expected to operate in some connection with an international monetary stabilization proposal (International Monetary Fund) which will be especially designed, among other things, to be in a position to help debtor countries meet foreign-exchange needs on current trade and service accounts.

7. Other Desirable International Action

What, of course, is widely realized as extremely desirable is that commercial policies, of debtor and creditor countries alike but especially of creditor countries, shall be gradually rearranged so as to be appropriate to the foreign investment position as it may develop for each country. More specifically, for the United States the need is for commercial policies that are consistent with the proposed revival of foreign lending. This will require, slowly and steadily, that changes in trade restrictions be made so as to permit borrowing countries, through the sale of goods to us, to service and ultimately repay loans. Perhaps the greatest hope here lies in the fact that foreign lending and its desirability in specific instances will be the subject of discussion and review by an international agency. It is such an agency that can be expected to see to it that necessary changes in commercial policy are suggested and are, in fact, actually made over the period of time during which such correction is necessary if there is to be a long-run, satisfactory outcome for the international capital financing which they are to manage.

8. Conclusion

The record of international capital financing in the nineteenth century contributed immensely to world progress. Except for a brief 6-year period in the 1920's, international capital financing in a substantial way has not existed in the present century since 1914, when its quantitative level surpassed any levels of the very short revival of the later period.

The International Bank for Reconstruction and Development provides an institution which should serve to restore foreign investment after the war. That financing, made under proper safeguards, can contribute to world progress. It can be profitable to lending countries, thus enlarging the gains that peace should be able to bring and reducing thereby, in some degree, the risk of future war.

Finally, it is of the utmost importance that every action that promises to contribute to reduce the risks of war should be taken. This is action to help achieve political and military security. It is in this way only that the third risk, the "war risk" in foreign investment, can be reduced. Many desirable international economic policies can have successful outcomes only if the risk of war can be reduced. This is true as well for international capital financing.

Chapter XXI

The Path from Bretton Woods

by HENRY C. WALLICH

AMONG plans for international reconstruction, none reach more deeply into fundamental questions of economic policy and theory than the Bretton Woods proposals. The debate on the plans has been vigorous, and most of the major issues separating supporters and opponents have become clearly defined. The present chapter is not primarily a plea for or against, but rather attempts to appraise certain weaknesses of the Monetary Fund, and to point out how they could be overcome by appropriate measures on the part of its management. However, it takes the view that, given a management strong enough to protect the Fund against the intense pressures of the postwar transition period, the Bretton Woods projects may be regarded as the best available means of handling foreseeable postwar monetary problems.

1. Loan Operations

Two major questions are posed by the Fund's prospective loan operations ("sales of exchange"): (1) How far can it afford to see its resources drawn into reconstruction activities, which will be the main source of postwar credit needs? (2) How much control does the Fund have over its loan operations? The answer to these questions must go far to determine one's attitude toward the Plan.

Although clause XIV-1 of the Fund proposal states, with deceptive simplicity, that "the Fund is not intended to provide facilities for relief or reconstruction . . . ,"[1] there can be no doubt that this prohi-

[1] *Articles of Agreement, International Monetary Fund and International Bank for Reconstruction and Development,* U. S. Treasury Department, Washington, 1944.

bition applies primarily to direct loans for specific purposes, rather than to an indirect use of its exchange loans for relief and reconstruction. It is frequently impossible to prove conclusively whether a stabilization loan is being used to increase consumption or to intensify reconstruction, since an industrial country need not import capital goods in order to be using the Fund's resources for reconstruction.[1] To avoid such indirect use, the Fund would have to bar reconstructing countries from obtaining any aid at all, and it is a safe guess that the war-damaged countries did not sign the Bretton Woods Agreements with any such understanding. It is a reasonable assumption that all reconstructing countries which may become debtors in the Fund will indirectly be using at least part of their borrowings for the ostensibly illicit purpose.

A moderate use of the Fund's resources for reconstruction is not necessarily an evil, however; on the contrary, it is preferable, *ceteris paribus*, to an equivalent draft for purely consumptive purposes. It is an error to think that, because reconstruction implies long-term capital investment, the exchange needs connected with it ought exclusively to be covered with long-term loans of the Bank type. The soundness of the Fund's loans depends, not upon the purpose for which they are employed, but upon their magnitude and upon the general balance of payments situation of the borrowing country.

This is easy enough to see. The Fund operates on the assumption that the balances of payments of its members will undergo more or less normal fluctuations and that the borrowings of the passive periods will be paid off with the surpluses of the active years. If this assumption is correct, there is no need to insist that the loans be used for exchange-generating purposes, since over a period of years the country will have enough exchange. It is evident, in fact, that the purpose which stabilization loans are ultimately made to serve does not matter, *provided their volume does not exceed probable future exchange surpluses*. The loans can be paid off as soon as these surpluses materialize. Unlike loans made by the Bank, they are not dependent upon the amortization of any capital investment for which they may indirectly have been used, or upon tax revenues. Insofar as the Fund's loans do indirectly serve for reconstruction purposes, and thus perhaps tend to generate a little foreign ex-

---

[1] A country, for instance, might indirectly use the Fund for reconstruction by importing foodstuffs with borrowed exchange and simultaneously shifting equivalent resources from consumer-goods output to reconstruction. Another country might import capital goods and shift resources into consumer-goods industries, thus in effect using the Fund for consumptive purposes.

change, the prospect of repayment is, if anything, better than if they had been employed to increase consumption.

The trouble is that neither of the uses to which stabilization loans can indirectly be put may offer good prospects of repayment, because for many of the reconstructing countries the assumption of normal swings in the balance of payments does not hold good (unless much larger long-term loans are forthcoming than now appear to be in prospect). It will take these countries several years, and probably a good deal of belt pulling, before they can get back to equilibrium, let alone develop a substantial surplus. Hence the outlook for an early repayment of their stabilization loans is dim, no matter what the money is used for. It is for these reasons, and not because of the long-term character of most reconstruction projects, that the use of the Fund's resources by reconstructing countries is dangerous.

If a sufficient volume of long-term loans is forthcoming from the International Bank and other sources, the Fund can permit moderate drafts by a reconstructing country, without too much fear of permanent unbalance. This raises the important question of how much control the Fund has over its loan operations. It is futile to debate whether or not the Fund's lending should be called "automatic"; there can be no doubt that all the forces of inertia, which in the case of bank lending are against the borrower, weigh here in his favor, and that normally there is a presumption that he will get his money. It is true that if a member should make very rapid and heavy withdrawals, or if it should exhaust, year after year, its annual allowance (25 per cent of its quota), the Fund may decide that its resources are being misused and may reject further demands.[1] Nevertheless, this power is not an adequate safeguard for the Fund if a large number of members simultaneously apply for moderate amounts. The sums which could quite legitimately be drawn out in this manner during 1 or 2 years would seriously jeopardize the Fund's liquidity if the demand should concentrate upon only a few currencies. The probability that during the transition period the demand will be large and concentrated is the main reason why the Fund should exercise stiff control over its lending.

A second reason for desiring more control during the transition period is the rapid growth in the exchange reserves of a number of

[1] If the offending member is engaged in reconstruction, the Fund could further buttress its disciplinary action by referring to the clause which prohibits the use of its resources for reconstruction. This *ad hoc* interpretation of the clause would probably be generally accepted as reasonable.

countries. Even while we have been talking about means to remedy the world shortage of dollars, the problem has silently solved itself in good part for quite a number of countries. In view of the limited supply of dollars available to the Fund, it would be desirable to restrict the use of the Fund by exchange-rich countries more thoroughly than is at present proposed.

A third reason for objecting to quasi-automatic lending during the transition period is the probability that all but a few members will invoke the Transitional Arrangements clause (XIV-2) and thereby maintain exchange control. Automatic and largely uncontrolled lending does not seem to harmonize with such conditions. It is appropriate in a situation where balances of payments fluctuate freely and are subject only to the indirect and slow influence of monetary and fiscal policies, so that borrowing, too, is in a sense automatic. Under exchange control, however, borrowing becomes a deliberate act: the authorities decide whether or not to license imports in excess of exchange receipts and thus determine directly the character of the balance of payments. It would seem logical to match this type of borrowing with equally deliberate lending on the part of the Fund.

Fortunately, the means are at hand, within the present framework of the Fund proposal, to give the agency the control which it ought to have during the transition period. All that need be done is to declare that some currency has become scarce. Since demand during these years is likely to concentrate upon a few currencies, chiefly the American and Canadian dollars, there is every prospect that these currencies will become scarce eventually. It would not seem to be out of harmony with the spirit of the plan to declare them scarce immediately, before the actual shortage has materialized. Thereafter the Fund is authorized to "apportion its existing and accruing supply of the scarce currency with due regard to the relative needs of members, the general international economic situation, and any other pertinent considerations,"[1] which is precisely what it ought to do from the outset. The fact that other members would then be authorized to impose exchange control and to discriminate against the scarce-currency countries should not be an obstacle. Exchange control will be well-nigh universal in any case, and discrimination is authorized only insofar as necessary in the light of availabilities of the scarce currencies.

[1] *Loc. cit.*, clause VII-3.

2. Structural Weaknesses

To the means of international payment existing so far—gold and certain "key" currencies—the Bretton Woods proposals add a third: a drawing right in the Fund. Whenever a member is paid "through the Fund," *i.e.*, receives payment in its own currency drawn from the Fund, its drawing right increases correspondingly. Unfortunately, the new medium is by far the least attractive of the three, because, unlike gold and free exchange, it does not necessarily enable its holder to make payment to countries whose currency is scarce.

From the viewpoint of the United States, whose currency enjoys the greatest probability of becoming scarce, this limitation of the drawing right is of minor importance. The Fund normally will have most of the other currencies; our trouble will be that we may not want them. Despite the lament of some American critics that our drawing right will thus be "worthless," this is not a defect peculiar to the drawing right. Gold, too, is of little use to us unless we want to buy more abroad than we sell; for us its sole advantage over a drawing right is the prospect that it will survive a new glacial period in international financial relations, whereas a drawing right, under such conditions, probably would become permanently frozen. For other members, however, most of them potential applicants for dollars, the fact that the drawing right does not guarantee access to dollars is a very serious handicap.

It is to be feared that this may occasion a new demonstration of Gresham's law. Members who are creditors in the Fund [1] would seem to have every reason to draw on the Fund before using their own reserves, since they incur no interest charges. From the Fund's viewpoint that operation would be desirable, since it would replenish currencies in short supply, so long as it did not intensify the demand for even scarcer currencies. Other members, however, might also be tempted to use the Fund as much as possible, in spite of small charges, in order not to miss out on their "fair share" of dollars. This practice the Fund would have to combat.

Another tendency on the part of members which it will have to fight may be that of avoiding the receipt of payments through the Fund, a

---

[1] A member is a creditor in the Fund if the Fund's holdings of its currency are less than 75 per cent of its quota. If the Fund's holdings are above 75 per cent of the quota, the member may be regarded as a debtor in the Fund, although it would not have received *net* assistance unless the Fund's holdings exceed 100 per cent. Any exchange it might have obtained up to that point would be merely the equivalent of its gold contribution.

practice which probably will soon be in evidence and for which devices will not be lacking. A preference might develop among members for dealing with countries which customarily do not pay through the Fund and are prepared to convert foreign holdings of their currency into gold,[1] and for using such countries as monetary centers, at the expense of other centers which offer payment mainly through the Fund. If the Fund should become very lopsided, payment through it will come pretty close to payment in blocked currency and may be strongly resisted. To put the brakes on this kind of thing, the Fund frequently may have to argue, bicker, and plead with its members to operate so as to keep it on an even keel as much as possible. All these troubles stem from the fact that there is a gap between the amount of any one currency which may be demanded and that which the particular member is required to supply.

A second string of troubles originates in the Fund's egalitarian treatment of all currencies, in a world which is plainly organized on the key currency principle. The Fund seems to have been constructed on the ostensible assumption that each country invoices its exports in its own currency, and that each country, therefore, pays for its imports in the currency of the exporter. Presumably, a universally acceptable arrangement could not have been formulated without this show of monetary democracy, for the authors of the Plan unquestionably knew that a few countries, mainly Britain [2] and the United States, conduct virtually all their foreign trade in their own currency (a few others to a lesser degree), and that most other countries accordingly conduct both their imports and their exports mainly in dollars, sterling, and a few other currencies. The great majority of the world's currencies hardly ever show up in international trade.[3]

The result is that, in the ordinary course of events, a key country may have no occasion to purchase a foreign currency from the Fund, since it ordinarily pays in its own. This leads to the very serious further consequence that the key currency may be drained from the Fund even

---

[1] Such conversions would not fall under clause V-6-*a*, which requires a country desiring to acquire another member's currency against gold to do so through the Fund, if it can be done with equal advantage.

[2] As long as sterling remains under control, British importers probably will have to make payment in some other currency to countries outside the sterling area. The same applies to other key currencies.

[3] In the great exchange markets of the world, therefore, these secondary currencies are without significance. Dealings in South American currencies in New York, for instance, are scanty, even when exchange control does not intervene; major sales and purchases of dollars and sterling against the various local units can be made only in the respective local markets.

if the key country has an even balance of payments.[1] Furthermore, as long as the key country stands ready to sell gold, as the United States has done since 1934, it may be completely unable to obtain aid from the Fund. The following example will illustrate this. Suppose that the United States has a passive balance of payments with, say, Latin America and an equivalent active one with, say, Europe. Our active balance will be covered in dollars which Europe may obtain from the Fund, assuming Europe's total balance to be passive. Our passive balance will likewise be covered in dollars which we pay to Latin America directly and which Latin America will add to her exchange reserves (perhaps in the form of gold, as long as the United States stands ready to sell it), assuming her total balance to be active. We are paid through the Fund but are forced, by the logic of our existing payment habits, to pay outside the Fund. Thus, although our balance of payments may be in equilibrium, the Fund would be losing dollars.[2]

A key country's inability to channel its payments at will through the Fund and thus to replenish the Fund's holdings may become embarrassing not only to the Fund but also to the key country itself. To continue with the above example, as long as the United States is prepared to sell gold, Latin America can convert its dollar holdings into gold.[3] The United States might prefer not to go on losing gold, but it could not obtain aid from the Fund, because all the Fund could do would be to offer Latin-American currencies ("pesos"), and these never enter into any of the transactions.[4] In order to be able to use the Fund, the United States would have to abandon its policy of selling gold freely. If Latin America then wanted to dispose of its dollars, the United States' obligation would be confined to redeeming its own currency by selling

---

[1] *Cf.* J. H. Williams, "International Monetary Plans: After Bretton Woods," *Foreign Affairs*, October, 1944, pp. 46–47.

[2] The definition of an active and an equilibrated balance of payments underlying the argument is the customary one which takes account of all autonomous items but disregards gold flows and induced capital movements. In the above example, the American balance is in equilibrium because our receipts from Europe are assumed to be equal to our payments to Latin America. Latin-American accumulation of dollars and the activation of our Fund subscription on behalf of Europe need not be considered, since they constitute an induced inflow and outflow of capital, respectively.

[3] This is what Latin America has done with a large part of its wartime dollar surplus.

[4] A rather tortuous interpretation of clause VIII-4 might in some cases offer a way out. This clause would obligate Latin America, under certain conditions, to repurchase "pesos" held by the United States. The United States, therefore, might obtain "pesos" from the Fund against dollars and demand repurchase by Latin America. But even if the Fund agrees to put this interpretation upon clause VIII-4, the obligation lapses, during the transition period, if Latin America maintains exchange control under the Transitional Arrangements clause, as it probably would.

"pesos" within the proper range of parity, which it could obtain from the Fund. Latin America in that case would acquire a larger drawing right in the Fund.[1]

Passing from illustration to reality, it becomes plain that the United States probably would not mind a drain of gold within reasonable limits, so that the difficulties standing in the way of Fund aid would not greatly matter. This attitude would not necessarily be shared, however, by other key countries, should they find themselves in the same position. It is not unthinkable that Britain, for instance, may eventually wish to resume a policy of selling gold freely. In that case, she would be able to draw on the Fund only insofar as her payments could be made in some key currency other than sterling.

The difficulties arising from the Fund's symmetrical construction in a key currency world may be summarized by saying that it fails to act as a clearing mechanism. It is simply a lending institution. In a properly functioning clearing mechanism, the in and out payments of a member should be offset against each other, if they are of equal magnitude. The member's net position in the clearing should always reflect its actual position vis-à-vis the other members. This could be accomplished if all payments were made through the clearing, or perhaps if the distribution of payments through and outside the clearing were random. In the Fund, however, it is biased in the sense that payments by key countries generally will go outside. Hence a member's net position in the Fund need not, and probably will not, reflect its true international position.[2]

How serious is this defect? In my opinion it is not grave enough to warrant a negative attitude toward the Fund. Unlike the earlier White and Keynes plans, the Bretton Woods project does not make a member's position in the Fund or Union the criterion for policy recommendations. It merely permits the imposition of universal exchange control, if a certain currency becomes scarce, and authorizes discrimination against the scarce-currency country, but not beyond what is warranted by each member's availabilities in that currency. Although this sounds pretty

---

[1] Since in most instances that might be a less desirable asset than dollars, Latin America may well remain content to hold on to its dollars. This would not hurt the United States, but the Fund's dollar shortage would remain uncured.

[2] The repurchase provisions will prevent a member which is internationally strong from being a debtor in the Fund, but they cannot make it become a creditor, since repurchase is not allowed to reduce the Fund's holdings of the repurchasing member's currency below 75 per cent of the quota. Nor would they suffice to prevent an internationally weak key country from being a creditor in the Fund, although they would go some distance toward correcting the situation.

grim, it need not cause undue alarm. What may happen, in other words, is that the Fund may experience a dollar shortage which reflects only a localized rather than a universal shortage among its members and that it may then authorize exchange control for all members, including those which have sufficient dollars. This would be serious if there were reason to think that the latter countries would otherwise have pursued a free-exchange policy. For a number of years, however, most countries will be engaging in exchange control and discrimination anyway, under the Transitional Arrangements clause, so that the additional sanction of these practices under the Scarce Currencies clause will add little that is new. Discrimination, moreover, is not authorized unless warranted by each member's dollar availabilities, so that the dollar-rich members— Latin America in the above illustration—could not legitimately discriminate. For these reasons, I can see no great harm in declaring the dollar scarce and have even suggested this as the normal *modus operandi* for the transition period.

The post-transition period is another matter, assuming that the earlier period is not merely a transition to some new emergency. By that time we hope to get along without exchange control in most countries. A Fund, therefore, which might be suffering from a chronic dollar shortage of its own, not representative of world conditions, and which for that reason would have to authorize universal exchange control, would be a real calamity.

Whether or not this threat would materialize will depend, in the first place, upon the size of the dollar or gold accumulations of countries receiving net payments from the United States, *i.e.*, upon the size of their active total balances. It will further depend on whether the Fund, the United States, or the rest of the membership are able and inclined to adopt measures which would cause these active balances to take the form of credits in the Fund rather than dollar or gold holdings. This, in turn, resolves itself into the question of making it possible and desirable for the United States to pay through the Fund instead of outside it. If attempts in this direction do not avail, a change in the Fund's statutes might be envisaged at that time, restricting the right to impose or maintain exchange control under the Scarce Currencies clause to members that actually need control. The amendment probably would have better chances of acceptance if accompanied by an American offer to contribute a few more dollars to the Fund.

3. Alternative—The Key Currency Approach

The key currency approach, suggested by Dr. Williams in his series of articles in *Foreign Affairs* [1] has been needlessly abused by some of its opponents and has been misused by others to lend intellectual respectability to a do-nothing attitude. It has never, however, been embodied in a detailed plan. The key currency approach does not necessarily involve splitting the world up into currency blocs, nor is it a device by which the United States could seek to escape its international responsibilities. It is simply an attempt to make the international mechanism to be created conform to the preexisting pattern of international financial relations. All credit systems naturally tend to group themselves around one or more centers which are known to be strong lenders. International credit relations have been no exception; before 1914 they were centered mainly on London. Trade, therefore, tended to be carried on mainly in sterling. Instead of pretending, as the Monetary Fund is forced to do, that all currencies are born equal (if not free), the key currency approach recognizes the inevitable asymmetry of the world's monetary organization and tries to build upon it a system of stabilization measures. It is, as a British commentator has said, the sort of thing that would naturally occur to a central banker.

It is not difficult to sketch the outlines of a key currency system. There would be one or more key countries—say the United States and Britain—and a number of member countries. The latter might be grouped in blocs around one of the key countries, or they might have direct relations with both of them. Since the bloc arrangement would require Britain to underwrite the net dollar requirements of its member countries and would also entail other inconveniences, the second arrangement would be preferable for most countries. The key countries, then, would lend dollars and sterling to each member country having a passive total balance, regardless of the state of its partial balance with the United States or Britain. The member countries, on the other hand, would hold part or all of their exchange reserves in the form of dollars and sterling whenever they had an active total balance. Dollars and sterling would be the normal means of international payments among all members, and the whole system would therefore be upon a dollar and sterling standard. Loans to the member countries would be closely controlled during the transition period, when the borrowing pressure

[1] Reprinted in J. H. Williams, *Post-war Monetary Plans and Other Essays*.

would be heavy, but could become more or less automatic later on, perhaps up to a certain quota. To prevent excessive borrowing by the key countries, the members might be authorized to demand gold redemption if their dollar or sterling balances rose above a certain level. Agreements would have to be made between the key countries and their members to avoid unnecessary exchange-rate movements, and indemnification for exchange losses would have to be arranged for whenever such movements did occur. Consultation regarding internal policies might also be provided for.

Such a system would be quite workable—it worked very well before 1914, the main differences being that London then was the only center and that the balances held there were private rather than official. What speaks against it is mainly the delicate character of the relationships involved. Borrowing is not impersonal, as under the Fund, but direct. Policy obligations are not to a general body, but to a specific country. The member countries must have considerable confidence in the integrity and good will of the key countries. The latter, in turn, risk the assumption of heavy burdens, or the emergence of paralyzing disputes, unless the member countries are willing to restrain themselves or to be restrained. Such a system is one that must grow up gradually; it can hardly be imposed from one day to the next. The mutual obligations and restraints are bearable only as long as they are implicit, the result of habit and experience. Explicitly formulated at a conference, they become unacceptable, no matter how hard the delegates work or how beautiful the scenery.

Under postwar conditions, the difficulties confronting sterling would be a further handicap. Britain would hardly be in a position to stand the strain which would be imposed upon her by the obligation to make widespread sterling stabilization loans and to meet the obligations vis-à-vis the United States which are implicit in the arrangement sketched above. Even a large dollar loan would probably not overcome this difficulty, for the British problem is not only one of solvency, the blocked balances question, but also one of breaking even as a going concern, the gap in the balance of payments. A system based on two key currencies thus would certainly limp rather badly for some time.

A system based purely on the dollar, on the other hand, would likewise meet with great difficulties. Britain probably would refuse to range herself under such a system and would try to salvage as much of the sterling area as possible. And since a good part of the world is in fact upon a sterling standard and because London is a great financial center, a pure dollar system would not be in harmony with the world's present financial organization. Finally, even those countries which economically lean more toward New York than toward London may be hesitant to bank upon, and with, the United States. We have not yet proved our sense of international responsibility; the experience of 1928, when we suddenly found domestic lending more interesting than foreign, can hardly have been forgotten. Wartime experience with our freezing controls, moreover, may have made some countries skeptical as to the advisability of carrying reserves in the form of dollar balances or even earmarked gold, when they might as well have gold safely in their home vaults.

For all these reasons, one must reluctantly conclude that the key currency approach does not offer an alternative preferable to the Fund, at least not in the immediate future, provided the Fund is properly managed. In the longer run, a development in a key currency direction seems wholly desirable. It would harmonize with the natural centralizing tendencies of the international credit system, would provide a uniform means of international payments, and would, in a sense, reproduce the conditions existing before 1914, when the world's monetary system was functioning at peak efficiency. Such a development may well take place under the regime of the Fund, if the latter succeeds in re-creating a reasonably free currency setup, for in that case the system's strong centripetal forces will have a chance to work themselves out. But like the pre-1914 gold standard, a key currency system will have to grow up gradually. An attempt to create it at one stroke is likely to lead to confusion and resentment and to bog down in a morass of bilateralism.

Part VI

SOCIAL SECURITY AND THE CONTRIBUTIONS
BY THE GOVERNMENT

Chapter XXII

Social Security

by EVELINE M. BURNS

OF THE many fields of social and economic policy bearing on reconstruction none is more liberally furnished with specific plans and programs than that which has come to be loosely identified as social security. The Beveridge Plan was only the first in a long line of concrete proposals which now includes, to mention only official documents, the Security Work and Relief Policies Report of the National Resources Planning Board, the Marsh Plan of the Canadian Advisory Committee on Reconstruction, and the various Interim Reports of the Australian Joint Committee on Social Security. Provisions for veterans have also been enacted in these countries which include, *inter alia*, measures to promote the economic security of ex-servicemen and women. In all these countries, too, with the marked exception of the United States, there is active cooperative planning by the government and the medical profession to expand health services and make them more generally available to the whole population.

Not all of these proposals have a direct bearing on the immediate problems of reconstruction, unless that term be defined so as to include the longer run. But in terms of the problems which have been of prime concern in this symposium, the programs which aim to assure *income security* have a very direct contribution to make. Indeed, at the present time there is a tendency to evaluate our existing social-security programs solely from the point of view of their adequacy to meet the demands of the reconversion period. This I believe to be a mistake. The need for assurance of income maintenance during the postwar dislocations is of course of the greatest importance. But it is equally important that amendments made at this time should be carefully scrutinized for the effect they are likely to exert on the ultimate development of a workable and socially satisfactory and permanent social-security system. This, however, requires a clear picture of the main outlines of a socially satisfactory long-run program.

I. The Objectives of a Satisfactory Program

Such a program must reflect both the social objectives of the time and the economic conditions of the country. To bring the problem into focus, we might imagine—I admit by some effort—that a unanimous Congress called in some social-security expert and said to him: "The people of the United States are rational, intelligent, and progressive. They want a social-security program that will satisfy three conditions and we want you to devise it. These conditions are: First of all, it must assure basic economic security against all the more common interruptions of private income. Second, the system must preserve to the greatest possible degree other important values in our society, and notably it should interfere as little as possible with the influences encouraging initiative. Third, the system should yield the greatest possible number of useful economic by-products, implementing, rather than running counter to, other accepted social and economic policies."

There are several points in this mandate that call for comment. Note for example that it would not matter to the social-security expert why the nation wanted to assure basic security to all. The policy might be based on a widespread concern for the welfare of the individual citizen; it might be because the nation thought it economically wise to provide for a specific minimum of purchasing power as a bulwark against internal economic collapse; it might be due to political fears that a democratic society could not long survive the presence of millions of incomeless people, or it might be that the society did not want to be bothered with continual improvisation of methods for providing for people who suffer interruptions of private income and have no other source of support.

Note too that this intelligent electorate does not ask that the system shall not interfere *at all* with individual or group initiative or exert *no* adverse influences on other important social values, but only that this interference shall be kept to the minimum consistent with achieving the goal of basic security for all. Being intelligent, this electorate realizes that it is impossible to remedy the great evils of insecurity without interfering in some measure with, for example, the perfect freedom of the citizen to do exactly what he likes with his own income. And note, finally, that our wise electorate is modest about the incidental advantages it hopes to secure from an orderly social-security program. It asks only for the largest possible number of desirable by-products consistent with attaining the main goal. It does not expect to solve *all* the evils of poverty and insecurity through a social-security program.

In carrying out his mandate our social-security expert would have three major decisions to make. He would have to determine the levels of social-security benefits and the conditions under which they were to be available. He would have to decide upon methods of financing and, in particular, the distribution of costs between different groups in the population and the period of time over which he would seek to bring expenditures and income into balance. Finally, he would have to select appropriate administrative agencies and assign responsibility among Federal, state, and local governmental units. Only the first two of these major problems will be dealt with in this chapter.

II. Eligibility Conditions and Benefit Levels

a. ELIGIBILITY CONDITIONS

Changes in the conditions under which social-security benefits can be secured have been among the most significant developments in the field of social security in the past thirty or forty years. Today our expert would have to decide between two major approaches. On the one hand is the view that social-security benefits should be available as a right, whereby people fulfilling prescribed qualifying conditions are entitled to money benefits payable at rates, and in contingencies, defined by law without having to demonstrate economic need. On the other hand, social-security benefits may be available on a discretionary basis, payable only after passage of a test of need and in amounts that reflect the extent of need. The institution of social insurance is generally regarded as reflecting the first of these theories; the poor law or public assistance (to use the more popular euphemism) expresses the second view. I prefer, however, to distinguish them by the terms "nondiscretionary" and "discretionary" systems, because both social insurance and public assistance have undergone modifications of form whereby each has tended to assume some of the characteristics of the other.

Between these two extremes, there is one possible compromise, which is that adopted in New Zealand and proposed in Australia for all income-security programs except children's and maternity allowances. This is to make stated social-security benefits a statutory right in the event of legally defined instances of income loss, but to reduce the amount of the payment by stated amounts as private income increases until, at some level of income, no security benefit is payable. Such a system is similar to social insurance in that payments are a matter of right in the defined circumstances, and their amount is determined by objective criteria (the provisions of the law and the money income of the claimant) which leave little room for the exercise of discretion on the part of the administrator. On the other hand, it has affinities to public assistance because there still remain traces of a needs or means test, though in much modified form.

One final compromise has been adopted by many countries in regard to certain security programs: namely, to provide payments in the statutory form for a limited period, and thereafter to revert to the discretionary system.[1]

In choosing between these principles governing the availability of social-security payments our expert would have to take account of a number of important variables. In the first place he would have to take account of the emotional associations attached to the needs or means test as such. In Great Britain the feeling is so strong that I cannot conceive of any planner developing a program containing this, to the British, so objectionable feature. It would too evidently run counter to prevailing social standards, for here the presence of a means test has come to be identified with the philosophy that underlay the old deterrent poor law.[2] In the United States the public attitude to any kind of means or income test is less easy to determine, though the strong support of the labor movement for the technique of social insurance would seem to indicate that the desire to avoid a discretionary system is widespread here, too.

[1] This is one of the points at issue between Sir William Beveridge and the British government's White Paper proposals. Beveridge would make unemployment insurance a statutory benefit so long as unemployment lasts. The government would continue the present British system of paying insurance benefit for only a limited period, thereafter providing for the worker and his family through unemployment assistance. Similarly, the National Resources Planning Board proposed to limit insurance benefits to the first 26 weeks of unemployment and thereafter to provide public work.

[2] This attitude to the means test, and by contrast to social insurance, which is a technique for avoiding its use, runs through the whole Beveridge Report. *Cf.* also, E. M. Burns, *British Unemployment Programs*, 1920–1938 (1941), pp. 239–252.

The second variable relevant to the determination of the conditions under which social-security payments are to be available is the possibility of defining by law an acceptable standard of average income and of the items that are to enter into the individual's income for the purpose of determining eligibility in the event that some such compromise as that in effect in New Zealand might be adopted. Here the United States is at a real disadvantage as compared with many other countries. As compared with Great Britain, the size of the country and other factors have resulted in a great heterogeneity of living standards and variety of methods of securing incomes which would create difficulties if the attempt were made to follow the New Zealand model. Furthermore, there are in the United States no such standardization of wages and general acceptance of the concept of a basic minimum wage as have resulted in New Zealand and Australia from an old and extensive system of wage regulation through courts of arbitration. The possibility of adopting a system based upon income declarations is, however, continually being increased by the tendency everywhere to widen the scope of the income tax so as to include lower wage brackets.

Finally, our expert would have to take into account the level of national income. The higher this is, the easier will it be for him to recommend the statutory or social-insurance technique, for the more easily will a wealthy country be able to afford and be willing to countenance a system which provides benefits based on potential, rather than on actual or demonstrated, need.

Faced with these considerations, I suspect that our expert would in the main be impressed by the increasing popularity of nondiscretionary payments and the tendency here as abroad to aim at social insurance as the method of assuring basic security which most accurately reflects prevailing social attitudes. His plan, in other words, would have to embody the principle of assured rights to stated payments in specified contingencies.

b. THE DETERMINATION OF BENEFIT LEVELS

The decision in favor of the widest possible use of the nondiscretionary technique has important repercussions on the decision as to the principle on which benefit levels are to be set. If it is indeed intended to assure security to all or almost all the population (including the lowest income groups) through this technique, the benefits must, for the vast majority of those covered, be sufficient to assure maintenance without recourse to any supplementary system.[1] The precise standard of living which is to constitute "maintenance" at any given time must of course be determined in the last resort by reference to the general levels of productivity and incomes in the community. On the one hand, rising general standards of living affect men's judgments as to what is a "proper" living standard for those who are at any time receiving socially provided income. Public opinion, which is a real fact of which economic planners must take account, will reject too great a disparity between those who are earning and those in receipt of public aid. Practically, this means that a satisfactory plan will have to include some provision for periodic revision of the assured standard in the light of broad trends in the national income. On the other hand, changes in the national income are relevant because they affect the extent to which social-security payments *can* be raised without departing from the second of the conditions that were laid down for our expert: namely, that the program should preserve to the greatest possible extent other important social values such as the encouragement of initiative. Our expert must at all times provide a margin between the assured minimum and what can be obtained by participation in production. Obviously, the prospects of guaranteeing security payments that at one and the same time assure an acceptable standard of living and yet still leave a comfortable margin as "bait" to induce active participation in production are increased as productivity and national income increase.

I suspect that our expert, when making his benefit proposals, would make a distinction between the unemployables and the employables. The aged, the permanently disabled, and dependent children and their mothers fall into one class, because they are people who for physical conditions or reasons of social policy are deemed to be out of the labor market. No serious economic harm would be done if these groups received security payments higher than the earnings they could hope to secure from participation in production. Hence, it would be possible to assure them a uniform minimum level of income based upon maintenance costs, which might be revised every 10 years or so in accordance with trends in the national income. Whether this maintenance level would include more or fewer "luxury" items at any given time would, within these limits, depend upon such considerations as the num-

---

[1] For an elaboration of this point see E. M. Burns, "Social Insurance in Evolution" and the ensuing discussion by Prof. E. W. Bakke, *American Economic Review Supplement*, March, 1944, pp. 199*ff.*

bers in these groups in relation to the numbers in the productive age classes and upon the relative importance attached to the welfare of the different groups (*e.g.*, the aged *versus* the young).

The problem of determining benefit levels for the employable population in a nondiscretionary system is much greater. In a country like the United States, characterized by great occupational and geographical differentials in wages, standards of living and to a lesser degree in living costs, the Beveridge solution, which involves a uniform minimum bearing some relationship to an acceptable maintenance standard, would for some groups and in some areas exceed normal earnings and would be unacceptable both economically and socially. Yet, given the intensity of the desire for wide coverage by the nondiscretionary system, the trend toward benefits based on maintenance will be inescapable. Only two alternatives would seem to be available to our expert. He could suggest a system in which benefits were frankly based upon maintenance, in which, however, both the real standard and its money expression varied regionally, and possibly also with urban and rural differentials (an elaboration of the principle that was adopted in setting the security wage under the Work Projects Administration). Or he could propose a minimum that was admittedly somewhat below an acceptable maintenance level and provide above that for differentials based upon earnings according to a relatively small number of wage classes. This second system might well be more costly, but it would enable a concession to be made to those who feel strongly that social differentials should also be reflected in social-security payments. In either case, however, allowances for dependents would be necessary. They can be avoided in a comprehensive nondiscretionary system covering even the low-income groups, only if there is considerable resort to supplementary public assistance (in which case the objective of the nondiscretionary system is sacrificed) or by limiting the duration of the payments to a relatively short period during which the recipient can reasonably be expected to supplement their inadequacy from his own resources.

III. Financing the Social-security Program

Decisions made concerning the level of benefits and the conditions under which they are to be payable, coupled with estimates of the incidence of the risks provided against, will roughly determine for any given year or period of years the anticipated expenditures on social-security programs. The purely financial questions are two in number: How are these costs to be shared between different groups in the population? How are they to be distributed over time?

a. THE DISTRIBUTION OF COSTS BETWEEN PERSONS

Recognizing the very real desire for a feeling of self-help and a sense of independence on the part of the majority of people, our expert would probably aim to raise part of the needed funds from an earmarked tax on income receivers as such. He would, in other words, recognize the important social value in typical social-insurance programs, which, by collecting part of the funds from those who are to benefit by the program, tend to lessen the feeling of charity previously associated with the receipt of socially provided income. Such a direct allocation of part of the costs to earmarked taxes on individuals has the additional advantage of keeping before the taxpayers (*i.e.*, the potential beneficiaries) the costs of programs of varying degrees of liberality.

But he would not be able to rely wholly on such taxes because the level of incomes of a significant part of the population is such that they could contribute their proportionate share only by drastic cuts into an already unduly low standard of living. Where then is the difference to come from? I believe it extremely unlikely that our expert in planning a social-security program for a rational society would make use of the pay-roll tax on employers. He would eliminate it because in the first place it is a bad tax, which, *inter alia*, runs counter to the second of the general conditions he was asked to comply with. In the short run, its impact varies greatly from firm to firm and industry to industry, varying with the elasticity of demand for the product, the proportion of labor in relation to other costs, the degree of unionization among employees, and the like. It may lead to uneconomic shifts as between labor and the use of capital equipment. Socially and politically, too, it is an unsatisfactory source of income for a program such as social security. Although there is not yet complete agreement among economists as to its ultimate incidence, there seems to be a broad measure of agreement that in the long run it is likely to be shifted to consumers or to wage earners, the precise direction of shifting depending on conditions of monetary supply and the level of economic activity at the time. Certainly in the vast majority of cases it does not ultimately rest with the employer. To the degree that its incidence is unpredictable, it is a disturbing influence in any rational tax program. To the extent that it is passed on to workers or consumers, it is a regressive tax which has little place in a program whose major objective is the greater economic security of the lower income groups. Politically, the tax has the disadvantage that it gives a small and easily organized group of taxpayers a disproportionate influence on policies relating to the character of the program, since their influence will always be exerted in the direction of keeping taxes down.[1]

Finally, I believe our expert would eliminate the employers' pay-roll tax because, in the kind of society for which he is planning, many of the arguments which have hitherto supported use of this tax in spite of its many disadvantages would be no longer valid or necessary. Its earlier importance as a guaranteed source of revenue for a service whose permanence was still in doubt would be less because the rational society we are presupposing has already decided to have a social-security program and, being rational, would ensure that the necessary appropriations were in fact made. Nor in such a society would it be any longer necessary, or indeed possible, to use the pay-roll tax as a psychological compensation to the worker for being asked to pay what, when first introduced, was in fact a new form of income tax. The workers' tax now is very generally accepted, and a rational society would certainly not be hoodwinked by the argument that as a result of the pay-roll tax the employer was also "contributing."

In a rational financing system, therefore, the difference between the yield of any practicable earmarked tax and total expenditures would have to be drawn from general tax funds. Our expert would, in other words, be likely to favor the financial principles adopted in New Zealand (namely, of an earmarked social-security tax payable by every income receiver plus a contribution from general tax revenues) rather than the recent Australian proposal for 100 per cent reliance on general tax funds or the Beveridge proposal to use the pay-roll tax as one of the three sources of social-security revenue. At the same time I am sure he would urge wide publicity for an annual statement of the expenditures, current and projected, of the different segments of the social-security system so that our intelligent society would always be in a position to know to what it was committing itself and which of the risks covered were proving most costly.

[1] This situation has already characterized to a marked degree the evolution of the state unemployment-insurance programs, where the interest of employer taxpayers, heightened by experience-rating systems, has operated as a powerful lobby against proposals to make the systems more adequate or liberal.

b. THE DISTRIBUTION OF THE COSTS OVER TIME

Our expert would be well aware of the fact that the financing of a program of the magnitude under contemplation has important economic effects upon the economy as a whole. Recalling the third of the requirements laid down in his mandate, he would certainly desire that so far as possible his social-security program should be integrated with broader economic policies and specifically with plans for a compensatory fiscal policy. Whether or not he would suggest meeting all expenditures in any given year from taxes collected in that year would therefore depend on prevailing general fiscal policies. Neither the pay-as-you-go principle nor the method of providing for full reserves or for automatic increases in the rate of tax irrespective of prevailing economic conditions would be appropriate to such a policy. Rather the decision as to what proportion of the costs of the program should be financed by taxes in any given year would be made annually, account being taken of the fact that deficit financing in some years involves collection of taxes more than sufficient to meet current outgoes in years when the level of economic activity is high. At the same time our present preoccupation with the problem of how to bring about investment of the current high level of savings should not lead to a neglect of an important economic aspect of reserves. For apart from the shorter run considerations which appear to be the focus of compensatory fiscal policies, it is at least conceivable that a society which, for example, wished to be very generous to its aged population in the future might face the necessity of enforcing an increase in national saving for the purpose of increasing the future capital equipment of the country, and thus the future level of productivity. But it is evident that such an attempt to increase the productivity of a future generation, thus putting it in a position to make relatively large payments to the aged of that date without excessive diminution of its own current living standards, would have to be accompanied by measures to ensure that the social-security reserves did in fact lead to a net addition to capital growth over and above what would otherwise occur, and not merely to a decrease in other types of taxes at the time the reserve is being accumulated.

IV. A Comparison with the Existing System

The social-security system which has been outlined would not only have a certain inner consistency but also make a more substantial contribution to economic stability during the reconversion period than that which we now have. It would assure at least a minimum of income to all, thereby providing a minimum guaranteed purchasing power for the economy, but it would also provide for upward variations in that minimum should the long-term upward trend in national income be continued. It would ensure coordination of social-security financing with the general fiscal policies of government and avoid distortion of business calculations by eliminating a tax on the use of labor.

The present system differs from this in many respects. It does not even assure income security to all Americans by either the social-insurance or the public-assistance techniques.[1] The social-insurance system itself has a thoroughly irrational structure. It pays benefits that for some groups now covered are too low for maintenance, and this inadequacy will become more glaring if, with the present pattern of benefit payments, the scope of the system is extended to bring in such typically low-paid groups as agricultural and domestic workers. On the other hand, it reflects the principle that when the minimum increases, the maximum must also, and may lead to an earmarking of an unnecessarily large proportion of national income for purposes of social security. Finally, in the case of the aged, it makes but a limited and long-delayed allowance, in fixing the money amount of cash benefits, for any upward trend in the national income.

The financing of the program is almost the reverse of what economic considerations would suggest. There is heavy reliance on a pay-roll tax, and the extent to which a government contribution is to be utilized in the future for the old-age and survivors insurance program is unspecified and apparently is to depend upon the relative strength of the political forces on every occasion when the question of raising the wage and pay-roll taxes comes up. The arrangements for spreading the costs over time are almost the reverse of what economic considerations would suggest. In the unemployment-insurance program, which would seem naturally to lend itself to some form of "compensatory financing" even with a uniform tax rate, the mounting reserves that have accompanied the fortuitous fact that the system began to function in a period of increasing business activity have almost everywhere been used as an argument for somewhat indiscriminate liberalizations or for the cutting of taxes. This last objective has been conspicuously successful through the device

---

[1] *Cf. Security, Work and Relief Policies*, National Resources Planning Board, 1943, especially Ch. 6.

of an experience rating system which makes no distinction between "stabilization of employment," resulting from better organization of production within the firm, and that due to an extremely tight labor market. As a result, at the very time when large reserves could have been accumulated to pay for more adequate benefits for a period of time longer than the 16 weeks most generally adopted in the states, taxes are being cut and the reserves are much lower than they could have been under such favorable employment conditions.

The position is similar in the old-age and survivors insurance program. Here the 1939 departure from the large reserve which was to serve as a source of income in later years was accompanied by no change in the principle of periodic increases in the tax rate. The scheduled increase to 1½ per cent in 1940 was indeed eliminated, but the tax rates originally provided for 1943 and thereafter were unchanged. Since 1943, Congress has annually refused to authorize the statutory increase to 2 per cent. The first change in rate fell due in a period of low economic activity and was postponed with every economic justification, but the second fell due at a time when every economic indication pointed to the desirability of tax increases.

Finally, the present "system" is essentially unstable. Two quite different social-security systems, social insurance and public assistance, exist side by side, and so far the second is, in terms of numbers of beneficiaries, by far the more important. The long experience of Great Britain has shown that it is impossible to isolate each system from the other. On the one hand, the preference for the nondiscretionary system leads, as America is already finding, to continual pressure for a broadening of coverage, to new risks, and new population groups. This, in turn, for the reasons outlined earlier, leads to pressure to reconsider the benefit structure and also to changes in the methods of financing in the direction of some contribution from general taxation. On the other hand, the assistance program itself brings pressures to bear on the insurance program. First, it becomes liberalized in an attempt to make it more acceptable to those who are excluded from insurance and, when liberalized, the assistance payments which are frankly based in principle on need throw into relief the low insurance benefits for the lower income groups and lead to renewed pressure to liberalize the insurance system. No balanced or orderly social-security program can be expected until the conditions of eligibility, benefits, and methods of financing for each program are determined in the light of the similar decisions to be made in regard to the other.

V. The Prospects for a More Orderly and Logical System

What are the prospects that in the near future the United States might adopt a social-security system that would satisfy the three conditions laid down at the beginning of this chapter? What is sought is a system that will (1) assure an effective minimum of economic security to all Americans, (2) preserve to the largest degree possible other important social and economic values such as initiative and freedom, and (3) achieve the greatest possible number of incidental economic advantages as a by-product? Frankly, I believe that the prospects are not very bright.

In the first place, there is a real technical obstacle due to the very great variations in levels of wages and standards of living in different parts of the country, between different occupational groups and, it must not be forgotten, between different racial groups. Economically, these differences obstruct adoption of any simple and single flat rate system such as Beveridge proposed for Great Britain. Socially, the enforcement of a standard of minimum adequacy of income, which would confer an especial benefit on Negroes in view of their generally lower living standards, would undoubtedly add an emotionally based opposition to the sufficiently serious economic obstacles. Here, as in so many other fields of social policy, national progress may be held back by the unsolved social and economic problems of the South. This is not to say that the problems are insuperable. Every increase in the productivity and standards of living of the South will simplify the task of the deviser of social-security programs. But the obstacle is one calling primarily for action outside the field of social security, and the needed action is of a fundamental and long-run character.[1]

In the second place, the attitude of organized labor is not favorable to the emergence of a more logical and economically satisfactory system. Labor in the United States is strongly individualistic and appears to attach as much importance as other groups to the maintenance of income differentials, *including their reflection in social-security payments*. This takes the form of demands that maximum benefits should be raised

[1] *Cf. Ibid.*, pp. 503–504, 514–515.

when minimum benefits are increased.[1] This attitude, if persisted in, will make it more difficult to bring up the lower benefits to any real level of adequacy and may well have unfortunate repercussions upon the public attitude to public social-security systems. For, given the prevailing attitude toward individual enterprise and government controls, it is evident that use of compulsion, in this case compulsion to devote a specific portion of private income to providing a cash annuity in old age, must be justifiable in terms that have a broad appeal. To use compulsion to assure at least a minimum of basic security in cash can be supported by a wide variety of arguments. But a people that have so emphatically indicated their desire to maintain the maximum possible scope for individual enterprise, compatible with assurance of security for all, may well hold that above that minimum level the choice as to both the amount of old-age cash income each person desires and the form in which that income shall be enjoyed (*i.e.*, through private savings, insurance, or home or farm purchase, and the like) should be left to the individual. In other words, compulsion on individuals to set aside a specific portion of income to assure a minimum old-age income of $30, $40, or $50 monthly is much easier to justify in broad social terms than compulsion to "save" in a specific form for a cash annuity of $120 upward.

In the third place, it is difficult to see how a rational and economically advantageous system can be expected as long as there is such widespread distrust of the actions of future Congresses and a fear of irrational and selfish pressure groups. I suspect that these very real social facts will for some time to come prevent adoption of the economically appealing arguments of those who, like Prof. Hansen or Mr. Ruml, urge that social-security financing should be subordinated to the general fiscal policies of government or, like Mr. Williamson, the Actuary of the Social Security Board, suggest the adoption of a "social budgeting" approach to the determination of benefit payments.

In the welter of current discussion about the inhibiting effect on business enterprise of "fears of government" and uncertainty as to government policy, it is often overlooked that workers, too, distrust government and suffer from uncertainty as to future policies. This lack of confidence that policies currently adopted will be implemented and

---

[1] Thus the Wagner-Murray-Dingell bill, which raises the minimum benefits in the old-age and survivors insurance program from $10 to $20 monthly, simultaneously raises the maximum from $85 to $120. Still more significant is the fact that during 1943, while 13 states raised the weekly maximum unemployment compensation benefit, only 3 of these raised the minimum as well, while 3 others raised benefits in the lower wage classes.

enforced by future Congresses has very real effects upon our social-security system. It leads to an overvaluation of the social-insurance approach because, rightly or wrongly, it is popularly believed that the payment of benefits at some future date will be more certainly assured if they are provided for in a law which embodies some kind of a contractual obligation between "government" and the contributors. It leads to tremendous emphasis on the sanctity of social-security reserves and to charges of ill faith when the government quite properly borrows from the contributors to finance current governmental expenditures. Until there is a more widespread acceptance of the ideas that all citizens should be entitled to some minimum income in the event of interruption of private income and that assurance of these payments will be a first charge on government expenditures, I suspect that the social-insurance approach with its *quid pro quo* implications and its separate reserves will be vigorously defended by those who are fighting for freedom from want and who recall that the proposal to provide even old-age assistance was regarded as a dangerous incitement to dependency only fifteen years ago.

The fear of irresponsible pressure groups will work in the same direction. From this point of view a social-insurance system is a conservative bulwark against continuous pressure of well-organized groups to raise security payments at every legislative session.

Fourth, a more rational social-security system can hardly be expected until there is a wider understanding of economic principles and in particular of the function and economic significance of reserves, on the part of the people as a whole and their legislators. From this point of view, the recent public and Congressional discussion of the projected increase in the pay-roll tax is far from encouraging, not only to those who desire a more rationally financed social-security system but to all those who are urging adoption of compensatory fiscal policies.

Finally, emergence of a more satisfactory program is likely to be delayed as long as there is a general unwillingness to countenance some redistribution of social-security functions and responsibilities as between the Federal government and the states. The needed changes in the unemployment-insurance laws to make this system play the important role of which it is capable during the reconversion period and thereafter are unlikely to come about so long as the decision has to be made by 51 separate legislative bodies. Nor are the chances of integrating the financing of this program with other fiscal policies very bright, for the same reason. Here the objective of a rational social-security system runs squarely up against another widely held social objective: *i.e.*, the maintenance of state autonomy. The social-security expert is entitled to feel that it is particularly unfortunate that the issue today appears to have crystallized around that part of the social-security program where change is most needed if it is to make a real contribution to the problems of economic reconstruction, *i.e.*, unemployment insurance.

VI. Summary

The task of the expert who would plan a more rational and economically satisfactory social-security system is not easy because it is of the essence of his problem to take account of prevailing social attitudes as well as economic forces. These attitudes and social values change from time to time, necessitating changes in social-security programs. Building upon the apparently widespread desire for a nondiscretionary guarantee of minimum income security, it was shown that this can be assured by a program that would also satisfy certain generally acceptable economic criteria, but it would differ in many respects from the present system. The prospects for early adoption of such a program in the United States are, however, not very encouraging.

Chapter XXIII

Government Contribution

by ALAN SWEEZY

I

THE IDEA that the government might be able to contribute to the community's income is relatively new. What the government spends has been thought of traditionally as *coming out of* the income of the people. This view is widely held even today. Editorial writers, businessmen, and politicians are constantly warning the public against the idea that government spending can contribute to the country's prosperity. Every dollar the government spends, they say, comes out of what someone has earned. The people have the choice of spending their money themselves or letting the government spend it for them.

From one point of view the traditional attitude toward government spending seems the merest common sense. When a person sends a check to the Collector of Internal Revenue or any of the other tax-collecting authorities, he is acutely aware of the fact that that much of his income is gone beyond recall. He also sees clearly enough that what he has lost the government has gained. It is only natural for him to generalize on the basis of his personal experience and to conclude that any money the government spends necessarily comes out of his earnings and the earnings of other people like him.

There are, of course, other sources from which the government could obtain money. In our modern economy the most important of these is the banking system. The government sells bonds to the banks (or to people who use them as collateral for bank loans) and the banks create additional deposits which the government uses to pay suppliers, contractors, and employees. If a shortage of reserves develops as a result of the expanded volume of deposits and an increased flow of currency into circulation, the central bank can step in to make up the deficiency. This is what has happened, for instance, during the war. From June, 1940, to June, 1944, bank holdings of government bonds increased more than $50 billion, demand deposits went up $28 billion, and currency in circulation increased $14 billion. The increased needs of the banks for reserves were met chiefly through a $13 billion expansion in Federal Reserve credit, a reduction of $5.5 billion in excess reserves, and a lowering of reserve requirements.

But, although students of economics have always realized that the government could obtain money without taking it from the taxpayers, they used to argue that in real terms government spending nonetheless reduced the people's income. As the government spends additional money created by itself, or by the banks for it, prices, according to the traditional argument, are forced up and people are thus deprived of part of the purchasing power of their incomes. Whatever goods and services the government gets are taken away from the people just as if the government had taxed them directly.

In the last decade or so most economists have become aware of the fact that this reasoning presupposes full employment of resources. For it is only if resources are already fully employed that the appearance of a new buyer, equipped with additional purchasing power, must necessarily divert some of them from their initial occupations. If there are unemployed resources to begin with, the additional spending may simply increase employment all around. This is, in fact, what happened during the recovery of the thirties and in the early stages of our preparation for war, up to the point where substantially full employment was reached. Instead of taking something away from the taxpayers, government spending actually increased their incomes.

Many people thought of the Work Projects Administration, for instance, as merely a device for transferring income from the rich to the unemployed. They complained bitterly that the "taxpayers' money" was being wasted on projects of which they did not approve. Actually, the WPA not only kept the unemployed alive but also increased the incomes of the rich and of the rest of the community. As the WPA workers spent their wages on food, clothes, fuel, shelter, and what few incidentals they could afford, producers in these fields experienced a welcome increase in the demand for their products. Retailers, farmers, manufacturers, workers, landlords, found their incomes increasing and in turn were able to buy more food and clothes and automobiles, and so on, further increasing the incomes of the people engaged in producing these things. Thus the beneficial effects of the WPA spending spread throughout the community.[1] Instead of complaining about the "waste of the taxpayers' money" as he rode past a WPA project, the wealthy stockholder should have been grateful for the increased dividends he was enjoying. And the farmer, as he drove his truck to town, should have thanked the WPA, not only for the new road he was riding on but also for the bigger check he was going to receive for his produce at the end of the trip.

Unfortunately, such association of cause and effect in connection with economic phenomena is rare. People today are at a particular disadvantage in that they still unconsciously think in terms of a full-employment world. They accept a balanced budget, for instance, as a self-evident goal of fiscal policy, forgetting—or never having realized—that the real purpose of a balanced budget is to prevent inflation in an economy where resources are fully employed (without help from the government) and that, as soon as the assumption of full employment is dropped, balancing the budget loses its fundamental *raison d'être*.

It is also still widely assumed that thrift is always a social, as well as an individual, virtue; that the more people save, the richer the whole community will be. This, too, is based on the assumption that resources are always fully employed, as well as on the assumption that more resources can always be profitably employed in building new capital goods. The real economic function of saving, as we can learn from any elementary textbook, is to release resources from the production of goods for current consumption. When a person saves part of his income, whether he buys securities, or holds a deposit idle in the bank, or puts currency in an old sock, he refrains from spending that much on consumer goods. The market for such goods is correspondingly reduced, producers hire less labor and buy less materials, and the labor and materials are free for use elsewhere. We can see this clearly enough in wartime. People are urged to save as much as possible, not because the government really needs their money—as already indicated, there are other sources from which it could get the money—but rather because labor and materials are needed in vast quantities for the prosecution of

---

[1] The only exceptions were the people on fixed interest or salary incomes who had to pay prices which had risen somewhat from their depression lows. But even they gained more in increased security than they lost in slightly reduced purchasing power. In 1931–1932 millions of salaried workers and rentiers found out that there were no "fixed" incomes.

the war and the government wants to reduce civilian competition for these resources as much as possible.

Saving also releases resources from the production of consumer goods in peacetime; the difference is that there may be no place for the resources to go. In a modern war the demand for labor and materials for its prosecution far exceeds the supply that would be forthcoming if reliance were placed on normal, voluntary saving alone. Strong measures to stimulate saving and to limit civilian purchases directly through rationing and production controls have to be taken. But in peacetime the amount of resources released through saving may easily exceed the amount for which profitable employment can be found in the production of new capital goods.

It is important to remember in this connection that saving is absorbed only through the production of additional capital goods. The large volume of replacement required to keep up the capital stock of a modern industrial society is taken care of, by and large, through the spending of depreciation allowances. Industry, in other words, covers in the price it charges the consumer the cost of replacing its capital equipment. In fact, it usually more than covers the cost. Numerous studies in recent years have shown that a considerable amount of improvement and expansion is financed out of depreciation quotas. The savings of individuals and the savings of corporations out of net profits must thus try to find an outlet in the building of additional capital goods. But the rate at which additional capital goods can be profitably built is determined by factors which have little or nothing to do with the rate of saving.

II

The most important of these factors are the rate at which new techniques of production and new products are being developed and new resources are being discovered, and the rate at which the economy (in terms of population and resources) is growing. Saving has no direct influence on any of these factors: it can only set labor and other resources free to be used in exploiting what investment opportunities there may be.

When the rate of change and growth in the economic system is high relative to the rate of saving, incomes, production, and employment are also high. And, conversely, when the development of new investment opportunities tends to lag behind saving, business is depressed, production is curtailed, and unemployment appears. The actual volume of saving is always kept in balance with the volume of investment through the rise or fall of incomes. When saving tends to be too large relative to investment, incomes decline and people perforce save less. We can talk about excess saving only in the sense of the excess which would exist if income were at a high level. The concept, properly understood, is nonetheless useful since it points to the cause of income's being low in certain periods or of the necessity for "outside" (*i.e.*, outside private investment) support to keep it from being low.

The factors determining investment have so far eluded statistical measurement. They are themselves so complex—especially the vast multiplicity of technological developments—and their effect is so much influenced by price and cost relations and by psychological and social factors that measurement perhaps always will be impossible. Predictions that the future will see even greater and more prolonged investment booms (relative to our greatly increased capacity to save) than we had in the nineteenth century cannot be definitely disproved. There is nonetheless important indirect evidence as to the long-run trend of investment demand (relative to saving) which makes such a conclusion seem fairly improbable.

One of the most important indications of the trend is the transformation of the United States from a capital-importing to a capital-exporting nation.[1] Until late in the nineteenth century, this country absorbed large amounts of capital from European, chiefly English, sources. With the increase of domestic income and wealth, however, the United States developed rapidly increasing capital resources of its own. Important investment outlets were taken over from foreign investors [2] and the flow of American funds to Central and South America began to assume significant proportions. By the beginning of the twentieth century, the export of American capital almost equaled the inflow of European funds and a decade later, on the eve of World War I, the balance had been tipped the other way. This country was already lending more to foreigners than it was borrowing from them. The war greatly accelerated the process of change. The United States emerged from it the leading capital-exporting nation of the world. Nor is there any reason to think that the depression and the present war have done anything to reverse

[1] For a convenient summary of the available statistical material, see the Brookings study by Cleona Lewis, *America's Stake in International Investments*, p. 455.
[2] The railroads for instance. *Cf.* W. Z. Ripley, *Railroads: Finance and Organization*, Ch. I.

the trend. On the contrary, the pressure of American capital to find outlets abroad is sure to be much greater after this war than it has ever been before.

The fact of America's change from a capital-importing to a capital-exporting country is well known. But its significance is not so generally realized. It indicates clearly that the country's ability (and disposition) to accumulate investment funds has increased faster than its ability to absorb them in home investment. As the growth of saving has caught up with and passed the growth in domestic investment opportunity, the alternatives—barring government fiscal policy directed toward redressing the balance—have been capital export or depression.

Another indication of the long-run trend of investment opportunity relative to the trend of saving is the increasing severity of depressions. This can be seen most clearly by comparing the depression of the thirties with what used to be called the "great" depressions of the seventies and nineties. Industrial production declined approximately 7 per cent in the seventies and 13 per cent in the nineties, contrasted with a fall of almost 50 per cent from 1929 to 1932.[1] Pig-iron production, a rough index of activity in the capital-goods sector of the economy, presents an equally striking contrast. The maximum decline in the seventies was 27 per cent and in the nineties about the same, while the drop from 1929 to 1932 was 80 per cent. Available consumption series tell the same story:

> The production of foodstuffs which had been relatively immune to preceding cyclical contractions, shows the impress of this depression unmistakably. For example, milk receipts in the New York metropolitan area, which have been recorded monthly for 44 years, show their first cyclical decline in the Great Depression, though it was not until January, 1932, that the shrinkage began. Non-food series that had usually responded to earlier contractions by a mere decline in the rate of increase—the shipment of cigarettes, the consumption of newsprint paper, the production of gasoline, electric current, and Portland cement—experienced a substantial decline.[2]

Depressions hit farmers primarily through their effect on the prices of farm products. Here again the greatly increased severity of the recent

---

[1] These figures are based on the Day-Persons index for the earlier, and the Federal Reserve Board index for the post-World War I period. *Cf.* A. F. Burns, *Production Trends in the U. S. Since 1870*, NBER, 1934, Ch. VI.

[2] W. C. Mitchell and A. F. Burns, *Production during the American Business Cycle, 1927–1933*, National Bureau *Bulletin 61*, 1936, p. 18.

depression is clear. In the seventies farm prices held their own—thanks largely to a strong export demand—relative to the prices of other commodities. In the nineties the farm index sagged below the general index, but the gap was less than 10 points. However, this is enough, considering the fact that the general index contains farm prices, to indicate real difficulties in the agricultural sector of the economy. By 1932, the farm index was 30 per cent below the general index of wholesale prices, which had itself fallen to 65 per cent of its predepression level.

These indirect evidences of the long-run trend of investment demand relative to the (potential) supply of saving are further supported by the fact of declining population growth and by what we know, in a general way, about the still undeveloped natural resources of the world. It is, of course, impossible to make any detailed predictions about the future volume of investment. There may well be periods in which investment will be large enough to support income without any outside help. But the broad trend is fairly clear, and it indicates that such periods are likely to be shorter and less frequent than in the past. We must expect, in other words, that much of the time private investment will not be large enough by itself to keep income at a reasonably high level.

A government contribution to incomes is still widely thought of as merely a recovery measure, a device for raising income, production, and employment from the depths of depression. Once recovery has been achieved, the contribution, according to this view, should be discontinued. This assumes, implicitly, that income has a natural tendency to maintain itself at a full-employment level, once that level has been reached. Unfortunately, there is no justification for such an assumption. As long as the community saves part of its income, less is returned to producers through the purchase of consumer goods and services than they are paying out in costs (plus profits). The deficiency must be made good through the purchase of new capital goods or through a government contribution to the incomes of people who will spend the additional money, or income as a whole will decline and the community will soon find itself back in the same depressed condition it started from. Nor is there any reason to expect that private investment will be sufficient, merely because income and production have reached a higher level, to keep them there. A higher level of production necessitates a larger volume of replacement. But, as already pointed out, that provides no outlet for the net savings of the community. Such an outlet can be provided only by the creation of additional capital goods, which depends fundamentally on the rate of change and growth in the economy and not on the volume of production itself.

Some writers have argued that ample investment outlets for all the saving the community may want to do could be provided through a more rapid increase in the consumption of the lower income groups. Why worry about new industries, new continents, and new population, they ask, when so many people who are already here want more of the things we are already producing? Their question suggests a perfectly good solution to the production and employment problem: the basic function of a government contribution is, in fact, to provide consumers with more money so that they can buy more and thus stimulate an increase in production and employment. But raising consumption does not provide a solution to the investment problem (at least not the solution investors are looking for). What the mass of consumers need is income, not capital. An investment trust or insurance company with a surplus of funds on its hands could, of course, give them away and thus provide people in the lower income brackets with more purchasing power. But this would not be investment. The investment trust or insurance company not only would receive no return on its capital, it would lose the principal as well.

As consumer purchases increased there would, to be sure, be some expansion in the consumer-goods industries, involving the creation of additional capital goods. Thus by giving away part of their savings, investors might create an outlet for the profitable investment of the rest. But even this would be only a temporary outlet. As soon as the additional capacity had been built, replacements would be financed out of depreciation, and investors would have to give away part of their remaining savings in order to expand consumption still further and create a new investment outlet. The process would, obviously, end up in a 100 per cent consumption economy.[1]

Since we cannot expect that investors will voluntarily give away part of their savings, we must be prepared for the use of a government contribution, not only in stimulating recovery from depression but also in maintaining prosperity in periods when the volume of private investment is not large enough to do the job alone.

---

[1] For further discussion of the relation between consumption and investment, see Dr. Emile Benoit-Smullyan's "Note" and my "Reply" in the December, 1944, issue of the *American Economic Review*.

III

For a few years after the war, the total volume of spending may be sufficient to maintain production and employment at a reasonably high level without the assistance of any government program designed specifically to increase incomes. Consumers have built up a big backlog of unsatisfied demand—for automobiles, refrigerators, household repairs, and all the other things they have been unable to get during the war—and also have, as a result of their wartime saving, an abnormally large reserve of purchasing power to draw on in making their demands effective. Unless there should be an offsetting loss of income as a result of unemployment in the process of shifting back to peacetime production, this deferred consumer demand should prove an important factor in maintaining employment during the transition to the "normal" peacetime economy. The danger of unemployment's getting there first, moreover, can be largely eliminated by a careful handling of the release of workers and materials from military to civilian production and by the provision of adequate unemployment compensation.

It is less clear as to whether producer demand for capital goods will be greater in the transition period than later on or not. Many producers have had to let replacements and improvements go during the war and, like consumers, will be anxious to make good the deficiencies. Others, now engaged in war production, will have to spend money on the reconversion of their plants to peacetime use. As against these "favorable" factors, however, must be set the enormous amount of new plant and equipment that have been erected during the war and the possibility that a large part of them will be adaptable to peacetime production.

Finally, the prospect of continued government expenditures for military purposes and for foreign relief and reconstruction at a rate much higher than before the war must be taken into account. Exact prediction as to how large these various quantities will be is clearly impossible.[1] The safe course is to be equally prepared for too much and for too little spending—or for a combination of both at the same time. Against the danger of too much spending, and particularly too much spending on goods which for some time will be in short supply, we shall need to continue certain price, rationing, and production controls.

---

[1] For a discussion of current expert statistical guesses, as well as of the analytical issues involved, see Gunnar Myrdal, "Is American Business Deluding Itself?" *The Atlantic Monthly*, November, 1944. Extensive references to the pertinent literature can be found in E. J. Howenstine, Jr., "The Economics of Demobilization," American Council on Public Affairs, 1944.

Against the opposite danger of too little spending (1) we should have a more adequate system of unemployment compensation and (2) we should plan, and be ready to launch, long-range programs for supporting income and employment.

IV

This brings us to the question as to what these programs should be. In the thirties the government's contribution to income was partly an incidental result of providing emergency relief to the 12 to 15 million unemployed, whose resources had been exhausted and whose situation had become desperate by 1932, and partly an application of pump-priming theory. Though of tremendous value in the crisis of 1932–1933, neither relief nor pump priming constitutes a satisfactory foundation for long-run policy. Relief spending is unsatisfactory, first of all, from the point of view of those directly affected. The WPA did far more to preserve the morale and skills—to say nothing of the physical existence—of the workers it employed and to contribute to the wealth of the country (in the form, *e.g.*, of roads, schoolhouses, sanitary installations, musical and theatrical performances) than it is commonly given credit for. But in spite of this, the employment it offered bore the stigma of relief, the wages it was allowed to pay were barely enough for subsistence, and the usefulness of its work was limited by restrictions as to materials, equipment, and supervisory staff and by the failure of many local government units to cooperate in the proper planning of projects. Obviously, none of these features would be satisfactory in a long-run program.

Relief spending has the further weakness that it tapers off as the emergency is eased. In 1936 and again in 1938, production and employment increased rapidly, largely as a result of WPA spending. On both occasions Congress, urged on by business leaders, cut the WPA appropriation without substituting any other type of expenditure for it, on the ground that business had improved and the need for relief had diminished. This was like killing the goose that laid the golden eggs. Although private investment had recovered from the panic of 1932–1933 and, in fact, was doing very well, it was not large enough, nor was there any reason to think that it would become large enough, to fill the gap between income and consumption at any reasonably high level of income. Given the basic conditions as to saving and investment of the thirties, a continuing government contribution of perhaps $5 to $6 billion would have been necessary to maintain even moderately full employment.

Pump priming suffers from the same basic weakness. As income increases, expenditures are reduced, leaving income without any support at the higher level. The result, barring the fortuitous appearance of a private-investment boom, is a lapse back into depression. The pump primers thought that the trouble in 1932 was merely that the pump had somehow run dry. With a sufficient amount of priming it would, they thought, catch on again and function as smoothly as ever. Actually the pump had become inadequate for its job. Under the circumstances what we needed was not pump priming but an auxiliary pump.

The government's long-run contribution to income should be made through channels which meet the following tests: (1) the purposes for which the money is spent should have general social approval; (2) participation in the programs should be free of any stigma of relief; (3) the expenditure should interfere as little as possible with the production of goods and services by private business.[1] All these conditions are satisfied in a high degree by public works of the traditional type—roads, bridges, schools, sewer systems, etc.—by low-cost housing, soil conservation, flood control, public-health services, and the like, and by social security.

It has been generally accepted for a long time that the government must provide the community with roads, schools, police and fire stations, post offices, sewer systems, etc. Popular realization of the need for adequate health and recreation facilities, for conservation measures, and for low-cost housing has been slower in developing but has now reached the point where these objectives too are strongly approved by the great majority of people. Finally, the popular demand for social security—approval is too weak a word—has grown so strong that representatives of all parties and groups, even the most conservative, have expressed themselves in favor not only of keeping what we already have, but also of extending the system to include categories of workers now left outside.

---

[1] Many types of public spending will provide a direct, as well as indirect, stimulus to private business. This point was vigorously stated by Prof. Hansen in a recent address: "I am convinced that we could raise our total productivity more by a twenty-billion-dollar public investment program than we could by a twenty-billion-dollar private investment program, and the public investment program would, moreover, have the effect of enlarging very greatly the area of profitable private investment." Excerpt published in *The Nation*, Oct. 21, 1944, p. 492.

In spite of strong popular support, however, no more than a beginning has been made in any of these fields. Plans for the expansion of public-health services (including the building of hospitals where present capacity is inadequate or totally lacking) were drawn up and discussed by the various agencies and groups concerned in the late thirties but had not yet been acted on in Congress when the war broke out. The United States Housing Authority was doing valuable experimental work in low-cost housing and slum clearance,[1] but the scale on which it was authorized to work was so small that it could meet only a small fraction of the need.

The social-security machinery set up was much more extensive, but the payment of benefits—the vital part of the program from the point of view of maintaining income and employment—was either postponed (old-age insurance) or so hedged in with restrictions as to fall far short of contributions (unemployment compensation). The result was a large excess of contributions over benefits which acted as a serious drain on the flow of purchasing power.[2] The system, moreover, has serious gaps in it. Benefits under both old-age and unemployment insurance are too small, no protection is afforded against the risks of permanent disability or temporary sickness, millions of workers in agriculture, domestic service, and certain other occupations, are left out entirely.[3]

These gaps should be filled and the relation of contributions to benefits should be revised, so that within a few years after the end of the war the system will begin to make a net contribution to community income. This does not at all mean that the contributory principle should be abandoned. People generally feel that it is right and proper that those who receive benefits should contribute to their financing. The workers' and employers' contributions protect the system from being regarded as a form of relief or charity. They guarantee that benefits will be received

---

[1] *Cf.* Nathan Straus, *The Seven Myths of Housing.*

[2] The nature of this drain is frequently misunderstood. The Treasury did not keep the actual money collected in an idle checking account, as is often implied, but rather borrowed the money from the Social Security Funds and spent it on other things. The effect was nonetheless deflationary since there was no increase in total expenditure and the Treasury consequently reduced its borrowing from savers and the banks. Money collected largely from consumers—people who would have spent it on goods and services themselves—was substituted in the government's spending for money obtained from those who, for the most part, would not have spent it.

[3] For a discussion of the gaps in the existing system, see Senator Wagner's remarks in the *Congressional Record* for June 3, 1943, pp. 5342–5347, and also "A Basic Minimum Program of Social Security," *Social Security Bulletin*, January, 1944. *Cf.* also Dr. Burns, Ch. XXII in this volume.

as a right and that the beneficiary will not be subject to investigation to determine what other income or assets he may have. But—and this is the important point for fiscal policy—the contributions need not equal the entire amount of benefits paid. Even our present system contemplates an *eventual* government contribution out of general funds.

The trouble is that this contribution is too far off in the future—it will not even begin for another 20 years or more. Meanwhile, if nothing is done to revise the system's financial setup,[1] we shall have to rely entirely on housing, conservation, and other public-works programs to provide the necessary government contribution to incomes. But expansion of these programs will not be easy. Most of them have encountered, and will continue to encounter, strong opposition from vested interests— the opposition of the owners of slum property to low-cost housing, for instance. This opposition will find powerful support in the still widespread notion that we cannot "afford" such public improvements. It is going to be difficult enough in any case to get an adequate government contribution; without help from social security it may well be impossible.

V

There is finally the question of finance; particularly whether a government contribution to income is consistent with a balanced budget. This question has come to the fore in recent discussion as a result of Dr. Beardsley Ruml's proposal [2]—and similar proposals by other experts in the field [3]—that the government adopt a definite policy of balancing the budget at a high level of employment, at the same time holding onto "the principle of progressive income taxes and estate taxes as the best way of reversing the tendency of purchasing power to come to rest." [4]

Dr. Ruml and the other budget balancers of this school apparently accept the thesis that saving tends to be excessive in the modern world and that unless some way is found to channel part of it back into the spending stream, we shall have chronic depression and unemployment.

---

[1] The contemplated extension of the system to cover categories of workers and types of risks now excluded will provide an excellent opportunity for revision of the financial setup as well since new benefit and contribution provisions will in any case have to be introduced.

[2] Beardsley Ruml and H. C. Sonne, *Fiscal and Monetary Policy*, National Planning Association, 1944.

[3] For instance, J. W. Gillman's prize-winning essay in the Pabst postwar employment contest. Gillman's specific tax proposals differ greatly from Ruml's, but both agree on the possibility of maintaining full employment with a balanced budget.

[4] Beardsley Ruml, "A Fiscal Program for High Employment," *The Nation*, Oct. 21, 1944, p. 491.

They are convinced, however, that the channeling can be done through taxation, which will enable us to avoid the psychological and political problems connected with a growing debt.

To accomplish the desired result, the taxes would have to fall on saving rather than on consumption. Government spending contributes to the flow of purchasing power and thus to the maintenance of production and employment, only if the money comes from people (or institutions) which would not have spent it themselves. Spending money raised by a sales tax is of no use since the consumers would have spent the money themselves if they had not had to pay the tax. The same is true, generally speaking, of excise, customs, pay-roll, and processing taxes.[1] The budget balancers realize this, of course, and are careful to point out that they are talking about income, inheritance, gift, and other taxes which are more likely to be paid at the expense of saving.

The trouble with taxation (of this kind) as a means of financing the government contribution is that, while it undoubtedly does reduce saving, it also reduces consumption. Quantitatively, chief reliance would have to be placed on an increase in the income-tax rates in the upper middle and lower middle brackets—roughly from $3,000 to $50,000 a year. Rates in the higher brackets are already very high and, more important, the bulk of the saving—in the aggregate, not per person, of course—is done by people in the middle brackets.

But there are strong reasons to think that these people will react to higher (peacetime) tax rates as much by cutting consumption as by reducing saving. The motives which lead people to save are very strong in our society. To accumulate a reserve for future contingencies and, beyond that, to build up a competence or, if possible, a fortune are goals which have become deeply imbedded in our psychology. They are reinforced, moreover, by the growth of institutions whose business it is to administer and thus to encourage saving: life insurance companies, building and loan associations, savings banks, trust companies, etc. The life insurance companies are particularly important. In the immediate prewar period it was estimated that their reserves were growing at the rate of $4 billion a year. Through their vigorous and persistent sales efforts they exert great pressure on people to keep on buying insurance, pressure which would undoubtedly continue whatever tax policy the

---

[1] It is more difficult to determine the effect of property taxes on spending, but most economists seem to agree that they also fall largely on people who would have spent the money themselves.

government might adopt. It seems fairly safe to predict that a majority of people in the middle income group would cut their expenditure on luxuries before they would reduce the amount of insurance they carried.

Another difficulty is that taxes must necessarily be levied in accordance with uniform rules. Allowance can be made for size of family and for certain special items such as medical expenses. But beyond these allowances, tax rates must be the same for saver and spender alike. Any attempt to discriminate against savers as such would break down on our deeply rooted—and, as far as the individual is concerned, quite justified—feeling that thrift is a good thing. The amount of saving done by different individuals and different groups of individuals in the same income bracket probably differs greatly. A professional man in a large city earning $10,000 a year and associating with people whose incomes are much larger is likely to save less, for instance, than a person in a small town with the same income whose neighbors and associates are all poorer than he is.

The great advantage of borrowing over taxation as a method of financing the government's contribution is that it scoops up saving wherever it may be without in the least disturbing consumption. No one is going to reduce his consumption spending in order to buy government bonds bearing a 2 per cent[1] interest rate. Borrowing makes it possible, moreover, to gather up the savings collected by insurance companies and other institutions which could not be reached at all by taxation. And, finally, borrowing gives the individual a valuable asset, whereas taxation leaves him with nothing. Even if society as a whole is no richer with the debt than without it, its advantages to the individual cannot be ignored.

It will certainly be desirable to have higher income taxes in the future than we had before the war, since they will help make the problem of saving more manageable. But, at the same time, we would be very unwise to rule out from the beginning the use of so effective and reliable an instrument of fiscal policy as borrowing.

---

[1] A reduction to 1 per cent after the war would be highly desirable and is not entirely out of the range of practical possibility.

Index

A

Agricultural Adjustment Administration, 56
Agricultural commodities, pricing of, 201
Agricultural production, postwar, 43–45, 47, 80
  prewar, 48–50
  suggested shifts of, 55–57
Agriculture, and employment, 36f., 57, 99
  foreign, 33, 36, 49
  and industry, relative importance of, 21
  mechanization of, 44, 51, 57
  and outlets for production, 36
  postwar policies of, 31f., 51, 57
  productivity of, 21f., 33, 55f., 58, 229
  wartime expansion of, 21f., 31f., 48f., 99
Allocations of markets by cartels, 218, 220, 222f., 228
  (*See also* Controls; Priorities)

B

Bakke, E. W., 386n.
Balance of payments, and exchange depreciation, 331f.
  postwar international policies with regard to, 329, 338f., 376
  in relation to International Monetary Fund, 343–346, 351, 367f., 372
  of United States, 326, 337
  (*See also* Bank Credit; Consumption)
Balogh, Th., 325, 334n.
Bank for Reconstruction and Development (*see* International Bank)

Bank capital, ratio to total assets, 246n., 250f.
Bank credit and loans, control of, 244n., 246n., 247, 251
  and government securities, 242f., 244n.
  in relation to balance of payments, 329
  in relation to earnings, 250f.
  during transition period, 240
  during upswing, 238
Bank investments (*see* Government bonds)
Banking, central, and control of inflation, 241f., 244
  and fiscal policy, 254
  in postwar period, 237–239, 398
Banks, commercial, 237f., 240f., 243n., 246–252
  and insurance, 249, 251
Baruch, B. M., 95n., 143
Benefits, social-security, 29, 259, 383–387, 391–395, 408f.
  unemployment, 112f., 115, 118–120, 138, 143, 193, 396, 405f., 408
  and vocational aid, 116–118
Benoit-Smullyan, E., 404n.
Berge, W., 218
Beveridge, Sir W. H., 113n., 258n., 325n., 384n.
Beveridge plan, 381, 387, 389, 393
Bilateralism (*see* Clearing agreements)
Birth rates, 149f.
Bissell, R. M., 40n.
Block, H. D., 61n.
Boileau Amendment, 56n.
Bone Committee, 225
Bourneuf, A., 363n.

413

Bratt, E. C., 61n.
Bretton Woods Agreements, aims of, 339f., 360
  and capital flight, 342
  and competitive depreciation, 331, 341
  and exchange control, 338f., 342–344, 350f.
  and full-employment policy, 326, 328, 330
  and international investment, 246, 346–349, 357–364
  and international trade, 348f., 364
  and key currencies, 371–373, 375–377
  and scarce currencies, 343f., 370
  and stable exchange rates, 337, 340–342
  (*See also* International Bank for Reconstruction and Development; International Monetary Fund)
British White Paper on Employment Policy, 20, 244n., 271, 384n.
Brookings Institution, 3, 60n., 72
Budget, balanced, 19, 88, 279, 299, 409
  (*See also* Business fluctuations; Employment; Fiscal Policy; Government)
Budget deficit, 89, 267–269, 275, 293
  postwar, 293f.
  during war, 275
Bureau of Agricultural Economics (BAE), 37–39, 41–43
Bureau of Labor Statistics (BLS), 37–39, 61n., 72, 146, 204
Burns, A. F., 402n.
Business fluctuations, 244–246, 256f., 266
  and budgets, 262–265, 293, 299
  and employment, 20
  and exchange depreciation, 331
  and foreign investment, 356–358, 401f.
  and income, 401, 407
  and international trade, 319f., 322, 327–329, 348
  monetary controls of, 245–247
  and taxes, 289, 292f., 299
  and transition period, 192–194, 244f., 257
Byrnes, J. F., 143, 186

C

Capacity, excess, and restrictive practices, 145, 219–222
  productive, 26, 35, 83, 133f., 163, 165, 172, 175f., 185, 315
Capital exports, 401f.

Capital formation, private, 19, 78, 83f., 87–89, 90n., 91f., 135f., 165f., 168, 293, 302, 304f., 353
  in the United States, value of, 134n., 147, 164, 261n., 355
  per worker, 80
  (*See also* Investment)
Capital-gains tax, 289
Capital goods, 23, 26, 28, 140, 153, 163–166, 316, 399f., 403–405
Capital investment abroad (*see* Foreign investment)
Capital movements (flights), 331f., 341
Capital replacement, costs of, 311f.
Capital requirements, 301, 305–308, 316
Capital resources, differences in, 353
Capital-stock tax, 288
Cartels, 8, 217–226, 228f., 232f.
  and American trade, 223f.
  and balance of payments, 220, 232
  and governments, 226–229
  and monopolies, 220f., 226
  output, prices and wages, 218–220, 222, 224, 227
  and patents, 224–226
  and war, 221f., 226
Cash (*see* Currency; Deposits)
Clayton, W. L., 143f.
Clearing agreements, 325, 328, 335, 338f., 356
Collectivism and international trade, 323f.
Committee for Economic Development, 34
Commodity agreements, international, 8, 219, 229–233
Commodity Credit Corporation, 56, 63n.
Compensatory fiscal policy, 299, 390, 407
Competition, in banking, 247
  and cartels, 218
  in postwar period, 195, 223, 247, 252, 282
Construction, employment in, 152, 154
  of new plants, in postwar period, 26–28, 34, 74, 172, 175, 312f.
    in wartime, 25f., 125, 130, 132f., 135, 163–165, 174, 304, 312
  in postwar period, 60, 92, 195, 206, 261, 269, 407
  and public works, 406f.
  rural, 44
  of schools (*see* Education)
  urban, 31, 302, 304
Construction industry, loans to, 248, 299, 410

INDEX 415

Consumer credit, and business fluctuations, 246, 299
  control of, 182, 194, 246
  decrease of, 302–305
  in postwar period, 307, 313
Consumers' durables, postwar expansion of, 25, 34, 139, 184f., 189, 195, 206, 404,
  postwar prices of, 194, 210, 257
  production of, 26, 71, 257
  purchases of, 18, 60, 87n., 210, 241
  shortages of, 15, 70, 215, 257, 405
  and total consumption, 210
Consumers' expenditures (*see* Consumption)
Consumption, and balance of payments, 329f.
  and capacity to produce, 16
  decline of, in depression, 402
    (*See also* Business fluctuations)
  and income, 3, 20, 30f., 78, 83f., 86, 88, 89n., 90n., 91, 118, 206, 261, 269, 274, 404, 406
  and investment, 11, 18, 256, 269, 280, 404
  postwar, 25, 45, 60, 84, 90f., 183, 207, 212, 214, 259f., 269, 404
  and taxation, 280, 298
  wartime, 71, 259
Contract termination (settlement, cancellation), 9, 27, 34, 95, 104, 114, 116, 124–129, 136–139, 143f., 187, 306–308, 309n.
  and administration, 142f.
  and pay rolls, 240
Control of monetary system, 237f., 243, 251
Controlled Materials Plan, 190
Controls, and administration, 182, 190
  direct vs. indirect, 181, 197f., 202f., 209
  interrelationship of, 7f., 34
  postwar, 2, 7f., 29f., 125, 181–186, 188–195, 208–210, 214–216, 241, 257, 281, 405
  of production and distribution, 197f., 209
  of spending, 244
Conversion to postwar economy, 30, 192, 206–208
Convertibility of war plant, 175
  (*See also* Reconversion)
Corporate tax, shifting of, 283f.
  (*See also* Income tax; Investment; Taxes)
Cost of living, postwar, 139, 184, 191, 207, 209f., 212

Cost of Living, wages and farm prices, 59, 61n., 65–70, 75f., 191–193, 197, 207, 209, 212
  wartime rise of, 9, 65
Costs of production, agricultural, 51, 201
  postwar, 175, 187, 189, 209–211
  and prices, 198f., 201–203, 207, 210–213
  and tariffs, 327
Cotton producers, postwar problems of, 32
Credit controls, 244–246
  selective vs. general, 245f.
Credit expansion, 206, 238, 251
Credits, agricultural, 57, 244f.
  (*See also* Bank credit; Consumer credit)
Currency, 1f., 7f., 240–242, 251, 301f., 304f., 309, 315f., 398
Cutbacks, 104, 113, 116, 126, 137f., 144, 158, 187, 190, 206–208
  (*See also* Contract termination; Demobilization)
Cycle (*see* Business fluctuations)

D

Danhof, C. H., 61n.
Deficit (*see* Budget)
Deflation, 27, 31, 239, 249, 251, 257, 270, 293
  control of, 253
  and international trade, 328f., 332n.
  (*See also* Business fluctuations)
Demand, aggregate vs. partial, 9
  deferred, 5, 145, 184f., 194, 206f., 239, 257, 301, 405
  deficiency of, 9–11, 60, 96, 254f.
  and employment, 6, 76f., 95, 214
  postwar, 11n., 83, 89n., 257, 271, 405
  and savings, 30, 260, 265
  shifts in, 27–29, 147, 193, 258
  support of, 4, 12, 193, 256, 270
  for United States exports, 192, 257
    (*See also* Consumption; Government contributions; Spending)
Demobilization, of controls (*see* Controls)
  military, 2, 27, 96, 104–107, 110, 138, 146, 184f., 188, 192
  regional differences in, 10, 103f., 108f., 113
  of resources, 104
  of workers, 2, 96, 98, 103–105, 107f., 110, 146, 184, 188, 192, 206, 405

Denison, E. F., 117n.
Deposit insurance, 251
Deposits, government, 397f.
  100 per cent reserves against, 244
  regional aspect of rise in, 9
  time, 241f., 248
  total, wartime increase of, 1, 7, 206, 241f., 301–305
Depreciation (*see* Reserves of business)
Depreciation policy, 400
Depreciation reserves, 19, 302–308, 312, 315
Depression (*see* Business fluctuations)
De Vegh, I., 322n.
Dickinson, H. D., 324
Dietary standards in the United States, 53
Diets, relative costs of, 56
Division of labor, international, 319–321, 324, 328f., 331
Dollar-and-cents pricing, 198
Douty, H. M., 61n., 62, 66n.
Downgrading, 59f., 74f., 191, 207
Dumping, 50
Du Pont, 218f.

E

Earnings (*see* Hourly earnings; Profits; Wage payments)
Education, 17, 31, 256, 262, 270, 293f.
  and demobilization, 107, 156f.
  (*See also* Training of workers)
Einzig, P., 325
Emergency Price Control Act (EPCA), 71n., 196, 200f.
Employment, agricultural, 79, 98n., 99, 101, 106, 153
  and agricultural production, 36, 45
  civilian government, 79f., 98n., 152
  and deficiency of demand, 11, 27
  and demobilization, 10, 27, 29, 75, 96, 103f., 106–113, 138, 146, 193, 207, 301, 314
  effects of wartime changes in, 154–158
  and fiscal policy, 78, 87f., 253, 258, 267–270
  and food consumption, 39, 42–45, 47
  and foreign trade, 23, 232, 246, 319, 322, 328f., 332n., 337–340, 348f.
  and free enterprise, 3

Employment, full, policies, 20, 76, 87f., 91, 112, 116–118, 214n., 257, 262f.
  postwar estimates of, 3, 16, 23–25, 30f.
  and gross national product, 5, 74, 78–80, 257–262
  and investment, 11, 88, 400–402
  and monetary control, 237, 239, 242, 251
  and national income, 60
  and reconversion, 211–214
  regional differences in, 10, 100–104, 109f., 146, 158–161, 188
  and savings, 19
  during war, 15, 61, 64, 98–103, 152f.
  (*See also* Productivity; Public investment)
Ensley, G., 258n., 268
Estate and gift taxes, 276f., 290, 294–296, 409f.
Excess-profits taxes, 275–277, 281–283, 288, 294, 297, 309f.
Excess reserves, 237, 246, 397f.
  and sterilization, 246
Exchange control, 323, 325, 326n., 328, 330–332, 335, 337, 342f., 349f., 369, 371n., 373f.
Exchange depreciation, 330f., 334n., 337, 341f., 349f., 356, 376
Exchange rates, postwar, 340
  postwar adjustment of, 341
Exchange stability, 10, 338, 340–342, 344, 349, 351
  and business fluctuations, 341
Exchange Stabilization Fund, U. S., 339
Excise taxes (*see* Sales taxes)
Expansion, classical theory of, 255
  postwar, 31, 33f., 213, 315f.
  postwar programs for (developmental programs), 20, 31, 34, 92, 262, 267, 293, 336, 338, 340, 348f.
Export bounties, 220f., 232, 341, 349
Export prices, 216, 350
Export subsidies in agriculture, 50, 52
Export surplus and gold, 246, 326
Exports, agricultural, 37n., 43–45, 47–52, 55, 192
  and balance of payments, 220, 330n.
  and cartels, 218, 221, 224, 227
  control of, 181, 223
  and employment, 337
  of machinery, 28, 192, 327

INDEX

Exports, net, and business investment, 261*f*., 269
   and revenue of foreign governments, 220
   of United States, demand for, 327*f*.

F

Fabricant, S., 72*n*.
Factors of production, relative returns to, 47*f*.
Farm land, prices of, 243, 245
Farm prices, 196*f*., 204, 207, 209, 229*f*., 402*f*.
   and incomes, 37*n*., 46–49, 203
   and industry, 32, 70, 229
   and output, 43, 46–50, 229
Federal Deposit Insurance Corporation, 251
Federal Housing Administration, 243*f*., 299
Federal Reserve Board, 72
Federal Reserve System and banking control, 237–247
Fiscal policy, 252–254, 262–271, 402, 411
   and central bank policy, 254
   and effects on employment and income, 87*f*., 266–269, 272, 292, 299*f*.
   need for flexibility in, 29, 208, 271, 292
   and postwar budgets, 260, 266–269, 271, 292, 299
   and reconversion, 256*f*., 399
   and social security, 390, 394–396, 409
   and taxation, 279, 409–411
Fixed costs, and output, 60, 70
Fixed incomes and government spending, 399*n*.
Food and Agriculture Organization of the United Nations, 33, 35, 51
Food consumption, per capita, 22, 37–42, 52
   and employment, 39, 402
Food distribution measures, 45, 53–56
Food needs in postwar period, 32, 37
Food prices, 22, 196*f*.
Food production and business fluctuations, 402
Foreign dollar balances, 206, 344
Foreign investment, and balance of payments, 358
   postwar estimates of, 19, 261*f*., 320, 354
   postwar policies toward, 336*f*., 346*f*.
   record of, 353–355, 401

Foreign investment, risks of, 356–359, 363, 365
   (*See also* Bretton Woods Agreements; International Bank for Reconstruction)
Foreign lending and standards of living, 355, 359
Foreign trade, and cartels, 218, 221–224, 232*f*.
   control of, 195, 223, 231, 324
   employment, and national income, 231, 319*f*., 322, 328*f*., 336, 348
   and planning, 320, 324
   postwar estimates of, 173, 231–233
   postwar policies toward, 319–321, 338, 348*f*., 351
   and reconversion, 175, 193, 223
   and technology, 321*f*.
   (*See also* Trade)
Formula pricing, 198
Free-enterprise society, 2*f*., 5, 247, 252, 254, 263, 320, 382*f*., 393*f*.
Free entry, 248
   and controls, 7, 195, 251, 254
Free exchanges, 337*f*., 340, 344, 348, 351, 370, 374
Free trade vs. restrictionism, 8*f*., 320
Freeze, price, 198
Full employment (*see* Employment)

G

G.I. Bill of Rights, 107, 122, 157
General Maximum Price Regulation, 196*f*.
Geographic (*see* Location; Regional problems; Regional development problems; Regional distribution)
Gibbons, C. A., 47*n*.
Gilbert, M., 37*n*.
Gillman, J. W., 409*n*.
Gold standard, 338, 370, 377
Gold sterilization, 246
Goldenweiser, E. A., 244*n*., 247*n*., 363*n*.
Goldsborough Bill, 246*n*.
Goode, R., 264*n*., 272*n*.
Government and risk, 247
Government borrowing, 292, 300, 395, 397, 408*n*., 411
Government contracts (*see* Contract termination)
Government contributions, to demand, 4*f*., 96, 195, 250, 255, 258–260, 267, 300

418 ECONOMIC RECONSTRUCTION

Government contributions, to income, 60, 90–92, 266, 293, 397–399, 403–407, 409–411
and social security, 391
Government expenditures, and employment, 87f., 111–116, 253, 265f., 292, 398
financing of, 265, 409f.
and individuals' spending, 5, 27, 31, 207, 241, 409–411
size of, 1, 207, 275
(*See also* Gross national product)
Government guarantee of private investment, 262, 267, 271
Government loan agencies, 249
Government-owned industry and cartels, 228
Government-owned industry, disposal of, 175, 177
Government participation in cartels, 219f.
Government planning, 29, 35, 178, 192f., 267, 292, 299, 323f., 381, 406
Government policies in the postwar period, 10f., 175, 195, 240, 250, 382
Government revenue, 7, 11, 263, 265–269, 271–280, 292–294, 398f.
Government securities, 7, 241–243, 248, 397
holdings of, 18, 241–243, 301f., 304f., 309, 316, 398
increase in, 19, 238, 301
interest payments on, 80, 259, 293, 411
prices of, 242, 244
Government-supported industry, 9, 69, 110, 124, 133f., 136, 140–144, 168, 171f., 219, 267
Graham, F. D., 333n.
Gross national product, and food consumption, 38–43
and government expenditures, 87–92, 147, 258–262, 266–270
and monetary expansion, 240
and national income, 3, 5, 84, 274
postwar estimates of, 74, 80–83, 172, 258–262
and taxes, 263–266, 275
(*See also* Wages)

H

Hagen, E. E., 40n., 258f., 263
Hancock, J. M., 95n., 143
Hayek, F. A., 329n.
Health services, 31, 262, 381, 406–408

Health standards, deficiency of, 17
Hill, M., 326n.
Hines, F. T., 143
Hinshaw, R., 322n., 334n.
Hold-the-line order, 197, 209
Hourly earnings, 59, 62f., 65f., 68, 70, 75f., 191
real, 66, 191f.
Hours of work, 3f., 6, 16, 25, 59–67, 69–72, 75f., 79, 82, 90, 97, 114f., 155, 188, 207, 257, 262, 270
in agriculture, 22, 51
Housing, investment in, 19, 407
need for, 17, 20, 25, 195, 262, 267, 408f.
(*See also* Credit controls)
Howenstine, E. J., Jr., 405n.

I

Import restrictions, 220–222, 230–232, 330, 334n., 349
Imports, agricultural, 37n., 45, 231
control of, 181, 323
elasticity of demand for, 327, 332–334, 348
and exchange rates, 341
and national income, 322, 327f.
postwar, 337
and prices, 216, 224, 231, 327
of raw materials, 231
Incentive pay, 62f., 69f.
Incentive prices, 194, 201, 203
Incentives, to investment, 280, 286
to production, 198, 201, 279f.
Income (*see* Consumption; Employment; Fiscal policy; Government)
Income payments, distribution and consumption, 87n., 256, 260
postwar, 91, 260f., 296
wartime rise of, 9, 65, 71, 85, 153, 275
Income security, 381f., 384, 392–396
Income tax, corporate, 283–289, 294–297, 309f., 409
individual, 275–277, 280, 285–297, 299, 409–411
(*See also* Taxes)
Incomes, postwar, 60, 146f., 192, 206, 220, 246, 259–262, 269, 274
regional differences in rise of, 9f.
savings, and investment, 19, 401
and social security, 385
spent or saved, 27, 83, 269

INDEX

Indebtedness of business, 302, 304*f*.
Industrial fluctuations (*see* Business fluctuations)
Industry, and the capital market, 7
  postwar expansion of, 34*f*.
  regional pattern of, 9
  structure and ownership of, 9
  wartime expansion of, 22*f*., 28
  (*See also* Expansion; Reconversion)
Inflation, 8, 27, 29–31, 182*f*., 187, 189, 191–194, 196*f*., 203, 206*f*., 216, 238*f*., 241*f*., 257
  control of, 209*f*., 215, 243–247, 253, 265, 293, 299, 399
  and government spending, 398*f*.
  and wartime pay rolls, 64, 66, 68*f*., 72, 187, 203
Interest payments (*see* Government securities)
Interest rates, 242–245
  and the capitalistic system, 254*f*.
  on foreign loans, 356
  and speculation, 244*f*.
International Bank for Reconstruction and Development, 246, 339*f*., 346–349, 351*f*., 357, 359–365, 367*f*.
  functions of, 360–362
  organization of, 362*f*.
International Labor Office, 24, 121*n*.
International Monetary Fund, loan operations, 366–369
  resources of, 344–346
  during transition period, 366–369
International trade (*see* Foreign trade)
Interrelationship of cost, prices, and profits, 203*f*., 213*f*.
Inventories (stocks), 19, 44–46, 130–132, 142, 144, 183*f*., 195, 207, 230, 260, 303, 306*f*., 311, 313–315
  control of, 127, 181, 183, 189, 194, 210
  wartime reduction of, 31, 127, 301*f*., 311, 316
Investments, agricultural, 57
  by banks, 243, 247*n*., 250*f*.
  private, postwar estimates of, 19, 171–175, 259–262, 269, 301–315, 402–404
  by government, 11, 132–134, 140
  in plant and equipment during war, 132–136, 163–166, 168–170, 304
  and prices, 214*f*., 255

Investments, and reconversion, 177, 210, 260*f*., 301, 307, 310
  and savings in postwar period, 11, 31, 89, 210, 237, 252, 260, 262, 390, 401, 403*f*.
  and technology, 400*f*.
  (*See also* Consumption; Employment; Fiscal policy; Government; Savings)

J

Jacoby, N. H., 249*n*.
Johnson, E. C., 244*n*.

K

Key currency principle, 350, 370–373, 375*f*.
Keynes, Lord, 339, 373
Kindleberger, C. P., 327, 333*n*.
King, W. I., 185*n*.
Kirkpatrick, N. B., 40*n*., 258*n*.
Kossoris, Max D., 114*n*.
Kuznets, S., 4, 37*n*., 38, 40*n*., 68

L

Labor, and social security, 393*f*.
  wartime gains of, 67, 76
Labor and administration, 121
Labor costs, unit, 72
Labor force, in agriculture, 22, 44, 51, 57*f*., 79, 99, 101
  composition of, 156–158
  industrial shifts in, 26, 57*f*., 74*f*., 81*f*., 101, 152–154
  mobility of, 70, 76*f*., 121–123
  postwar size of, 6, 68, 74, 79, 90, 111, 148–151, 256–258, 314
  regional shifts in, 100–103, 109*f*., 158–161, 177
  during transition, 103–109, 112–116, 188, 207
  wartime controls of, 182, 185, 192
  wartime expansion in, 1, 15*f*., 61, 97–100, 121, 147
Labor policy, 111–114, 189, 193
Labor relations, 5, 123, 193, 292
Labor turnover, 82, 121, 155
Lange, O., 324
Lend-Lease, 49
Leontief, W. W., 214*n*.

Lerner, A. P., 265f., 270, 324
Lester, R. A., 111n., 119n.
Lewis, C., 401n.
Life insurance, rising importance of, 248–250, 410f.
Liquid assets, of business and individuals, 7, 241f., 301–304
  postwar uses of, 309–315
  wartime rise in, 7
  (*See also* Savings)
Little Steel Formula, 67, 76
Loan operations, of the International Monetary Fund, 366–374
  under key currency system, 375–377
Location, and reconversion, 171f.
  of war production, according to cities, 170f., 176
    according to regions, 100, 109f., 166–171
Longstreet, V. M., 247n.
Lutz, H. L., 298

M

Machlup, F., 244n.
McNary-Haugen Program, 50
Maffry, A., 322n., 358n.
Man-hour output (*see* Productivity)
Manufacturing establishments, 126n.
Marriage rates, 149f.
Marschak, J., 88n.
Marshall, A., 333
Mayer, J., 60, 72
Mead Bill, 246n.
Means test, 383–385, 409
Meany-Thomas Report, 37n.
Missouri Valley Authority, plans for, 20
Mitchell, W. C., 402n.
Mobility of labor (*see* Labor force, mobility of)
Mond, Sir Alfred, 227
Monetary policies, 245, 270
  international, 323, 336–339, 349–352
Monetary problems, 7, 237f., 367
Money flow, banking system control of, 7, 238, 241–243
Monopolies, import, 323
Monopolistic practices, 76, 224, 252
Monopoly, and banks, 247f.
  and war-plant disposal, 142

Multilateral trade within a bloc, 328
  postwar, 335, 339
  and standard of living, 339
Multiple exchange rates, 341
Multiplier, 89, 274, 329n., 330n., 398f., 406
Murray Bill, 35
Myers, R. J., 61n.
Myrdal, G., 15, 19, 405n.

N

Nathan, R. R., 97n.
National income, estimates of postwar, 4f., 72, 252f., 260–262
  and fiscal policy, 299
  and food consumption, 39f.
  and full employment, 3, 31, 60, 75, 97
  and imports, 231
  and income payments, 86
  and investments, 261n.
  and military pay rolls, 15
  and the public debt, 11, 19f., 45, 299
  and savings, 11
  secular rise of, 20
  and social security, 385f., 391
  and taxation, 84, 279, 299
  (*See also* Consumption; Employment; Fiscal policy; Government; Gross national product; Income)
National Labor Board, 193
National Planning Association, 79n., 258–260, 261n., 268
National Resources Planning Board, 40n., 97n., 120n., 381, 384n., 391n.
Net national product (*see* National income)
Nondurable goods, consumption of, 87n., 241
  output of, 23, 25f., 70f.
  for war, 27
  postwar output of, 60, 404
  postwar prices of, 210
  (*See also* Food)
Nurkse, R., 331n.

O

Office of Price Administration (OPA), 60, 130, 187, 197–200, 203, 210
Office of War Mobilization and Reconversion, 104, 105n., 143

INDEX

P

Palyi, M., 354n.
Parity, 43, 46f., 50, 52, 56, 201
Patent arrangements, 218
Patterson, R. P., 128n.
Pay-roll taxes, 17f., 263, 276f., 291, 294, 388–392, 395, 410
Pay rolls (*see* Hourly earnings; Wage payments)
Perloff, H. S., 40n.
Population, estimates of postwar, 40n.
  growth of, and savings, 400, 403
  regional distribution of, 10
  urban, and its importance for agriculture, 57
Price control, general vs. selective, 196f., 215
  and gross national product, 90
  methods of, 198, 203, 208
  of multiple-product firms, 200, 202f.
  during transition, 206–209, 214–216
  wartime, 72, 124, 182, 185, 196–200
Price Control Bill, 71n.
Price movements, 204
Price policies, 5, 17, 29, 44, 46, 52, 91, 95, 189, 194, 199, 208, 211–216, 292
  of cartels, 218
Price relationships, interindustry, 208, 213f.
Prices, control of, 60, 70, 184, 187
  of farm products, 43–47, 50, 52, 55–58, 70, 191, 194
  as regulating the free economy, 255
  of surplus property, 139–142
  and wages, 71, 76, 187, 189–192, 269
  of war materials, 69
Priorities and allocations, 71, 181–183, 186, 189, 191, 209, 241
Production, civilian, 15, 27, 137, 163
  decline of in depressions, 402
  expansion of, as ultimate aim, 70
  and foreign trade, 25
  and international agreements, 225
  and markets, 175
  postwar, 23, 25, 60, 75f., 79, 172, 178, 184, 188, 192–194, 207f., 212–214, 223, 239, 404f., 410
  and reconversion, 27, 105, 109, 114, 175, 188, 190–192, 207
    (*See also* Reconversion)
Production, for war, 15, 27f., 99, 105, 109, 113, 125, 130, 137, 152, 163, 165f., 183, 186–188, 197, 202f., 206, 209, 257, 281, 306f., 310, 405
  wartime expansion of, 4, 8, 22f., 69, 72
Production shifts and price control, 202
Productivity, of agriculture (*see* Agriculture)
  and fiscal policy, 266, 292
  of foreign loans, 358, 360
  and foreign trade, 349
  and population distribution, 10
  postwar changes in, 4, 25, 60, 72–75, 80–83, 155, 211–213, 258n., 262, 266, 269, 292, 349, 400
  and quality deterioration, 81, 155, 185f.
  and wages, 68f., 71, 269
  wartime rise in, 212
Profits, 266, 400
  of banks, 247n., 250f., 282
  inventory, 85n.
  at low-capacity levels, 16
  postwar, 86, 184, 210f., 213–215, 248, 269, 273, 283–285, 296
  during transition, 187, 208, 308–310
  undistributed (*see* Savings)
  wartime, 60, 199–205, 212, 215, 280, 283, 305
Propensity to spend income and savings, 18, 206
  (*See also* Consumption and income)
Protection (*see* Quotas; Tariffs)
Public debt, and full employment, 253
  growth of, 11, 19, 410f.
  interest on, 293, 411n.
    (*See also* Government securities)
  repayment of, 11, 253, 277, 279, 299
  states' shares in, 160
Public investment, and employment, 11n., 78, 87, 115, 267–270, 400–410
  need of, 11, 35
    (*See also* Government contributions)
Public utilities, employment in, 152, 154
  taxation of, 283
Public works, in postwar period, 31, 116, 143, 293, 299, 407, 409
  during transition, 28f., 113n., 115, 143, 193, 257
Purchasing power, and deflation, 16
  and demand, 30, 145, 193, 269f., 382, 391, 405
  excess, 71, 265

Purchasing power, and government spending, 398, 409*f.*
  and unemployment compensation, 112, 408
  and taxation, 265*f.*, 294, 300
  (*See also* Demand)

Q

Quotas, licenses and other restrictive practices, 323, 325, 326*n.*, 328, 330*f.*, 334*f.*, 349

R

Rationing, of food, 22, 181, 191
  postwar, 189, 191, 194, 209, 241
  wartime, 71, 72, 124, 181, 299
Raw-material prices, 230
Raw materials, control of, 230*f.*
Readjustment, suggestions for, 116*f.*
Real estate, prices of, 243
Real property, investment in, 18*n.*
Real wages, 66*f.*
  (*See also* Hourly earnings; Wages)
Reconstruction, international, 366–368
  (*See also* International Bank for Reconstruction and Development)
Reconversion, of agriculture, 31–34
  costs of, 310–314
  differences in, 187
  and employment, 95–123, 153–157
  financing of, 7, 126, 129, 139, 144, 211, 213, 239*f.*, 301, 305–308, 310–316, 405
  of plants, 26, 171–175
  policies for, 28, 183–193
  and prices, 208, 210–213, 313*n.*
  and social security, 380, 391*f.*
  and taxes, 282*f.*
  (*See also* Production)
Regional development programs, 31
Regional distribution of war production, 100–103, 108*f.*, 133, 142, 158–161, 166–171, 173–176
  and contract termination, 124, 142, 187*f.*
Regional problems, 9*f.*, 76, 97, 104, 113*f.*, 116, 146, 158–161, 173, 175–178, 256, 393
  of cotton producers, 32
Relative returns (*see* Factors of production)

Rent control, postwar, 194
Research, need for, 20, 92, 142, 262
Reserve requirements, 244, 247, 251, 398
Reserves, of business, 301–307, 313*f.*
  (*See also* Liquid assets; Savings)
  excess (*see* Excess reserves)
  international, 335, 340, 344–347, 368, 370, 375
  rise of, 7, 237, 246
  and social security, 395
Resources, conservation of, 232
  postwar shifts of, 220
  use of, 20, 168, 172, 178, 216, 336, 400
Restrictive practices (*see* Cartels; Quotas)
Revenue (*see* Government)
Ripley, W. Z., 401*n.*
Risks, bank, 247, 249–251
  government's underwriting of, 262
  investment and taxation, 295, 297
Robertson, D. H., 321
Robinson, R. I., 239*n.*, 251*n.*
Ruml, B., 18, 52, 253*n.*, 265, 394, 409

S

Sales taxes, 18, 263–265, 275–277, 290, 294, 297*f.*, 410
Savings, of business and individuals, 19, 26*f.*, 206, 239, 241, 252, 301*f.*, 305–308, 314*f.*, 400
  and capital formation, 354*f.*, 390, 399
  corporate, 19, 31, 86, 213, 240, 301*f.*, 304, 400
  and demand, 30, 184, 257
  estimates of, 11, 18, 31, 241*f.*, 269, 353
  and insurance, 248*f.*, 394
  and investment, 237*f.*, 248*f.*, 255, 261, 401–403, 406
  investment and taxation, 265*f.*, 272–274, 280, 285
  and social security, 390
  and spending, 193, 206, 241, 261*f.*, 355
  wartime, 399*f.*, 405
Scarce currencies, 326*f.*, 343*f.*, 369*f.*, 373*f.*
Scarce materials, controls of, 181
Scarce resources, best use of, 8, 183, 185, 189*f.*, 281
Schüller, R., 325*n.*
Schumacher, E. F., 325
Securities and Exchange Commission, 240

INDEX

Selling costs of reconversion, 310*f.*
Seltzer, L. H., 244*n.*, 246*n.*
Shavell, H., 38
Simmons, E. C., 246*n.*
Slater, A., 302
Slichter, S. H., 40*n.*, 97*n.*, 115*n.*, 118*n.*
Small War Plants Corporation, 240
Smith, H. D., 271
Smithies, A., 253*n.*, 274*n.*
Social insurance, 115, 118–120, 383–395
   vs. security, 383–385, 387, 392
Social security, and compulsion, 394
   coverage of, 61, 392
   and exchange rates, 341
   financing of, 18, 86, 291, 293, 383, 387–392, 394*f.*, 408*f.*
   future of, 112*n.*, 113*n.*, 148, 151, 259, 382, 389–393, 395*f.*, 409
   need for expansion of, 17, 29, 75, 91, 119*f.*, 262, 383, 407*f.*
   and spending, 11, 266
Social-security payments (*see* Benefits)
Sonne, H. Chr., 18, 258*n.*, 269, 409*n.*
Spending, importance of steady flow of, 5, 193, 207
   patterns of, 2
   (*See also* Consumption; Demand; Investment)
Spot Authorization Order, 186
Stabilization Act, 197
Stabilization Extension Act, 200
Stagnation, 20, 255
   and monetary system, 238, 252
Standard of living, 5, 241, 327, 336, 338–340, 348*f.*
   and national product, 16
   and public services, 17, 266
   and social security, 385–388, 390, 393
Standards for pricing, 201
Straus, N., 408*n.*
Subsidies, 197, 202*n.*, 216, 220
   to agriculture, 56*f.*
   (*See also* Export bounties)
Surplus-property legislation, 34, 43, 47, 143*f.*
Surplus-property policies, 95, 124*f.*, 129–132, 134, 136, 139–142, 144*f.*, 183, 190, 210
Surpluses, agricultural, and their distribution, 45, 47, 54–57

T

Taft, Sen. R. A., 293
Tariff reductions, 252, 325*f.*
Tariffs, and cartels, 220, 222, 224, 227, 232
   and economic nationalism, 325–327
   existing vs. newly imposed, 334
   and export surplus, 246
   growth of, during depression, 320
   postwar revenue from, 295
Tax accrual of business, 30, 307, 309, 313
Tax policy and individuals' spending, 27, 30, 270, 285, 409–411
Tax structure, 5, 7, 71, 252, 264–266, 268, 276, 278–280, 286, 289, 291, 293, 298*f.*, 388
Taxation and depreciation, 287, 302*f.*, 305
Taxes, on business, postwar, estimates of, 84, 264, 272, 277
   corporate income, 283–287, 295*f.*, 309
   effects of, on income and employment, 7, 263–266, 272–274, 277–279, 409–411
   excess profits, 281–283, 288, 294
   and gross national product, 84*f.*, 91, 262–264, 266, 272, 275*f.*, 292, 409*f.*
   on individuals, 30, 87*f.*, 272, 277, 290*f.*, 294
   individual income, 288*f.*, 294–297, 410
   and inflation, 238, 244, 265, 289, 293, 299
   and profits, 263, 266, 273, 283–286
   and purchasing power, 263, 265, 409*f.*
   and revenue, 7, 19, 44
   state and local, 91, 297*f.*, 389*n.*, 392
   during transition, 193, 257
   wartime rise of, 275*f.*, 299, 312*f.*
   (*See also* Business fluctuations; Consumption; Corporate tax; Estate and gift taxes; Excess-profits taxes; Fiscal policy; Government revenue; Gross national product; National income)
Temporary National Economic Committee, 248
Termination (*see* Contract)
Terms of trade, 8, 224, 327*n.*, 332, 348
   and real income, 332*n.*
Textiles, demand for, 32, 241
Time deposits (*see* Deposits)
Trade, freedom of, 24, 35, 252, 323*f.*, 326, 337
   (*See also* Foreign trade)

Trade barriers, and cartels, 221f., 224, 227, 232
  relaxation of, 5, 10, 24, 232f., 252, 320, 325f., 349, 364
Trade policies, 95, 322f., 328, 332f.
Training of workers, 156f., 162, 193, 211, 213, 256
Transfer of workers vs. transfer of industry, 211
Transition vs. long-run, 6f., 27, 270, 381f.
Unit costs add productive capacity, 17
  (*See also* Controls; Reconversion)
Transportation, employment in, 152, 154
  need for development of, 20, 267
  wartime rise of, 23
Treasury vs. central-bank control, 237–239

U

Unemployment (*see* Employment; Fiscal Policy; Government contributions)
United Nations Relief and Rehabilitation Administration (UNRRA), 51
U.S. Chamber of Commerce, 5
U.S. Employment Service, 116, 121–123

V

Veterans' benefits, 259, 293
Veterans' readjustment, 156f.
Veterans' Readjustment Act (*see* G.I. Bill of Rights)
Veterans' rights, 34, 381
Viner, J., 326n., 363n.

W

Wage control, 65f., 103, 182, 187, 198, 203
Wage differences and social security, 393
Wage payments, 59–61, 63–69, 74, 86, 90, 96, 115, 189, 191, 203f., 207, 240, 257
Wage policy, 5, 17, 29, 71, 76, 91, 95, 124, 189, 193, 262, 292
Wage rates, differences in, 9, 256
Wages, agricultural, 57
  and cost of living, 66–68, 191f., 207
  and gross national product, 74, 85, 96
  in manufacturing, 61–64
  and prices, 16, 59f., 69–72, 85, 193, 198, 269
  and productivity (*see* Productivity)
Wagner, Senator R. F., 408n.
Wagner-Dingell Bill, 17, 394n.
Wagner-Spence Bills, 240, 249
Waite, W. C., 56n.
Walsh, R., 253n.
War Food Administration, 197
War Labor Board (WLB), 61n., 62, 65–67, 69f., 76
War Manpower Commission (WMC), 121, 138, 182
War Production Board (WPB), 136, 138, 143, 164, 182, 186, 190, 197
Warriner, D., 33
Waugh, Dr. F. V., 53
Webb-Pomerene Law, 218
Weiler, E. T., 129n.
White, H. D., 339, 373
Whittlesey, C. R., 331n.
Williams, J. H., 363n., 372n., 375
Williamson, W. R., 394
Willis, J. B., 251n.
Wilson, C. E., 310n.
Witte, E. E., 112n.
Wolfbein, S., 158
Work Projects Administration (WPA), 387, 398, 406
Woytinsky, W. S., 103n.

Y

Yates, P. L., 33f.

NG